Egypt: The Lower Kingdom

European University Studies

Europäische Hochschulschriften
Publications Universitaires Européennes

Series XXIII
Theology

Reihe XXIII Série XXIII
Theologie
Théologie

Vol./Bd. 828

PETER LANG

Frankfurt am Main · Berlin · Bern · Bruxelles · New York · Oxford · Wien

Sudhir Kumar Minj

Egypt: The Lower Kingdom

An Exegetical Study of the Oracle of Judgment against Egypt in Ezekiel 29,1-16

PETER LANG
Europäischer Verlag der Wissenschaften

Bibliographic Information published by Die Deutsche Bibliothek
Die Deutsche Bibliothek lists this publication in the Deutsche Nationalbibliografie; detailed bibliographic data is available in the internet at <http://dnb.ddb.de>.

Zugl.: Frankfurt (Main), Phil.-Theol. Hochschule Sankt Georgen, Diss., 2005

ISSN 0721-3409
ISBN 3-631-54579-7
US-ISBN 0-8204-9808-4

© Peter Lang GmbH
Europäischer Verlag der Wissenschaften
Frankfurt am Main 2006
All rights reserved.

ACKNOWLEDGEMENTS

The present research was submitted as a doctoral dissertation to the Faculty of Theology at the Philosophisch-Theologische Hochschule Sankt Georgen in Frankfurt on-the-Main in January 2005, and is published here in a revised form.

I am grateful to Prof. Dr. Hans-Winfried Jüngling, SJ, who directed this doctoral dissertation. He showed much interest in the topic and guided me through this research with valuable suggestions, observations on the usage of terms, phrases, expressions and ideas, and encouragement for me to further elucidate any new insights or clarifications that my work succeeded in reaching. Again and again he drew my attention to a new or relevant article, review or book relating to my topic. His own bibliography served as a basis for the initial stage of this research. He was also always available whenever I needed to discuss any point or idea. While working through the last part of the dissertation, his constant encouragement gave me the confidence to bring it to a conclusion.

I thank Prof. Dr. Helmut Engel, SJ, the Rector of the Faculty, Hochschule Sankt Georgen, who served as the Second Reader for this study, providing many useful suggestions to improve the dissertation for publication. I would also like to thank him for working on my behalf to obtain a stipend for me that made my stay and study in Sankt Georgen possible.

My gratitude goes to my superiors, for allowing me to pursue the doctoral study, to my colleagues at St. Albert's College, Faculty of Theology (Ranchi), and friends who have supported me in this research in their own way. I am also grateful to the German Jesuit Province and to the Jesuit community of Sankt Georgen, where I lived for three years while completing this research. Words of appreciation are due to Mr. Anthony Gomes (Bombay) and to Dr. David Donald (USA), who reviewed the manuscript for language and style.

Finally, my special thanks go to the Anna Ruths-Stiftung, its Supervisor Dr. Gregor Seikel and his colleagues, foremost Mrs Anna Ruths, the foundress of the Stiftung, both for supporting this study financially from the beginning of the research to the delivery of the manuscript for publication, and for the warm, encouraging friend she has been from the beginning. Mrs. Ruths' keen interest in my current research and future work has been truly remarkable. I am very indebted to her.

Sudhir Kumar Minj
Frankfurt on-the-Main, Germany
January 2006

TABLE OF CONTENTS

CHAPTER SIX
THE USAGE OF שׁוּב שְׁבוּת "BRING BACK [FROM] CAPTIVITY"
TO DENOTE GOD'S SAVING ACTION FOR EGYPT 141

CHAPTER SEVEN
RESTORATION OF EGYPT: EZEKIEL 29,13-16
FURTHER EXPLANATION OF THE ORACLE OF SALVATION 175

INTRODUCTION

0.1. Research orientation of the dissertation

Egypt is primarily known as the "house" and "land" of slavery in the Old Testament. This echoes in Moses' address to the people when he leads the Israelites out of Egypt: "Remember this day in which you came out from Egypt, out of the house of slavery, for by a strong hand the LORD brought you out from this place" (Ex 13,3; cf. Deut 6,12). The expression, "Egypt – the house of slavery," became part of the preamble of the Decalogue: "I am the LORD your God, who brought you out of the land of Egypt, out of the house of slavery" (Ex 20,2).[1] The prophets of the Old Testament take pain to remind Israel of her liberation from Egypt by the hand of the LORD and warn her against the tendency to return into it. They see it as a dangerous state of affairs that preceded Israel's faith in the LORD. From this it becomes clear that Israel's slavery in Egypt is directly bound up with her profession of faith in the LORD.

Ezekiel interprets Israel's political alliance with Egypt differently. On the one hand it seriously violates Israel's special relationship with the LORD and on the other hand it thwarts His plan of salvation for her. Israel's dependence on Egypt for her political security amounted to her return to Egypt from where the LORD had delivered her with a mighty hand. Ezekiel condemns not only Israel's tendency to go back to Egypt, but also the latter's role in persuading Israel to do so, especially through her boasting and self-pride (cf. Ezek 29,3).

However, the prophetic books do not present Egypt only as Israel's enemy. The oracle of Isaiah (19,23-25) surprisingly speaks about God's salvation for Egypt (and Assyria). The promise of God's salvation is here pronounced for Israel's traditional arch enemy: "Blessed be Egypt my people, Assyria work of my hands, and Israel my inheritance" (cf. v.25). This oracle of salvation is framed between two oracles of judgment against Egypt (Isa 19,1-16 [19,17-25] 20,1-6). Ezekiel announces a similar oracle of salvation to Egypt (Ezek 29,13-16). So also, Jer 46,26b speaks about the restoration of Egypt. However, the texts on the laws and statutes underline the role of Egypt as the house of slavery: "You shall not abhor an Egyptian, because you were a sojourner in his land" (Deut 23,8b). In other

---

[1] Egypt's relation with Canaan shows that much of the Biblical history is tied to it. Cf. KITCHEN, "History of Egypt: Chronology," in *ABD* II, 321. *Please note* that the footnotes of this text will, following the ordinary German convention, provide only the authors' last name and the abbreviated title of the relevant work. A full bibliography of all cited works is set forth at the end of this book.

words, although Israel became a slave in Egypt, she is reminded that it gave her refuge.

The oracles against the nations[2] constitute the middle part of the book of Ezekiel (1-24 [25-32] 33-48).[3] Here Ezekiel gives the oracles against Ammon, Moab, Edom, the Philistines (25,1-17), Sidon (28,20-24) and Tyre (26,1-28,19), on the one hand, and against Egypt (29-32) on the other hand. Thus, the foreign oracles have two main units: 1) against Tyre (Ezek 26-28), and 2) against Egypt (Ezek 29-32). This division is specially marked by their date formulas. In Ezek 26,1 the chronological date is March/April 587[4] whereas in Ezek 29,1 the seven independent units of oracles against Egypt begin, six with chronological dates, where the second date formula contains two word-events, indicating two independent oracles (29,1-7-21 and 30,1-19).

Except the third undated oracle, all other oracles against Egypt are dated, and save the second oracle, they are all chronologically ordered:[5]

1. The oracle against Pharaoh, the big crocodile	(29,1-16)	17 Jan. 588
2. The land of Egypt given as booty to Nebuchadnezzar	(29,17-21)	8 Apr. 572
3. The day of the LORD in Egypt	(30,1-19)	without date
4. The LORD breaks the arms of Pharaoh	(30,20-26)	10 Apr. 588
5. The destruction of the cosmic tree (= Pharaoh)	(31,1-16)	2 June 588
6. The lament over Pharaoh, over Egypt and her hordes	(32,1-16)	15 Mar. 586
7. The lament over descent of Egypt into Sheol	(32,17-32)	29 Mar. 586

These oracles against Egypt are thematically different (on Pharaoh: 29,1-16; 30,20-26; 31,1-18; 32,1-16; on Egypt: 29,17-21; 32,17-32),[6] they use different literary forms, and each of them shows progressive development of the oracles. The judgments announced in the successive oracles are increasingly severe. There is also an oracle of salvation in the 'Egypt-oracles' which is skilfully placed between the first (29,1-12) and the last oracle of judgment (29,17-21).[7] While the

---

[2] Cf. in Isa 13-21; 23; 34; Jer 25,15-38; 46-51; Ezek 25-32;35; 38,1-39,20; Am 1,3-2,3, Obad, 1,2-2; Nah 1,1.9-3,19; Zeph 2,3-15; Zech 9,1-8. See also HAYES, "The usage of oracles against foreign nations," in *JBL* 87 (1968), 81f. BOADT observes that in the book of Ezekiel, "they are intended to reinforce the program of reconstruction envisioned by the prophet." See his "Rhetorical Strategies," in LUST (ed.), *Ezekiel and His Book* (BEThL 74), 196.

[3] Three-parts eschatological structure (i.e., judgment of Israel - judgment of nations - salvation to Israel) is found also in Isa (1-12 [13-23] 24-35), Jer LXX 1-25,14 [25,15-38; 46-51] 26-36), and Zeph 1-2,3 [2,4-3,8] 3,9-20). In Ezekiel, the foreign oracles are also encircled by two oracles of salvation to Israel (24,25-27 and 33,21-33). See POHLMANN, *Hesekiel, 1-19*, 366; FUHS, *Ezechiel 1-24*, 7.

[4] GREENBERG, *Ezechiel 1-20*, HThKAT, 24.

[5] KUTSCH, *Die Chronologischen Daten*, 71. See also GREENBERG, *Ezechiel 1-20*, 24; LANG, *Ezechiel*, 32-42; MAY and ALLEN, "Ezekiel", in *IB* VI, 59-60.

[6] ZIMMERLI, *Ezechiel 25-48*, BKAT 13/2, 697.

[7] On the relation of the first and the last oracle against Egypt, see p.62, No. 3.7: 'The nexus.'

first oracle of judgment looks forward to this oracle of salvation (29,13-16), the last oracle of judgment keeps its glance at it, which is the main topic of this dissertation.

Ezekiel's oracles of judgment against Egypt, and especially his oracle of salvation to her, have not been sufficiently commented upon. Although it has been overlooked in research, the exegetical and theological significance of the oracle of judgment against Egypt (cf. 29,1-12) and particularly of her salvation (cf. 29,13-16) need to be acknowledged. The oracle of salvation evinces an extraordinary way in which God dealt with Egypt. God's promise of salvation to Israel, spoken several times in the book of Ezekiel,[8] is announced here in favour of Egypt, and this does not occur by sheer chance: Ezekiel states it here intentionally because he sees it as a paradigm for Israel in exile. It is a sign that gives hope to the exiles of Judah and the dispersed of Israel (cf. 4,4-8) and guarantees their future restoration, which he announces in Ezek 33-48. Thus, the promise of salvation to Egypt reflects God's plan of salvation for Israel.[9] It contains three basic elements: "to gather together" (the dispersed tribes of Israel and Judah), "to bring [them] back" (from their captivity) and "to settle" them (in their homeland). In Ezek 29,13-16, Ezekiel applies the same elements of God's saving deeds to Egypt that are primarily used for Israel. The transference of these prerogatives from Israel to Egypt, her "arch rival," is remarkable both from exegetical and a theological point of view.

0.2. History of interpretation of the oracle of Salvation
0.2.1. Commentaries

In the modern scholarship in Ezekiel, an outstanding commentary by W. Zimmerli (*Ezechiel 1-24*, BKAT 13/1 [1969]; and *Ezechiel 25-48*, BKAT 13/2 [1969]), is particularly notable as it applies form-critical and traditio-critical methods of interpretation, which made a major advance over the historical and text-critical approaches of earlier Ezekiel-study, substantially succeeded in sorting the original

---

[8] Cf. Ezek 11,17; 20,34.41; 34,13; 36,24; 37,21; 39,25f.; also 16,53; 28,25. Contrary to such hope see: SCHARTZ, "Ezekiel's dim view of Israel's restoration," in *SBL* 119/1 (2000), 43-67.

[9] This theological viewpoint has not been sufficiently recognised in the some of the notable commentaries, like POHLMANN (*Hesekiel 20-48*, 22/2 [2001]); BLOCK (*Ezekiel, 25-48*, NICOT 33/2 [1998]); GREENBERG (*Ezekiel 20-37*, AB 22B [1998]); ZIMMERLI (*Ezechiel 25-48*, BKAT 13/2 [1969]); monographs, e.g., PREMSTALLER, *Fremdvölkersprüche*, FzB 104 (2005); SCHÖPLIN (*Theologie als Biographie*, FzAT 36 [2002]); KRÜGER (*Geschichtskozepte*, BZAW 180 [1989]); FECHTER, (*Bewältigung der Katastrophe*, BZAW 208 [1992]); BOADT (*Ezekiel's Oracles against Egypt*, BibetOr 37 [1980]); HOSSFELD (*Untersuchungen*, FzB 20 [1977]); LANG, (*Ezechiel*, 1981), GARSCHA (*Studien*, 1975); symposium, e.g., LUST [ed.], (*Ezekiel and his book*, BEThL 74 [1986]); and book, e.g., VOGELS, (*God's Universal Covenant*, 1979).

text out from later additions,[10] and raised theological[11] concerns underlying the text. He considers the collection of oracles against the nations (Ezek 25-32) to be an editorial composition either by Ezekiel himself or the final redactor, while the oracles themselves are grounded in the prophetic tradition (cf. Am 1,1f.). Thus, the six preceding oracles of judgment against the nations come as a warning for the seventh nation in the series, i.e., Egypt, against which the most severe judgment is announced.[12] Like the oracles against Tyre, the oracles against Egypt centre on two figures, namely, Pharaoh and Egypt: the hubris of Pharaoh has made Egypt a temptation for Israel. This conflicts with God's plan of salvation for Israel, and thus Pharaoh and Egypt come under God's judgment.[13]

In Zimmerli's opinion, the first oracle of judgment against Egypt (29,1-16) is not a collection of separate oracles (cf. vv.1-6a, 6b-9a; 9b-16), but a series of related oracles of judgment against Egypt.[14] He does not ascribe to the theory that Ezekiel, in his oracle of salvation to Egypt at the end of the first oracle of judgment (29,13-16; cf. Isa 19,23f. Jer 46,26;), was expressing a sentimental feeling toward either Israel's connection to Egypt (cf. Deut 23,8) or the Jewish diaspora there, which existed since the sixth century B.C.[15] (cf. Deut 17,16), although Zimmerli does observe a sign of anti-Egyptian feeling in Ezek 20; 23; the "position of the surrounding nations" may also have expected a resurgence of Israel.[16] Unfortunately, he does not elaborate on this point further. His great contribution in Ezekiel studies notwithstanding, Zimmerli seems to overlook one significant theological aspect in the oracle of salvation to Egypt, namely, it reinstates the hope of future restoration of Judah (Israel). This failure seems to occur, because Zimmerli considered the single announcement of salvation to Egypt - and for that matter, equivalent announcements to any nation other than Israel (cf. 11,17; 28,25f, 34,13) - to be an editorial addition to the book of Ezekiel.[17]

The earlier commentaries and studies[18] focused mainly on literary text-critical analysis of the book of the prophet Ezekiel. Therefore, few have made similar

---

[10] KECK (ed.), *NIB*, VI, 1092.

[11] CHILDS, *Introduction to the Old Testament*, 362.

[12] ZIMMERLI, *Ezechiel 25-48*, 579-581.

[13] ZIMMERLI, *Ezechiel 25-48*, 702.

[14] ZIMMERLI, *Ezechiel 25-48*, 706.

[15] Gottwald, *Politics of Ancient Israel*, 140.

[16] ZIMMERLI, *Ezechiel 25-48*, 715.

[17] ZIMMERLI, *Ezechiel 25-48*, 712.

[18] E.g., ZUNZ, *Bibelkirtisches II, Ezechiel*, ZDMG 27 (1873); KEIL, *Ezekiel*, 1882; CORNILL, *Ezechiel*, 1886; BERTHOLET, *Hesekiel*, KHAT 12 (1897); and *Hesekiel*, HAT 13 (1936); KRAETZSCHMAR, *Ezechiel*, HAT 3 (1900); JAHN, *Ezechiel*, (1905); HEINISCH, *Ezechiel*, HSAT 8 (1923); HERRMANN, *Ezechielstudien* (1908); and *Ezechiel*, KAT 11 (1924); HERNTRICH, *Ezechielstudien*, ZAW 61 (1932); G. COOKE, *Ezekiel*, ICC 19 (1936); IRWIN, *Problem of Ezekiel*, (1943); HOWIE, *Date and Composition*, SBL MS 4 (1950); FOHRER, *Ezechiel*, HAT 13 (1955); and LAMPARTER, *Zum Wächter Bestellt*, BAT 21 (1968).

observations with respect to Ezekiel's oracles against Egypt and, particularly, the oracle of salvation to Egypt. A few commentators such as, Bertholet (*Hesekiel*, HAT 13, 105), Heinisch (*Ezechiel*, 141), Herrmann (*Ezechiel*, KAT 11, 198-199) and Lamparter (*Zum Wächter Bestellt*, BAT 21, 218), think it a later addition. The particular method and approach that the earlier commentators used, which limited their interpretation, and above all because most of them considered this oracle of salvation to Egypt to be an editorial addition, such commentators failed to notice the theological import of the oracle for Israel, namely, that it gives hope to the exiles of Judah and the restoration of Israel.

Zimmerli's research found large acceptance by the scholars who came after him and they make use of his theological observations "within older critical framework."[19] Younger commentaries[20] tend to take more of a literary-critical approach to the book,[21] but they also take into account the historical-critical findings.[22] Even here, however, the oracle of judgment against Egypt, particularly the role of to Egypt's salvation in relation to the future salvation of Israel, remains unclear or omitted altogether.

Some of these commentaries that try to interpret the salvation oracle from the aforementioned point of view come close to seeing the relation between Egypt and Israel. W. Eichrodt (*Hesekiel 1-18*, ATD 22/1 [1959]; and *Hesekiel 19-48*, ATD 22/2 [1966]) is one commentator who recognizes that the fate of Egypt resembles the fate of Judah, indicating the beginning of a pattern of prophetic universalism.[23] However, it is not very clear whether Eichrodt means there is similarity only in respect of judgment or also with regard to salvation. In either case, he does not express clearly that Ezekiel intends to use the salvation of Egypt as a model for God's future act of salvation for Israel. Therefore, like Zimmerli, Eichordt fails to elaborate on the full implication of his statement.

J. W. Wevers (*Ezekiel*, NCB 33 [1969]), who is of the view that the original form of Ezekiel's oracle was "concise, even bordering on the cryptic," but became longer in the history of tradition, considers 29,1-16 to be a collection of four related oracles that are also affected by editorial expansion, which is very obvious in vv.9b-12 except in 16b.[24] As such, he does not try to show that theologically it is closely connected with the future hope of Israel.

---

[19] CHILDS, *Introduction to the Old Testament*, 360.

[20] E.g., FISCH, *Ezekiel*, 1978; CRAIGE, *Ezekiel*, 1983; COOPER, *Ezekiel*, NAC 17 (1984); CODY, *Ezekiel*, OTM 11 (1984); FUHS, *Ezechiel 1-24*, NEB AT/21 (1984) and *Ezechiel, 25-48*, NEB AT/22 (1988); HALS, *Ezekiel*, FOTL 19 (1989); BLENKINSOPP, *Ezekiel*, 1990; VAWTER and HOPPE, *Ezekiel*, ITC (1991); KLEIN, *Ezekiel*, 1998; and few others.

[21] KECK (ed.), *NIB*, VI, 1094.

[22] KECK (ed.), *NIB*, VI, 1090.

[23] EICHRODT, *Hesekiel 19-48*, 278.

[24] WEVERS, *Ezekiel*, 35.221-222.

L. C. Allen (*Ezekiel 1-19*, WBC 28 [1994]; and *Ezekiel 20-48*, WBC 29 [1990]) considers 29,9b-16 a "redactional supplement," a literary expansion, which continues "a message of Egypt's fate of desolation," yet limiting it by fixing the period of exile.[25] Allen, indeed, sees 13-16 as yet another phase of punishment of Egypt, although tempered and contrasting with v.5, but he finds no discernible reason for its reappraisal.[26] He does not view it as a salvation oracle, and as such, he fails to recognize it as a precursor to the restoration of Israel.

B. Vawter and L. J. Hoppe[27] (*Ezekiel*, ITC, 1991) consider 29,1-16 as three separate oracles and give a very brief and simple explanation of the text. They take the oracle of salvation as an "exceptional text," but despite drawing on Deut 23,7b to note Israel's relation to Egypt, they fail to state any further theological meaning of this oracle for the salvation to Israel.

D. I. Block (*Ezekiel 1-24*, NICOT 33/1 [1997]; and *Ezekiel 25-48*, NICOT 33/2 [1998]), who sees three oracles as displaying formal similarities, that heighten force from the first to the third oracle in 29,1-16, seems to agree with Zimmerli (*Ezechiel 25-48*, 715-716) that much of this text is an editorial addition.[28] He terms 29,13-16 as a "modified restoration oracle" from the oracles of Israel's restoration, and indicates a correspondence between the two concluding statements in 29,16 and 28,24 that explains God's promise of hope for Egypt.[29] Still, Block does not adequately show how the statement reinforces the hope of Israel's restoration.

M. Greenberg (*Ezekiel 1-20*, AB 22 [1983]; and *Ezekiel 21-37*, AB 22B [1998]) takes a holistic view of the book of Ezekiel, tries to make sense of the text and structure in his analysis and interpretation, and favours the authenticity of the texts. In approach and method, he stands opposed to Zimmerli. His observations on the structure and his comments on the difficult texts and grammatical peculiarities of the oracles against Egypt are remarkable. He explains the oracle of hope for Egypt primarily as a result of a behaviour that was exactly the opposite of Israel's other foreign neighbours: Egypt did not rejoice at Israel's defeat. He also notes that this promise of hope is not repeated again.[30] However, it should be noted that Greenberg does not comment on the relationship between this oracle of salvation for Egypt and that for the future salvation of Israel.

K.–F. Pohlmann (*Hesekiel 1-19*, ATD 22/1 [1996]; and *Hesekiel 20-48*, ATD 22/2 [2001]) follows a literary-critical approach to the book of Ezekiel, examines the history of origin and redaction of the text complexes and reconstructs their original order. He holds the view that the oracles against the nations are re-worked to accommodate the exilic view. Thus, the earlier text complexes 1-24 and 33-48

---

[25] ALLEN, *Ezekiel*, xxx; cf. 104.

[26] ALLEN, *Ezekiel*, xxx; cf. 106-107.

[27] VAWTER and HOPPE, *Ezekiel*, 135-138.

[28] BLOCK, *Ezekiel 25-48*, 131-133.

[29] BLOCK, *Ezekiel 25-48*, 144.

[30] GREENBERG, *Ezekiel 21-37*, 611.

were made to rest on the exile-oriented oracles against the nations[31] and served as proof of the LORD's sovereignty.[32] In view of the restoration of Israel, the LORD establishes a just order and salvation by submitting the nations to judgment. Thus, the oracles against Egypt reflect Israel's attitude toward Egypt in Ezek 17 and broaden its scope further (cf. Ezek 15-17).[33] Pohlmann concludes that the aim of the oracle against Egypt (cf. 29,1-16) is to correct self-pride which stands in opposition to the LORD. However, he fails to address the theological implication of the oracle of salvation to Egypt (cf. 29,13-16) for restoration of Israel which I argue the prophet intends to emphasize.

0.2.2. Monographs

G. Hölscher (*Hesekiel. Der Dichter*, BZAW 39 [1924]) is of the opinion that the reworking and supplementary additions have left the genuine texts of Ezekiel wildly overgrown.[34] He opines that 29,13-16 is a later addition and, moreover, that it is neither a salvation-oracle nor indicate any sympathy for Egypt other than that, that Egypt no more exists in Delta or rules over the nations.[35] Thus, Hölscher does not see any role for this Egyptian salvation oracle in connection with the promise of salvation for Israel.

H. G. Reventlow (*Wächter über Israel*, BZAW 82 [1962]) traces the background of the form-tradition of Ezekiel's salvation oracles in Lev 26. The announcement of a curse is seen as God's judgment, while the blessing directly as its opposite.[36] For Ezekiel, the nations play a significant role in Israel's taking possession of the land and in their punishment ("scatter [them] among the nations," "disperse [them] through the countries," cf. Lev 26,33), but equally so in their blessing ("bring [them] out from the people," "gather [them] from the countries," cf. Ezek 20,34).[37] The nations are also witnesses of God's dealing with Israel; above all, He has a similar plan for both of them, i.e., recognition of His sovereignty.[38] Nevertheless, Reventlow somehow fails to indicate the theological aspect that the promise of salvation to Egypt provides an example to inspire hope of restoration for Israel.

J. Garscha (*Studien zum Ezechielbuch*, 1975), who makes a redaction-critical study of Ezekiel 1-39, thinks that the important question regarding the Oracles

---

[31] POHLMANN, *Ezechiel 20-48*, 366.

[32] POHLMANN, *Ezechiel 20-48*, 443.

[33] POHLMANN, *Ezechiel 20-48*, 401.

[34] HÖLSCHER, *Hesekiel. Der Dichter*, 144.

[35] HÖLSCHER, *Hesekiel. Der Dichter*, 146.

[36] REVENTLOW, *Wächter über Israel*, 65-66.

[37] REVENTLOW, *Wächter über Israel*, 134-135.

[38] REVENTLOW, *Wächter über Israel*, 136.138.

against the foreign nations (Ezek 25-32) is whether it results from an editor's reworking of the pre-existing form provided by the prophet himself or a secondary redactor.[39] In his view, Ezek 29-32 is accounted for as a deutero-Ezekielian addition that includes 29,9b-16.[40] Thus, due to his aim and approach, Garscha has failed to see the oracle of salvation for Egypt from its theological perspective, which Ezekiel presents as a mirror of Israel's future salvation.

Although F.-L. Hossfeld (*Untersuchungen*, FzB 20 [1977]) studies the composition and theology of the selected chapters of the book of Ezekiel, he omits Ezek 29 from this study. Therefore, his study cannot contain a concrete and direct opinion on the role of the oracle of salvation for Egypt with regard to the salvation of Israel.

W. Vogels («Restoration de l'Égypte», *Biblica* 53 [1972], and *God's Universal Covenant* [1979]) does point to the use of God's salvific action for Israel also for Egypt in 29,13-16.[41] Although he gives an interesting theological and biblical interpretation of the oracle from the point of view of "universal salvation" and "universal covenant," he does not address the significance of the oracle of salvation to Egypt for the future restoration of Israel.

L. Boadt (*Ezekiel's Oracles against Egypt*, BibetOr 371 [1980]) takes a literary and philological approach to the study of Ezekiel's oracles against Egypt. By constantly referring to parallels from NW Semitic languages, from other biblical texts and from the book itself, he carefully analyzes every verse and offers quite convincing arguments on the reliability of the texts. His observations on various stylistic features and other insights on the oracles are useful for an interpretation of the texts. However, the theological relevance of the promise of restoration to Egypt in relation to the future restoration of Israel is not discussed. One can only assume that this point was not raised primarily because of the particular method and scope of his study.

T. Krüger (*Geschichtskozepte*, BZAW 180 [1989]), in the fifth chapter of his study, attempts to reconstruct the history of redaction of the historical concepts in the book of Ezekiel.[42] He deals briefly with the problem of the oracles against the foreign nations. In his view, before the incorporation of Ezek 25-32 in the final redaction of the book of Ezekiel, it existed as an independent collection of oracles whose final editorial composition was not completed before the end of the exiles. Because his study has a different aim, and devotes little space to the text, it does not discuss the relation of the oracle of salvation for Egypt to the future salvation of Israel.

Among the more recent monographs, F. Fechter (*Bewältigung der Katastrophe*, BZAW 208 [1992]) has dealt with Ezek 29 in his elaborate study of literary

---

[39] GARSHA, *Studien*, 132.

[40] GARSHA, *Studien*, 194-195.

[41] VOGELS, «Restoration de l'Égypte» *Biblica* 53, 485; and *God's Universal Covenant*, 91.97.

[42] KRÜGER, *Geschichtskozepte*, 307-308.

aspects, structure and redaction of the selected oracles on the foreign nations in the book of Ezekiel. He concludes that the salvation oracle (29,13-16) is a re-working of the original material - a correction of 9b-11a.12.16b and a supplement, which fixes the period of judgment of Egypt.[43] This salvation oracle in the prophetic oracles of the Old Testament is peculiar for a foreign nation. However, the function of Ezek 29,13-16a is not to serve as a salvation oracle, but to limit the oracle of judgment 29,1-12.16b.[44] After the catastrophe of Jerusalem and exile to Babylon, Ezekiel's oracles were proved genuine and he was accepted as a true prophet. Thus, the history of tradition wanted to incorporate them in the canon before the final redaction of the book took place.[45] All the same, Fechter fails to take note that this oracle was intended by Ezekiel to be a mirror for the exiles, giving them a hope of restoration to Israel.

Among the most recent monographs, V. PREMSTALLER, (*Fremdvölkersprüche des Eezechielbuches*, FzB 104 [2005]) provides a systematic presentation of the foreign oracles in the book of Ezekiel with a translation and outlines of each oracle, as well as an exegetical explanation. He sees the restoration of Egypt as part of the third oracle of judgment, which restricts the previous judgment by setting a fixed time-limit. To this he attributes a direct application of the promises of salvation to Israel.[46] However, Premstaller nowhere shows the theological implication of this salvation oracle, i.e., how it casts a ray of hope of salvation for the exiles of Israel.

Among others, E. VOGT (*Untersuchungen zum Buch Ezechiel*, AnBib 95 [1981]), K. SCHÖPLIN (*Theologie als Biographie*, FzAT 36 [2002]) and LUST, ed., (*Ezekiel and his book*, BEThL 74 [1986]) could also be named here. All of these scholars, because of the different aims and perspectives of their studies, fail to take note of the theological purpose of the oracle of salvation of Egypt in relation to Israel. The general view that it was a later editorial addition could be called upon as the primary explanation for their overlooking this aspect of the salvation oracle. The lack of a previous treatment of the salvation oracle to Egypt in relation to the future restoration of Israel presents the motive for the present study of the oracle of salvation to Egypt in Ezek 29,13-16.

---

[43] FECHTER, *Bewältigung der Katastrophe*, 220. 223.248.

[44] FECHTER, *Bewältigung der Katastrophe*, 253. Here Fechter cites FUHS, *Ezechiel 25-48*, 161f.; REVENTLOW, *Wächter über Israel*, 156f.; COOKE, *Ezekiel*, 328; and ZIMMERLI, *Ezechiel 25-48*, 712-716.

[45] FECHTER, *Bewältigung der Katastrophe*, 253.

[46] PREMSTALLER, *Fremdvölkersprüche*, 149.

0.3. Methodology:

The methodology followed in this research is exegetical-theological. Taking text-criticism, structural and semantic analysis of Ezek 29,1-16 as a basis, it employs a diachronic-synchronic approach to understand the fundamental concepts of the salvation oracle ("to gather" and "bring back") in order to grasp the significance of these terms for Egypt. The theological significance of the oracle is extracted through further explanation of the oracle of salvation in the final chapter.

An attempt has been made to examine the MT (chapter two), where variant readings appear (in the BHS), and the research provides explanation for them, attempting to determine the correct reading, especially where some doubt currently exists on such choice. Boadt[47] has strongly argued for the authenticity of the texts of the oracles against Egypt from a philological point of view. His work is also extensively referred herein.

The structural analysis (chapter three) of the text attempts to show the unity of the main literary components and to illuminate the relationship of the smaller sub-units within the whole structure of the oracle. Attention has been paid to Ezekiel's use of literary forms and style in the oracles against the foreign nations.[48] The semantic analysis (chapter four) seeks to arrive at the correct meanings and expressions of certain words and phrases used in the oracle through their usages in the Old Testament texts. On the basis of such usages, their meanings will then be investigated and interpreted in the context of the oracle.

A specific inquiry into two fundamental concepts of the oracle of salvation in the subsequent chapters five and six will take up the meaning and the usage of the verb קבץ ("to gather") and of the expression שׁוּב שׁבוּת ("to bring back [from] captivity"), and examine their significance in relation to the salvation of Egypt. These concepts reveal God's dealing, i.e., His saving action for Egypt. This analysis will then lead to further explanation in the final chapter (i.e., chapter seven), which is a practical commentary on the oracle of salvation.

The whole inquiry is preceded by an overview of the oracles against Egypt within the chain of oracles of judgment against the nations (cf. chapter one). Such placement will give a larger context to the oracle of salvation to Egypt.

---

[47] BOADT, *Ezekiel's oracles,* BibetOr 37 (1980); see also GREENBERG, *Ezekiel 21-37,* AB 22B (1998).

[48] E.g., the use of the particles, e.g., יַעַן/לְכֵן/כִּי/הִנְנִי, the literary forms, e.g., date, word-event, address [son of man], orientation, command to prophesy, message and the recognition formula, and the literary techniques, e.g., chiasmus, parallelisms, alliteration, repetition, etc., show Ezekiel's literary skill and his theological motive.

CHAPTER ONE
THE ORACLES OF JUDGMENT AGAINST EGYPT
IN THE CHAIN OF ORACLES AGAINST THE NATIONS:
AN OVERVIEW

Chapter One is an overview of the oracles of judgment against the nations (Ezek 25-32), showing the larger context of Ezek 29,1-16, and helping us to see how the first and the last oracle are structurally as well as literarily linked together. Here we make only a passing reference to the other foreign oracles. Instead, we have taken up the seven oracles of judgment against Egypt (Ezek 29-32) separately and elaborated their main themes. We have also discussed their interrelation to one another, showing their compositional unity.

1.1. The oracles of judgment against the nations (Ezek 25-28)

The second part of the book of Ezekiel[1] consists of the oracles of judgment against the nations. They highlight the reconstruction of Israel as expressed in Ezekiel's vision (cf. chaps. 33-48) and so they play a significant role in the overall structure of the book of Ezekiel.[2] Ezekiel announces God's judgment against seven nations/cities that remind the reader of the seven nations mentioned in the Book of Deuteronomy (7,1), nations that the Israelites drive out in order to possess the Promised Land. The series of oracles against the nations begins with four short and similarly formulated oracles against Ammon (25,1-7), Moab (25,8-11), Edom (25,12-14), and the Philistines (25,15-17), but the oracles against Tyre (26,1-28,19) are formulated differently. They are longer and structurally they are similar to the oracles against Egypt. A short oracle of judgment against Sidon (28,20-24) is found at the end of the 'Tyre-oracles.'[3] The oracles of judgment against these six foreign nations and cities is followed by an oracle of salvation for Israel (28,25-27), used as a tactical literary intervention before announcing harsh judgment against Egypt in the next series of oracles of judgment.

---

[1] I.e., chaps. 1-24 (Israel); chaps. 25-32 (Nations); and chaps. 33-48 (Israel).

[2] BOADT, "Rhetorical strategies," in LUST (ed.), *Ezekiel and His Book*, BEThL 74, 196.198.

[3] The list of names of the nations/cities follows geographical orientation, clockwise from north to south and back to the north (of Israel). Egypt, the seventh nation in the list, breaks this continuity; see ZENGER (ed.), *Stuttgarter Altes Testament*, 1649.

1.2. The oracles of judgment against Egypt (Ezek 29-32)
1.2.1. The oracle of salvation to Egypt (29,13-16)

Ezekiel 29,13-16 is the only oracle of salvation in the oracles against the nations in the book of Ezekiel[4] and it refers to the restoration of Egypt that will take place at the end of 40 years (29,13). Here the "forty years" refers to the period of judgment of Egypt (29,11.12). It is an Exodus motif which reminds us of Israel's 40 years of wandering in the desert. Thus Ezekiel draws a parallel between God's dealing with Israel (11,16-18; cf. 28,24-26) and Egypt (29,13-16).

This oracle of salvation to Egypt highlights four basic actions of God: 1) He gathers the Egyptians from their dispersion; 2) He brings them back out of captivity; 3) He causes them to dwell in Pathros; and 4) He makes them a lowly kingdom. Egypt's new existence as a lowly kingdom has implications for Egypt as well as for the nations and for the house of Israel. Egypt becomes the lowest of all the kingdoms. This means that 1) Egypt shall not exalt herself over the nations; and 2) she shall not rule over the nations (v.15). It implies that the nations will not live under the shadow of Egypt. For the house of Israel, it means that 1) Egypt shall no longer be confidence for Israel, in other words, Israel will no longer depend on her; and 2) it will be a reminder of their past infidelity to the LORD whenever they turned to them, instead of turning to Him.

1.2.2. Pharaoh: the big crocodile; Egypt: An unreliable reed (29,1-12)

The first oracle of judgment against Egypt (10th year/10th month/12th day) chornologically dates 6th January 587,[5] and consists of three short oracles (3b-6a; 6b-9a; 9b-12). It begins with a solemn introduction and contains a date formula, the word-event formula, the address to the prophet as 'son of man,' and a command to direct himself for his prophetic oracles. The command indicates that the oracles relate to Pharaoh and the whole of Egypt (1-3a).

All three oracles use metaphors. The first oracle uses the metaphor of the "big crocodile" living in the Nile. Its main accusation is hubris, expressed by the crodile's claim: "The Niles is mine and I made it for myself." This saying of the crocodile implies that Pharaoh considers himself as the creator of Egypt, i.e., of its wealth and greatness which is an affront to God's authority and power.

The "big crocodile"[6] refers to Pharaoh, the Nile where it lies[7] refers to Egypt, and the fish of the Nile refer to Egypt's inhabitants. The announcement of

---

[4] Compare Hos 8,8-10; Isa 19,23-25; cf. 66,18-21.

[5] PARKER and DUBBERSTEIN, *Babylonian Chronology*, Chicago (1942), 25-26.

[6] The crocodile represents a mythical animal, the primeval enemy of God's creation (cf. Ps 74,13f.; Is 27,1; 51,9; Job 7,12).

[7] Ezek 32,2 gives further description of the Nile-crocodile: It bursts forth (תָּגַח) its streams, troubles (תִּדְלַח) the waters with its feet and stamps (תִּרְפֹּס) their streams.

judgment includes Paharaoh and the the inhabitants of Egypt. The vocabularies used in the announcement of judgment, e.g., wilderness, (cf. Num 14,29), food, etc. express the exodus motif.

The second oracle uses the metaphor of the "staff of reed." Here the focus shifts from Pharaoh to Egypt. The second accusation against Egypt relates to her relationship with the house of Israel, which is exemplified by the reed's nature. It is feeble and it characterises Egypt's "unreliability" (cf. Is 36,6; 2Kgs 18,21), proving her deceptive character.[8] Indirectly, the "reed" also refers to the physical condition of the banks of the Nile where it grows (cf. Ex 2,2). Thus the second oracle shows its relationship with the first oracle. God announces the "sword" as a judgment that will cut off man and beast, making the land of Egypt desolate.

The third oracle repeats the metaphorical saying of the crocodile, which relates to the pride of Egypt, while the announcement of judgment refers to the destruction of man and beast and the desolation of the land for "forty years". This is Exodus terminology, whereas the "dispersion" of the Egyptians reminds the exile motif.

1.1.3. The judgment of Egypt through Nebuchadnezzar (29,17-21)

This short oracle (27th year/ 1st month/ 1st day) comes seven years after the first oracle, and chronologically dates 16th April 571,[9] which is the latest oracle in the book of Ezekiel.

There is no direct motive here for a judgment against Egypt,[10] but the lack of reward for the army of Nebuchadnezzar that sieged Tyre is given as an indirect motive. The Thirteen years' siege of Tyre by Nebuchadnezzar's army is interpreted as a "service" to the LORD, for which he gives Nebuchadnezzar Egypt as wages for his army and personal compensation.[11] The manner in which this is realized is described in terms of pillage of the land of Egypt and carrying off her hordes as booty.

Here Ezekiel abrogates and reformulates his earlier oracles against Egypt, not realized so far, in the light of the (partial) fulfilment of his oracles against Tyre, giving some clue as to how his earlier oracles could be interpreted. Ezekiel is not concerned about the fulfilment of his oracles nor does he lose faith and conviction

---

[8] It may refer to Hophra (589-570) when Egypt quietly watched the fall of her ally in 587. See "History of Egypt: Intermediate-Saite period," in *ABD* II, 362.

[9] PARKER and DUBBERSTEIN, *Babylonian Chronology*, Providence (1956), 28. 16th April 570 is calculated according to the autumn Calendar but according to the spring calendar it corresponds to 26th April 571.

[10] Egypt's logistical support of Tyre against Nebuchadnezzar's thirteen years' siege cannot be ignored as one of the reasons, for connecting the fall of Tyre directly with the fate of Egypt.

[11] Theologically, Nebuchadnezzar is seen as the LORD'S agent; see CORRAL, *Ezekiel's Oracles against Tyre*, 7.

over the lack of their fulfilment. This is proved by the assurance he gets from the LORD himself on the true nature of his prophetic mission.

1.2.4. The Day of the LORD (30,1-19)[12]

Ezek 30,1-19 is the only oracle against Egypt that is not dated, but its placement after 29,17-21 shows that it further develops the preceding oracle, as 30,3 clearly shows the near end and destruction of Egypt. This destruction is going to be carried out by Nebuchadnezzar, the king of Babylon (30,10; cf. 29,18;). Ezek 30,1-19 also continues the hordes-motif (30,4.10.15) mentioned in 29,19.[13] The motif of the "Day of the LORD" (30,1-9) sharpens the threat of God's judgment against Egypt.[14] Ezek 30,1-19 also makes a detailed description of the threat of destruction announced in 29,1-21 and bridges the distance to mythic and cosmic aspects of judgment described in chaps. 31-32.[15]

The Day of the LORD[16] makes it clear that the LORD will punish Egypt by the sword, bringing a day of gloom over her. It will destroy her supports and devastate the entire land.[17] The hordes of Egypt will be carried into captivity and her national foundations will be torn down. Even the cities and the nations which helped her will not be spared. It describes the woes of Egypt because of God's judgment and shows the similarity between the fate of Egypt and Judah/Israel (cf. Ezek 7). Here sword is a key-word, used as a means of God's judgment against Egypt and against her helpers, namely, Cush, Put, Lud, the Arabs,[18] the Lybians and the "sons of the covenant."[19]

The hordes[20] of Egypt and her foundations (יְסוֹדֹתֶיהָ cf. 11,3), i.e., the army chiefs, the leaders, and the helpers (עֹזְרֶיהָ v.7), symbolise two main structures of Egypt's might. The cutting off of the basic sources of supply for the army and the

---

[12] In BOADT's opinion, the relation between 30,1-19 and 29,17-21 is deeper than reference to Nebuchadnezzar; namely, both emphasize the desolation of the land in the judgment against Egypt. See his *Ezekiel's Oracles*, 11.

[13] הֲמוֹן ("hordes") occurs 66 times in the Old Testament; 45x in Isa, Jer, and Ezek. Ezekiel attests 26 occurrences including 16 times in chaps. 29-32. See BOADT, *Ezekiel's Oracles*, 11. For its etymology and meaning see, MÜLLER, „הָמָה", in *ThWAT* II, 449-454.

[14] ZIMMERLI, *Ezechiel 25-48*, 728.

[15] BOADT, *Ezekiel's Oracles*, 57

[16] Is 13,6ff.; Joel 2,1; 4,14; Zeph 1, 7; Ezek 7, 7.12

[17] Please note the repetition of the expression "from Migdol to Syene" (29,10.6).

[18] During the Saite Dynasty, the Egyptian army comprised the Greeks, Ionians, Rhodians, Carians, Lybians, Phoenicians, and Jews besides the native Egyptians. See GREENBERG, *Ezekiel 21-37*, 621

[19] By the expression "sons of the covenant" ZIMMERLI considers the Israelites, who had established a colony in Elephantine. See his *Ezechiel 25-48*, 731.

[20] Boadt (*Ezekiel's Oracles*, 71) prefers to render הֲמוֹן as "troops" (cf. v.10) in contrast with "foundations" (יְסוֹדֹת); Zimmerli (*Ezechiel, 25-48*, 733) translates it as "pomp".

destruction of the country's foundations indicate utter destruction of Egypt. Besides, the supports of Egypt (סֹמְכֵי מִצְרַיִם v.6), which include its idols and princes (v.13), fortified cities (v.15), and warriors (v.17), as well as its helpers (עֹזְרֶיהָ v.7), i.e., the auxiliary tribes, constituting other vital elements of the nation's power. God's judgment envisages the destruction of all these structures and sources of power.

God, who has judged and punished Tyre by Nebuchadnezzar's sword, now turns to execute his judgment against Egypt.[21] As a result of his judgment, 1) the hordes of Egypt will be put to an end (הִשְׁבַּתִּי); 2) the Nile will be made dry (חָרָבָה); 3) the land and everything in it (מְלֹאָהּ) will be devasted (הֲשִׁמֹּתִי); and 4) the idols and the images (גִּלּוּלִים and אֱלִילִים)[22] of Memphis, and her prince (נָשִׂיא) will be destroyed (וְהַאֲבַדְתִּי).[23] It also shows the helplessness of the gods and idols of Egypt and of her prince.[24] Finally, the list of names of her cities points to all-encompassing judgment against the entire land of Egypt.

1.2.5. Pharaoh's arms are broken (30,20-26)

For those who doubted the authenticity of Ezekiel's oracles against Egypt,[25] the next oracle (30,20-26) comes as a greater shock. It is dated 11th year/1st month/7th day (19th April 586) and relates to the second year of the siege of Jerusalem.[26] This short oracle speaks plainly that God has already broken one arm of Pharaoh, i.e., Egypt's supports, strongholds and foundations, and that He is soon going to break the other as well so that he can no longer hold a sword. The latter may refer to a severe blow to her army that will break her military might.

On the contrary, God will strengthen the arms of Nebuchadnezzar and put His sword in his hand. The oracle does not dispute the fact that God is going to use Nebuchadnezzar as His instrument to execute His judgment against Egypt. It is through Nebuchadnezzar's arm that God's sword will bring desolation to the land and disperse her inhabitants. Sword (29,8; 30,6.11.17.22.24) and the dispersion of

---

[21] Nebuchadnezzar's thirteen years' siege of Tyre ended with a treaty in 573 B.C. (March/April 571 B.C.), but Tyre managed to maintain her independence. The siege emptied her treasuries and Nebuchanezzar's army could not gain substantial booty for it. Nebuchadnezzar decided to campaign against Egypt in his 37th year which is 568-567 B.C.

[22] אֱלִילִים - גִּלּוּלִים echo the holiness Code in Lev 26. See BOADT, *Ezekiel's Oracles*, 77.

[23] God is the subject of these verbs of action, indicating that God Himself judges Egypt.

[24] BOADT argues that although נָשִׂיא refers to Pharaoh here, Ezekiel leaves it ambiguous intentionally so that diminutively it could be interpreted to mean a mere tribal chieftain rather than a great divine-Pharaoh. See his *Ezekiel's Oracles*, 77.

[25] Ezekiel's oracles against Tyre did not materialise fully in the manner he had predicted. This may have encouraged Judah's reliance on Egypt to avert the inevitable catastrophe befalling her through Nebuchadnezzar of Babylon.

[26] KEIL, *Ezekiel*, COT 9, 257.

the Egyptians (29,12;30,26), these two motifs are repeated here, showing their literary relation with the earlier oracles.

1.2.6. Pharaoh's comparison with the cosmic tree (31,1-18)

The the fifth oracle is an allegory.[27] The rhetoric in v.2, "To what you are like in your greatness," intimates a reference to Pharaoh and to his hordes. But the description of the cosmic tree (cf. 31,3-9) maintains suspense until v.10, "Therefore thus says the Lord GOD," which makes it clear that it is an oracle of judgment against Pharaoh. The greatness and envious beauty of the Lebanon-cedar are described in vv.3-6 and vv.7-9, respectively.[28] Nourished by rain and deep waters, it grows high and lofty; its branches grow long with foliage; the birds of the air flock to its large branches, the beasts multiply under it and all the nations dwell under its shade.[29] It excells all cypresses and plane tress, a sheer envy of all the trees of Eden. Although it dominates the heavens and the deep ocean (cf. Gen 1,2), it fails to realise that its majestic growth and beauty are the results of God's action. So, Pharaoh's "self-glory" or "pride" (31,10 cf. 29,3; 32,2), underlies the motive for its judgment.

God's judgment is described in prophetic perfect. He has delivered the cosmic tree into the hands of the most powerful and cruel of nations who cuts it down, leaving its trunk on the hills and scattering its branches in the valleys.[30] The birds and the beasts who sought its protection earlier, now prey upon its carcass (ruin). The nations are shocked at its ruin when God humbles (lit. drives out גֵּרַשׁ) its haughtiness. The descent of the mighty cedar to the Underworld is characterised by mourning, stopping of streams, restraining of abundant waters and the trembling of the nations, highlighting God's judgment. The reference at the end to Pharaoh and his hordes lying in disgrace in Sheol with the uncircumcised and with those fallen by the sword (cf. 32,18), points to its relation with the next oracle of judgment against Egypt.

1.2.7. A dirge over Pharaoh (32,1-16)

The sixth oracle of judgment is a lament over Pharaoh. It is spoken allegorically and it illustrates an unceremonious exit of the great Pharaoh from the land of the living and humbling of his pride. Pharaoh is metaphorically spoken of as a young lion with strength and prowess, ultimately referring to its might and pride that provokes God to haste his judgment against it.

---

[27] Cf. 1 Kgs 5,13.

[28] Cf. Ps 80,11; 109,16.

[29] Cf. Ezek 28,13; Isa 51,3. See also Judg 9,7-15.

[30] For the possible inspiration on the allegory of Lebanon cedar, see Isa 14,9-10; 10,33-34.

In Egyptian thought, the lion was "associated with royalty or divinity."[31] As a young lion, Pharaoh typifies power and superiority that is over-confident of victory.[32] But in his pride, Pharaoh is blinded and fails to realise that he is not a young lion but a self-indulgent sea-monster that God will capture in his net and pull from the water, leaving it on the dry ground as a prey for the birds of the air and the beasts of the field. The carcass of the sea-monster will be thrown all over the mountains[33] and valleys. Its fluid will soak the land and its blood fill the river-beds, befitting its pride and guilt.

The imagery of catching the dragon with a net, dragging it out of water and leaving it on the dry, open ground, reflects the Babylonian myth about the battle between Marduk and the Sea-Dragon Tiamat, a symbol of primeval chaos. Marduk captures Tiamat in his net, subdues it and thus gurantees order in the universe, which had been threatened by Tiamat.

The heavens will be covered with clouds, darkening the stars, the sun and the moon. They will fail to give their light, and the other great luminaries will also be darkened. This celestial phenomenon reveals a gloom and hopelessness on the Day of the LORD, and echoes the plague of three days and nights of utter darkness in Egypt (cf. Ex 10,21-22). The hearts of people and kings will be dismayed at the sight of Egypt's fate and horror of its destruction by the sword (חֶרֶב)[34] of Nebuchadnezzar. However, God's judgment against Egypt does not imply only destruction, but also its re-establishment, which he assures by purging the land and cleaning the Nile-streams (cf. 32,13-14) that had been defiled by the sea-monster and by Pharaoh's blood.[35]

1.2.8. A Dirge over Egypt: Her going down to Sheol (32,17-32)

The seventh oracle of judgment is a dirge over Egypt. It describes Pharaoh's going down to Sheol with his hordes (32,17-32), which makes a fitting conclusion to the oracles of judgment against Egypt. God brings Egypt, her hordes, and her helper-nations (cf. 30,4-18) to the lowest places of the earth. Although Pharaoh (Egypt) was mighty and incomparable in his life-time, he is thrown into Sheol in the company of the uncircumcised and those slain by the sword, where Assyria and her whole assembly, Elam and all her hordes, and Meshech-Tubal and all her hordes already belong. They all lie there, carrying their reproaches with them,

---

[31] BOADT, *Ezekiel's Oracles*, 130.

[32] It is comparable with the king of Judah, cf. 19,3,5b.

[33] Mountains are seen as the last place of refuge in times of calamity. Here they are seen as a refuge against God's judgment, but they will not protect Egypt from God's judgment; cf. Ezek 7,16; Jer 25,33. See BOADT, *Ezekiel's Oracles*, 137; see also his comment on Ezek 30,11b and 12b, in the same, p.115f.

[34] חֶרֶב ("Sword") is a key-word in the oracles of judgment against Egypt.

[35] Blood is seen as what defiles or fauls the land; cf. the Egyptian plague in Ex 7,17.

although warriors of the past. Edom and her kings and her chiefs, the princes of the north, and all the Sidonians (the Phoenicians), have met the same fate despite their great valour. In the same way, Egypt will be crushed and forced to lie with the uncircumcised and those slain by the sword, symbolizing her final humiliation.

The final destination of Pharaoh and his hordes in the Underworld debases and disgraces Egypt completely, rendering her devoid of all power and glory. Pharaoh's hubris and claim to divinity meet a fitting end in this humiliation and inglorious existence in the lowest parts of the Underworld, in the company of the impure and the unfortunate, bereft of any possibility of life.

1.3. Conclusion

The oracles against the foreign nations in the middle section of the book of Ezekiel are neither superfluous nor mere preludes[36] or transitional[37] texts. They highlight the reconstruction of Israel as expressed in the third section of the book, thus playing a significant role in the overall structure of the book of Ezekiel. The first six nations in the list, preceding the main oracles of judgment against Egypt, are reminiscent of a classical prophetic tradition, using the number "seven" in the oracles of judgment as found in Am 1,1ff.

The seven oracles of judgment against Egypt use metaphorical language to achieve unity (cf. theme of Pharaoh and Egypt). The judgment against Egypt becomes increasingly severe. Pharoah, the big crocodile, who boasted to be master of the Nile and presumed himself to be a god, is judged by the Sovereign LORD, which results in his dead corpse being left to lie in the open, his land being laid desolate and her population scattered. God cuts off both of Pharoah's arms, felling him like a cedar of Lebanon that is cut down and strewn in the valley. The casting of Pharaoh into the Underworld together with his hordes, the source of his power and boasting, shows the utter humiliation of Pharaoh's might and boasting while re-establishing the sovereignty of the LORD.

---

[36] BOADT, "Ezekiel," in *ABD* II, 711 cited in CORRAL, *Ezekiel's Oracles against Tyre*, 1.
[37] BLOCK, *Ezekiel 25-48*, 3.

CHAPTER TWO
TEXT CRITICICAL ANALYSIS OF EZEKIEL 29, 1-16

The overview of Ezekiel's oracles against the nations in the previous chapter makes it clear that the oracles of judgment against Egypt (chaps. 25-32) constitute the main part of his oracles of judgment against the nations. It also highlights the placement of the first and the last oracles against Egypt (29,1-16 and 29,17-30,19), which also happen to be his first and the last oracles in the book, next to each other in the composition.

In the present chapter, we present a text-critical analysis of the first oracle of judgment against Egypt in Ezek 29,1-16. L. Boadt has thoroughly investigated the text philologically from Ugarit, and D. Barthélemy has pointed to some problematic texts.[1] By and large, the text is free from any serious dispute. All the same, we have noted variant readings in the MT, which in some cases seem to be helpful in understanding the text and its meaning. The text and translation of each verse is given separately, and wherever variant Readings appear in the MT (cf. BHS), they have been indicated with Arabic number in the Hebrew text and have been discussed. Thus, this chapter examines and evaluates the MT in interpreting the text, especially where variant Readings appear.

2.1. Ezek 29,1-16:

29,1:

בַּשָּׁנָה֙ הָעֲשִׂירִ֔ית בָּעֲשִׂרִ֕י בִּשְׁנֵ֥ים עָשָׂ֖ר לַחֹ֑דֶשׁ
הָיָ֥ה דְבַר־יְהוָ֖ה אֵלַ֥י לֵאמֹֽר

In the tenth year, in the tenth month, on the twelfth of the month
the word of the LORD came to me saying:

LXX renders בִּשְׁנֵים עָשָׂר as μιᾷ while Aquila and Theodotion render it as τῇ δωδεκάτη (= שנים עשר). LXX[B] attests δωδεκάτῳ and the Vulgate translates it as *undecima die*. In rendering בַּשָּׁנָה הָעֲשִׂירִית ("in the tenth year") as ἐν τῷ ἔτει τῷ δωδεκάτῳ ("in the twelfth year") by LXX[B], L. Boadt cautions about the danger of depending on LXX for the study of the book Ezekiel.[2] If one accepts the date "in

---

[1] BARTHÉLEMY (ed.), *Critique Textuelle* 3, 239-244.

[2] BOADT, *Ezekiel's Oracles*, 17. COOKE and ZIMMERLI think that "in the twelfth year" as given in LXX[B] is an attempt to correct the sequence after 26,1; see COOKE, *Ezekiel*, 325 and ZIMMERLI, *Ezekiel 25-48*, 703.

the twelfth year," corresponding to Dec./Jan. 586/585[3], in LXX[B] as correct, then it would mean that the oracle was delivered after the fall of Jerusalem.[4] This, however, does not agree with the historical events relating to the siege of Jerusalem by the army of Nebuchadrezzar of Babylon, which lies in the background of this oracle. The MT בַּשָּׁנָה הָעֲשִׂירִית "in the tenth year," (= 6th Jan. 587)[5] agrees with the historical situation reflected in v.7. Zimmerli thinks that δωδεκάτῳ ("twelfth") in LXX[B] may be a retrograde attempt to correct the MT in view of "in the eleventh year" in 26,1 and an attempt to establish a historical sequence.[6] But if one accepts "in the twelfth year" as given in LXX [B], one faces an insurmountable difficulty in explaining "in the eleventh year" in 30,20 and the next date in 31,1 that presupposes subsequent historical date/events in relation to 29,1.[7]

According to D. I. Block, LXX's reading of MT בִּשְׁנֵים עָשָׂר as as μιᾳ (= בְּאֶחָד) may be a case of pseudo-dittography of the next word לַחֹדֶשׁ, which is rendered *undecima die* (eleventh day) in the Vulgate, and apparently reinstates עָשָׂר in the text.[8] Zimmerli presumes that here the date may have been wrongly exchanged for the month.[9] But historically, MT "in the 10th year, in the 10th month, on the 12th of the month" (29,1) refers to nearly one year's siege of Jerusalem[10] by the Babylonian army which was a little more than six months before the fall of Jerusalem.[11] This date corresponds to the occasion when Hophra (588-570 B.C.), Pharaoh of Egypt, made his army march to relieve Jerusalem which prompted Nebuchadnezzar to lift the siege of Jerusalem temporarily (cf. Jer 37,3ff).[12] These historical events support the date given in the MT. Therefore, LXX's rendering of of 29,1 is not reliable in resolving the complexity of this date.

---

[3] HAYES and HOOKER maintain that the Babylonians did not lay siege to Jerusalem until 10 *Tebet* in Zedekiah's ninth year (588-587) which is January 587 B.C. Ezekiel's oracle against Egypt came on 12 *Tebet* of the 10th year of the exile. See their *A New Chronology*, 98. A. MALAMAT places Hophra's intervention against Nebuchadnezzar's siege of Jerusalem at the end of winter and in the spring of 587 B.C., i.e., after a full year of its siege, and somewhat more than a year before its end, thus, on 12 *Teberth*, the 10th year of exile, corresponding to 7 January 587 B.C. See his "The Last Kings of Judah," in *IJE* 18/3, 152-153.

[4] BOADT, *Ezekiel's Oracles*, 17.

[5] MAY, "Ezekiel: Introduction," in *IB* VI, 56.

[6] ZIMMERLI, *Ezekiel 25-48*, 703.

[7] ZIMMERLI, *Ezekiel 25-48*, 703; see also COOKE, *Ezekiel*, 325.

[8] BLOCK, *Ezekiel 25-48*, 133, fn. 15.

[9] ZIMMERLI, *Ezekiel 25-48*, 703.

[10] It refers to the second siege of Jerusalem (588-587 B.C.). The first siege of the city began in 598 B.C. and it ended in 597 B.C. with the first deportation to Babylon, cf. 2Kgs 24,10ff.

[11] A little over six months after this date (i.e., June/July 587 B.C.), Jerusalem fell to the Babylonians. See BLENKINSOPP, *Ezekiel*, 127.

[12] COOKE, *Ezekiel*, 325; BLENKINSOPP, *Ezekiel*, 128.

29,2:

בֶּן־אָדָם שִׂים פָּנֶיךָ עַל־פַּרְעֹה מֶלֶךְ מִצְרָיִם
וְהִנָּבֵא עָלָיו וְעַל־מִצְרַיִם כֻּלָּהּ

Son of man set your face against pharaoh, king of Egypt,
And prophesy against him and against all Egypt.

After the command "Turn your face", the preposition אֶל ("to") would be normally expected; instead עַל ("against") appears in 29,2 and 35,2.[13] In both these places, BHS equates עַל with אֶל. Boadt observes that עַל and אֶל are used interchangably in Ezekiel, sometimes even in the same verse (21,2; 22,13; 23,5.42; 38,12; 44,3), and that the distinction between the two prepositions was sometimes confusing in dictation.[14] Yet, he thinks that the interchange cannot be ascribed merely to the confusion of distinguishing *ayin-aleph* in the dictation, since there is clear evidence of the distinction between them in other sources.[15] It cannot be ascribed to phonetic confusion, since the interchange is found also in those texts where this confuision does not arise.[16] This change from אֶל to עַל could be partly due to Aramisation, as Aramic does not use אֶל with a personal object.[17] Zimmerli observes that according to the strict Hebrew usage, here as well as in 1,17 and 10,12, עַל is used instead of אֶל that is expected, blurring the range of meaning of אֶל and עַל, are used interchangably in the book of Ezekiel without any hard and fast rule; although a change from עַל to אֶל occur rarely.[18]

Boadt maintains that in NW Semitic, the prepositions may have a wide range of overlapping semitic meaning (e.g., in the use of *b* and *l*, `*l* and *l* in UT) due to a frequent interchange between אֶל and עַל in the OT tradition. But there is evidence in 8th cent. Aramaic and in classical Hebrew that the preposition אֶל was clearly distinguished from עַל, and had the meaning "to", but in the 6th century and later a growing tendency arose to change אֶל to עַל. Up to the Exile, variation between the two preopositions was used more for stylistic effect and balance than for grammatical reasons. Of the nine occurrances of שִׂים פָּנֶיךָ אֶל / עַל in Ezek (cf.,

---

[13] Compare it with v.10 where there a change from the usual עַל to אֶל. On the meaning of עַל ("against") see VOGT, *Lexicon*, 128.a.

[14] BOADT, *Ezekiel's Oracles*, 19.

[15] BOADT, *Ezekiel's Oraclest*, 19; see also COOKE, *Ezekiel*, 27; BROKELMANN, *Hebräische Syntax* §108c.

[16] BOADT, *Ezekiel's Oracles*, 19-20.

[17] BOADT, *Ezekiel's Oracles*, 20. See also *BDB*, 757a.c.-b(a). *BDB*'s (41a.2) observation on the use of אֶל is noteworthy: "There is a tendency in Hebrew, esp. manifest in S K Je Ez, to use אֶל in the sense of עַל; sometimes אֶל being used exceptionally in a phrase or construction which regularly, and in accusative with analogy, has עַל; sometimes, the two prepositions interchanging, apparently without discrimination, in the same or parallel sentences."

[18] ZIMMERLI, *Ezekiel 1-25*, 6.

6,2; 13,17; 21,2.7; 25,2; 28,21; 35,2; 38,2), only in 29,2 and 35,2 has the preposition עַל been employed with שִׂים פָּנֶיךָ.[19] These characteristics of use, make it clear that its usage in 29,2 is not stylistic, but rather lays special emphasis on the prophetic oracle. Therefore, although the suggestion of BHS to change עַל to אֶל makes good sense in 29,2, שִׂים [פָּנֶיךָ] עַל is a standard biblical form even though שִׂים אֶל is also found OT (Job 5,8; 13,33; 23,33).[20]

29,3:

דַּבֵּר[3] וְאָמַרְתָּ כֹּה־אָמַר אֲדֹנָי[4] יְהוִה הִנְנִי עָלֶיךָ
פַּרְעֹה מֶלֶךְ־מִצְרַיִם[5] הַתַּנִּים[6] הַגָּדוֹל הָרֹבֵץ בְּתוֹךְ יְאֹרָיו[7]
אֲשֶׁר אָמַר לִי יְאֹרִי[8] וַאֲנִי עֲשִׂיתִנִי[9]

Speak and say, thus says the Lord GOD:
Look, I am against you Pharaoh, king of Egypt,
The big crocodile that lies in the midst of his Niles;
Who says: 'Mine is the Niles and I made it for myself.'

This verse offers a number of textual difficulties. In the Old Greek דַּבֵּר is lacking and it is often omitted as a gloss.[21] Ehrlich goes to the extent of saying that Ezekiel does not use it in such combination.[22] Zimmerli considers it unusual in the stereotype, introductory formulaic expression,[23] while Greenberg takes it as a "shortened form of the solemn parallelism of 14,4 and 20,3."[24] This combination occurs in 14,14; 20,3; 33,2 and Lev 1,2; 18,2; 23,2; Num 5,12; 6,2.[25] While the Priestly style commonly uses דַּבֵּר וְאָמַרְתָּ, Ezekiel's use of אָמַר may be explained as pleonastic, to create a dramatic effect (cf. in Ezek 11,16; 12,10; 17,12; 33,10-12).[26] Although דַּבֵּר וְאָמַרְתָּ do not make a parallel pair, Boadt defends the usage in 29,3a and finds its omission from the Old Greek as an attempt to smoothen its unusual usage.[27] However, since דַּבֵּר וְאָמַרְתָּ expresses exactly the same sense, the usage of this pair here is rather unusual for Ezekiel and may explain the omission of דַּבֵּר in LXX.

---

[19] BOADT, *Ezekiel's Oracles*, 20-21.

[20] BOADT, *Ezekiel's Oracles*, 20-21.

[21] WEVERS, *Ezekiel*, 223; ZIMMERLI, *Ezekiel 25-48*, 703; BOADT, *Ezekiel's oracles*, 21; ALLEN, *Ezekiel 20-48*, 102, fn. 3; BLOCK, *Ezekiel 25-48*, 135; GREENBERG, *Ezekiel 21-37*, 601.

[22] EHRLICH, *Randglossen*, 15. Bd., 111.

[23] ZIMMERLI, *Ezekiel 25-48*, 703.

[24] GREENBERG, *Ezekiel 21-37*, 601.

[25] ALLEN, *Ezekiel 20-48*, 102; see also BLOCK, *Ezekiel 25-48*, 134.

[26] BOADT, *Ezekiel's Oracles*, 22.

[27] דַּבֵּר וְאָמַרְתָּ appears in Ex 6,29f., Num 18,26; Isa 45,19; Prov 4,20 and their reverse in Gen 21,1; Isa 40,27; see BOADT, *Ezekiel's Oracles*, 22-23.

The appellation אֲדֹנָי is lacking before יְהוִה in Old Greek, although אֲדֹנָי יְהוִה occurs 310 times in the OT, of which 217 occurrances are found in Ezekiel alone.[28] This makes it a special form in Ezekiel although many doubt its authenticity and consider אֲדֹנָי a late addition on the ground that Boadt has raised, that LXX's rendering of this divine name is not always consistent.[29] Boadt is of the opinion that there may be an early tradition behind its use, and points to some older texts in the OT in support of this view (cf. Gen 15,2; 2Sam 7,18ff., Jos 7,7; Judg 6,22; and esp. Ex 15,17). He also claims that Ugaritic provides similar examples of a parellel use of double names, which are found in the latter text (cf. in parallel colons in Ex 15, 17ff.) and witnessed also in poetic verses (e.g., Pss 35,22; 71,5; 86,5f; 130,1f; 135,5; Isa 3,17; 49,14).[30]

מֶלֶךְ־מִצְרַיִם is missing in the Old Greek, but BHS adds this phrase after פַּרְעֹה (29,2.3; 31,2.21.22; 32,2; only פַּרְעֹה in 30,25x2; 32,31) in the book of Ezekiel. In the book of Exodus, where most of the occurrances appear (115x), there are only five instances in which מֶלֶךְ־מִצְרַיִם is added after פַּרְעֹה (6,11.13.27.29; 14,8), and one in which it stands alone (cf. 14,5). The five occurrences where מֶלֶךְ־מִצְרַיִם is added to פַּרְעֹה in the book of Exodus show a turning point in the narrative and emphsize the person of Pharaoh in relation to the people of Israel rather than the people or the land. The reason for its ommssion in Ezek 29,3 in the Old Greek is because it was considered to be otiose, an unnecessary phrase, and apparently a late addition to the text.[31] Its usage in 29,3 and in other places (e.g., vv.18.19), functions as a 'qualifier' in apposition to Pharaoh as a person. It is used in specific refererence to the person of Pharaoh, just as the "inhabitants of Egypt" (v.6), the "Egyptians" (v.13), and the "land of Egypt" (vv.9.10.12.19.20) are used with reference to the people of Egypt and their land, respectively. Thus, there is no need to omit it.

MT הַתַּנִּים, a plural form of תַּן (n. m. sg.), generally means "jackals" (cf. Isa 13,22; 34,13).[32] That meaning does not fit in this context, since here it refers to the Niles (plural) as its natural habitat in which it is hunted with a fishing hook (cf.

---

[28] BOADT, *Ezekiel's Oracles*, 23. For a detailed discussion on this topic see „Der Gottesname im Buche Ezechiel", ZIMMERLI, *Ezechiel 25-48*, 1250-1258.

[29] Cf. κύριος occurs 140 times, κύριος κύριος 57 times, κύριος θέος or ὁ θέος 16 times; see DALMANN, „Der Gottesname Adonaj und seine Geshichte", 15. For a summary of various findings by different critics on the topic see BOADT, *Ezekiel's oracles*, 23.

[30] BOADT, *Ezekiel's oracles*, 23-26; see also Pss 30,9; 38,16; 130,3 (with shortened form יָהּ for יְהוִה), Am 7,8, and Mic 1,2, as well as Ex 23,17; Isa 10,16 and the Elohistic Psalms 54,6; 62,13; 68,33, its reverse in Ps 66,18f., in a chiastic structure in Pss 71,5; 130,1b-2a; 135,5 and Isa 49,14. For further discussion, see in the same, pp.23-26.

[31] ALLEN, *Ezekiel 20-48*, 102.

[32] ALLEN, *Ezekiel 20-48*, 102; see also ZIMMERLI, *Ezekiel 25-48*, 703.

v.4). Many manuscripts correct it as הַתַּנִּין "crododile," a sea-animal.[33] Boadt thinks that הַתַּנִּים in 29,3 refers to the mythological הַתַּנִּין (cf. Isa 27,1; 51,9; Job 7,16; Ps 74,13) that God defeats.[34] He argues that since Ezekiel uses הַתַּנִּים in 29,3 (cf. 32,2), the final *mem* could be a scribal confusion for "ן" in הַתַּנִּין ("jackals") or, the scribes corrected that Aramized masculine plural *nun*-ending to the standardized Hebrew masculine plural *mem*-ending. He gives examples of interchange between *mem-nun* attested in Semitic languages, like: Akkadic, Ugaritic, Moabitic, Hebrew and Arabic, which may explain the confusion of *mem-nun* in Ezekiel (33,26: עֲשִׂיתֶן as Aramaic type m. pl.; 13,20: אַתֶּם as f. pl., 34,31 אַתֶּן as m. pl.; 26,18: אִיִּן for אִים; and 30,13: נֹף instead of מֹף).[35] So, MT הַתַּנִּים in v.3 is a special form of the usual plural הַתַּנִּין, which is supported by Barthélemy.[36]

Syriac renders MT יְאֹרָיו (m. pl. + cstr. 3m. sg.) as *nhrwt'* (= יְאֹרִים m. pl.). Likewise LXX reads it as οἱ ποταμοί (m. pl.). יְאֹר (sg.) is commonly thought to derive from an Egyptian root *i(t)rw* which means "river" or "the Nile."[37] Its use in singular generally refers to the river Nile and its plural יְאֹרִים refers to its channels in the Delta region.[38] In practice, however, the Niles referred also to its branches.[39] In view of its plural-usage (יְאֹרָיו [3a]; יְאֹרֶיךָ [vv.4.10]), LXX and Syriac suggest a plural reading also in 3b.9b, although BHS maintains its singular usage in the last two occurrances.[40] Boadt holds the opinion that singular usage in 9b may have been a stylistic variation, as in Pss 5,10; 7,2f; 17,11f., and a few other examples in Ezekiel.[41]

MT עֲשִׂיתֻנִי (pf. 1c. sg. + suff. 1c. sg. homonym[42]) is difficult to explain in this verse.[43] LXX translates it ἐποίησα αὐτούς, "I made them;" Syriac has `*abdth* (= עֲשִׂיתִיו suff. 3m. sg.), and BHS suggests עֲשִׂיתִים (suff. 3m. pl.). Grammatically, the object suff. 1c. sg. ("myself") in MT עֲשִׂיתֻנִי does not agree with the context, and so it is taken as a special case of the verbal dative suffix.[44] Cooke thinks that the

---

[33] הַתַּנִּים in Gen 1,21 refers to "sea-creature." See also RUPRECHT, „Das Nilpferd im Hiobbuch", *VT* 21 (1971), 209-231.

[34] BOADT, *Ezekiel's oracles*, 26; see also GREENBERG, *Ezekiel 21-37*, 601.

[35] BOADT, *Ezekiel's Oracles*, 26.

[36] BARTHÉLEMY (ed.), *Critique Textuelle* 3, 239-241.

[37] LAMBDIN, "Egyptian Loan Words," in *JOAS* 73 (1953), 151; see also BLOCK, *Ezekiel 25-48*, 135.

[38] BLOCK, *Ezekiel 25-48*, 135.

[39] BOADT, *Ezekiel's oracles*, 28.

[40] ALLEN, *Ezekiel 20-48*, 103; see also BOADT, *Ezekiel's Oracles*, 29.

[41] Ezek 18,25; 18,29; 20,7; 20,8; 22,18; 22,18; 34,26; 44,30; 11,6; see BOADT, *Ezekiel's oracles*, 29.

[42] DAVIDSON, *Hebrew and Caldee Lexicon*, 617.b.

[43] See a summary of its discussion in BARTHÉLEMY (ed.), *Critique Textuelle* 3, 239-241.

[44] BOADT, *Ezekiel's oracles*, 29-30; see also GREENBERG, *Ezekiel 21-37*, 602.

omission of the objectival suffix is idiomatic[45] while Zimmerli presumes that due to
וַאֲנִי emphatic, the original עֲשִׂיתִים was tranferred to עֲשִׂיתִנִי.[46] Greenberg agrees
with David Kimhi that there is no direct object of the verb in עֲשִׂיתִנִי.[47] Presumably,
the object suffix of עָשָׂה refers to the object preceding it (יְאֹר); in such case,
Hebrew usually takes the verb בָּקַע and not עָשָׂה to denote "to make/create a river."
In fact, like the ruler of Tyre, Paraoh supposed himself to be god who made the
Niles."[48] Joüon-Muraoka suggest that the object suffix should not be read as an
accusative object but as a dative object.[49] Thus, עֲשִׂיתִנִי in v.3 is an exceptional case
of obj. suff. 1c. sg. acc. while it is interpreted in the dative[50] "I made it for myself."

In conclusion, we could say that עָשָׂה does not have a direct accusative object
anywhere in the text. The object preceding it, namely, יְאֹר is its supposed object
and the pronomial objective suffix should be interpreted in the dative.

29,4:

וְנָתַתִּי חַחִיים[10] בִּלְחָיֶיךָ וְהִדְבַּקְתִּי דְגַת־יְאֹרֶיךָ[11] בְּקַשְׂקְשֹׂתֶיךָ
וְהַעֲלִיתִיךָ מִתּוֹךְ יְאֹרֶיךָ[11A] וְאֵת כָּל־דְּגַת יְאֹרֶיךָ[12] בְּקַשְׂקְשֹׂתֶיךָ תִּדְבָּק[13]

But I will put hooks in your jaws,
And make the fish of your Niles to stick to your scales;
And I will bring you out from your Niles,
And all the fish of your Niles will stick to your scales.

Cairo (Geniza) and many other MSS read the MT חַחִיים as חַחִים (n. m. pl. from חָח
sg.= hook), as in *Qere*, and in 19,4.9. and in 38,4. It seems that חַחִיים was
mistakenly written in the place of חַחִים (= thorn). Moreover, there could not be
another form of the plural of חָח since it is not attested in other places where it
occurs. Therefore, the second *yodh* in חַחִיים may be a case of dittography and
should be corrected as suggested in *Qere*.

LXX, Syriac and Vulgate read MT יְאֹרֶיךָ in the singular. בְּקַשְׂקְשֹׂתֶיךָ תִּדְבָּק is
lacking in LXX and וְאֵת כָּל־דְּגַת יְאֹרֶיךָ is lacking in Old Greek.[51] Ehrlich observes
that if וְאֵת is taken as the direct object marker of כָּל־דְּגַת יְאֹרֶיךָ and if בְּקַשְׂקְשֹׂתֶיךָ
תִּדְבָּק could be taken as a relative clause then כָּל־דְּגַת יְאֹרֶיךָ may be considered a

---

[45] COOKE, *Ezekiel*, 330; see also KAUTZSCH, *GESENIUS' Hebrew Grammar*, 364, §117f.

[46] ZIMMERLI, *Ezechiel 25-48*, 703.

[47] GREENBERG, *Ezekiel 21-37*, 602.

[48] EHRLICH, *Randglossen*, 111.

[49] JOÜON-MURAOKA, *Grammer of Biblical Hebrew*, 440, §125ba.

[50] BARTHELEMY (ed.), *Critique Textuelle* 3, 241. BOADT gives other examples: Ezek 5,25;
16,21.52; 21,32; 27,10; 28,3; 29,3; 31,8; 32,11; 37,15; cf. 12,11; 44,7). See his *Ezekiel's
Oracles*, 30.

[51] BOADT, *Ezekiel's Oracles*, 31; BLAU, "Zum Angeblichen Gebrauch von את", in *VT* 4 (1954),
8; ZIMMERLI, *Ezechiel 25-48*, 703.

second object phrase of וְהַעֲלִיתִיךָ (4bα).[52] Greenberg calls it a case of *anacoluthon* that is possible due to a syntactical contamination[53] whereby the grammatical subject[54] of the verb תִּדְבָּק, which is a noun phrase, i.e., דְּגַת יְאֹרֶיךָ וְאֵת כָּל־, becomes the object of the first verb וְהַעֲלִיתִיךָ.[55] Boadt offers two other reasons: *first*, its chiastic structure with וְהִדְבַּקְתִּי / תִּדְבָּק makes an inclusion, employing identical words/phrases as a rhetorical device; and *second*, an expansion of the phrase דְּגַת יְאֹרֶיךָ (4aβ) with new details in וְאֵת כָּל־דְּגַת יְאֹרֶיךָ (4bβ), creates a parallelism comparable to Sumerian and Ugaritic couplets.[56] The repetition of בְּקַשְׂקְשֹׂתֶיךָ in 4b (smoothened by its omission in Old Greek) need not be judged as dittography, but must be seen as an expanded parallelism.

29,5:

וּנְטַשְׁתִּיךָ הַמִּדְבָּרָה אוֹתְךָ וְאֵת כָּל־דְּגַת יְאֹרֶיךָ[14]
עַל־פְּנֵי הַשָּׂדֶה תִּפּוֹל לֹא תֵאָסֵף וְלֹא תִקָּבֵץ[15]
לְחַיַּת הָאָרֶץ וּלְעוֹף הַשָּׁמַיִם נְתַתִּיךָ לְאָכְלָה

I will leave you and all the fish of your Niles in the desert;
You will fall on the open field;
You will not be gathered together and you will not be assembled;
I will give you for food to the beasts of the land and to the birds of the air.

Following Targums, MSS read MT תִקָּבֵץ as תִּקָּבֵר ("be buried").[57] BHS suggests to read תִּקָּבֵר. But תִּקָּבֵר is not supported by other versions even the Vulgate supports MT[58] and LXX renders it καὶ οὐ μὴ περισταλῇς. The Greek verb περισέλλω is translated אָסַף in Isa 58,8 and Sir 38,16 and it is generally used to denote care for the corpse (Tob 12,13).[59] אָסַף and קָבַץ can have a similar meaning

---

[52] EHRLICH, *Randglossen*, 111. BLAU ("Zum Angeblichen Gebrauch von אֵת", *VT* 4, 8) calls it object by attraction through אֵת.

[53] GREENBERG explains that the subject "all the fish" of the intrans. vb "shall stick" (4bβ) is preceded by the object marker 'ēt under the influence of the preceding transitive construction (4bα) as though it were absorbed into it. See, GREENBERG, *Ezekiel 21-37*, 603. He cites other examples of *anacoluthon* in 17,21 and 20,16.

[54] The emphatic אֵת at the beginning of a circumstanial clause may also be used as a "nominative" subject. See, BLOCK, *Ezekiel 25-48*, 135; other texts with emphatic אֵת used in the nominative sense: Ezek 10,20; 16,4f; 17,21; 35,10; 43,7; 44,3, 47,17.18.19; see BOADT, *Ezekiel's oracles*, 31.

[55] BOADT, *Ezekiel's Oracles*, 31-32.

[56] BOADT, *Ezekiel's Oracles*, 33. He cites more examples of parallelism in Ps 29,1-2.3.5.8; Gen 49,22; Jdg 5,23, Pss 67,4.6; 113,8; 98,5; 133,2; Jer 2,13; Job 37,4; Cant 2,15; and in Ezek 19,10; 22,2; 30,3; 36,10.

[57] קבר ("to bury") is used to mean "to gather"/"be gathered" in the company of the ancestors, e.g., Jer 8,2 and 25,33; see FOHRER, *Ezekiel*, 167; and HERRMANN, *Ezekiel*, 186.

[58] GREENBERG, *Ezekiel 21-37*, 603.

[59] BARTHÉLEMY (ed.), *Critique Textuelle* 3, 242.

of "to gather" or "be gathered," "care" and "concern"[60] (cf. אָסַף: "to gather," "be gathered", cf. Judg 2,10; Gen 25,8.17; 35,29; 49,29.33; 2Kgs 22,20; "care", cf. Ps 27,10; קָבַץ: "to gather," "be gathered" [of flock, persons], cf. Isa 60,7; Ezek 29,5; Mic 2,12; 4,6; Zph 3,19.20; [of the dispersed], cf. Ezek 29,13; Mic 4,12; Isa 66,18; Joel 4,2).[61] Greenberg thinks that in the post-biblical period, קָבַץ attained a sense of burial in a transferred sense and so אָסַף and קָבַץ are used as a pair.[62] Similarly, Zimmerli, Cornill, Hölscher, Toy, Herrmann, Bertholet and Fohrer think that תִּקָּבֵר attained the sense of burial by transferance of meaning that originally belongs to תִּקָּבֵץ.[63] So קָבַץ carries the sense of gathering the remains of a dead person[64] as required by the text. There is definintely too little evidence in the Versions for תקבר; therefore it is better to keep the MT תִּקָּבֵץ.[65]

29,6:

וְיָדְעוּ כָּל־יֹשְׁבֵי מִצְרַיִם כִּי אֲנִי יְהוָה
יַעַן הֱיוֹתָם¹⁶ מִשְׁעֶנֶת קָנֶה לְבֵית יִשְׂרָאֵל

Then all the inhabitants of Egypt will know that I am the LORD.
For, they were a staff of reed to the house of Israel.

LXX translates MT הֱיוֹתָם (inf. cstr. + suff. 3m. pl.) ἐγενήθης (Aor. pass. 2sg. "you were"). BHS suggests reading it as הֱיוֹתְךָ "your being" (suff. 2m. sg.). Many versions and commentators are of the opinion that הֱיוֹתָם in 6b is due to the assumption that the subject of 6a is the subject also of 6b[66] whereas v.7 suggests הֱיוֹתְךָ to be its proper reading. Cooke has no difficulty in keeping the MT and he renders it, "they have been." So, the "inhabitants of Egypt" (6a) remain the subject also of הֱיוֹתָם in 6b.[67] Boadt offers another solution by reading it הָיִיתָ (2m. sg.), with a dative suffix, and affirms that the change from הֱיִיתֶם (2m. pl.) to הֱיוֹתָם (qal inf. + suff. 3m. pl.) is not due to orthographic change between yodh and waw. He thinks that probably due to a misunderstanding of considering 6a as part of 6b, כָּל־יֹשְׁבֵי מִצְרַיִם (6a) was mistaken as the subject of הֱיִיתֶם (2m. pl. "you were"), necessitating its correction to הֱיוֹתָם (inf. suff. 3m. pl. "they were") to correspond with the subject. In the long run, this shift of subject from 3m. pl. to 2m. pl.

---

[60] ALLEN, *Ezekiel 20-48*, 102; In Ezek 11,17: וְקִבַּצְתִּי and וְאָסַפְתִּי are used in the sense of "gathering"/"assembling" the scattered. Cf. Ezek 39,17: הֵאָסְפוּ / הִקָּבְצוּ in the same sense.

[61] *BDB*, 62a.2a.c and 867d.2-868a.1.

[62] GREENBERG, *Ezekiel 21-37*, 604.

[63] ZIMMERLI, *Ezekiel 25-48*, 704.

[64] BLOCK, *Ezekiel 25-48*, 135.

[65] BARTHÉLEMY (ed.), *Crtitique Textuelle* 3, 242.

[66] ZIMMERLI, *Ezekiel 25-48*, 704; see also BOADT, *Ezekiel's Oracles*, 36.

[67] COOKE, *Ezekiel*, 327.

between v.6 and v.7 (for Egypt) was not seen as strange.[68] Allen considers it a case of dittography of *mem* in הֱיוֹתָם prompting כָּל־יֹשְׁבֵי מִצְרַיִם to be taken wrongly as its subject. He thinks that the particle יַעַן in 6b begins a new sentence which relates directly with לָכֵן in 8a. By its content too, it relates closely with v.7 (2m. sg.). For this reason probably, LXX, Syriac and Vulgate rendered היה in pf. 2m. sg. (הָיִיתָ "you were") irrespective of the error of the interchange between *waw/yodh*.[69] This explanation seems better than the commonly suggested הֱיוֹתְךָ and the one given by Boadt (הֱיִיתָם). In spite of this, it is preferable to keep the MT הֱיוֹתָם since it allows enlarging the scope of the oracle to include the inhabitants of Egypt, mentioned as the hordes of Pharaoh in 19c.[70]

29,7:

בְּתָפְשָׂם בְּךָ בַכַּפְּךָ[17] תֵּרוֹץ וּבָקַעְתָּ לָהֶם כָּל־כָּתֵף[18]
וּבְהִשָּׁעֲנָם עָלֶיךָ תִּשָּׁבֵר וְהַעֲמַדְתָּ[19] לָהֶם כָּל־מָתְנָיִם

> When they held you with their palm,
> You crushed and tore open all their shoulders;
> And when they leaned on you,
> You broke and shook all their loins.

Boadt maintains that בַכַּפְּךָ ("with your palm") is grammatically possible with final ךָ taken as a possessive pronoun, but that was thought to be otiose even by the Masoretes. Therefore, MSS edit the MT (בַכַּפְּךָ) to read with *Qere* as בְכַף ("with palm") thus, the final pronominal suff. 2m. sg. is omitted in favour of the preceding בְּ and *kap* is doubled. As a general rule, the suffix-ending with a part of the body can be dropped in בַכַּפְּךָ because it is already supplied by the preceding prepositional phrase בְּךָ.[71] Greenberg thinks that בַכַּפְּךָ is a scribal error (suff. בְ understood as haplography of בְּךָ).[72] LXX and Syriac rightly correct it as בְכַפָּם ("by their palms").[73]

In Boadt's view, the position of בַכַּפְּךָ before the following verb in the end-position indicates the use of emphatic כִּי, which finds support in the Ugaritic. He suggests taking the suffix ךָ in בַכַּפְּךָ as כִּי emphatic. Comparing it with Isa 58,5 הֲלָכֹף כְּאַגְמֹן רֹאשׁוֹ ("Is it to bow down his head like a rush"), he concludes that בַכַּפְּךָ in v.7 could be taken as an infinitive construction in which the temporal-

---

[68] BOADT, *Ezekiel's Oracles*, 36.

[69] ALLEN, *Ezekiel 20-48*, 102.

[70] 2Kgs 18,21//Isa 36,6 speaks of Pharaoh as a broken reed, a figure of speach that is used for Egypt, whereby the figure refers not just to Pharaoh but to all Egypt.

[71] BOADT, *Ezekiel's Oracles*, 37.

[72] GREENBERG, *Ezekiel 21-37*, 604.

[73] BERTHOLET, *Ezekiel*, KAT 12, 152.

marker כְּ in conjunction with the verb כָּפַף means "to bend down," thus rendering it, "when you bent over."[74] But this explanation is not very convincing because it fails to explain the rare combination of the prepostion בְּ that is joined to it. Therefore, reading of *Qere* (בְכַּף) seems to be a better solution.

LXX (χείρ) and Syriac (אידיהון) correct MT כָּתֵף "shoulder" (cf. 29,18; 25,9) to כַּף "hand", but more accurately it should be rendered as "palm." Block thinks that LXX and Syriac's rendering of כָּתֵף as כַּף have been influenced by two parallel texts (Isa 36,6; 2Kgs 18,21).[75] He takes *lectio difficilior*, which is also the reading of MT and keeps the text as it is.[76] Greenberg explains it as a gradual climax of increasing injury from hand to shoulder; in other words, the reed pierces not only the palm but splits their shoulders as well.[77] In Zimmerli's opinion, following the previous half verse (cf. בְכַּפְּךָ), כָּתֵף was written to avoid the doubling in כַּף.[78] Ehrlich thinks it illogical that a reed should harm shoulder or other parts of the body other than the palm where it is held, and so he favours כַּף.[79] This argument seems logical, but the MT makes a point in that it shows gradual development which relates to "shaking their loins."

LXX renders MT וְהַעֲמַדְתָּ ("and you caused to stand") καὶ συνέκλασας (Aor. ptc. acc. 1sg. act. "and you broke"), but BHS suggests reading it וְהִמְעַדְתָּ (מָעַד "and you caused to shake"). Greenberg thinks that there is a *metathesis* of הִמְעַד to הַעֲמַד, i.e. of *ayin-mem* here, and refers to Ps 69,24: וּמָתְנֵיהֶם תָּמִיד הַמְעַד ("and make their loins tremble continually"), supporting his argument to change וְהַעֲמַדְתָּ to וְהִמְעַדְתָּ.[80] Driver favours MT, which also finds support in Akkadic and Arabic where it carries a sense of "bruising" or "causing something to be knocked down."[81] In Allen's opinion, Driver's suggestion looks like a linguistic display, an attempt at a *tour de force*.[82] MT וְהַעֲמַדְתָּ certainly does not make proper sense in the context and it should be emended to read וְהִמְעַדְתָּ as Vulgate, LXX and Targums read.[83]

---

[74] BOADT, *Ezekiel's Oracles*, 37, fn. 54; cf. Ezek 7,9; 18,5; 30,3; 33,10; Isa 36,6//2Kgs 18,21.

[75] BLOCK, *Ezekiel 25-48*, 136; ALLEN (*Ezekiel 20-48*, 103) calls it a case of "assimilation".

[76] BLOCK, *Ezekiel 25-48*, 136.

[77] GREENBERG, *Ezekiel 21-37*, 605.

[78] ZIMMERLI, *Ezechiel 25-48*, 704.

[79] EHRLICH, *Randglossen*, 111.

[80] GREENBERG, *Ezekiel 21-37*, 605; see also, BOADT, *Ezekiel's Oracles*, 39; BARTHÉLEMY (ed.), *Crtitique Textuelle* 3, 243.

[81] DRIVER, "Linguistic and Textual Problems," in *Biblica* 35, 229; see also BLOCK, *Ezekiel 25-48*, 136.

[82] ALLEN, *Ezekiel 20-48*, 103.

[83] BARTHÉLEMY (ed.), *Crtitique Textuelle* 3, 244.

29,8:

לָכֵן כֹּה אָמַר֙ אֲדֹנָי[20] יְהוִֹה
הִנְנִי מֵבִיא עָלַיִךְ חָרֶב וְהִכְרַתִּי מִמֵּךְ אָדָם וּבְהֵמָה

Therefore, thus says the Lord GOD:
Look, I will bring a sword upon you and cut off man and beast from you.

The divine name אֲדֹנָי is lacking in two MSS of Old Greek, and is often deleted as a gloss (cf. 13a.16b). Wevers maintains that אֲדֹנָי יְהוִֹה is the usual name in the MT of Ezekiel. He points out that, "G testifies, as now known from Papyrus 967, to a single name throughout. Apparently 'LORD' as the perpetual Qere for 'Yahweh' crept into the text and only 'Yahweh' should be read throughout Ezekiel."[84] But since MT is consistent in keeping אֲדֹנָי יְהוִֹה, there is no reason to omit it from the text.

29,9:

וְהָיְתָה אֶרֶץ־מִצְרַיִם֙ לִשְׁמָמָה וְחָרְבָּה
וְיָדְעוּ כִּי־אֲנִי יְהוָה
יַעַן אָמַר[21] יְאֹר[22] לִי וַאֲנִי עָשִׂיתִי[23]

And the land of Egypt will become waste and desolation;
Then they will know that I am the LORD.
Because he said: The Nile is mine and I made it.

LXX (also Syriac and Vulgate) renders MT אָמַר (qal pf. 3m. sg.) τοῦ λέγειν σε (אָמְרְךָ inf. + suff. 2m. sg.) "you say." Block thinks that אָמַר in v.9 has been influenced by v.3 where it stands without any pronomial suffix.[85] For the same reason, Allen terms it as a case of assimilation of v.3.[86] As a general remark, one should take note of the flexible and often changing usage of person and number of the subject/object in vv.8-10: e. g., from עָלַיִךְ (2m. sg.) in v.8b to וְהָיְתָה in 9a (3f. sg.) and וְיָדְעוּ (3m. pl.) in 9b, to אָמַר (3m. sg.) or אָמַרְךָ (2m. sg.) in LXX, Syriac, and the Vulgate in 9c.[87] LXX's rendering of אָמַר as אָמְרְךָ in 9cα also agrees with the next object of the following verb in 10a: אֵלֶיךָ וְאֶל־יְאֹרֶיךָ (2m. sg.).[88] However, Boadt prefers to keep the MT, which seems to be a better option because it (9c) re-emphasizes the main accusation against Pharaoh (3bβ) and keeps the focus on Pharaoh.

As in 3bβ so also here in 9bβ, עָשִׂיתִי apparently lacks an object. LXX supplies αὐτούς (pron. relat. 3m. pl.) and reads "I made them." It is an emphatic statement

---

[84] WEVERS, *Ezekiel*, 52.
[85] BLOCK, *Ezekiel 25-48*, 140.
[86] ALLEN, *Ezekiel 20-48*, 103.
[87] Note the use of 3m. sg. in vv.10b-12; see GREENBERG, *Ezekiel 21-37*, 609-610.
[88] ZIMMERLI, *Ezekiel 25-48*, 704.

with אֲנִי as its subject, comparable to the similar affirmation or formulaic saying: אֲנִי יְהוָה דִּבַּרְתִּי וְעָשִׂיתִי ("I the LORD have spoken and I will do [it]") in 17,24; 22,14; 24,17; 36,36; 37,14 and two other occurrances in Isa 38,15 and Gen 41,34.[89] This may explain why עָשָׂה does not have any pronomial suffix in 3bβ and in 9bβ. It may be proved also by other texts enumerated above.

29,10:

$$\text{לָכֵן הִנְנִי אֵלֶיךָ וְאֶל}^{24}\text{־יְאֹרֶיךָ}^{25}\text{ וְנָתַתִּי אֶת־אֶרֶץ מִצְרַיִם}$$
$$\text{לְחָרְבוֹת}^{26}\text{ חֹרֶב}^{27}\text{ שְׁמָמָה}^{28}\text{ מִמִּגְדֹּל סְוֵנֵה}^{29}\text{ וְעַד־גְּבוּל כּוּשׁ}$$

Therefore look, I am against you and against your Niles;
And I will give the land of Egypt to wastes, a waste of desolation
from Migdol to Syene till the border of Cush.

BHS conjectures a deviation of form from עָלֶיךָ וְעַל to אֵלֶיךָ וְאֶל. According to the sense required in the context, עָלֶיךָ וְעַל would be an expected phrase as in 3b (הִנְנִי עָלֶיךָ פַּרְעֹה). The preference of MT for אֶל to עַל reveals a tendency to change עַל to אֶל due to Aramaic influence, as discussed above (see the explanation above on p.33f.). The context also demands the preposition עַל as a normal usage. Boadt, who favours keeping MT, explains that a preference of אֶל to עַל is due to the strong influence of *aleph* in 9c-10a, whereby an alliteration has been created.[90]

Although Aramaisation in the choice of עַל to אֶל is quite acceptable, as is their alliteration, a change from the commonly expected usage nevertheless reflects the particular intention of Ezekiel. In the given context it should be viewed as an attempt to create a sharp contrast that displays God's opposition in the accusation dialogue. This explains the intentional deviation from the normal usage. Therefore, אֵלֶיךָ וְאֶל is to be preferred to the normally expected עָלֶיךָ וְעַל.

Syriac reads MT יְאֹרֶיךָ in the singular, but LXX renders it πάντας τοὺς ποταμούς σου ("all your rivers"), harmonising it with v.3. MT יְאֹרֶיךָ (m. pl.) refers to all its channels although יְאֹר (sg.) may also assume its channels (pl.).

Many commentators regard חֹרֶב in לְחָרְבוֹת חֹרֶב שְׁמָמָה (10b) as dittography and wish to omit it altogether.[91] Wevers takes חֹרֶב לְחָרְבוֹת as "a bound verbal noun," and שְׁמָמָה as its "cognate modifier," but he does not rule out a possible

---

[89] BOADT maintains that the "use of עָשָׂה in this absolute form has the ring of a legal formula in which the action that is referred to is well-understood by all. It strongly empasizes the unexpected but obvious conclusion." See his *Ezekiel's Oracles*, 40.

[90] BOADT gives other examples of alliteration of other (alphabetical) sounds, like of *aleph* v.3c, *kaph* and *qoph* in v.4 of *beth* and *peh* in v.7 and vv.12-13, of *mem* in 2a and 3. See his *Ezekiel's Oracles*, 41.

[91] BOADT, *Ezekiel's Oracles*, 42.

dittography.[92]   Cooke recognises it as dittography and translates it as "wastes, a waste of desolation."[93] LXX, Syriac and Targums render לְחָרְבוֹת in sg. and read לְחָרְבָּה ("a waste"), while LXX and Vulgate render it καὶ ῥομφαίαν (חֶרֶב "large sword"), but this is lacking in Syriac, perhaps deleted as dittography. LXX, Syriac and Targums render שְׁמָמָה καὶ ἀπώλειαν (and a waste) and perhaps read as וּשְׁמָמָה. Boadt thinks that חָרְבוֹת and שְׁמָמָה make a formulaic group as found in Isa 61,4; Jer 49,13; Ezek 35,3f). So, לְחָרְבוֹת חֹרֶב שְׁמָמָה, all three having the same sense, is an *asyndeton* bound by the first word in absolute plural form.[94] The occurrence of this group of words in other places with similar meaning favours MT even though its rendering presents a challenge. Wevers' suggestion, "utter waste and desolation" (a bound verbal noun with cognate modifier) is a reflection on v.8, which seems to be the simplest proposition.

29,11:

לֹא תַעֲבָר־בָּהּ רֶגֶל אָדָם וְרֶגֶל בְּהֵמָה לֹא תַעֲבָר־בָּהּ
וְלֹא תֵשֵׁב אַרְבָּעִים שָׁנָה

No foot of man shall pass through it and a foot of beast shall not pass through it;
And she will be uninhabited for forty years.

29,12:

וְנָתַתִּי אֶת־אֶרֶץ מִצְרַיִם שְׁמָמָה בְּתוֹךְ אֲרָצוֹת נְשַׁמּוֹת
וְעָרֶיהָ בְּתוֹךְ עָרִים מָחֳרָבוֹת[30] תִּהְיֶיןָ שְׁמָמָה[31] אַרְבָּעִים שָׁנָה
וַהֲפִצֹתִי אֶת־מִצְרַיִם בַּגּוֹיִם וְזֵרִיתִים בָּאֲרָצוֹת

I will make the land of Egypt a desolation among the lands that are desolate,
And her cities shall be desolated for forty years,
among the cities that are laid waste;
And I will scatter the Egyptians among the nations
And disperse them through the countries.

MT uses מָחֳרָבוֹת (*hophal* ptc. 3f. pl. "laid waste" cf. Ezek 26,2 pf.) but at least one MS changes it to נַחֲרָבוֹת (cf. 30,7, *niphal* ptc. 3f. pl. "be desolate"). It is frequently read as חֲרֵבוֹת as in 36,55 ("desolate" adj.) and the prefix *mem* is deleted as a case of dittography of the preceding *mem*-ending in עָרִים.[95] *Hophal* and *niphal* verb

---

[92] WEVERS, *Ezekiel*, 224. The additional element חֹרֶב in the original phrase לִשְׁמָמָה וְחָרְבָּה (9a), is a crux of interpretation of 10b, prompting one to amend it as a dittography of the preceding word לִשְׁמָמָה.

[93] COOKE, *Ezekiel*, 327.

[94] BOADT, *Ezekiel's Oracles*, 42. ZIMMERLI (*Ezechiel 25-48*, 704) suggests its solution in comparison with v.9 (parallelism): (10b) לְחָרְבוֹת חֹרֶב שְׁמָמָה // לִשְׁמָמָה וְחָרְבָּה (9a) where חֹרֶב (10b) is inserted to show its relation with v.8 as also its progression.

[95] FOHRER, *Ezechiel*, HAT 13, 167. See also JOÜON, «Notes Philologiques», in *Biblica* 10, 308; and BLOCK, *Ezekiel 25-48*, 140.

forms have a passive sense. Their difference lies in that *hophal* is a fully passive form while *niphal* is medio-passive in meaning. Boadt observes that the usage of a *hophal* participle is determined by the prevalence of *mem* alliteration in the verse.[96] This explanation is plausible, but it concerns not merely the stylistic alliteration of *mem* but its real passive meaning, which gives better sense to the verse than its *niphal* counterpart.[97]

שְׁמָמָה is lacking in Old Greek, so also in 30,7 and is considered to be a later addition. However, when "and her cities among the ruined cities"[98] (12bα) is taken as a complement of the verb וְנָתַתִּי (cf. v.12a) and תִּהְיֶין is taken as the verb of the next clause "will be a desolation for forty years"[99] (12bβ), then שְׁמָמָה fits properly in the text, rendering a fitting sense as the final statement (complement clause) of judgment in v.12a. Moreover, since it concludes the oracle in v.12, its usage here does not seem to be an addition.

29,13:

כִּי³² כֹּה אָמַר אֲדֹנָי³³ יְהוִה מִקֵּץ אַרְבָּעִים שָׁנָה
אֲקַבֵּץ אֶת־מִצְרַיִם מִן־הָעַמִּים אֲשֶׁר־נָפֹצוּ שָׁמָּה

For, thus says the Lord GOD:
At the end of forty years, I will gather the Egyptians
from the peoples where they are dispersed.

The conjunction כִּי is attested in LXX[A] but lacking in LXX and Syriac, and its addition in BHS is uncertain and is considered to be secondary. However, כִּי has a specific function in v.13 because it refers to "the implication of the limitation of forty years."[100] Block thinks that its function is deictical because it points to an exegetical clause which explains the complement phrase "forty years" of the verb תִּהְיֶין in the previous verse (12bβ).[101] It is a significant conjunction in the verse which introduces another phase of the oracle[102] and holds a key to interpretation of the text. Therefore, it should be retained.

---

[96] BOADT, *Ezekiel's Oracles*, 45.
[97] Its rendering in *hophal* expresses a state of existence from which Egypt cannot think of her resurgence except through a divine intervention (vv.13-14).
[98] BOADT, *Ezekiel's Oracles*, 44.
[99] BOADT, *Ezekiel's Oracles*, 44.
[100] ALLEN, *Ezekiel 20-48*, 103.
[101] BLOCK, *Ezekiel 25-48*, 140.
[102] GREENBERG, *Ezekiel 21-37*, 607.

29,14:

וַשַׁבְתִּי אֶת־שְׁבוּת מִצְרַיִם וַהֲשִׁבֹתִי[34] אֹתָם אֶרֶץ פַּתְרוֹס
עַל־[35]אֶרֶץ מְכוּרָתָם וְהָיוּ[36] שָׁם מַמְלָכָה שְׁפָלָה

And I will bring back the captivity of Egypt,
And I will bring them back to the land of Pathros, to the land of their origin;
And there they will be a low kingdom.

LXX renders וַהֲשִׁבֹתִי as καὶ κατοικιῶ αὐτούς ("and I will cause them to dwell"),
Vulgate renders "*et conlocabo eos*" and Syriac אותב, thus they assume it to have
been derived from the root ישׁב (*to dwell*).[103] However, וַהֲשִׁבֹתִי derives from the
root שׁוב ("to return"). BHS follows MT, which may be rendered "I will
return/bring back" (from שׁוב). It is a repetition of the previous idea (cf. v.14a:
וְשַׁבְתִּי) whereas the gradual development of the oracle presupposes progress of
thought. Therefore, the rendering of LXX καὶ κατοικιῶ (וַהוֹשַׁבְתִּי > ישׁב "and I will
inhabit"/"cause to dwell")[104] thus, "I will bring back the captivity … and cause them
to dwell in Pathros … and they will be there a low kingdom" (LXX), correctly
shows this development of the oracle.

LXX translates וְהָיוּ שָׁם as καὶ ἔσται ("and it will be" [fut. 3m. sg.], MT has
waw consec. Pf. 3c. pl.) to correspond with תִּהְיֶה שְׁפָלָה (3f. sg. "she will be a low")
in v.15a. However, in 15a תִּהְיֶה stands for the land of Egypt, while in 14c וְהָיוּ
denotes the people of Egypt. Logically וְהָיוּ connects the final clause (14c) with its
preceding clause (14b) and makes a correct rendering of the present verse as
required by the text.

29,15:

מִן־הַמַּמְלָכוֹת[37] תִּהְיֶה שְׁפָלָה[38]
וְלֹא־תִתְנַשֵּׂא עוֹד עַל־הַגּוֹיִם וְהִמְעַטְתִּים לְבִלְתִּי רְדוֹת בַּגּוֹיִם

She will be the lowest of all the kingdoms;
She will not exalt herself again above the nations;
And I will make them small, never to rule over the nations.

LXX (as well as Syriac) renders מִן־הַמַּמְלָכוֹת as παρὰ πάσας τὰς ἀρχάς ("beyond
all the kingdoms") and connects it with 14c. Probably for the same reason, it omits
תִּהְיֶה שְׁפָלָה as an unnecessary addition because the beginning of 15a is taken as a
complement to 14c (cf. LXX emends תִּיְהֶה). But the meaning of מִן־הַמַּמְלָכוֹת
seems to be comparative,[105] denoting, "than"/"from the kingdoms." The literary
structure of 15a also shows that it begins a new verse that explains the significance

---

[103] ZIMMERLI, *Ezechiel 25-48*, 705.

[104] BOADT renders it "restore" in both places. See his *Ezekiel's Oracles*, 46.

[105] BERTHOLET, *Hesekiel*, 153.

of being "lower than the kingdoms." Although the nuance may not be striking, it does give an expected progression to the thought. Therefore, it makes sense to retain it.

29,16:

וְלֹא יִהְיֶה[39]־עוֹד לְבֵית יִשְׂרָאֵל לְמִבְטָח
מַזְכִּיר עָוֹן בִּפְנוֹתָם אַחֲרֵיהֶם וְיָדְעוּ כִּי אֲנִי[40] אֲדֹנָי יְהוִה

It will no more be reliance for the house of Israel,
A reminder of sin, when they turned to them;
And they will know that I am the Lord GOD.

In 16a one is confronted with the difficulty of the number of the pronomial subject. MT has יִהְיֶה (fut. 3m. sg.), but different translations e.g., LXX, Syriac, Targums and Vulgate read it יִהְיוּ (fut. 3m. pl.). The usage of 3rd person masculine singular for Egypt as its subject is somewhat awkward here, since the 'land' [of Egypt] is taken as feminine throughout (cf. 15b). Its masculine form could refer to the 'people' [of Egypt], but that is usually taken in 'plural' sense. Strictly speaking, יִהְיֶה cannot denote the people of Egypt in this clause, although its masculine plural form (יִהְיוּ) could. In view of the plural form of the rest of the verse (cf. וְיָדְעוּ in 15b), changing יִהְיֶה to plural has some support.[106] Zimmerli suggests that since Egypt has been referred to in 3rd person masculine plural throughout and also in later occurrences, יִהְיוּ refers to Egypt.[107] Ehrlich suggests that if לְ in מִבְטָח is regarded as dittography of the preceding *lamed* in יִשְׂרָאֵל and if מִבְטָח is to be taken as the subject of יִהְיֶה instead of מִצְרַיִם being its subject, then MT יִהְיֶה is possible.[108] However, it is also quite likely that by using יִהְיֶה, MT intended to denote Pharaoh, ruler of Egypt, which is quite possible.[109] Moreover, v.16 is the conclusion of the first part of the oracle (29,1-16), which began by referring to Pharaoh, king of Egypt (cf. 2a), as the "great crocodile" (3b), and thus may refer back to the beginning of the first oracle. This argument supports a consideration of יִהְיֶה in MT as establishing a conclusive link with 3b (in reference to Pharaoh); therefore, it (MT) should be retained.

2.2. Conclusion:

The text critical analysis has shown some of the peculiarities of the text. LXX's rendering of the date (12th year/10th month/1st day) is an attempt at harmonisation

---

[106] WEVERS, *Ezekiel*, 225.

[107] ZIMMERLI, *Ezechiel 25-48*, 705.

[108] EHRLICH, *Randglossen*, 112.

[109] BLOCK, *Ezekiel 25-48*, 141.

with the date in 26,1. The command (+ indicative) formula דַּבֵּר וְאָמַרְתָּ is not superfluous, but shows the importance of the "word-event" in v.1. The change in the preposition used, from אֶל to עַל shows a mark of Aramaisation in late Hebrew, but is also a stylistic change meant to stress a point. מֶלֶךְ־מִצְרַיִם, the apposition to Pharaoh, even without any definite article, has a definite sense because of its relation to "Egypt" (pr. n.). הַתַּנִּים (pl.) usually refers to jackals, but here one would expect the form הַתַּנִּין to denote a crocodile. It shows another case of Aramaisation, here of the Hebrew plural ending (*mem*) to Aramic plural ending (*nun*) and vice-versa. The plural form of יְאֹרָיו indicates the Nile and its canals. The usage of the verb עֲשִׂיתִנִי without direct object poses some difficulty of interpretation. Frequent changes in the gender of personal pronouns in 6b-9a render the interpretation of the text difficult, as they do not always refer to the preceding subject/object in the oracle, but also to the previous oracle (3b-6a). A similar difficulty is observed in vv.13-16 (cf. v.16). The use of the three nouns לְחָרְבוֹת חֹרֶב שְׁמָמָה in v.10 poses another difficulty in rendering their proper meaning. However, their use is not, as it may appear, altogether superfluous. Although וַהֲשִׁבֹתִי ("I will restore" from שׁוּב v.14) makes sense, it should be rendered as LXX renders it (καὶ κατοικιῶ "and I will inhabit" from the root יָשַׁב) to show the development of the oracle. The use of the appellation אֲדֹנָי for God (cf. v.16) in the recognition formula seems late.

CHAPTER THREE
STRUCTURAL ANALYSIS OF EZEKIEL 29, 1-16

This chapter presents a structural analysis of Ezek 29,1-16. This first oracle of judgement against Egypt consists of a solemn introductory formula, i.e., date, word-event, orientation, and command formula (vv.1-3a), and introduces the oracles of judgement against Egypt (chaps. 29-32), concluding with an oracle of salvation for Egypt (vv.13-16). The oracle consists of three small oracles of judgement (vv.3b-6a; 6b-9a; 9b-12), marked by distinct forms indicating their beginning and end, which also determine the literary unity of the small oracles within the larger unit of the oracle. The manner in which these oracles develop a thematic element and build up an overall unity within the oracle shows Ezekiel's literary skill, which, despite repetitious use of certain phrases and vocabulary, gives a stylistic quality to the composition.

3.0. General observation

The literay composition of chapter 29 has two parts,[1] 29,1-16 and 29,17-21, which are distinguished by different date (cf. vv.1.17) and recognition formulas (vv.16.21).[2] Slightly different formulations of the date formulas, i.e., "In the tenth year, in the tenth month, on twelfth of the month," (v.1) and "In the twenty-seventh year, in the first month, on the first day of the month," (v.17) indicate the two different historical situations in which these oracles of judgment against Egypt were delivered. These two dates also happen to be Ezekiel's earliest and the latest prophecies against Egypt.

Within the general structure of chapter 29, the internal unity of 29,1-16 and of 29,17-21 are quite clear. Both parts contain oracles of judgment against Egypt and an oracle of hope. In the first part, the oracle of hope (vv.13-16) is given for Egypt while in the second part, it is given for the house of Israel and for the prophet Ezekiel (v.21). The compositional unity of these two parts, or, the relation of the first oracle (29,1-16) to the second (29,17-21) is not at once clear. Due to their different historical dates, they should be standing logically on two ends of the entire composition; instead, they stand next to each other. This displays the prophet's compositional motive and skill, for by standing close to one another, they make a literary frame to the oracle of slavation for Egypt (29,13-16).

An interpretative clue to the literary relationship of the three small oracles to each other and to 29,1-16 and 29,16-21 taken as a whole, lies in the reference to

---

[1] ZIMMERLI, *Ezechiel 25-48*, 679; ZENGER, *Stuttgarter Altes Testament*, 1655f.

[2] HALS, *Ezekiel*, 204. Chronologically, 29,17-21 is the last oracle, which continues through 30,1-19, and closes with a shortened recognition formula in v.19.

Nebuchadrezzar, king of Babylon, and his thirteen-year siege of Tyre (Ezek 26-28), which is qualified as a 'service' to the LORD (v.18).

The fulfilment of Ezekiel's oracles of judgment against Egypt are seen as a reward for Nebuchadrezzar's success in humbling the pride of Tyre. This is an immediate motive for judgement against Egypt, but the remote cause is Pharaoh Hophra's ([588-569] Jer 37,5-8; cf. Jer 44,30f.) interference in the political affairs of Judah (Jerusalem) which is seen as a hinderence to God's plan for her. This is the case notwithstanding the accusation of Egypt's unreliablity, especially in keeping her treaty obligation to Jerusalem when the army of Nebuchadrezzar laid siege to the city.[3] Ezek 29,6 makes an indirect reference to this event that serves as a thematic link (cf. desolation, dispersion) between 29,1-16 and 29,17-21(+ 30,1-19). Keeping this in mind, let us see how 29,1-16 is organized as a unit.

3.1. Ezek 29,1-3a

1 In the tenth year, in the tenth month, on the twelfth of the month,
   the word of the LORD came to me saying:
2a Son of man set your face against Pharaoh, king of Egypt,
2b And prophesy against him and against all Egypt.
3a Speak and say:

The first oracle begins with a date formula and a word event formula to the prophet (v.1) who is instructed to orient himself toward the adressee, Pharaoh, king of Egypt (2a), commanded to prophesize against him (Pharaoh) and the whole of Egypt (2b), and is told to speak the message (3a). Thus, vv.1-3a solemnly introduces not only the first oracle (29,1-16) but also the whole series of oracles against Egypt (Ezek 29-32).

The introduction begins with שָׁנָה + בַּ (v.1) instead of the usual verbal phrase וַיְהִי (cf. 40,1) and closes with a דַּבֵּר + וְאָמַרְתָּ (*piel* impv. + *qal* impv. 3a). The use of דְּבַר (n. subj.) in v.1 and דַּבֵּר (vb) in 3a (cf. לֵאמֹר in v.1 and אָמַרְתָּ in 3a) make an inclusion of this opening unit. In other words, the opening is marked by the word-event formula. The prophet receives a revelation from the LORD and he is asked to deliver it.

Because דַּבֵּר and וְאָמַרְתָּ have the same meaning, their paired use seems to be unnecessary. Greenberg considers it a shortened form of a parallelism (cf. 14,4; 20,3).[4] The imperative sense of וְאָמַרְתָּ emphasizes the significance of God's commandment. The revealed "word" constitutes the proper subject of the verb הָיָה and the lack of the *waw*-temporal modifier makes it an indicative sentence. The prophet is not addressed by his proper name, but by a common epithet, 'Son of

---

[3] MAIER, *Ägypten- Israels Herkunft und Geschick,* 19f.166f.210f.
[4] BOADT, *Ezekiel's Oracles,* 21; GREENBERG, *Ezekiel 21-37,* 601.

man' (2a), which can be applied to any one. The instructions to the prophet in v.2 form a parallel AB//AB pattern and show the gradual development of God's command:

2a Set your face (A) against Pharoah (B)
2b And prophesy (A) against him (B).

Pharaoh is used as a proper name and is further qualified by his title, "king of Egypt" in 2a, but is addressed by pronoun "he" in 2b. "All Egypt" constitutes an additional element. The introduction contains, in a nutshell, the whole extent of the addressee(s) that come under God's judgment.

The three imperatives and an indicative with the force of an imperative, שִׂים פָּנֶיךָ / וְהִנָּבֵא / דַּבֵּר / וְאָמַרְתָּ in a chain (2-3a) make the composition of this introduction very compact. While שִׂים פָּנֶיךָ עַל directs the prophet's orientation to the final recipient of the message, וְהִנָּבֵא explains its purpose. Ezekiel's commission to prophesize includes to "speak and say," which is an integral part of his prophetic mission. So, the command to the prophet, his commission and the message he receives to deliver, all are presented together in the opening formula.

The verbal phrase שִׂים פָּנֶיךָ עַל "turn your face to" is peculiar to Ezekiel. The combination of a verb + part of body + directional preposition intends to give a dramatic effect to his message. The name "Pharaoh" is followed by an apposition, "king of Egypt," a title that explains its signifcance. The Egyptian word "Pharaoh" designates a 'big house' and originally referred to the "royal living quarters" in the "palace complex of Memphis" and by extension it signfied king or ruler of Egypt.[5] Therefore, the addition of the apposition to "Pharaoh" seems to be redundant, which may explain its omission in the LXX.[6]

וְעַל־מִצְרַיִם כֻּלָּהּ "and against all Egypt" (2b) is a new addition that, by implication of "king of Egypt," takes into account the king and the land, and expands the scope of God's judgment (cf. vv.4-5). "All the inhabitants of Egypt" in the recongnition formula (6a) refers back to "all Egypt" (2b). Thus, this introduction contains, in a telescopic way, two main aspects of the oracles - Pharaoh and Egypt – around which the oracles of judgment are developed in subsequent units.

---

[5] HERRMANN, *Ezechiel*, 185, Fn. 2.

[6] FREEDY and REDFORD consider it as a late scribal gloss. See their "The Dates of Ezekiel," in *JAOS* 90 [1970], 471, No. 37; see also BLOCK, *Ezekiel*, 135, No. 23.

3.2. Ezek 29,3aα-6a

3b   Thus says the Lord GOD:
3bα   Look, I am against you Pharaoh, king of Egypt, the big crocodile,
3bβ   That lies in the midst of his Niles;
3bγ   Who says: Mine is the Niles and I made it for myself.
4aα   But I will put hooks in your jaws;
4aβ   And make the fish of your Niles stick to your scales.
4bα   I will bring you out from your Niles;
4bβ   And all the fish of your Niles will stick to your scales.
5a   I will leave you and all the fish of your Niles in the wilderness.
5b   You will fall on the open field;
5bα   You will not be gathered together;
5bβ   And you will not be assembled.
5c   I will give you for food to the beasts of the land and to the birds of the air.
6a   Then all the inhabitants of Egypt will know that I am the LORD.

The first sub-oracle begins with a message "thus says the LORD," the particle הִנְנִי and the challenge formula "look I am against you," a new reference to the addressee, "Pharaoh, king of Egypt, the big crocodile." It is followed by the accusation, consisting of the proud saying (hubris) of Pharaoh (3bγ). The announcement of judgment begins directly, without any particle "but I will give (נתן)..." (4aα) and is developed in 4aβ-5c and expressed in a metaphor. The oracle concludes with a recognition formula, "All the inhabitants of Egypt will know that I am the LORD" (6a).[7]

In Ezekiel, the message formula frequently precedes God's accusation. In 3aα it is followed by a demonstrative particle, הִנְנִי. It calls attention to and states the accusations against Pharaoh (3bβ-3bγ). It is expressed in a "confrontation" or a "duel formula" ("I-You").[8] Thus, הִנְנִי עָלֶיךָ (3bα) relates directly with פַּרְעֹה and מִצְרַיִם כֻּלָּה (v.2).

The use of the metaphor הַתַּנִּים הַגָּדוֹל "the big crocodile" is attributitive and draws a parallel with מֶלֶךְ־מִצְרַיִם, which highlights the motive for the accusation. The metaphor evokes an imaginative effort to ascertain the exact nature of the accusation against Pharaoh, thereby widening the scope of judgment in vv.4-5. The sequence of the accusation moves from Pharaoh, king of Egypt, to the big crocodile, and to the Niles where the big crocodile lies (רבץ) secure.

The announcement of judgment includes the "big crocodile" and כָּל־דְּגַת "all the fish" inhabiting the Niles (v.4). The pronomial suffix ending in יְאֹרֶיךָ (n. sg. + pron. suff. 2m. sg.) restores the oracular saying once again to a duel form (cf. 4-

---

[7] WESTERMANN, *Grundformen*, 131.

[8] BLOCK calls it a "challenge formula". See his *Ezekiel 25-48*, 130; see also VAN ROOY, "Parallelism, Metre and Rhetoric," in *Semitics* 8 (1982), 90-105.

5bβ), which was briefly disrupted by a metaphorical description of its habitation[9] and the hubris of the crocodile: לִי יְאֹרִי וַאֲנִי עֲשִׂיתִנִי.[10] The brief description of the big crocodile (3m. sg. cf. 3bα-3bβ) is remarkable. The announcement of judgment is developed through an intervention "but" (cf. *waw* and pf. of נתן) and is spoken in a metaphor:

4aα	But I will put hooks in your jaws	וְנָתַתִּי חַחִיִּים בִּלְחָיֶיךָ
4aβ	And make the fish of your Niles stick to your scales	וְהִדְבַּקְתִּי דְגַת־יְאֹרֶיךָ בְּקַשְׂקְשֹׂתֶיךָ
4bα	I will bring you out of your Niles	וְהַעֲלִיתִיךָ מִתּוֹךְ יְאֹרֶיךָ
4bβ	And all the fish of your Niles will stick to your scales	וְאֵת כָּל־דְּגַת יְאֹרֶיךָ בְּקַשְׂקְשֹׂתֶיךָ תִּדְבָּק׃

4bβ seems to be a repetition of 4aβ, but all the same, it shows certain development. The attribute וְאֵת כָּל[11] expands the noun object דְּגַת. Its first verb וְהִדְבַּקְתִּי "I will cause to stick" (causative 4aβ) and the subsequent action תִּדְבָּק "they will stick" (intrans. active 4bβ) prepare a background for further development of judgment: God brings out (עלה 4b) and leaves (נטשׁ 5a) them; consequently, they "fall" (נפל 5b) and are not "collected" (אסף 5bα) and not "gathered" (קבץ 5bβ). The use of the pronoun "you" is noteworthy in the whole description.

At another level, the successive usage and movement from "the fish of your Niles" (4aβ) to "all the fish of your Niles" (4bβ), to "you and all the fish of your Niles" (5a), builds a climax towards the announcement of judgment. The usage of the defenite object marker (את) is another notable literary element here. The pair verbs אסף (5bα) and קבץ (5bβ) show a parallelism.[12] Similarly, הַמִּדְבָּרָה (5a) and הַשָּׂדֶה (5b), and הַשָּׁמַיִם and הָאָרֶץ (5c) offer examples of pair-words.

29,5c builds a climax of 5bα and 5bβ: Instead of being collected and gathered,[13] the fish and the crocodile will become "food" for the beasts and the birds (5c).[14] The picture of God's judgment that began by addressing Pharaoh and Egypt (v.2) is expanded to include God's opposition (3aβ), is charged with accusation

---

[9] רבץ means "to lie"/"couch in a den." The preposition בְּתוֹךְ signifies a space, a place that it occupies rather than an enclosure which contains it. This may explain why the preposition בְּ is not prefixed directly to יְאֹרָיו.

[10] The suffix ־נִי in עֲשִׂיתִנִי is to be taken as dative and not as direct object, thus: "and I made (it) for myself." See JOÜON-MURAOKA, *Grammar of Biblical Hebrew*, 441, §125b n.2.

[11] The particle את occurs at least 11 times before a noun in the book of Ezekiel. See ROOKER, *Biblical Hebrew in Transition*, 88-89.

[12] WATSON, "Hebrew Word Pair *'sp//qbz*," in ZAW 96, 426-434.

[13] This is a metaphorical way of speaking about a burial.

[14] Instead of a respectful burial, the cropse of the crododile lies in the open, being food for birds and animals, indicating the greatest humilation of the fallen.

(3bα.3bβ), and a judgment is announced against them (vv.4-5). "All the inhabitants of Egypt" (6a) in the recognition formula shows that the judgment is against Egypt.[15]

3.2.1.Conclusion

The first oracle of judgment begins with a message formula (3aα) addressed to פַּרְעֹה מֶלֶךְ־מִצְרַיִם (3aβ) and concludes with the the recognition formula referring to כָּל־יֹשְׁבֵי מִצְרַיִם (6a). The two statements of the judgment oracle, i.e., hubris of the big crocodile לִי יְאֹרִי וַאֲנִי עֲשִׂיתִנִי (3bβ) and the announcement of judgment by the LORD נְתַתִּיךָ לְאָכְלָה (5c), show deep contrast. The former refers to the pride of the crocodile while the latter reveals the sovereign power of the LORD, which reduces the pride of the crocodile to nothing. The spatial movement of the oracle, i.e., from בְּתוֹךְ יְאֹרָיו (3bα) to מִתּוֹךְ יְאֹרֶיךָ (4bα) and then from הַמִּדְבָּרָה (5a) to הַשָּׂדֶה (5b), and from הָאָרֶץ (5c) to הַשָּׁמַיִם (5c) symbolically express the expanse of the whole cosmos over which the LORD rules.

3.3. Ezek 29,6b-9a

> 6b   For they were a staff of reed to the house of Israel;
> 7aα When they held you with their palm,
> 7aβ You crushed and you tore open all their shoulders;
> 7bα And when they leaned on you, you broke,
> 7bβ And you caused to shake all their loins.
> 8a   Therefore thus says the Lord GOD:
> 8b   Look, I will bring a sword upon you,
> 8c   And I will cut off man and beast from you.
> 9a   And the land of Egypt will become waste and desolation;
> 9aα Then they will know that I am the LORD.

The second sub-oracle begins differently. It lacks the usual message formula, "Thus say the LORD." Instead, it begins directly with the particle יַעַן (*protasis*) and the "accusation" (against Egypt, cf. 6b: "you"), which is developed in v.7 in two parallel verses similar to v.4. The "announcement of judgment" begins with the particle לָכֵן (*apodosis*) and the "message formula" (8a), while the particle הִנְנִי begins the announcement of judgment (8b), developed further in 8c-9a and closes with a "recognition formula" (9a).

To begin with, the addressee, a pronoun (6b: inf. cstr. of הָיָה + suff. 3m. pl.) is not specified here. Therefore, there is some ambiguity about the identity of the

---

[15] GREENBERG, *Ezekiel 21-37*, 609.

addressee (Pharaoh? Egypt? Inhabitants? Reed?). It poses some syntactical difficulty. Since יְעַן (6b) follows immediately from 6a, it is presumed that it refers to the "inhabitants" (6a), but the inf. cstr. form of היה (f. pl.) does not correspond to it; "Pharaoh, king of Egypt" (3m. sg.) is out of the question even though "staff of reed"[16] apparently refers to him (v.7). The announcement of judgment (8b.9a) refers to the "land" of Egypt and it is presumably the addressee here.

A new metaphor in introduced in the accusation (6b). Egypt is compared to a "staff of reed" (cf. Isa 36,6//2Kgs 18,21).[17] V.7 illustrates and develops the basic nature of the reed, which focuses on Egypt's unreliablity in relation to the house of Israel. Their parallelism (7a//7b) reflects the consequence of Israel's reliance on Egypt:[18]

7a When they held/you crushed/and you tore	בְּתָפְשָׂם/ תֵּרוֹץ / וּבָקַעְתָּ
7b When they leaned/you broke/and you shook	וּבְהִשָּׁעֲנָם/תִּשָּׁבֵר/וְהַעֲמַדְתָּ

The first colon, a circumstantial clause, states the circumstance for the incumbent action. It is followed by a short, one-word colon that describes its consequence and the third colon enumerates its final consequence. The phrases בְכַף ("with palm"), כָּל־כָּתֵף ("every shoulder"), and כָּל־מָתְנָיִם ("all their loins") vividly express it .

יְעַן (protasis 6a) + accusation and לָכֵן (apodosis 8a)[19] + message formula + הִנְנִי + judgment is typical of this sub-oracle. "Sword" is a new element introduced in the judgment against Egypt and עָלַיִךְ in מֵבִיא עָלַיִךְ חָרֶב עָלַיִךְ "I will bring sword against you" (8b) denotes the land of Egypt.[20] The focus of judgment is neither "Pharaoh" nor the "inhabitants" (2a.3b.4a), but the "land" of Egypt (6b-7 cf. 2b).

The announcement of judgment is metaphorical: The sword will "cut off" (כרת) "man and beast" (אָדָם וּבְהֵמָה 8c) and will make the land "waste and desolation"

---

[16] Wevers takes "staff of reed" to be the subject proper in 6b. See his *Ezekiel*, 224.

[17] The reed was, as it still is, a common plant in marshy places along the banks of the Nile. Its use in the text could allude to an association with the Nile where the great crocodile lives, with the distinction that by alluding to the supple nature of the reed, a new dimension would likely be added to Egypt's character.

[18] Its construction בְ + inf. suff. 3m. pl. / impf. 3m. pl. / *waw-consec.* + pf. 2m. sg., is noteworthy.

[19] VAN DIJK, *Ezekiel's Prophecy on Tyre*, 93.

[20] In Hebrew, "land" is usually feminine therefore the pronomial suff. 2f. sg. in the prepositon עַל (8b) and a common plural-ending (cf. 9aα וְיָדְעוּ) cannot denote Pharaoh (3m. sg.). It cannot denote to the "people of Egypt" either which is usually masculine. Therefore, the only other possibility is that it denotes the "land." In this regard, note the verb וְהָיְתָה "will be" (*waw*-consec. pf. 3f. sg.) in 9a and compare it with הֱיוֹתָם "they were" (inf. cstr. + suff. 3m. pl.) in 6b. BOADT suggests to read הֱיוֹתָם in 6b as הֱיִיתָם "you were to them" (pf. 2m. sg. + proleptic dat. suff. 3m. pl.). He changes the verbal form to correspond with the object (2m. sg.) in vv.4-5 without affecting the gender of the pronomial suffix-ending, so that it continues to correspond to Pharaoh in v.3, rather than to the inhabitants of Egypt in v.6. See his *Ezekiel's Oracles*, 36.

(לִשְׁמָמָה וְחָרְבָּה 9a). The new announcement of judgment shows a definite progress from the previous one (cf. vv.4-5). As the sword severs all, the subject of the recognition formula shifts from "the inhabitants of Egypt" (6a) to a more general expression through the all-inclusive pronominal subject "they" (9aα).

3.4. Ezek 29,9b-12

9b   Because he said:
9bβ   The Nile is mine and I made it.
10a   Therefore look, I am against you and against your Niles;
10b   I will give the land of Egypt to wastes, waste of desolation
        from Migdol to Syene till the border of Cush.
11a   No foot of man will pass through it;
11b   And a foot of beast will not pass through it;
11c   And she will be uninhabited for forty years.
12a   I will make the land of Egypt desolation among the lands that are desolate;
12b   And her cities shall be desolated for forty years
        among the cities that are laid waste.
12cα   And I will scatter the Egyptians among the nations;
12cβ   And I will disperse them through the countries.

The third sub-oracle also begins directly with the causal particle יַעַן (*apodosis*) and the accusation (9b),[21] which repeats the proud claim of Pharaoh (cf. 3bβ). It is followed by לָכֵן (*apodosis*) + הִנְנִי and the opposition formula, "therefore, look, I am against you," (10a) and the announcement of judgment which is very similar to the first sub-oracle (cf. 4aα), "I will give (נתן) the land of Egypt..." (10b), and developed further in vv.11-12. There is no usual closing formula in 12cβ.

The judgment further develops the previous announcement of judgment, i.e., desolation of the land (9a). How the sword (8b) will desolate it is expanded territorially "from Migdol to Syene," paticularized in that it will destroy man and beast (11b cf. 8c.), and affect its cities and country-side (land) for a definite period of time; till that period expires, its population will remain dispersed and scattered throughout the countries.

The usage of the causal particle יַעַן as the opening of the third sub-oracle (9b; cf. 6b) shows its immediate (syntactical; cf. also thematic) relationship with the second sub-oracle, while both oracles together also display their unity with the first oracle of judgment. Moreover, by repeating the same motive for judgment, i.e., the "hubris" of Pharaoh, the big crocodile (9bβ; cf. 3bβ), the first and the third sub-oracles make a thematic inclusion of the whole oracle of judgment (29,1-12). Its structure, namely, יַעַן + the accusation (9b) and לָכֵן + הִנְנִי + the opposition

---

[21] MULDER, „Die Partikel Jaᶜan", *Syntax and Meaning*, OTS XVIII (1973), 49-83.

formula + the announcement of judgment is peculiar to this sub-oracle of judgment where the message formula is missing.

The closing of the judgment-oracle is unconventional because it lacks the usual recognition formula. In fact, there is no closing formula in a technical sense. All the same, if vv.13-16 could be separated as an oracle of salvation to Egypt (with כִּי beginning a resumption clause [cf. 13a] and a final recognition formula [cf. 16b]), then the final statement of judgment, indicating complete dispersion of the inhabitants after the land has been devasted, thereby showing the climax of God's judgment (cf. 12cβ), could still be considered a logical conclusion of the third sub-oracle of judgment against Egypt.

מִגְדֹּל (a Hebrew word denoting "ford" or "tower") is used as the proper name of the place in lower Egypt (Nile Delta) and סְוֵנֵה (Syene/Aswan) as that of the place in upper Egypt (south) until the border of Kush (10a), indicating the northern and southern boundaries of Egypt, and preparing the background for the fourth oracle (vv.13-15). It also points to a maximum expansion of judgment against Egypt, i.e., from "you and your Nile" (10a) to "the land of Egypt" (10b), even "from Migdol to Syene till the border of Cush" (10b). In v.11 the consequence of the judgment is described in AB//BA pattern:

11a) No foot of man will pass through it   לֹא תַעֲבָר־בָּהּ רֶגֶל אָדָם
11b) and a foot of beast will not pass through it   וְרֶגֶל בְּהֵמָה לֹא תַעֲבָר־בָּהּ

It is an expansion of אָדָם וּבְהֵמָה in 8c, where they are objects of the verb כרת, but in v.11a.11b they are subjects of the verb עבר where בָּהּ refers to the land of Egypt (cf. 10a.9a). The construction of v.12 is complex due to the second clause, וְעָרֶיהָ בְּתוֹךְ עָרִים מָחֳרָבוֹת ("and her cities [shall be a desolation] among the cities that are laid waste"). It may not be established beyond all doubt whether the passage should be understood as a second complement of 12a or as the subject of the following clause. As part of 12b, it would place the "desolation for forty years" at the centre of God's judgment, while "scattering and dispersion" (12c) would illustrate the final consequence of judgment, bringing the third sub-oracle and the three series of related oracles of judgment to a climax and logical conclusion.

The parallelism in 12cα-12cβ explains why the land of Egypt will become desolate. Moreover, it also shows the correspondence between the judgments in v.5 and v.12, indicating how they are going to be fulfilled:

v.5 You will not be collected/not gathered   לֹא תֵאָסֵף/וְלֹא תִקָּבֵץ
v.12 I will scatter/I will disperse them   הֲפִצֹתִי/זֵרִיתִים
12cα I will scatter the Egyptians among the nations   וַהֲפִצֹתִי אֶת־מִצְרַיִם בַּגּוֹיִם
12cβ And disperse them through the countries   וְזֵרִיתִים בָּאֲרָצוֹת

3.5. Ezek 29,13-16

13a   For thus says the Lord GOD:
13b   At the end of forty years I will gather the Egyptians from the peoples,
13bα Where they are dispersed;
14a   And I will bring back the captivity of Egypt;
14b   And I will bring them back to the land of Pathros,
      to the land of their origin;
14c   And there they will be a low kingdom.
15a   She will be the lowest of all the kingdoms;
15b   She will not exalt herself again above the nations;
15c   And I will make them small never to rule over the nations.
16a   It shall no more be reliance for the house of Israel,
16b   A reminder of sin when they turned to them;
16c   And they will know that I am the Lord GOD.

The oracle of salvation to Egypt begins with כִּי and the message formula "thus says the LORD" (13a); further, it announces the end of the "forty years" of judgment and the beginning of the reversal of previous judgment. The process of restoration and its various aspects, i.e., its results are developed in 13b-16b, concluding with the final recognition formula, "And they will know that I am the LORD" (16c).

The conjunction כִּי "for" expands the oracle but what precedes it can hardly be its basis, although it is closely linked with this conjunction.[22] As such, it is not used in the resumptive[23] sense. It may be rendered in the adversative sense, "but" or "however."[24] In either case, it is a key to interpreting the oracle of salvation, which explains the significance of the expression "at the end of the forty years" (13b) and of the desolation of the land of Egypt and her cities for "forty years" (cf. 11c.12b). Therefore, כִּי links 13b directly with the previous oracle of judgment, indicating that the judgment against Egypt was to last for a definite, time only- for "forty years."[25] It leaves room for God's new intervention against the grim view of Egypt outlined in the previous oracles:

---

[22] WEVERS, *Ezekiel 20-48*, 225; see also GREENBERG, *Ezekiel 21-37*, 482.

[23] HALS, *Ezekiel. Forms*, 207.

[24] The conjunction כִּי denotes "that," "because," "for" (KAUTZSCH, *GESENIUS' Hebrew Grammar*, 305, §104.1.a.; *BDB* 471c). Here it could be rendered in the adversative sense "but," "for" (cf. Ezek 16,59; 25,6, 32,11). JOÜON-MURAOKA points out that it "probably derives from the casual one, and must have developed in cases where there is virtual equivalence between for and but." See their *Grammar of Biblical Hebrew*, 641, §172.c.; also SCHOORS, "The Particle kī," *OTS* XXI (1981), 240-276.

[25] The forty years' duration of judgment of Egypt and the dispersion of the people may connote the forty years' period of exile of Israel to Babylon as punishment (cf. Ezek 4,6) and her new exodus (Ezek 20,32-44), reflected in the exodus of Egypt and the return of her captives to Pathros. See ZENGER (ed.), *Stuttgarter Altes Testament*, 1656.

v.5   You will not be collected/and not be gathered   לֹא תֵאָסֵף/וְלֹא תִקָּבֵץ
v.8c   I will cut off man and beast from you   וְהִכְרַתִּי מִמֵּךְ אָדָם וּבְהֵמָה
v.12   I will scatter/disperse them   הֲפִצֹתִי/זֵרִיתִים

Here, the כִּי clause (13a) generates a positive response and inaugurates God's unique saving intervention to gather (קבץ 13b) Egypt "from the people" (מִן הָעַמִּים 13b), which recalls the word-pair בַּגּוֹיִם in 12cα. The final clause "where they were dispersed" (אֲשֶׁר־נָפֹצוּ שָׁמָּה 13bα) refers to בָּאֲרָצוֹת in 12cβ. Thus, כִּי establishes a close link between the third oracle of judgment (cf. v.12) and the oracle of hope (v.13). The clause "Where they were dispersed" (נָפֹצוּ 13bα) makes a final assessment of the judgment against Egypt (cf. v.12), which is now open to God's renewed intervention.

The formulation of the oracle of salvation for Egypt is adapted from God's promise of restoration to Israel (cf. 11,17; 20,34.41; 28,25 etc.).[26] Vv.14-15 describe in detail different aspects of the restoration of Egypt, i.e., her new existence and its final goal, namely, recognition of God's sovereignty.

3.5.1. The result of God's new initiative

14a   And I will bring back the captivity of Egypt   וְשַׁבְתִּי אֶת־שְׁבוּת מִצְרַיִם
14b   And bring them back to the land of Pathros   וַהֲשִׁבֹתִי אֹתָם אֶרֶץ פַּתְרוֹס
14c   And there they will be a low kingdom   וְהָיוּ שָׁם מַמְלָכָה שְׁפָלָה

The announcment of restoration of Egypt (14a.14b) may be compared with other texts which speak about her restoration (e.g., Isa 19,18ff.; Jer 46,26; Zeph 3,10; Zech 14,18f.).[27]

3.5.2. The result of the new initiative with respect to Egypt

15a   She will be the lowest of all the kingdoms   מִן־הַמַּמְלָכוֹת תִּהְיֶה שְׁפָלָה
15b   She will not raise herself again over the nations   וְלֹא־תִתְנַשֵּׂא עוֹד עַל־הַגּוֹיִם
15c   And I will make them few   וְהִמְעַטְתִּים לְבִלְתִּי רְדוֹת בַּגּוֹיִם
       never to rule over the nations.

The preposition מִן (15a) should be taken in a comparative sense in 15a.[28] It offers an explanatory note on the nature of the "low kingdom" (מַמְלָכָה שְׁפָלָה 14c) which is specified by "She will not exalt herself again" (וְלֹא־תִתְנַשֵּׂא עוֹד 15b).

---

[26] FUHS, *Ezechiel 25-48*, 159. Suffix 3m. pl. in יֵדַע has a collective noun in 16b. See ROOKER, *Biblical Hebrew in transition*, 95.

[27] FUHS, *Ezechiel 25-48*, 159.

[28] BERTHOLET, *Ezekiel,* KAT 12, 153.

God's intervention, "I will make them small" (הִמְעַטְתִּים 15c), emphasizes the new status of Egypt (cf. 14c), made specific by the infinitive noun clause "never to rule over the nations" (לְבִלְתִּי רְדוֹת בַּגּוֹיִם 15c). The new status of Egypt, "the lowest of all the kingdoms" (15a), contrasts sharply with the proud claim of the crocodile, "Mine is the Niles and I made it for myself" (3bβ; cf. 9bα). No doubt, v.15 shows gradual transformation of Egypt.

3.5.3. The result of the new initiative with respect to the house of Israel

The restoration of Egypt has great significance for the house of Israel (16a.16b):

16a And it shall no more be reliance   וְלֹא יִהְיֶה־עוֹד לְמִבְטָח
16b A reminder of sin when they turn to them   מַזְכִּיר עָוֹן

"And it shall no more be" (וְלֹא יִהְיֶה־עוֹד) signals a change in the situation of Egypt in relation to Israel. מִבְטָח is the implicit subject of יִהְיֶה, but as it is far removed from its predicate verb by its prepositional prefix, it commands a neutral subject.[29] מִבְטָח looks back to מִשְׁעֶנֶת קָנֶה (6b) and establishes a unity with the second oracle. The expression מַזְכִּיר עָוֹן (16b) is a neutral term.[30] A similar usage is found in 21,28: עָוֹן לְהִתָּפֵשׂ וְהוּא־מַזְכִּיר "but he will remind them of their guilt and take them captive," which confirms its neutral sense. "When they turn to them" (בִּפְנוֹתָם אַחֲרֵיהֶם 16b), a circumstantial adverbial clause, is a complement to the noun phrase מַזְכִּיר עָוֹן. The "habitual" or "durative" sense of the adverbial clause gives a clue to the interpretation of this verse. Israel did not turn to Egypt just once (cf. 29,6b), but has shown a habitual tendency to do so, while Egypt herself has been in league with the house of Israel. The meaning of פנה "to turn"[31] implies to seek help or support, and connotes an alliance between them which, however, goes against Israel's essential nature in relation to the LORD. Egypt had a vested political interest that determined her actions toward Jerusalem, irrespective of any alliance and mutual understanding between them.[32] This gives some hint of why God pronounces judgment against Egypt.

---

[29] GREENBERG, *Ezekiel 21-37*, 607.

[30] DRIVER, "Linguistic and Textual Problems," *Biblica* 35, 300.

[31] פנה occurs 13 times in Ezekiel. It occurs 25 times in the later prophets and 32 times in former prophets. The Pentateuch attests the highest number of occurrencees (Deut 16x, Ex 6x; Num 5x).

[32] In General, Egypt had a keen interest in Syria-Palestine where it often sought to augment its control, and saw Babylon as a threat. This is proved by Neco II's (610-595) campaigns, viz., his battle against Josiah at Megiddo, against Nebopolassar at Harran in 610-609 B.C. (cf. 2Kgs 23,28-30), and against Nebuchadnezzar's army at Carchemish (Hamath) in 605 B.C.; it is also shown by Psammetichus II's campaign against Khatu (Phoenicia) in 590 B.C., and Hophra's/Apries (588-568) attack of Sidon and Tyre and his calculated but short-lived adventure

3.6. Reveiewing the structure of Ezek 29,1-16

The first oracle of judgment against Egypt (Ezek 29,1-16) displays a complex structure. This becomes clear only when we closely observe its vocabulary. The five units of this oracle are:

1) 1-3a	introduction:	A historical date: 7th January 587[33]
2) 3b-6a	first oracle:	Saying of the big crocodile: "Mine is the Niles and I made (it) for myself."
3) 6b-9a	second oracle:	Egypt is a "staff of reed" for the house of Israel.
4) 9b-12	third oracle:	Saying of the great crocodile: "The Nile is mine and I made (it)."
5) 13-16	fourth oracle:	An oracle of hope "After 40 years I will gather the captives of Egypt, And I will bring back the captives of Egypt And I will bring them back to Pathros; And they will be there a low kingdom."

3.6.1. Brief explanations of the structures
3.6.1.1. The introduction to the oracles (29,1-3a)

The opening unit begins with a date formula followed by a word-event formula and closes with a command to the prophet, indicated by an imperative-indicative: דַּבֵּר וְאָמַרְתָּ. The word דבר in vv.1.3a makes a perfect inclusion of the unit. This opening formula serves as an introduction not only to the first oracle but also to the whole series of oracles against Egypt.

3.6.1.2. The first oracle of judgment (29,3b-6a)

The first oracle begins with a message formula, "Thus says the Lord GOD" + הִנְנִי, calling attention to the accusation, while the announcement of judgment begins directly with *waw*-consec. + נתן (pf.) and closes with the recognition formula: "And all the inhabitants will know that I am the LORD."

3.6.1.3. The second oracle of Judgment (29,6b-9a)

The second oracle begins with a causal particle יַעַן + a construct (inf.) of הָיָה (הֱיוֹתָם), giving a motive for accusation. The accusation begins with an adverb בְּ +

---

during Nebuchadnezzar's siege of Jerusalem in 587 B.C. See HAYES and HOOKER, *A New Chronology*, 88-91.97; and WISEMANN, *Chronicles of Chaldeaen Kings,* 31.

[33] COOKE, *Ezekiel,* 325; PARKER and DUBBERSTEIN puts this date in December/January of 588/587 B.C. See their *Chronology* (1942), 28; also BOADT, *Ezekiel's Oracles,* 17; Allen, *Ezekiel 20-48,* 104; GREENBERG, *Ezekiel 21-37,* 601; BLOCK, *Ezekiel 25-48,* 133.

a construct (inf.). It is followed by לְכֵן + the message formula, "Thus says the Lord GOD," followed by הִנְנִי and the announcement of judgment. The oracle closes with a recognition formula: "And they will know that I am the LORD."

3.6.1.4. The third oracle of judgment (20,9b-12)

The third oracle also begins with a causal conjunction יַעַן + perfect of the verb אָמַר repeating the motive for accusation (cf. 3bβ). It is followed by a לְכֵן + הִנְנִי construction, indicating the announcement of judgment without any new message formula. This oracle has no formal ending; instead, the climax of desolation of the land is announced in two parallel statements of judgment, bringing it to its logical conclusion:

> 12cα I will scatter the Egyptian among the nations
> 12cβ And I will disperse them through the countries.

3.6.1.5. The fourth oracle: An oracle of hope (29,13-16)

The oracle of hope begins with the particle כִּי and a message formula "Thus says the Lord GOD" (cf. v.3), announcing the end of 40-years' of judgment, and heralding God's new saving intervention. The oracle closes with the full form of the recognition formula: "And they will know that I am the Lord GOD."

The three oracles of judgment in 29,3-12 are highly organised through the use of the deictic particle הִנְנִי, the relative conjunction אֲשֶׁר, the causal conjunction יַעַן, the final result conjunction לְכֵן and the use of the verbs נתן and הָיָה, which bind each of these oracles of judgment together.

This can be seen easily in the first oracle where הִנְנִי gives an orientation for the accusation against Pharaoh and is followed by אֲשֶׁר, which begins the motive for accusation, and the verb וְנָתַתִּי, which announces judgment against him.

A	(3aβ)	הִנְנִי עָלֶיךָ פַּרְעֹה מֶלֶךְ־מִצְרַיִם
B	(3bβ)	אֲשֶׁר אָמַר לִי יְאֹרִי וַאֲנִי עֲשִׂיתִנִי
C	(4aα)	וְנָתַתִּי חַחִיים בִּלְחָיֶיךָ

We find a different construction in the third oracle, which begins with יַעַן, indicating the motive for accusation, and is followed by לְכֵן and הִנְנִי, which give orientation to the accusation, and the verb וְנָתַתִּי, which announces judgment.

B' (9bα)   יַעַן אָמַר יְאֹר לִי וַאֲנִי עָשִׂיתִי
A' (10a)   לָכֵן הִנְנִי אֵלֶיךָ וְאֶל־יְאֹרֶיךָ
C' (10b.12a)   וְנָתַתִּי אֶת־אֶרֶץ מִצְרַיִם לְחָרְבוֹת

There is a change in the preposition in the third oracle from the normally expected עַל to אֶל in A' to emphasize the orientation to the accusation. The motive for accusation (cf. יַעַן) is placed before the orientation for it (cf. לָכֵן). Moreover, a causal conjunction יַעַן is preferred to a relative conjunction אֲשֶׁר to announce the accusation. By making this change in the order and the use of particles, the accusation is made more forceful. The causal function of יַעַן implies a motive for judgment whereas the function of אֲשֶׁר is that of a relative conjunction that connects the saying in 3bβ with its preceding verses (3aα.3aβ). The announcements of judgment in C and C' begin with *waw* + perfect of נָתַן but their specific contents are different.

In the instruction to orientation given to the prophet in the opening unit, there is an indication of the LORD's confrontation with Pharaoh (v.2), who is addressed in the third person, making him the recipient object to which the prophet turns and delivers the message. It is a solemn way of introducing the prophet to his audience and of opening the oracles that follow. The phrase עַל פַּרְעֹה מֶלֶךְ מִצְרַיִם (2a) is repeated again at the beginning of the first unit (A) (cf. עָלֶיךָ in 3aβ) where it takes the form of a duel and is addressed in the second person in which Pharaoh, king of Egypt, stands in the centre in relation to the Land of Egypt. It also distinguishes him from his metaphorical character: הַתַּנִּים הַגָּדוֹל הָרֹבֵץ בְּתוֹךְ יְאֹרָיו (3bα).

The "big crocodile" is not an apposition to Pharaoh, similar to "king of Egypt," but a new metaphorical title that depicts his character, giving a basis for its hubris. In the third oracle (A') the orientation to accusation is placed in the context of a contest. Pharaoh as a personal name is lacking in A' (10a) and instead, he is addressed in the second person, singular.

In C (the first oracle) the judgment is stated allegorically. It aims at the destruction of the life of the Niles, i.e., the destruction of the great crocodile and its fish by hunting the crocodile and taking it out of its Niles and its fish along with it. On the other hand, in C' (the third oracle) the content of judgment is direct. It relates to the devastation of the land of Egypt by scattering its inhabitants among the nations and dispersing them through the countries.

The theme of the "house of Israel" occurs once each in the judgment and in the salvation oracle (6b; 16a):

6b   יַעַן הֱיוֹתָם מִשְׁעֶנֶת קָנֶה לְבֵית יִשְׂרָאֵל
16a   וְלֹא יִהְיֶה־עוֹד לְבֵית יִשְׂרָאֵל לְמִבְטָח

The repetition of the house of Israel in the second oracle of judgment and in the oracle of salvation makes another level of unity with the rest of the oracles of this chapter. In the second (6b) and the fourth oracle (16a), this theme is expressed through the verb הָיָה and both uses refer to a negative experience of the house of Israel. This theme of the house of Israel within the oracles of judgment against Egypt reminds us of the central role of the house of Israel in the oracles against Egypt and against the nations. Moreover, the hope of salvation of Egypt and of the other nations is linked with God's plan of salvation for the house of Israel.

The verbs, נָתַן "to give" (= "to make") and הָיָה "to be" in reference to the land of Egypt are closely related to God's act of creation and occur in the announcement of judgment against Egypt in 9a.10b.19b.20a, while there is a repetition of "forty years" in 11c.12b.13b that restricts the judgment to a definite period.

3.7. The nexus between the first and the last oracle (Ezek 29, 1-16 & 29, 17-30,19)

At the end of the first oracle of judgment against Egypt in 29,1-16, the reader turns immediately to the next oracle in 29,17-21. But here lies the danger of considering it as a continuation of the series of oracles following the first oracle in 29,1-16 unless, of course, one takes note of the new date formula in 29,17. This new date formula indicates not only the beginning of a new unit but it also reminds the reader of a chronological gap between these two oracles.

The first oracle of judgment against Egypt dates 10th day, 10th month, 12th year (29,1), which corresponds to 6th January 587 B.C., whereas the next oracle (29,17-21) dates 27th year, 1st day, 1st month (v.17), corresponding to 26th April 571 B.C.[34] Chronologically, both the poles of Ezekiel's prophetic activity, whereby the last oracle is placed interestingly directly next to the first oracle, and in fact, next to the oracle of salvation (29,13-16), instead of keeping it at the end of the series of oracles against Egypt (i.e., after 32,17-32; cf. 40,1). This placement makes it clear that the aforementioned oracle of judgment is closely linked with the oracle against Tyre, which also takes place within a very short period of time soon after the fall of Tyre, thus, having a very compact temporal unity with it through which the fulfilment of the last oracle (29,17-21) is guaranteed. Moreover, the last oracle does not end in 29,21 as one might think, but continues through 30,1-19 and in this way the first part of the last oracle (i.e., 29,17-21) is developed fully in the second part (i.e., 30,1-19). However, the next four oracles (30,20; 31,1; 32,1; 32,17; cf., 33,21; 40,1) from a continuous chronological series, yet date prior to the date given in 29,17.

---

[34] PARKER and DUBBERSTEIN, *Chronology* (1942), 28.

30,1-19, which accounts for a series of seven oracles against Egypt, is undoubtedly a new oracle, but as it lacks a date formula of the type normally used in the oracles against Egypt to distinguish them as independent units, this undated oracle is placed next to 29,17-21, which interrupts the chronological sequence of the oracles. Thus, 29,17-21 and 30,1-19 are both clubbed together as a single piece (cf. 29,17-30,19) in the composition. This, however, interrupts the theme (cf. Pharaoh) dealt with in 29,1-16; 30,20-26; 31,1-18; 32,1-16. All the same, 30,1-19 shows a thematic unity (cf. Egypt) with 29,17-21, even though the literary *genre* of 30,1-19 is different ("lamentation"), which distinguishes it from 29,17-21. This arrangement shows Ezekiel's literary skill and theological aim, evincing that the fulfilment or non-fulfilment of his oracles remained immaterial to his personal faith and conviction.

Whether it was Ezekiel's intention and not a misplacement of the last oracle in the composition remains a point of discussion. Many commentators have tried to explain the placement of the last oracle of judgment against Egypt (29,17-21; cf. 29,17-30,19) next to the first oracle of judgment (29,1-16) rather than seeking to keep it at the end.[35] It is in this context, that the usage of the date formula in the oracles against the nations becomes significant, i.e., in identifying different oracles and, above all, in determining their chronological sequences.

Although the last oracle (29,17-21) is juxtaposed to the first oracle (29,1-16), 29,13-16, which is an oracle of salvation, does not strictly belong to the first oracle of judgment (i.e., 29,1-12). All the same, its close relationship with the oracle of judgment cannot be doubted. Indeed, this relationship makes it clear that the oracle of salvation is an integral part of God's judgment (cf. Ezek 26,36; 39,28). Thus, the oracle of salvation (29,13-16) plays an intermediary role between the two oracles of judgment. The opening verse of the salvation oracle, "for at the end of forty years" (v.13), points to the fulfilment of the definite period of judgment against Egypt (vv.11.12), thereby preparing necessary background for placing the

---

[35] BOADT (*Ezekiel Oracles*, 10-11) considers it an appendage. Similarly, COOKE (*Ezekiel*, 328-329) also thinks that it is an appendix to Ezekiel's oracles against Egypt (29-32), which came as a result of the partial fulfilment of his earlier oracles against Tyre (Ezek 26,1; cf. ZIMMERLI, *Ezechiel 25-48*, 718). COOKE's inference is based on the date given in 29,17, i.e., 27th year, 1st day of the 1st month which corresponds to 26th April 571 (PARKER and DUBBERSTEIN, *Chronology* [1942], 25f.), when Nebuchadnezzar ended thirteen years of siege against Tyre (cf. GREENBERG, *Ezekiel 21-37*, 611). It is also the latest date in the book (COOKE, *Ezekiel*, 329) as the oracle in 40,1 precedes it. The failure of fulfilment of Ezekiel's oracles against Tyre had raised doubts on the authenticity of his prophecies but Ezekiel was not unduly perturbed by it, nor did he make any effort to change or correct them (FOHRER, *Ezekiel*, 169), but waited until a new situation emerged (i.e., the fall of Jerusalem in 587) when he realised that God was going to fulfil his oracles also against Tyre through His judgment against Egypt (GREENBERG, *Ezekiel 21-37*, 611). Nebuchadnezzar marched against Amasis II, who had succeeded Hophra in 568/567 as Pharaoh of Egypt, but this campaign against Egypt is much debated (COOKE, *Ezekiel*, 329; GREENBERG, *Ezekiel 21-37*, 611; ZIMMERLI, *Ezechiel 25-48*, 718). BLOCK (*Ezekiel 25-48*, 147) argues in favour of the fulfilment of the oracles.

last oracle proximately close to the first oracle, which predicts the destruction of Egypt, desolation of the land and its cities, and dispersion of her inhabitants.

On the question of placing 30,1-19 (vv.1-9: the Day of the LORD; vv.10-19: the development of judgment) next to 29,17-21 (the judgment of Egypt), Bertholet correctly recognised that 30,1-19 follows from 29,17-21 rather than from 29,1-16 (Contrary to Hitzig) and argued that Ezekiel intentionally placed this closely related unit of oracles (29,17-21; 30,1-19) here, instead of putting it at the end, where the smallest (and the latest) oracle had already found its proper place.[36] Moreover, 29,1-16 and 29,17-30,19, both speak of dispersion (cf. 29,12) and exile of the Egyptians (cf. 30,17.18), thereby resonating a similar motif.

Boadt disagrees with Cassuto (*Arrangement*, 25-32) that 30,1-19 was placed together with 29,17-21, or that such placement can be supported, on the basis of their "association" namely, because both the parts (29,17-21 and 30,1-19) mention "hordes" and "Nebuchadnezzar," king of Babylon.[37] Boadt maintains that, since the insertion of the last oracle (29,17-21) between 29,1-16 and 30,20-26 already interrupts the chronological sequence, Ezekiel placed the only undated oracle against Egypt (30,1-19) next to the last oracle (29,17-21) to make a unified narrative.[38] No new date formula was required for the oracle in 30,1-19 because it did not make a separate unit of oracles, but rather continued the 'last oracle'. Notwithstanding some points of literary affinity, e.g., "hordes" (29,19; 30,4.10.15) and "Nebuchadnezzar" (29,18; 30,10), a deeper relationship is apparent between 29,17-21 and 30,1-19, which is their emphasis on "desolation" of the land and "dispersion"/"exile" of the inhabitants of Egypt.[39] The desolation of the land comes out forcefully in humbling the pride of Egypt, causing her to acknowledge the LORD.

The logic behind extending the main text (cf. 29,13-16) on either side, i.e., 29,1-12 on the one hand and 29,17-30,19 on the other hand, may well be that these two extremities of the oracles constitute the immediate literary context. The accusations and the announcement of judgment against Egypt in the first oracle (29,1-12), as well as its thematic development (cf. 29,17-21) are brought to a climax both in the Day of the LORD and in the development of judgment (30,1-19) through the destruction of the cities of Egypt, her gods, helpers, supporters, army and prince. Thus, the desolation of the entire land of Egypt and the dispersion of her inhabitants, offer proper background against which to display God's saving intervention - the restoration and salvation of Egypt.

Through its placement at the centre, the oracle of salvation (29,13-16) not only functions as a bridge between the oldest and the latest oracles of judgment in the book of Ezekiel, but also points to the final aim of the oracles as such: Egypt (and

---

[36] BERTHOLET, *Hesekiel*, KHAT 12, 157.

[37] Please note the reference to "hordes" in both the parts (29,19; 30,4.15).

[38] BOADT, *Ezekiel's oracles*, 10-11.

[39] BOADT, *Ezekiel's oracles*, 11.

also the nations and Israel) should come to recognise the LORD by seeing His saving deeds for her. Thus, God's judgment and salvation are both means through which His awesome presence and His holy name are revealed, motivating Egypt to acknowledge Him. In this sense, the two oracles of judgment on the either side of the oracle of salvation are closely related to it and with each other.

3.8. Conclusion:

The structural analysis shows a clear unity of the first oracle of judgment in 29,1-16, which is marked by a date (v.1) and a recognition formula (v.16). The next date appears in v.17, making the beginning of another oracle of judgment (29,17-21). Within this overall structure, the introduction, 1-3a, and the sub-oracles, 3aβ-6a, 6b-9a, 9b-12, 13-16, can be easily distinguished. The introduction (1-3a), contains the date of the oracle and the LORD's address to the prophet as "Son of man," instructing him to direct his prophecies against Egypt (v.2). All these are framed by an inclusion that is marked by דבר and אמר in v.1 and 3aα.

Vv.3aβ-12, the first oracle of judgment, consists of three small oracles against Egypt, which build a closely knit units. The first oracle (3aβ-6a) is marked by a "message" and a "recognition" formula. The "message formula" is followed by הִנְנִי, predicating the first accusation against Egypt: Look I am against you, Pharaoh...Who says: "Mine is the Nile; I made (it) for myself." The second oracle (6b-9a) begins with causal יַעַן and closes with a "recognition" formula (9a). יַעַן announces the second accusation: "Because you were a staff of reed to the house of Israel." The announcement of judgment begins with a resumption לָכֵן: "Therefore, Thus says the Lord GOD...I will bring a sword against you." The third oracle (9b-12) begins with a causal יַעַן but it ends differently. Instead of a recognition formula, there is an elaboration of judgment, reaching its climax in scattering and dispersion of the Egyptians. Here too, יַעַן states the accusation: Because he said, "The Nile is Mine; I made (it)." The consquent announcement of judgment begins with לָכֵן: "Therefore Look, I am against your Niles. I will give the land of Egypt to wastes, a waste of desolation." The repetiton of the saying of the big crocodile in the first and third oracles results in the "inclusion" of the oracle of judgment against Egypt.

The use of וְנָתַתִּי in the announcement of judgment (cf. 4a.10b) shows another element of unity of the oracles in 3aβ-12. Its position in both the occurrences, i.e., at the beginning of the announcements of judgement, is noteworthy. It occurs twice in the first and the third oracle (cf. 4a.5c and 10b.12a). The second oracle is constructed mainly by using the verb הָיָה "to be" in the accusation and in the intervention of judgment (6b.9a). It is used to state the result of judgment against the land of Egypt in 12b. The verb ידע occurs in the "recognition formula"

(6a.9aα.16c) and הִנְנִי is used in the first and the third oracle to announce God's accusation in 3aβ.10a.

The fourth oracle (vv.13-16) which is an oracle of hope, begins with the particle כִּי and a message formula and concludes with a recognition formula. הָיָה is used again (cf. 14c.16a) to make the basic statements regarding Egypt's new existence.

The oracles are directed towards two objects: 1) Pharaoh, king of Egypt and 2) the whole of Egypt. Greenberg observes[40] that the "object of address and reference" change frequently, and such movement becomes much more complicated with the change of pronouns. As the text moves forward, the oracles exhibit the following shifting use of pronouns:

- "they" in 6a.6b (m. pl. referring to the inhabitants),
- "you" in v.7 (3m. sg. referring to Pharaoh),
- "you" in v.8 (2f. sg. referring to the land),
- "she" in 9a (3f. sg. referring to the land),
- "they" in 9b (3m. pl. referring to the inhabitants),
- "he" in 9c (3m. sg. referring to Pharaoh),
- "you" and "your" in 10a (2m. sg. referring to Pharaoh),
- "in her" in v.11 (3f. sg. referring to the land),
- "she" in v.12 (3f. sg. referring to the land),
- (its) "inhabitants" in vv.12-13 (3m. pl),
- "she" in v.15 (3f. sg. referring to the land),
- "he" in 16a (3m. sg. referring to the low kingdom in v.15), and finally
- "they" (3m. pl. referring to the inhabitants).

"Desolation" is one of the main motifs in the oracle of judgment against Egypt and it runs throughout all three oracles (cf. 5a.9a.10b.12a). The restoration of the land of Egypt as a low kingdom after "forty years of desolation" (v.14) presents a great contrast to the oracles of judgment, but it is an integral part of such judgment. It emphasizes God's new intervention for Egypt, similar to His salvation to Israel.

---

[40] GREENBERG, *Ezekiel 21-37*, 609

CHAPTER FOUR
SEMANTIC ANALYSIS OF EZEKIEL 29,1-16

Through text critical and structural analysis of 29,1-16 in the preceding two chapters, we offered a critical interpretation of the text and examined the stylistic interaction of its individual units and sub-units. This exercise has revealed the tight unity of the first oracle of judgment. Chapter Four discusses the meaning and significance of the text through semantic analysis of the oracle.

4.1. Introduction to the oracles (29,1-3a)

בַּשָּׁנָה (v.1) "In the x year" in the introductory date formula[1] is a superscription to the oracles of judgment against Egypt (Ezek 29-32) and indicates the beginning of a new section. In 11 occurrences it begins with וַיְהִי but this is not the case in Ezek 29,1 and 40,1; here the date formula begins with a temporal preposition בְּ and the substantive שָׁנָה. This change from the usual form in 29,1 and 40,1 indicates the beginning of a section: i.e., 29,1 begins the oracles against Egypt and 40,1 begins the oracles of hope for Israel. Thus, the change (שָׁנָה + בְּ) is a stylistic feature to evoke the reader's attention.

The word דבר plays a special role in 29,1-3a, where it constitutes the "word-event formula" and is used as a verb to announce the revealed word. The WEF occurs 50 times in the book of Ezekiel. In 43 occurrences, it begins with an imperfect of היה and in seven occurrences it begins with a perfect.[2] Excluding 1,3, it occurs six more times in the oracles of judgment against Egypt (29,1.17; 30,20; 31,1; 32,1.17) and, in 30,1, it is used with the imperfect (וַיְהִי). The usage of הָיָה (pf.) in the WEF in the oracles against Egypt is noteworthy.[3] Seven times היה is immediately followed by בֶּן־אָדָם (but cf. Ezek 1,3), but in 24,20 it is constructed differently and בֶּן־אָדָם is missing.

---

[1] Cf. in Ezek 1,1 (cf. 1,2); 8,1; 20,1; 24,1; 26,1; 29,1.17; 30,20; 31,1; 32,1.17;33, 21; 40,1.

[2] ZIMMERLI (*Ezechiel 25-48*, 1251) notes 50 occurrences of the WEF in Ezekiel, 41 occurrences are constructed with imperfect and 9 with perfect, but he has wrongly included 26,1 in the constructions with perfect. 24,20 is constructed with perfect but it is not a new revelation; rather it reports a previous revelation that was made in 24,15.

[3] Cf. היה (impf.) + Date in Ezek 1,1; 8,1; 20,1; 26,1; 29,17; 30,20; 32,1.17; 33,21; (pf.) + WEF in 1,3 (with a date in v.2); 41,1 (with a Date); 32,1,17; 30,20; 29,1.17; 26,1; (impf.) + WEF in 24,1; 26,1; Ezek 40,1 contains a 'hand-event' formula.

Grammatically הָיָה (pf.) and וַיְהִי (*waw* + impf.) function as two different temporal modifiers.[4] הָיָה (pf.) denotes completed action but וַיְהִי (*waw* + impf. cf. 30,1) has a conversive sense of the perfect. Thus, הָיָה/וַיְהִי דְבַר־יְהוָה אֵלַי are rendered: "The word of the LORD came to me." The meaning and the temporal sequence of the WEF is not affected by *waw*-conversive + impf.

The divine name יהוה occurs 434 times (435x with 21,14) and אֲדֹנָי יְהוָה ("Lord GOD") occurs 217 times in the book of Ezekiel.[5] In the WEF (50 occurrences), יהוה (without אֲדֹנָי) stands in construct with דבר.[6] The absence of אֲדֹנָי in the WEF raises some doubt on possible expansion of יהוה at some stage in the Ezekiel tradition. It means that the WEF preserves an older tradition concerning the usage of the divine name יהוה, whereas אֲדֹנָי יְהוָה may be a later expansion. אֲדֹנָי יְהוָה is used as a stylistic term to express the majesty of God's name (*plur. excellentiae*[7]), as is also found in the use of the plural form אֱלֹהִים.

On the other hand, אֲדֹנָי occurs 449 times in the OT. Of these, 55 occurrences are found in the Psalms and 14 in the Lamentations. It occurs 134 times אֲדֹנָי standing alone, while in 315 occurrences it is used with יְהוָה (cf. 310x אֲדֹנָי יְהוָה and 5x יְהוָה אֲדֹנָי).[8] אֲדֹנָי יְהוָה generally occurs in those texts that are related to the older covenant traditions (cf. Gen 15,2; 2Sam 7,18ff. 28f.; Jos 7,7; Judg 6,22; Ex 15,17), the old literary form that Ezekiel revived consciously in his oracles.[9]

Ezekiel uses אֲדֹנָי יְהוָה as a "literary device" to form a parallel structure as is done in certain OT texts, particularly the Psalms.[10] Ezekiel's interest in reviving this older form (אֲדֹנָי) as an address to God's name in combination with יְהוָה had a background[11] that becomes clear in chapters 40-48, where he speaks about a new Israel and a new Priestly Code. The role and the place of the foreign nations and of Egypt are not eclipsed in this plan. On the contrary, it is through their role,

---

[4] LAMBDIN, *Introduction to Biblical Hebrew*, §110 and §123.

[5] ZIMMRLI, *Ezechiel 25-48*, 1250.

[6] OT attests 110 (+ 1 cf. Ezek 24,20) occurrences of WEF using the form דְבַר־יְהוָה (without אֲדֹנָי); it occurs 98 times in the Prophetic books (Isa 1x; Jer 30x; Jonah 2x; Hagg 5x; Zech 9x; Dan 1x; Ezek 50x), 12x in the Historical books and once in the Pentateuch (cf. Genesis). In 84 occurrences, וַיְהִי precedes WEF, and in 27 occurrences WEF uses הָיָה, of which 17 relate to a date formula (Jer 1,2; 25,3; Ezek 1,3; 24,20; 26,1; 29,1.17; 30,20; 31,1; 32,1.17; Hagg 1,1; 2,1; 2,10; Zech 1,1; 1,7; Dan 9,2).

[7] KAUTZSCH, *GESENIUS' Hebrew Grammer*, 398, §124.

[8] EISSFELDT, "אָדוֹן אֲדֹנָי", in *ThWAT* I, 66, and ZIMMERLI, *Ezechiel 25-48*, 1250-1258.

[9] BOADT, *Ezekiel's Oracles*, 23.

[10] Ps. 30,9; 35,22; 38,16; 71,5; 86,5f., 130,1f., 135,5; cf. Isa 3,17; 49,14; Mic 1,2); see also BOADT, *Ezekiel's Oracles*, 24-25; EISSFELDT, "אָדוֹן אֲדֹנָי", in *ThWAT* I, 75.

[11] Ezekiel is not the only one who uses אֲדֹנָי יְהוָה (cf. Isa 3,15; 10,24; Jer 1,6; 2,19.22;4,10; 7,20; 14,13; 32,17.25; 44,26; 49,5; 50,31). Jeremiah uses it several times in combination with יְהוָה צְבָאוֹת as also found in Isaiah. See EISSFELDT, "אָדוֹן אֲדֹנָי", in *ThWAT* I, 66.

particularly the role of Egypt that this motive, i.e., recognition of the LORD's sovereignty, comes into focus.

As in other basic forms of the OT, יְהוָה is the basic constituent of the WEF. In Ezekiel four basic formulaic groups are associated with this type of material:[12]

1) וַיְהִי / הָיָה דְבַר־יְהוָה אֵלַי (*Wortereignisformel*) Revelation of the word formula
2) כֹּה־אָמַר אֲדֹנָי יְהוִה (*Botenspruchformel*) Message/Messenger formula
3) נְאֻם אֲדֹנָי יְהוִה (*Gottesspruchformel*) Messenger's speech/Signatory formula
4) וְיָדְעוּ כִּי אֲנִי יְהוִה / אֲדֹנָי יְהוִה (*Erkenntnisformel*) Recognition formula

Two other formulaic sayings could be added to this common group, although they are not as frequent in the book of Ezekiel:

5) יַד־יְהוָה / אֲדֹנָי יְהוִה (*Botenauftrag*) Commissioning formula .
6) שִׁמְעוּ (אֶת)דְּבַר יְהוָה / אֲדֹנָי יְהוִה a *Paraenetic* address formula.

Ezekiel's usage of the divine name in the WEF is a sign of authenticity, to show that his prophetic utterances are not his own, but God's word revealed to him, a mere human being, whom God himself commands to announce a message to the intended recipient. Ezekiel's experience of the divine vision relating to his call and commission to prophecy (Ezek 1,1-3,21) lies heavily behind all this, making him constantly aware of his mortal nature on the one hand and, on the other hand, of the holiness of God, who reveals His own word to him.

בֶּן־אָדָם refers to man as such, and may be rendered by "son of man" or simply, "humankind".[13] This is a set form by which, in Ezekiel, God addresses the prophet, emphasizing his human and mortal nature.[14] It is also closely connected with the word-event formula. Of the 41 occurrences of וַיְהִי + WEF, 33 have בֶּן־אָדָם following the WEF directly, whereas in 5 occurrences (cf. 7,1; 21,23; 22,1; 27,1 37,15) we find וְאַתָּה בֶן־אָדָם, and thrice it is used differently.[15]

שִׂים פָּנֶיךָ עַל "turn your face to" (v.2) is a special form found only in Ezekiel.[16] The verb + part of body + directional preposition are used here to create a dramatic effect. It allows the reader to recall the previous pantomimes of the prophet which

---

[12] ZIMMRLI, *Ezechiel 25-48*, 1251; and his *Gottes Offenbarung* (1963). See also GRETHER, *Name und Wort Gottes* (1934); HAYES, *Form Criticism*, 151.

[13] HAAG, „בֶּן־אָדָם", in *ThWAT* I, 684.

[14] בֶּן־אָדָם occurs 93 times in Ezekiel including seven occurrences in 'Egypt-oracles,' and 23 times with an emphasis וְאַתָּה בֶּן־אָדָם. See HAAG, „בֶּן־אָדָם", in *ThWAT* I, 686; see also HOUK, "בֶּן־אדם as literary criteria," in *JBL* 88 (1969), 184ff

[15] In 17,12 בֶּן־אָדָם is followed by an imperative; in 18,1 it is followed by an interrogative and in 24,1 a date formula interrupts it.

[16] I.e., in Ezek 6,2; 13,17; 21,2; 21,7; 25,2; 28,21; 29,2; 35,2; 38,2. See WEIR, "Aspects of the Book Ezekiel," in *VT* 2 (1952), 101.

he acted out to announce God's judgment against Israel (cf. 4,1f.; 5,1f.; 6,1f.; 12,3f.17f.; 21,23f.; 24,15f.). Its usage is metaphoric and he is not asked to set off to Egypt. The preposition עַל ("to") gives a clue, i.e., the prophet is told to orient himself toward the addressee to whom he is to announce the oracle of judgment.

The use of פַּרְעֹה מֶלֶךְ־מִצְרַיִם is found mostly in Priestly writing in Genesis and Exodus[17] and several times in Ezekiel. פַּרְעֹה is a title of an Egyptian ruler that is used as a personal name here (cf. vv.2.3).[18] The technical meaning of the Egyptian word Pharaoh denoted from early times "big house", symbolizing a royal palace or official buildings, and, since Thuthmose III, and generally in new Egypt, it symbolized the person of the king.[19] The apposition מֶלֶךְ־מִצְרַיִם, a late addition, explains his designation proper. The title מֶלֶךְ refers to a great emperor as against a petty king (e.g., of Judah)[20] while מִצְרַיִם denotes the land of Egypt as such. So, מֶלֶךְ־מִצְרַיִם in apposition to פַּרְעֹה (cf. 2a) could be a stylistic feature that creates a favourable parallelism with מִצְרַיִם כֻּלָּהּ (2b).

דַּבֵּר וְאָמַרְתָּ[21] (impv. + ind.) is a *hapax legomenon*. Boadt considers the use of this paired-verb as Ezekiel's individual style and points out that it occurs frequently in the Priestly tradition[22] and its usage in other Old Testament texts shows poetic parallelism.[23] In Ezekiel (except in 29,3) its usage is always marked by some intervening words and phrases:

3,11:	וְדִבַּרְתָּ אֲלֵהֶם וְאָמַרְתָּ אֲלֵיהֶם
14,4:	דַּבֵּר־אוֹתָם וְאָמַרְתָּ אֲלֵהֶם
20,3:	דַּבֵּר אֶת־זִקְנֵי יִשְׂרָאֵל וְאָמַרְתָּ אֲלֵהֶם
20,27:	דַּבֵּר אֶל־בֵּית יִשְׂרָאֵל בֶּן־אָדָם וְאָמַרְתָּ אֲלֵהֶם
29,3:	דַּבֵּר וְאָמַרְתָּ
33,2:	דַּבֵּר אֶל־בְּנֵי־עַמְּךָ וְאָמַרְתָּ אֲלֵהֶם

Ezek 3,11 refers to Ezekiel's commission to speak to his fellow countrymen in exile, and 3,16f. confirms this by affirming his role as a "watchman." In 14,4 he is commanded to speak against the house of Israel, and condemn her idolatry. In 20,3.27 he is asked to speak to the elders of Israel concerning their rebellion

---

[17] FECHTER, *Bewältigung der Katastrophe*, 227; PREMSTALLER, *Fremdvölkersprüche*, 143.

[18] ZIMMRLI, *Ezechiel 25-48*, 704.

[19] WOLFGANG and WOLFAHRT, *Lexikon der Ägypotologie* IV (1982), 1021. See also RINGGREN and FARBY, „מִצְרַיִם", in *ThWAT* IV, 1099-1111.

[20] DUGUID, *Ezekiel and the Leaders of Israel*, VT.Suppl. 56 (1994), 31.

[21] It occurs 22 times in the Old Testament: Lev 9x; Num 8x; Ezek 5x.

[22] E.g., Lev 1,2; 18,2; 23,2.10; 25,2; 27,2; Num 5,12; 6,2; 8,2; 15,2.18.38; 33,51; 35,10. Ezekiel's use of these paired verbs shows his familiarity with the tradition. See, BOADT, "Textual Problems in Ezekiel," in *JBL* 97/4, 497.

[23] Gen 21,1; Ex 6,29-30; Isa 30,9-10; 40,27; 45,19; Prov 4,20; see BOADT, "Textual Problems in Ezekiel," in *JBL* 97/4, 497.

against the LORD. In 33,2 he is asked to speak to his countrymen, warning them to heed to the word of he who is a "watchman" of Israel (cf. 3,16f.). Moreover, both verbs command separate indirect objects in 14,4; 20,3.27; 33,2.[24] Thus, it is clear that the paired verbs דַּבֵּר וְאָמַרְתָּ refer to Ezekiel's command and commission to serve as prophet. Similarly, the paired-imperatives הִנָּבֵא וְאָמַרְתָּ are also attested to in Ezek 13,2; 21,14.33; 30,2; 34,2; 36,3; 37,12. Beyond this, there are also other occurrences of the paired verbs interrupted by other words or phrases, having meaning dissimilar to 29,3.

דְּבַר (n. 1β) relates to the revelation of God's word, whereas דַּבֵּר (vb 3a) indicates the prophet's action, i.e., the announcement of the revealed word, which is God's judgment of Egypt. So, there is a play of words here on the usage of the root-word דבר in the revelation of the word (i.e., "word event") and the "command/commission" to the prophet to announce it. It reveals that the usage of דַּבֵּר with וְאָמַרְתָּ is not a simple stylistic feature that is used here, to "command" the prophet to "announce" the "revealed word" as the "message", but that the "command to announce" is intimately related to the revelation itself. In this way, דַּבֵּר-דְּבַר achieves internal unity and 'inclusion'. In view of 29,21, which speaks about God's vindication on behalf of the prophet, the connection between דַּבֵּר / דְּבַר (speak/word) seems quite significant. God's vindication of the prophet refers to the fulfilment of his oracle of judgment against Egypt (cf. דַּבֵּר 3a), which he had received from Him. The "content" (i.e., the message דְּבַר 1β) that is revealed to the prophet and the commission to speak (דַּבֵּר 3a) introduce the oracles against Egypt and דַּבֵּר-דְּבַר, by their relation to the vindication of the prophet (21b), give a glimpse of the oracles' fulfilment.

4.2. The first oracle (29,3b-6a)
4.2.1. The accusation against Pharaoh (3aα-3bβ)

In 3b, הִנְנִי announces God's accusation and וַאֲנִי (pron. 3bβ) points to self-assertion of the big crocodile.

3b Look, I am against you Pharaoh,	הִנְנִי עָלֶיךָ פַּרְעֹה מֶלֶךְ־מִצְרַיִם
3bβ who says: Mine is the Niles and I made it.	אֲשֶׁר אָמַר לִי יְאֹרִי וַאֲנִי עֲשִׂיתִנִי

The saying לִי יְאֹרִי וַאֲנִי עֲשִׂיתִנִי (3bβ) is a *Hoffartsmonolog*,[25] a "proud claim" (= hubris) of the crocodile and an open defiance of God's sovereignty as its Creator. In comparison to the other texts in Ezekiel (cf. 12,25.28; 17,24; 22,14; 36,36;

---

[24] BOADT, "Textual Problems in Ezekiel," in *JBL* 97/4 (1978), 497.

[25] EISSFELDT, "אָדוֹן אֲדֹנָי", in *ThWAT*, I, 76; see also BOADT, *Ezekiel's Oracles*, 30.

37,14), where God affirms He will accomplish what He has spoken, this saying depicts the crocodile as a would-be god.[26] Here דבר (vb) relates to God's word, while לִי + עשֹה־נִי relates to the crocodile's claim, highlighting the latter's disposition.[27] The use of the pronominal suffixes 1st person singular in the statement of the crocodile intimates this.

הַתַּנִּים הַגָּדוֹל "the big[28] crocodile" alludes metaphorically to Pharaoh, king of Egypt. A crocodile can live both on the land (cf. Ex 7,9.12; Deut 32,3; cf. Ps 91.13; Ezek 32,2) and in the water (cf. Gen 1,28; Isa, 27,1; 51,9; Ps 74,13; 148,7; Job 7,12). In the text, תַּנִּין is translated as "crocodile," "serpent," or "dragon." In the creation-myth, the dragon is associated with the sea-monster.[29] Here תַּנִּין/תַּנִּים alludes to the act of creation. It is a symbol of chaos that God subdues when He establishes order at the beginning of creation. Similarly, sea/water is a symbol of dread, deluge and destruction. In an Egyptian hymn it also symbolizes military might.[30] The figure of the big crocodile, lying in the Nile-streams, and his hubris portray a danger to life and the order of God's creation. By his defiance, hubris and chaos, the crocodile poses a threat to God's purpose in creation.

הָרֹבֵץ ("who lies") describes the crocodile's attitude and its state of being, 'it lies securely' (cf. Ps 23,2; Is 17,2; Zeph 3,13, Job 11,19).[31] Jacob's blessing to his sons (Gen 49,25) and Moses' blessing to the children of Israel (Deut 33,13) use רבץ in the sense of "lying" where it relates metaphorically to Joseph.[32] Sometimes it is followed by another participial clause וְאֵין מַחֲרִיד ("and no one would make [you] afraid" cf. Job 11,19; Is 17,2; Zeph 3,13) that specifies the meaning of רֹבֵץ, namely, lying securely without fear of any threat. Ezek 32,2 then describes another characteristic of the crocodile beyond that found in 29,3, bringing his pride into sharp contrast:

וְאַתָּה כַּתַּנִּים בַּיַּמִּים וַתָּגַח בְּנַהֲרוֹתֶיךָ
וַתִּדְלַח־מַיִם בְּרַגְלֶיךָ וַתִּרְפֹּס נַהֲרוֹתָם:

But you are like a dragon in the seas; you burst forth in your rivers,
And trouble the waters with your feet, and foul their rivers.

---

[26] VOGELS, *God's Universal Covenant*, 89

[27] עָשָׂה denotes God's action of doing or making or, bringing something to fulfilment.

[28] In a theological sense, the LORD is called "great" and this expresses the greatness of his divine character; therefore, its usage as a title for Pharaoh is in itself already a critique of Pharaoh. See JENNI, "גָּדוֹל *gādôl* great," in *TLOT* I, 305-306.

[29] Cf. Ps, 74,13; Job 7,14; cf. Ps 91,13.

[30] PREMSTALLER, *Fremdvölkersprüche*, 144.

[31] רבץ ("to lie") occurs 36 times in the OT. See WASCHKE, „רבץ", in *ThWAT* VIII, 321.

[32] BOADT, *Ezekiel's Oracles*, 28.

In Ezek 32,2, the גיח ("to burst") and דלח ("to tread") correctly express the grandiose feeling of the crocodile. Thus, הַתַּנִּים as a metaphor for Pharaoh, describes Egypt's attitude, but despite its grandiose feeling, it is only a creature (Gen 1,21; Ps 148,7). The Priestly narrative (cf. Ex 7,8f//Ex 4,2-5) speaks about Aaron throwing his staff on the ground before Pharaoh and his servants turning it into a reptile, a crocodile (לְתַנִּין; RSV renders it as "serpent"). In ancient Egyptian cultic practice, הַתַּנִּין was viewed as a fearful and awesome sea-creature, which remained the inaccessible "LORD of the water".[33] Blenkinsopp thinks that the application of this image to Pharaoh is appropriate because the crocodile-cult was "associated with the divine ruler in Egypt".[34] Boadt thinks that the physical shape of Egypt along the long and winding Nile-course may have suggested the analogy of the crocodile. The text contains more than the semantic meaning of *far⁽un* and the cultic association of תַּנִּין with the ruler; rather, drawing an analogy to Egypt's geo-physical shape along the course of the Nile, it evokes the mythological aspect of the crocodile, which lies in the background. He points to this "mythological material" in Ugarit, which is closely linked with the "theme of *hubris* and the chaos-dragon" in the oracles against other nations. He also maintains that the "original *Chaoskampf* is moralized" in God's battle against foreign gods to establish his rule.[35] J. Day maintains that Egypt's depiction as a dragon could allude to her oppression of the Israelites, leading to their Exodus and final deliverance at the sea (Ex 14; cf. Ps 77,17-21). He also points out that Isa 51,10 demythologizes this chaos-conflict, depicted in Exodus through the ultimate defeat of Pharaoh and the Egyptians, and confirms God's victory over the sea.[36]

J. Day[37] points out that Gunkel was the first one to recognise "the mythical character of various passages in the Old Testament which speak of a conflict between the LORD and the sea and a dragon or dragons, variously called Leviathan, Rahab, etc." However, he wrongly characterizes them as being appropriated by the Israelites from the Babylonian myth of Marduk's victory over Tiamat as narrated in the epic of Enuma Elish, as Israelite-origin is actually Canaanite rather than Babylonian. The original Ugarit myth describes Baal's conquest over *Yamm* (sea) and *Mot* (death), by which he finally overcomes chaos and establishes order in creation. Pss 74,12-17 and 89,10-15 allude to God's conflict with the dragon, while Ps 104,6-9; Job 38,8-11 and Prov 8,29 allude to His control over the primordial sea. *Yamm* actually represents the dragon and is identified with it.[38]

---

[33] BOADT, *Ezekiel's Oracles*, 27. H. FRANKFORT remarks that the Egyptian god Sobek was manifest in the crocodile "represented the power of the Nile to rise and fertilize the land." See his *Ancient Egyptian Religion*, 26. See also GREENBERG, *Ezekiel 21-37*, 612.

[34] BLENKINSOPP, *Ezekiel*, 128.

[35] BOADT, *Ezekiel's Oracles*, 27.

[36] DAY, *God's Conflict*, 96-97.

[37] DAY, *God's Conflict*, 2-16.

[38] BOADT, *Ezekiel's Oracles*, 27.

Baal's victory[39] over Mot and the dragon contains "seasonal elements" that indicate a victory-celebration, reminding them of Mot's battle with the dragon, which people held at the end of each annual cycle, just before the beginning of the New Year. There are a number of Old Testament texts alluding to God's conflict with the dragon and the sea, in which Baal's victory over the dragon and the sea was associated with creation, and the imagery may have been taken from the Canaanites. However, it is not Baal, but El, who is associated with creation (cf. Gen 14,19.22).

In using the mythological dragon to identify Pharaoh,[40] Ezekiel alludes to this above mentioned background. Just as God made Israel his own possession by taking her out of Egypt and making a covenant with her, so too He now promises to make a new Israel by defeating foreign gods and her arch rival, Egypt. So, Pharaoh personifies the chaos-dragon that defies God's sovereignty in creation and thus, the motif of *Chaoskampf* plays a significant role here.[41]

The feast of the Tabernacles, celebrated in autumn, serves as a background for the *Sitz im Leben* of this *Chaoskampf* (cf. Ps 74; 93;29). The feast was associated with the enthroning of the LORD, and it hailed the New Year in pre-exilic Israel. בְּצֵאת הַשָּׁנָה "at the end of the year" (Ex 23,16) and תְּקוּפַת הַשָּׁנָה "at the end of the year" (Ex 34,22) refer to this feast.[42] The occasion of this celebration highlights the sovereignty of the LORD in creation.[43] The association of both of these motifs could be made with his announcement of salvation for Egypt "at the end of forty years" (v.13), making her a lowly kingdom (v.14). Thus, the revival of Egypt at the end of a specified period of judgment affirms the LORD's victory over the proud and chaos-mongering crocodile and His enthronement as the sovereign LORD over all: He alone decides and guides the destinies of the nations.

In the overall structure of the book, the oracles against the nations reflect God's plan for Israel. Therefore, although Ezekiel delivers oracles of judgment against the house of Israel, he still gives words of hope to Israel in the midst his oracles against the nations (cf. 28,24-26; 29,21).[44] Despite Israel's profanity and defilement, God will act to save her for the sake of His holy name (cf. 36,22f.), so that she may truly live by keeping His ordinances (36,27). Ezekiel's vision of a

---

[39] DAY, *God's Conflict*, 17-18.

[40] In Egyptian Folklore Pharaoh is seen as the embodiment of the divinity who is responsible for the annual rising of Nile, which makes the land fertile. His saying in 29,3 means that he is the master of the Nile. Thus, he poses as the mythical dragon in the ocean, who tries to eat up *Re* (sun) daily as it goes down, and yet he is daily subdued by *Re*. See GASTER, *Myth*, 624-625.

[41] God reminds Job that He is the creator of the Behemoth (Job 40,1ff. cf. v.15) and affirms that everything under heaven belongs to Him (v.3).

[42] DAY, *God's Conflict*, 18-20.

[43] In this regard, please note the Hubris of the crocodile which makes the claim, "Mine is the Nile; I made it for myself." (Ezek 29,3).

[44] HÖFFKEN, "Zu den Heilszusätzen," in *VT* 27, 407.

new order for the house of Israel (chaps. 40-48), who is reborn through the exile and her new exodus from the nations, hints at this.

The process of creating a new Israel involves destroying the forces that are detrimental to her relationship with the LORD. The so-called "other gods" of the foreign nations and the role of Egypt in particular are seen from this perspective. Therefore, God's action is two-fold: destruction and death of the old Israel through exile, out of which a new people with a "new heart" will be born, while his judgment of the foreign nations will lead them as well to accept His dominion. The latter is seen as God's battle against other "forces" and "gods" to re-establish His rule. Ezekiel uses the mythological תַּנִּים to denote Pharaoh from this perspective, demythologizing the "forces" and "gods" contending against the LORD. It is thus clear, that Ezekiel does not use the imagery of תַּנִּין under the influence of an Egyptian myth, although he does mention Egypt as the origin of Israel's idolatry, concerning her rebellious attitude with the time of her wandering in the desert (20,6.13f.).

4.2.2. The announcement of judgment (4aα-4bβ)

The two-part announcement of judgment against the crocodile consists *first*, in putting (נתן 4aα) hooks (חַח) in the jaws (לְחִי *a hapax* cf. Deut 18,3) of the crocodile (4aα) and causing the fish of the Niles to stick to them (דבק 4aβ), and *second*, bringing out (עלה 4bα) the crocodile from the Niles (4bα) and the fish sticking to it (דבק 4bβ). The judgment is primarily against Pharaoh (4aα.4bα), but has consequences also for the inhabitants of Egypt (cf. 4aβ.4bβ).

The announcement of judgment is spoken in a metaphor that is taken from the *Sitz im Leben* of Egypt. It depicts the hunting of a Nile-crocodile, which was done usually with a hook.[45] Zimmerli notes that the crocodiles were usually captured by hooking their jaws (לְחִי).[46] The corpse of these huge reptiles were very often not buried, but left in the desert or on hills (cf. 5a) so that the birds and the wild animals could eat their flesh (cf. 32,5-6).[47]

Gunkel thinks that the fish of the Niles allegorically symbolise סֹמְכֵי מִצְרַיִם ("supports" or "supporters" 30,6) and כָּל־עֹזְרֶיהָ ("helpers" 30,8).[48] Thus, in vv.4-5, the "fish of Niles" do not necessarily denote the inhabitants of Egypt, but rather the "supporters" and "helpers" of Pharaoh. Fate of Pharaoh affects their fate as well, so that when Pharaoh is judged, they also fall under the same judgment. It highlights

---

[45] חַח ("hook") occurs only in the Old Testament, in Ex 35,22; 2Chr 33,22; Isa 37,29; 2Kgs 19,28 and in Ezek 19,4.9; 34,14; 38,4.

[46] ZIMMERLI, *Ezechiel 25-48*, 708.

[47] GUNKEL, *Schöpfung und Chaos*, 76-77.

[48] GUNKEL, *Schöpfung und Chaos*, 75

the role of Pharaoh's supporters, who helped Egypt to hold her domination over other nations (29,15).

4.2.3. The expansion of judgment (5a-5c)

The judgment announced in 4aα-4bα (וְנָתַתִּי / וְהַעֲלִיתִיךָ) is expanded in 5a-5c (נְתַתִּיךָ and וּנְטַשְׁתִּיךָ) and it includes three spatial elements, מִדְבָּרָה and הַשָּׂדֶה (5b), הַשָּׁמַיִם and הָאָרֶץ (5c), showing its dynamic development. Three sets of pair-words הַמִּדְבָּרָה // הַשָּׂדֶה[49] (5a.5b), תִּקָּבֵץ // תֵּאָסֵף[50] (5bα.5bβ) and הָאָרֶץ // הַשָּׁמַיִם (5c) keep its intensity.[51] Boadt notes another example of הַשָּׂדֶה // מִדְבָּרָה in Joel 1,19 and its reverse in Jos 8,24 הַמִּדְבָּרָה // הַשָּׂדֶה.

In the first place, נתן occurs at vv.4.5.10.12 to announce judgment, and here is translated as "to give," "put" or "make", while עלה "to bring" (4bα hiphil), like בוא "to bring" (8b hiphil), displays a similar function in the judgment. דבק "to stick" or "cling", which occurs twice in v.4, shows a close dependence of the fate of the inhabitants (or supporters) on the fate of Pharaoh, and נטש "to leave," "abandon" or "forsake" (5a) expresses the utter helplessness of Pharaoh and the inhabitants.

Although מִדְבָּר occurs 15 times in Ezekiel, it occurs only once in the oracles against the nations, at 29,5, but it occurs 10 times in chap. 20, which recalls the history of Israel's infidelity.[52] There, it is described how Israel forsook her LORD (= infidelity) several times, yet He still had pity on her. The use of נטש and מִדְבָּר in the judgment against Egypt create an association to Israel's wilderness experience, but without the aforementioned pity. שָׂדֶה is used in combination with מִדְבָּר (cf. Ezek 26, 6.8; 32,4) also to refer to punishment, as it describes an unwelcoming and unfriendly place.

In the pair-verbs קָבַץ // אָסַף, which expresses a similar idea ("to gather"), the second verb, i.e., קָבַץ, is thought to be a scribal error for קָבַר, which is considered more appropriate in 5a, where the text refers to corpses in the context of a burial as attested to in Jer 8,2; 25,33 (אָסַף // קָבַר) and Hos 9,6 (קָבַץ // קָבַר), although קָבַץ // אָסַף is also used in other texts.[53] W. G. E. Watson,[54] while observing that קָבַץ // אָסַף is "exclusive to classical Hebrew," points out that of the various combinations of this pair of verbs, אָסַף // קָבַץ is the most common and the paired verbs have

---

[49] Cf. Joel 1,19: מִדְבָּר // הַשָּׂדֶה; Jos 8,24: בַּמִּדְבָּרָה // בַשָּׂדֶה; see BOADT, *Ezekiel's Oracles*, 35.

[50] קָבַץ and אָסַף occur often in Ezekiel. See ROOKER, *Biblical Hebrew in Transition*, 157.

[51] BOADT, *Ezekiel's Oracles*, 35.

[52] FECHTER, *Bewältigung der Katastrophe*, 231.

[53] BAODT indicates other paired verbs in Isa 11,12; 13,14; 43,9; 62,9; Ezek 11,17; 39,17; Mic 2,12; 4,6.11f., Hab 2,5; Jon 2,16; Zeph 3,8; see his *Ezekiel's Oracles*, 35, fn. 52.

[54] WATSON, "Hebrew Word-Pair," in *ZAW* 96, 426-429.

similar meanings except in two places: i.e., Jer 8,2 and 25,33, as already pointed out above, where קבץ denotes "non-burial", and more specifically in Hos 9,6. Thus, Watson favours amending קבץ to קבר in Ezek 29,5. However, Ezek 29,5 uses קבץ to denote its primary sense of "to be gathered," which also closely relates to the following verses: v.12 (פוץ "scatter"; and זרה "disperse") and v.13 (קבץ).

The two concepts לְחַיַּת הָאָרֶץ (cf. 32,4; 44,31) and וּלְעוֹף הַשָּׁמַיִם ("earth" and "heaven") represent the totality of place and space available for living beings. Otherwise, Ezek 31,6.13; 34,5.8; 38,20; 39,4.17 use the more usual expression, חַיַּת הַשָּׂדֶה, similar to חַיַּת הָאָרֶץ.[55] Thus, they include the whole of creation on earth and in the heavens, and these are made witnesses to God's sovereign judgment on Pharaoh.

4.2.4. The recognition of the LORD (6a)

The first sub-oracle closes with a recognition formula, וְיָדְעוּ כָּל־יֹשְׁבֵי מִצְרַיִם כִּי אֲנִי יְהוָה (cf. 9aα). Here "knowledge" and the proof saying "I am the LORD" together constitute the so-called "recognition formula." Here כֹּל is an all-inclusive term denoting totality and it means the "whole people." According to Zimmerli,[56] Ezekiel uses the recognition formula to make the LORD known to all people, and the content of this knowledge is contained in the statement of his self-revelation: "I am the LORD" (אֲנִי יְהוָה). God takes the initiative to make himself known to the people, and this is a characteristic feature of the "preamble of the Decalogue or the postscript of the Holiness Code." By proclaiming the self-revelation of the LORD, Ezekiel focuses attention on the future salvation of Israel, which God is going to bring about.

Ezek 37,12 attests a secret purpose of the LORD's actions. His initial intervention may be divine judgment, but His ultimate purpose is the salvation that is intimately connected with it (cf. 29,13: כִּי כֹה־אָמַר אֲדֹנָי יְהוָה), which He carries out irrespective of any merit of Israel and the nations, but because of His holy name. His saving intervention is a sign for the people, signifying His power and control over events, which leads them to recognise Him as the LORD.

אֲנִי יְהוָה is used as a proof saying in the pre-classical prophets (cf. 1Kgs 20,13-14.22.28.35-43)[57] and in the Priestly writings, especially in the books of Exodus, Leviticus and Numbers.[58] However, its usage is not attested to in later books until the time of Ezekiel. Ezekiel revives this old form of the proof saying in his oracles, not merely as a concluding formula, but also to indicate the final aim of the

---

[55] FECHTER, *Bewältigung der Katastrophe*, 232-233.
[56] ZIMMERLI, "Special Form," 526; see also his *Gottes Offenbarung*, 46.
[57] ZIMMERLI, "Special Form," 526; see also his *Gottes Offenbarung*, 41-119, esp. p.54ff.
[58] ZIMMERLI, *Gottes Offenbarung*, 57-61.

oracles.[59] As such, it forms an integral part of the recognition formula in the oracles. It is also remarkable to note that out of 947 occurrences of יד״ע in the OT, 99 occur in Ezekiel, and 54 of them are in the recognition formula.[60]

In two texts in Ezekiel (2,3f. and 28,25f.), Zimmerli examines how the revelation of God's word, its announcement and fulfilment, come together in the recognition formula of the oracles.[61] These texts, *one* concerning Ezekiel's commission (2,3) and the *other* relating to the restoration of Israel (28,25), show a link between God's "word" and His "deed", namely, how God executes His word through His judgment/promise in the sight of Israel and of the nations. It signifies fulfilment of His revealed word, i.e., His "message". Therefore, knowledge of God is related to fulfilment of His "word", which leads people to knowledge of Him. Here, God is not only the "subject" of His action but also its final "aim" (object). This affirms knowledge of God to be the final motive of the closing formula, so that the people acknowledge His sovereignty.

4.3. The second oracle (29,6b-9aα)
4.3.1. The accusation (6b-7bβ)

The second sub-oracle offers another motive for the judgment that is directed against the land of Egypt. מִשְׁעֶנֶת קָנֶה "staff of reed" is a new accusation against Egypt and it applies to כָּל־יֹשְׁבֵי מִצְרַיִם "all the inhabitants of Egypt" (6a),[62] but in function, מִשְׁעֶנֶת קָנֶה relates to the "house of Israel".

"Reed" (קָנֶה[63]) is commonly found on the banks of the Nile and in the marshy places adjacent to river, providing natural habitat for the Nile crocodile. In this way, it becomes directly associated in the oracle with the Niles and the Nile crocodile. On the other hand, the Nile, because of its vital role in the prosperity of the land, symbolizes Egypt. This seems to be the background of the metaphor "staff of reed" (מִשְׁעֶנֶת קָנֶה), which is found also in Isaiah[64] and refers to the land of Egypt. The object of the reference becomes clear also from the announcement of judgment (vv.8-9). Here, a reading of הֱיוֹתָם in 6b is significant as it is made to relate wrongly to כָּל־יֹשְׁבֵי in 6a.[65] Boadt amends this reading to הֱיִיתָ (pf. 2m. sg.)

---

[59] ZIMMERLI, *Gottes Offenbarung*, 42-54; cf. p.51.

[60] ZIMMERLI, *Gottes Offenbarung*, 42-43,

[61] ZIMMERLI, *Gottes Offenbarung*; 48.

[62] Cf. הֱיוֹתָם (inf. cstr. + suff. 3m. pl.), יֹשְׁבֵי (ptc. cstr. 3m. pl.) and מִשְׁעֶנֶת (cstr. 3f. sg.).

[63] קָנֶה occurs 62 times in the OT with 22 occurrences only in Ezekiel: in 27,19; 29,6; 40,3.5x3.6x2.7x3.8; 41,16x3.17x2; 42,18x2.19x2.

[64] Isa 36,6; cf. 2Kgs 18,21; and Ezek 29,6; see ZIMMERLI, *Ezechiel 25-48*, 710.

[65] ZIMMERLI, *Ezechiel 25-48*, 704.

and adds the 'proleptic dative' *mem*-suffix to it, reading it הֱיִיתָם.[66] LXX, Syriac, and Vulgate read הֱיוֹתְךָ by amending the pronominal dative *mem*-suffix to ךָ (2m. sg). Both of the changes make קָנֶה מִשְׁעֶנֶת refer to Pharaoh[67] (cf. 3aβ). However, in Isaiah (cf. Isa 36,6//2Kgs 18,21), the metaphor is used primarily for Egypt; also here, in 6b, it is conveniently used for the land of Egypt.[68]

Isa 36,2 recalls Sennacherib's assessment of Hezekiah's reliance on Egypt, which is like a splintered staff of reed to which Pharaoh is likened.[69] Israel's reliance on support from Egypt is echoed also in Isa 30,1-6; 31,1-3. Ezekiel makes use of the reed metaphor from Isa 36,6 in 29,6b-7 to describe Egypt's character as the object on which Israel erroneously relies for protection against the new threat from Babylon.

The poetic description of the interaction between the staff of reed and its interlocutor illustrates the basic nature of Reed. It responds to every successive interaction of its interlocutor diabolically, creating a helpless and utterly pathetic condition for its interlocutor as well as for itself:

When they held, you crushed and you tore   בְּתָפְשָׂם/תֵּרוֹץ/וּבָקַעְתָּ

When they leaned, you broke and you caused to shake   וּבְהִשָּׁעֲנָם/תִּשָּׁבֵר/וְהַעֲמַדְתָּ

It gives the following construction:

7a: בְּ + inf. cstr. + suff. 3m. pl. / prep. suff. 2m. sg. + impf. / וְ-perf. + impf

7b: וְ + בְּ + inf. cstr. + suff. 3m. pl. / prep. + suff. 2m. sg. + impf. / וְ-perf. + impf.

The above construction of the performative conjunction and *waw*-afforrmative conjunction[70] skilfully demonstrates an increasingly intense interaction between two interlocutors, Egypt and the house of Israel, as shown by the use of the subject-object pronouns "they-you," "you," and "you-their" in v.7.

The description of inflicting injuries on palms, shoulders and loins indicates injury being inflicted on the whole body. It brings out a sense of "totality"[71] as expressed in 5c, highlighting the catastrophic harm that reliance on the reed brings to its partner. In short, Egypt is weak and it cannot be used as a source of support; Israel's alliance with Egypt and her search for support from Egypt is a sure source of destruction for both partners. Thus, Ezekiel expresses a view similar to Jeremiah's on the confrontation with Babylon, and this highlights the real motive

---

[66] BOADT, *Ezekiel's Oracles*, 36.

[67] PREMSTALLER, *Fremdvölkersprüche*, 146.

[68] FECHTER, *Bewältigung der Katastrophe*, 246; see also ZIMMERLI, *Ezechiel 25-48*, 710.

[69] BARNES, *Studies in the Chronology*, HSM 48, 106-109

[70] KAUTZSCH, *GESENIUS' Hebrew Grammar*, 125f., §47a.c.

[71] PREMSTALLER (*Fremdvölkersprüche*, 146) thinks that כָל־כָּתֵף refers to the entire territory.

for judgment in 6b-7bβ, which is not Egypt's failure to help Israel but her confrontation with Babylon.[72]

4.3.2. The announcement of judgment (8a-9aα)

The announcement of judgment (8a-9aα) introduces חֶרֶב ("sword"), a new motif in the judgment against Egypt. It is a favourite theme in Ezekiel and it is used in the announcement of judgment against the house of Israel and against the nations.[73] It was first used for judgment against Israel (6,3), but is here applied to Egypt (v.8). Of the 411 occurrences of חֶרֶב in the OT, 84 usages are found in Ezekiel[74] and 28 of these are found in the oracles against Egypt.[75] It reflects the "sword" as a special means of God's judgment against her. While two similar expressions מֵבִיא עֲלֵיכֶם חֶרֶב (6,3) and מֵבִיא עָלַיִךְ חֶרֶב (29,8), occur in Ezekiel in relation to judgments against Israel and Egypt, respectively, other variations are also present in other places:[76]

Ezek 11,8:	Sword you fear and sword I will bring upon you	חֶרֶב יְרֵאתֶם וְחֶרֶב אָבִיא עֲלֵיכֶם
Ezek 14,17:	Or if I will bring a sword upon that land.	אוֹ חֶרֶב אָבִיא עַל־הָאָרֶץ הַהִיא
Ezek 33,2:	If I bring a sword upon her (i.e., a land)	כִּי־אָבִיא עָלֶיהָ הָרֶב
Lev 26,25:	And I will bring a sword upon you	וְהֵבֵאתִי עֲלֵיכֶם חֶרֶב

The above texts show the sword as a weapon of war and devastation, and as a means of God's judgment. He brings it to judge Israel and the nations. Ezekiel speaks about the sword of the LORD again in 30,24 (וְנָתַתִּי אֶת־חַרְבִּי בְּיָדוֹ "And I will put my sword in his hand") and in 32,10 (בְּעוֹפְפִי חַרְבִּי "when I brandish my sword"). The oracle presents two clear pictures of God's judgment by the sword, namely, it purges the "land of Egypt"[77] by "removing" all its inhabitants and it wreaks "desolation" (8c-9a):

---

[72] ZIMMERLI, *Ezechiel 25-48*, 710.

[73] SCHÖPFLIN, (*Theologie als Biographie*, 51-52) interprets the sword as a concrete reality of war on the one hand and, on the other hand, anticipates it through the interpretation of war-victory as God's judgment, depicting the concept of the LORD's punishment. It is a means of God's judgment along with pestilence, famine, fire, wild-beasts, and dispersion in Ezekiel (cf. 5,2.12.17; 14,12-20; cf. v.21). STACEY considers it as a means of prophetic drama; see his *Peophetic drama in the Old Testament*, 199-201.

[74] BOADT *Ezekiel's Oracles*, 40; ANDERSEN and FORBES (*Vocabulary*, 323) lists 91 occurrences. See also MANDELKERN, *Concordantiae*, 423-425.

[75] Note the occurrences of חֶרֶב in Ezekiel's oracles against Egypt: 29,8; 30,4.5.6.11.17.21.22. 24.25; 31,17.18; 32,10.11.12.20.21.22.23.24.25.26.27.28. 29.30.31.32.

[76] BOADT, *Ezekiel's Oracles*, 40.

[77] This phrase occurs 63 times in OT of which 10 occurrences are found in Ezekiel in 19,4, 20,8.36; 29,9.10.12.19.20; 30,25; 32,15. See PREMSTALLER, *Fremdvölkersprüche*, 147.

וְהִכְרַתִּי מִמֵּךְ אָדָם וּבְהֵמָה — And I will cut off man and beast from you

וְהָיְתָה אֶרֶץ־מִצְרַיִם — And the land of Egypt will become

לִשְׁמָמָה וְחָרְבָּה — a waste and desolation

The consequence of bringing the sword against the land is to destroy man and beast. This expression is *merismus* and it is all-inclusive, encompassing all living beings, human and animal.[78] Ezekiel also uses this expression in other places to denote every man and beast (4,14; 14,15; 32,14; 33,28; 36,34).

To "cut off" and to "destroy" the living world is the primary characteristic of חֶרֶב. It may denote "slain by the sword" חַלְלֵי־חָרֶב / חֶרֶב (cf. 31,17.18), e.g., of the warriors: בְּחַרְבוֹת גִּבּוֹרִים אַפִּיל הֲמוֹנֶךְ "I will cause your hordes to fall by the swords of might men" (32,12). Destruction by a sword also implies "waste and desolation" (לִשְׁמָמָה וְחָרְבָּה) of the land. A direct consequence of bringing the sword against the land is to scatter and disperse its inhabitants (v.12), carrying away its hordes (v.19) and plundering the land (v.19).

Ezekiel may have taken the sword-motif from the "thought world of the Holiness Code in Lev 17-26," where it occurs frequently[79] as the LORD's instrument to punish the people of Israel for their violation of the covenant (cf. Lev 26,25). Its use is closely connected with their "scattering" (אֱזָרֶה v.32), laying their land to "waste" (שְׁמָמָה vv.31.33),[80] and "ruining" their cities (חָרְבָּה vv.31.33). In Ezek 26 it is used against Tyre (9x) in a similar sense. It is seen as a punitive means by which God purifies[81] His people and their land and in accordance with His covenant with them. Thus, the sword is not a means to cut off, remove, cancel or abrogate the covenant by destroying man and beast, but a tool to bring the people back to God and bind them more closely with Him.

Ezekiel's use of חֶרֶב in 29,8 implies the same idea stated above. Because Egypt has sought to oppose Babylon by her alliance with Israel, she has tempted Israel into rebellion against her LORD. Israel's political alliance with Egypt is a sign of her infidelity. Moreover, Egypt's role in Israel's politics is also seen as a serious breach, similar to Israel's covenant-infidelity to the LORD. Thus, Israel and Egypt have both provoked God's judgment by sword.[82] Here, a direct relationship between the sword and the breaking of the LORD's covenant is established and used as a comprehensive term to denote punishment for disloyalty. In vv.8-9, it is employed to cut off (כרת) people, and to make the land a waste (חָרְבָּה) and

---

[78] BOADT, *Ezekiel's Oracles,* 43.

[79] BOADT, *Ezekiel's Oracles,* 40.

[80] MEYER, „שָׁמֵם", in *ThWAT* VIII, 241-251, cf. 242.244.

[81] The purpose of bringing a sword is usually described by the verb כָּרַת (cf. 29,8; Num 9,13) and in this sense, it also denotes removing every mark of covenant-infidelity.

[82] The bringing of a sword as a means of judgment against Israel's infidelity in Lev 26 and its usage in Ezek 29,8 reflect the latter's Priestly connection. See BOADT, *Ezekiel's Oracles,* 40.

desolation (שְׁמָמָה).[83] In v.8, "to cut off" expresses primarily the action of the sword, and it means destroying living beings and rendering them non-existent. By extension, it also means uprooting the inhabitants from their native place and sweeping them off to a new and hereto unfamiliar place. In this way, it cuts off, separates, removes and upsets, bringing existence to an end.[84]

כרת occurs 30 times in the Old Testament.[85] The book of Leviticus uses "to cut off" in a customary and ritual sense that primarily denotes a sacral removing someone who has disobeyed the covenant. In other words, it signifies removing and separating someone who has rejected living in accordance with the covenant, and thus constitutes a threat to the sacred character of the community. In the book of Kings and in the prophets, it frequently denotes removing something, someone or a people as punishment.[86] God's judgment in these texts is stereotypical, "I will cut off." In Ezekiel, "I will cut off man and beast" contains a complete expression[87] that encompasses destruction of all living creatures, man and beast alike.[88] It also means that without His further intervention, it would be absolutely impossible to imagine a revival of the land. The announcement of judgment in 8b sufficiently intimates this.

חָרְבָּה and שְׁמָמָה are used several times in connection with הֶרֶב in Lev 26,25ff. These uses highlight the implications of bringing the sword against the land, i.e., the destruction of man and beast and the desolation of the land. חָרְבָּה ("waste," "dry land") is derived from the same root as הֶרֶב and its meaning is synonymous with שְׁמָמָה ("desolation").

לְשְׁמָמָה וְחָרְבָּה is found only once in the OT, in Ezek 29,9, and its reverse is found in Jer 44,6 (לְחָרְבָּה וּשְׁמָמָה). The same root has been used once in Ezek 35,7 (לְשְׁמָמָה וּשְׁמָמָה), and rendered "waste and desolation" or a "desolate waste." In four occurrences, שְׁמָמָה is paired with מְשַׁמָּה and is rendered: "a desolate waste" (Ezek 6,14; 33,28.29; 35,3). Nine times לְשְׁמָמָה occurs in the prophetic books with or without חָרְבָּה / וְחָרְבָּה,[89] whereas חָרְבָּה / וְחָרְבָּה occurs 10 times without / שְׁמָמָה לְשְׁמָמָה and is rendered as "waste and desolation."[90]

---

[83] PREMSTALLER points that the element לשממה + אֶרֶץ + היה is used only against Judah (compare 12,10; 14,15f; 36,43). See his *Fremdvölkersprüche*, 147.

[84] HASEL, „כָּרַת", in *ThWAT* IV, 356-367; cf. 359; and KUTSCH, "כרת *krt* to cut off," in *TLOT* II, 637. See also SCHUNCK, „כָּרָה", in *ThWAT* IV, 318-322.

[85] I.e., in Pentateuch 4x, Historical books 4x and in the Prophets 22x.

[86] It occurs 4 times in the Historical books and 10 times in the Prophets.

[87] See Ezek 14,13.17; cf. vv.19.21; 25,13 and 29,8; 32,13.

[88] Other texts where אָדָם וּבְהֵמָה occurs: Ex 9,19.22; Num 31,47; Jer 7,20.21; 21,6; 27,5; Hag 1,11; Jonah 3,7 and Zech 1,3); see BOADT, *Ezekiel's Oracles,* 43.

[89] שְׁמָמָה occurs 43 times in the OT: in Isa 5x, Jer 11x, Lam 1x, Ezek 19x, in others 7x.

[90] Cf. Lev 26,31.33; Neh 2,3.17; Prov 17,1; Jer 27,17; 44,2; Ezek 25,13; 30,12; 35,4

From the usage of חָרְבָּה and שְׁמָמָה in relation to bringing the sword against Israel (וְהֵבֵאתִי עֲלֵיכֶם חֶרֶב cf. Lev 26,25),[91] it may be concluded that וְחָרְבָּה לִשְׁמָמָה underlines the punishment for Israel's violation of the covenant relationship and is also applied against Egypt in Ezek 29,9.[92] Dispossession and removal of the inhabitants makes the land desolate. From another perspective, the judgment against the land may be seen as God's way of cleansing disloyalty from the land. It is His way of beginning the restoration of the land.

4.4. The third oracle (29, 9-12)
4.4.1. The accusation and judgment (9bα-10b)

The third oracle begins by repeating the motive for accusation stated in the first oracle with slight alterations:

3bβ	Mine is the Niles and I made it for myself.	לִי יְאֹרִי וַאֲנִי עֲשִׂיתִנִי
9bα	The Niles is mine and I made it.	יְאֹר לִי וַאֲנִי עֲשִׂיתִי

The first position of לִי in 3bβ emphasizes the possessive pronoun "mine". Instead, in 9bα יְאֹר (subject) stands in the first position and consequently receives greater emphasis. The announcement of judgment (10b) is directed against the land of Egypt, made prosperous by the Nile-floods. This makes the statement of Pharaoh in 9bα bolder, and focuses on the basis of his hubris. In other words, the whole claim is about יְאֹר, which lies at the centre of Egypt's life and prosperity. Thus, vv.9b-12 (cf. vv.11-12) further supplement 3aα-6a.

God's word has the intrinsic character of bringing itself to fulfilment.[93] The fulfilment of His revealed word (message) brings those who witness it to recognise the LORD. Here, we are faced with God's word and its fulfilment, which focuses on bringing Israel and the nations to acknowledge Him. The juxtaposition of the crocodile's boasting with the causational nature of God's word and deed (message and fulfilment), contrasts the two sayings of Pharaoh on the one hand and, on the other hand, the word of the LORD in relation to the motif of "making"/"doing" (or not making/doing), which leads to a recognition of the LORD.

The big crocodile claims that it has made the Niles.[94] When paraphrased, it means that the crocodile is the master of Egypt's resources and prosperity, which come by annual flooding of the Niles. If this claim were to be drawn to its final conclusion, it would imply that, on account of bringing prosperity to Egypt, the

---

[91] BOADT, *Ezekiels Oracles*, 40.

[92] KAISER, „חָרַב I", in *ThWAT* III (1982), 160-164; cf. 163.

[93] Cf. Isa 55, 10-11 shows a close relationship between God's word and its fulfilment.

[94] The use of וַאֲנִי (cf. 29,9) makes the second part of the saying emphatic.

Egyptians should acknowledge Pharaoh as their god. But the announcement of God's judgment comes as a sharp critique to the false claim of the crocodile, and this leads them to acknowledge Him as the LORD.

The claim of the big crocodile centres on the Niles, but the issue underlying it is overridden by the predicate verb עָשִׂיתִי. Boadt points out that this characteristic of the LORD's saying, belongs exclusively to His activity and domain, which also holds the guarantee of fulfilment.[95] The claim of the big crocodile, by contrast, is a sham and a lie, a false attempt to usurp a divine stature. Therefore, the nature and meaning of עָשָׂה is the key to understanding the implication of the saying of the crocodile in 3bβ and its repetition in 9bα.

The use of the verb עָשָׂה in the 'absolute form' without referring to any object, resembles a legal formula, and "the action that is referred to is well-understood by all."[96] It is employed by the suzerain to enumerate the many deeds of benevolence that he has bestowed on the vassal and its purpose is to make those deeds known to all. Here, the acts of violating treaty provisions or the vassal's breach of the contract of fealty[97] are weighed to establish the nature of the crime, leading to judgment of the perjurer for violating vassal-oaths and for disloyalty to the agreed upon provisions of the treaty. If עָשָׂה is used in 3bβ.9bα with reference to the vassal-treaty, then Tsevat[98] maintains it implies the sanctity of the oath, awe of the suzerain, and the vengeance of the deity invoked in enactment of a vassal-treaty. He therefore maintains that in Ezek 17,11-21; 21,23-29; and 29,14-16 Ezekiel refers to "political perjuries of vassals." This would mean that עָשָׂה has been used in 3bβ.9bβ from the perspective of a treaty background, in which case the claim of the crocodile would highlight its unbridled pride and boasting.[99] However, we cannot push the treaty-motif in Ezek 29,3.9 beyond its connotation of highlighting the great pride that it wants to emphasize.

The expression וְנָתַתִּי אֶת־אֶרֶץ מִצְרַיִם "I will make[100] the land of Egypt" occurs twice in the OT (cf. Ezek 29,10b.12a) and it is the LORD's fitting response to the boastful claim of the crocodile.[101] Just as the position of יְאֹר lays emphasis on the hubris of the crocodile, אֶת־אֶרֶץ מִצְרַיִם counterbalances his claim by announcing

---

[95] E.g., Ezek 17,24: אֲנִי יְהוָה דִּבַּרְתִּי וְעָשִׂיתִי "I the LORD have said and I will do it;" see also Ezek 22,14; 24,17; 36,36; 37,14). See BOADT, *Ezekiel's Oracles*, 40.

[96] BOADT, *Ezekiel's Oracles*, 40.

[97] TSEVAT, "Neo-Assyrian Vassal Oaths," in *JBL* 73, 199.

[98] TSEVAT, "Neo-Assyrian Vassal Oaths," in *JBL* 73, 201.

[99] Although Ezekiel speaks about Israel's unfaithfulness in relation to her covenant relation with YHWH in Ezek 16 and her restoration (Ezek 36-37), he does not deal with this theme in Ezek 29-32. But see JÜNGLING, "Eid und Bund in Ez 16-17", in ZENGER [ed.], *Der Neue Bund im Anten*, 113-148.

[100] The active verb form וְנָתַתִּי occurs 136 times in the OT with 58 occurrences in Ezekiel alone, and it is rendered: "I will give/have given," "I will make/put".

[101] The big crocodile is the implicit subject of the verb אָמַר in 9b.

judgment directly against the land. So, just as the emphasis of the boasting of the crocodile shifts from "to me/mine" (3bβ) to the "Niles" (9bβ), the announcement of judgment in 10b relates directly to what the Niles symbolize, i.e., the land of Egypt; God's judgment focuses directly on this.

Ancient Egypt comprised the territory along the Nile from its delta in the north (Lower Egypt) upstream until approximately the fourth cataract.[102] The important cities of Egypt were situated mainly between the Nile's delta and the First cataract, with Syene (Aswan) as its southernmost city. The Nile's flooding swamped its lower plains every year, bringing deposits of fertile silt. This explains the hubris of the crocodile concerning the Nile and the prosperity of Egypt, according to which he regards himself as the maker of Egypt's wealth and prosperity. Giving the land of Egypt to "wastes, a waste of desolation" (לְחָרְבוֹת חֹרֶב שְׁמָמָה) is God's fitting response to the proud claim of the crocodile.

לִשְׁמָמָה וְחָרְבָּה in 9a has been reversed in 10b to לְחָרְבוֹת שְׁמָמָה, and חֹרֶב is inserted between them. This posed a difficulty for the interpreters who have been discussed in the text-critical and structural analysis set forth in chapters 2 and 3 of this research. The entire noun phrase may be taken as a complement to וְנָתַתִּי in which the first cognate חָרְבוֹת is modified by the preposition לְ and the apposition phrase חֹרֶב שְׁמָמָה stands as its modifier. There must be a reason for Ezekiel's choice of usage here. Boadt points to Isa 61,4 and Jer 49,13 where חֹרֶב occurs in combination with the paired words,[103] where חָרְבוֹת שְׁמָמוֹת // שְׁמָמוֹת חֹרֶב and לְשַׁמָּה לְחֶרְפָּה // לְחֹרֶב...לְחָרְבוֹת sequences appear respectively, describing desolation and ruin. The use of חֹרֶב ("dryness," "drought") in these texts refers to places of habitation, like cities in Isa 61,4 or to Bozrah in Jer 49,13.[104] Thus, in Ezek 29,10b, חֹרֶב is employed to denote the destruction of the inhabited places or cities of Egypt, whereas לְחָרְבוֹת שְׁמָמָה seems to be a general reference to the land of Egypt.

The expression מִמִּגְדֹּל סְוֵנֵה וְעַד־גְּבוּל כּוּשׁ "from Migdol [to] Syene, till the border of Kush" points to the demarcation of the boundary of Egypt, and shows the extent of its territory (10b).[105] Since מִגְדֹּל[106] and סְוֵנֵה[107] lay on the northern

---

[102] During the reign of Thuthmose III (18th Dynasty), Egypt's southern boundary reached up to Napata, near the Fourth Cataract. See BREASTED, *Geschichte Ägyptens*, German trans. by RANKE, 175; see also HARRISON, *Introduction to the Old Testament*, 116-117; MURNANE, "History of Egypt: New Kingdom," in *ABD* 2, 348-349.

[103] BOADT, *Ezekiel's Oracles*, 42.

[104] שְׁמָמָה generally refers to the land, whereas חָרְבוֹת refers to the cities of Egypt (cf. v.12).

[105] SÆBØ, „Grenzbeschreibung und Landideal", in *ZDPV* 90 (1974), 14f.

[106] The Hebrew word מִגְדֹּל means a "fortress tower" but it also signifies a place in the Nile-Delta, today identified with Tell el-Kheir, east of the Suez Canal. It played a significant role in defending against threats from other Asiatic powers. See BLOCK, *Ezekiel*, 142; see also OREN, "'Migdol' Fortress in North-Western Sinai," in *Qad* 10 (1977), 71-76.

and southern extremes of Egypt, they may have been used to denote geographical localities mentioned in 10b and in 30,6. וְעַד־גְּבוּל כּוּשׁ "till the borders of Cush", a Nubian territory, refers to the southernmost boundary of Egypt, and *merismus* denotes the whole land of Egypt.[108] A similar expression is found in the book of Judges 21,1: לְמִדָּן וְעַד־בְּאֵר שָׁבַע "from Dan to Beer-Sheba," referring to the whole land of Israel where the tribes of Israel had settled.

4.4.2. The first expansion of judgment (11a-11c)

The first expansion of judgment consists of three short, negative statements: לֹא תַעֲבָר־בָּהּ רֶגֶל אָדָם וְרֶגֶל בְּהֵמָה לֹא תַעֲבָר־בָּהּ "man…beast shall not pass through it" (11a.11b) and וְלֹא תֵשֵׁב "and she shall be uninhabited" (11c), resulting in desolation of the land, lasting for אַרְבָּעִים שָׁנָה "forty years". The use of "man and beast" in this verse (cf. 8c) once again emphasizes the idea of "totality". The key element of desolation, i.e., "uninhabited", and its restricted time-limit, "forty years", are taken up in the oracle of hope in vv.13-16.

The expression אַרְבָּעִים שָׁנָה occurs 35 times in the Old Testament. In 15 occurrences it refers to Israel's wanderings in the desert (מִדְבָּר),[109] once it refers to Israel being delivered into the hands of the Philistines (Judg 13,1), and three times it relates to the period of desolation of the land of Egypt (Ezek 29,11.12.13). The remaining 16 occurrences refer to the age of persons (e.g., Kenan, Isaac, Esau, Saul), Israel's period of peace, Eli's years of leadership, or to the years of the reign of kings. אַרְבָּעִים שָׁנָה is used to indicate a specific age or length of time and to denote a ripe, mature age (Gen 25,20; 26,34). Other times it indicates a significantly long period, number of years, or a complete term, e.g., Neh 9,21: "For forty years you sustained them in the desert."[110] It is also used to indicate a period of Israel's testing and punishment (cf. Judg 13,1)[111] and to refer to the LORD's punishment of all the Israelites who came out of Egypt (Josh 5,6 cf. Num 14,26ff., 26,64.65; Deut 2,14-16). Ezekiel uses the expression in a similar sense to denote a period of judgment in 29,11.12.13.

---

[107] סְוֵנֵה is identified with the modern Aswan on the First Cataract of the Nile. It was a strategic location in the south for launching conquests of the Nubian territory. See BLOCK, *Ezekiel,* 142.

[108] BOADT, *Ezekiel's Oracles,* 43.

[109] Cf. Ex 16,35; Num 14,33.34; 32,13; Deut 1,3; 2,7; 8,2.4; 29,4; Josh 5,6; 14,7; Am 2,10; 5,25; Ps 95,10; Neh 9,21.

[110] Other texts: Ex 16,35; Num 14,33.34; 32,13; Deut 1,3; 2,7; Neh 9,21.

[111] See also Num 14,33.34; 32,13; Deut 8,2.4, Ps 95,10; Judg 13,1; Ezek 29,11.12.

4.4.3. The second expansion of judgment (12a-12cα)

The second expansion of judgment repeats the motif of "desolation of the land" (cf. 10b) with a new formulation, laying emphasis on the desolation of Egypt, specially its "land" (12a) and "cities" (12b), as the "scattering and dispersion"[112] of the inhabitants (12cα.12cβ) will result in making the land desolate.

The verb פוץ ("to scatter") occurs in Deut 4, 27; Isa 24,1; 28,25 (וְהֵפִיץ), in Deut 28,64 (וֶהֱפִיצְךָ) and in Jer 9,16 (וַהֲפִצוֹתִים). In these texts, the scattering of Israel is seen as God's judgment for neglecting the covenant. The verb זרה ([I] "to scatter") occurs once in Mal 2,3. Ezekiel uses וַהֲפִצֹתִי בַגּוֹיִם // וְזֵרִיתִים בָּאֲרָצוֹת (cf. פוץ hiphil + בַּגּוֹיִם // זרה piel + בָּאֲרָצוֹת)[113] mainly in reference to the punishment of the "house of Israel" (cf. 12,15; 22,15; 36,19) and of Egypt (29,12; 30,23.26). In four occurrences (Deut 4,27; 28,25.64; Isa 24,1) פוץ denotes the scattering of Israel. In Ezek 34,5.6, וַתְּפוּצֶינָה and נָפֹצוּ refer to the scattering of the sheep because the shepherds of Israel have not taken care of them. Ezekiel employs פוץ / זרה in 12cα.12cβ in a similar sense to denote punishment of Egypt by scattering and dispersion, but for a 40 years' period.

4.5. The oracle of salvation (29, 13-16)

The oracle of salvation begins with כִּי and connects with the phrase"forty years" in 11c.12b.13b,[114] an interpretative link between מִקֵּץ אַרְבָּעִים שָׁנָה "at the end of forty years" (13b) on the one hand and, on the other hand, וְלֹא תֵשֵׁב אַרְבָּעִים שָׁנָה "she will not be inhabited for forty years" (11c) and תִּהְיֶין שְׁמָמָה אַרְבָּעִים שָׁנָה "she will be desolate for forty years" (12b). The development of this oracle relates to the restoration of Egypt as the lower kingdom, which will have new implications for the nations and for Israel.

---

[112] פוץ בַּגּוֹיִם // זרה בָּאֲרָצוֹת are generally used to denote the punishment of Israel and the nations, e.g., Ezek 11,16; 12,15; 20,23; 22,15; 30,23.26 cf. 36,19. פוץ occurs 21 times and זרה 17 times in the later prophets with the maximum occurrences in Ezekiel (9x); see ANDERSEN and FORBES, *Vocabulary*, 313.400. See also RINGGREN, „פוץ", in *ThWAT* VI, 544-547.

[113] PREMSTALLER, *Fremdvölkersprüche*, 148.

[114] KEIL, *Ezekiel*, COT 9, 248.

4.5.1. The beginning of restoration of Egypt (13a-14b)

The first part of the salvation oracle touches three points:

1) To gather the Egyptians from their dispersion
2) To bring back the captives of Egypt
3) To restore them to the land of Pathros, the land of their origin.

The salvation of Egypt begins with the announcement of the end of the forty years of judgment, which inaugurates the programme of restoration and rebuilding. It turns the earlier announcements of judgment (12c.12cα; cf. 8a.11a) upside down. Egypt will be restored through a gathering of its people from their dispersion, a bringing back out of their captivity, and their return to Pathros. The rebuilding focuses on the place of Egypt's origin, known as Pathros.

The substantive קֵץ from the verb-root קצץ means "to cut off," "to hew off". מִקֵּץ (קֵץ + מִן) occurs 23 times in the Old Testament.[115] Except in Jer 50, 26, all other occurrences denote the end of a specific time, but also the beginning of a new event. Thus, מִקֵּץ signifies a cut-off date, ending the previous situation and beginning a new intervention. There are four occurrences where it occurs in combination with "forty" (cf. 29,12b):

Gen 8,6:	וַיְהִי מִקֵּץ אַרְבָּעִים יוֹם
Num 13,25:	וַיָּשֻׁבוּ מִתּוּר הָאָרֶץ מִקֵּץ אַרְבָּעִים יוֹם
Deut 9,11:	וַיְהִי מִקֵּץ אַרְבָּעִים יוֹם וְאַרְבָּעִים לַיְלָה נָתַן יְהוָה
2Sam 15,7:	וַיְהִי מִקֵּץ אַרְבָּעִים שָׁנָה וַיֹּאמֶר אַבְשָׁלוֹם אֶל־הַמֶּלֶךְ

The judgment against Egypt was spoken in terms of desolation of the land for a period of 40 years (12b). Its restoration at the end of 40 years is not automatic, but comes as a sign of God's saving intervention (13b), which is indicated by מִקֵּץ. It separates the period of judgment from that of restoration, signalling the dawn of a new era of God's salvation to Egypt.

אֲקַבֵּץ אֶת־מִצְרַיִם "I will gather the Egyptians" indicates concretely how God will restore Egypt. He will gather the Egyptians from the nations where they were dispersed: אֲקַבֵּץ אֶת־מִצְרַיִם מִן־הָעַמִּים אֲשֶׁר־נָפֹצוּ שָׁמָּה (13b.13bα). This is a complete reversal of the judgment against Egypt.[116] It is highlighted by use of the corresponding verbs of action (קבץ in direct contrast to פוץ), and is also reflected by its complement מִן־הָעַמִּים "from the peoples" (13b), which counter-balances בַּגּוֹיִם "among the nations" (12c).

---

[115] Note the occurrences of מִקֵּץ in the OT: Pentateuch 9x, Historical books 7x; Prophets 7x.

[116] Compare it with 12cα.12cβ and 5β. The announcement of judgment is absolute in the case of Tyre, without any hope of restoration, cf. Ezek 26,21; 27,36; 28,19.

The verb קבץ occurs 127 times in the Old Testament.[117] In the prophetic books, the greatest number of occurrences are found in Isaiah (20x), Jeremiah (8x), Ezekiel (15x) and Micah (5x).[118] In 40 of these occurrences, the LORD is the subject who gathers Israel (and the nations: 6x) for judgment or brings them back from their dispersion among the nations to their own homeland, thereby restoring their fortunes (31 occurrences including once for Egypt).[119]

קבץ occurs twice in Ezek 29-32 (cf. 29,5.13). In 29,5 it is used in the passive in a negative sense, "not be gathered" (קבץ *niphal*), but its use (in *piel*) in v.13 is positive. There, the Egyptians are mentioned specifically as a people whom He promises to gather;[120] otherwise it is used to refer to the salvation of Israel (cf. 11,17; 20,34.41; 28,23; 34,13; 39,27). In this sense, הָעַמִּים sheds some new light because, where the dispersion of the people is usually announced in relation to בַּגּוֹיִם ("among the nations"), their gathering is generally announced in relation to מִן־הָעַמִּים ("from the peoples"). Its rendering in Deut 30,1ff (cf. Deut 4,27 in LXX and Vulgate) is noteworthy, as בְּכָל־הַגּוֹיִם is there rendered as "from the nations" in a usual sense[121] and מִכָּל־הָעַמִּים in v.3, is translated "from the nations," although it is generally rendered "from the peoples." In v.3 the use of הָעַמִּים denotes "families of nations" from whom God will mark out his peoples and gather them up, bringing them back to the land of their fathers.

גּוֹיִם usually denotes the nations or peoples (= Gentiles),[122] whereas עַמִּים denotes "peoples" or "nations" or "small groups of people"/"peoples".[123] In 13b, הָעַמִּים is not a variation, but a general use of the term to signify the different groups of people from whom the scattered of Egypt will be gathered. Just as אֲקַבֵּץ "I will gather" indicates God's personal choice and initiative, so too does מִן הָעַמִּים suggest His preference, so that the whole clause expresses God's personal choice to gather the Egyptians from different groups of people.

שׁוּב שְׁבוּת ("bring back captivity")[124] is a classical technical Hebrew expression and it expresses another aspect of God's saving action for Egypt. He promises to bring back the captives of Egypt. Elsewhere, Ezekiel uses this expression twice in reference to the restoration of the fortunes of Sodom and Samaria and of their

---

[117] I.e., in Pentateuch 6x; Deuteronomic history 24x; Prophets 64x; and in the Writings: 33x.

[118] MANDELKERN, *Concordantiae*, 1007-1008. Their distribution according to different verb-forms: *hithpael* (9x); *niphal* (31x); *piel* (49x); *pual* (1x); and *qal* (38x).

[119] Please see its treatment in Chapter Five.

[120] קבץ is used only once for the salvation of nations; see MOMMER, "קבץ", in *ThWAT* VI, 1149.

[121] In Ex 19,5, בְּכָל־הָעַמִּים expresses the idea, "from many small groups of peoples" or "from families of peoples"; other occurrences in Ezekiel, cf. 11,17; 34,13; cf. 36,24; 37,12.21.

[122] *BDB*, 156c.

[123] *BDB*, 766b-766d.

[124] DIETRICH, „שׁוּב שְׁבוּת, die endzeitliche Wiederstellung", in *BZAW* 40, 1-66.

villages, as well as for the house of Israel (16,53), when He will bring back Jacob from captivity (39,25).

E. Preuschen[125] and E. L. Baumann[126] maintain that שְׁבוּת is derived from the root שׁבה whereas E. L. Dietrich thinks that originally שְׁבוּת derived from שׁוּב, but later was confused with שְׁבִית (from שׁבה).[127] The verb root שׁבה "to take captive" occurs eight times in the Old Testament,[128] and שְׁבִית ("captivity") occurs 14 times,[129] and שְׁבוּת ("captivity") occurs 29 times. In certain cases, both the forms can be appropriately rendered "captive(s)", and except in Num 21,29, other occurrences of שְׁבִית/שְׁבוּת use the root שׁוּב.

שׁוּב שְׁבוּת occurs in Jeremiah (7x), Ezekiel (3x), Zephaniah (2x), and once each in Joel, Amos, Ps 85 and Deuteronomy, where it has been used to express the "reversal" of judgment.[130] In some but not in all of the occurrences, it means reversal of fortune by bringing back from captivity.[131] In Ezek 29,14, it denotes a reversal of God's judgment against Egypt, which elaborates further His promise of salvation announced in v.13. Here שׁוּב שְׁבוּת signifies a complete reversal of his earlier judgment. It means reversing the fortunes of those Egyptians whom He scattered and dispersed in other countries earlier, but now promises to bring back out of their captivity.[132] Isa 19,23-25 (cf. Jer 46,26b) speaks a similar oracle of salvation for Egypt, suggesting that Ezek 29,14 probably knew it.

וַהֲשִׁבֹתִי (hiphil 1c. sg.) derives from שׁוּב "to return" or "turn back," but it also denotes a "return to God" or "turn to God". In hiphil and in polel it means to "bring back" or "restore".[133] But its semantic range goes beyond its basic meaning and signifies "to withdraw," "return," or turn back."[134] In hiphil, its occurrences connected with physical movement implicitly bear a theological sense, e.g., Israel's return from exile (Jer 12,15) or the causing of the sea to return to its place (Ex 15,19).[135] In the books of the prophets, it means to turn and remove God's anger from his people (Jer 18,20); to bring Israel back to Him or to convert Israel

---

[125] PRUSCHEN, „Die Bedeutung von שׁוּב שְׁבוּת", in ZAW 15, 1-74.

[126] BAUMANN, „שׁוּב שְׁבוּת, eine exegetische Untersuchung", in ZAW 47, 17-44.

[127] This confusion is easily noticed in Jer 29,14; 6,39; Ezek 16,53 and 39,25.

[128] I.e., 2Kgs 6,22; Job 42,10; Ps 68,19; 85,2; Jer 49,39; Ezek 16,53x2; 39,25.

[129] Cf. Num 21,29; Jer 29,14; 49,39; Ezek 16,53x5; 39,25; Zeph 2,7; Ps 85,2; 126,4; Job 42,10; Lam 2,14).

[130] BRACKE, "שׁוּב שְׁבוּת: A reappraisal," in ZAW 97, 233-244; cf. 236f.; other texts: Ps 126,4f., Lam 2,14; Hos 6,11 (God's refusal to restore his people); see in the same, 242.

[131] Cf. Jer 29,14; 30,3; 31,23; 33,7; Ezek 16,53; 39,25; Zeph 3,20; Deut 30,1ff.

[132] In the Old Testament it is used only for Israel: Am 9,14; Joel 4,1; Hos 6,11; Jer 30,3.18; 33,7.11; but note its use for Moab in 48,47; for Ammon in 49,6 and for Elam 49,39. See PREMSTALLER, Fremdvölkersprüche, 149, fn. 89.

[133] KOEHLER and BAUMGARTNER, Lexicon in Veteris Testamenti, 951-953.

[134] HOLLADAY, (ed.), Hebrew and Aramaic Lexicon, 362-363.

[135] FARBY and GRAUPNER, „שׁוּב", in ThWAT VII, 1136.

to God (Neh 9,26.29).[136] Joined to an object, it usually means to "put back" (cf. Gen 29,3), to "bring back" (cf. Gen 24,5; Ezek 29,14) or to "restore" (Gen 40,13; Ezek 29,14).[137]

פַּתְרוֹס[138] ("Pathros"), in Egyptian *petorēs*, means "southern land," and thus it signifies that geographical region in Lower Egypt where God plans to settle the captivity of Egypt. Gathering and bringing Egypt back out of captivity are God's prerogatives, which demonstrate his primary saving action that includes settling them in their native land. Here וַהֲשִׁבֹתִי ("I will bring back" 14b) fails to express this latter sense and to build up consequent development of restoration. LXX translates it καὶ κατοικιῶ (= וְהוֹשַׁבְתִּי "and I will cause [them] to dwell" (in Pathros), and thus renders the sense better here (cf. Ezek 36,11.33). Settling them in Pathros, their native land, means returning them to the place where their original "roots" lie and thus bringing end to their dispersion.

עַל־אֶרֶץ מְכוּרָתָם "to the land of their origin" explains the significance of Pathros. מְכוּרָה means "origin," while its verb-root כָּרָה (I) signifies "to dig," "excavate," "dig through," and as a noun כָּרָה means "cistern" or "well". It occurs 13 times in the OT. Now, מְכוּרָתָם "their origin" and מְכֹרֹתַיִךְ / מְכֹרֹתָיִךְ "your origin"/"ancestry" occur only in Ezekiel 29,14; 16,3; 21,35. Outside Ezekiel, כרה occurs in Gen 26, 25, Ex 21,33 and Num 21,18 in reference to digging a well.

The contexts in which מְכוּרָה and כָּרָה are used suggest that their meaning is closely related to the settlement of the land, e.g., digging a well for daily use and, in this sense, they denote a "native land" or a "place of birth".[139] Indirectly, it indicates the place or land where they begin their settled-life and begin to grow as a people, so that the place becomes associated with them and their origin. What it finally means is that the LORD who promised to gather and bring back Israel, and make them dwell in their Land (cf. 11,17; 20,34.41.42; 28,25; 34,13; 36,24; 37,21; 39,27),[140] promises to do exactly the same thing for Egypt, namely, to gather them and bring them back out of their captivity, causing them to dwell in Pathros, their native place (מְכוּרָה). Returning them to their place of origin (i.e., "roots"; cf. מַגֵּזַע יִשַׁי "stump of Jesse" in Isa 11,1 that God promises to revive) also makes them

---

[136] FARBY and GRAUPNER, „שׁוּב", in *ThWAT* VII, 1136.

[137] HOLLADAY, *Hebrew and Aramaic Lexicon*, 362-363; KOEHLER and BAUMGARTNER, *Lexicon in Veteris Testamenti*, 952-953.

[138] Cf. Isa 11,11; Jer 44,1.15 and Gen 10,14; 1Chr 1,12; see ZIMMERLI, *Ezechiel 25-48*, 713. BLOCK points to *misrayim, patrôs* and *kûš*, in the order of names in Isa.11,11 (Jer 44, 1.15); see his *Ezekiel 25-48*, 143; see also PRITCHARD, *ANET*, 290.

[139] BOADT, *Ezekiel's Oracles*, 46. For other occurrences, see: כָּרוּ in Ps 57,7; 119,85; Jer 18,20.22; כָּרָה in 2Chr 16,14; Ps 7,16; and כֹּרֶה in Prov 26,27 with a meaning, "to dig," "excavate," "cut out" a pit, well; cf. in Prov 16,27 כֹּרֶה is rendered "to plot".

[140] BLOCK, *Ezekiel 25-48*, 143; see also, VOGELS, *God's Universal Covenant*, 94.

realize that their birth-place (Pathros) is a gift of not just any piece of land but of the southern land, associated with their origin.

4.5.2. A new existence of Egypt (14c-15a)

מַמְלָכָה שְׁפָלָה "a low kingdom" expresses a new existence of Egypt (14c-15a). Ezekiel uses this expression three times, in Ezek 17,14 and 29,14.15. Elsewhere, the Old Testament attests only three more occurrences.

Ezek 17,13 gives an account of the successful siege of Jerusalem by Nebuchadnezzar's army and his personal visit to Jerusalem to take Jehoiachin prisoner, carry him into captivity to Babylon, and place his uncle Mattaniah (Zedekiah) on the throne, putting him under oath (2Kgs 24,10ff.).[141] In view of this incidence, 17,14, states a new state of Judah. M. Tsevat takes מַמְלָכָה שְׁפָלָה to mean a "vassal state"[142]. In 17,14 מַמְלָכָה שְׁפָלָה is spoken of in terms of a punishment of Israel. But in 29,14.15 it is used in the context of a restoration of Egypt. Both announce a new state of existence, i.e., Israel and Egypt have both been made low. This is a prerequisite condition for existence under the LORD's eye. For Israel, her humbled condition in captivity is one, temporary, historical-political event, but also points to her disposition as a people who must wholeheartedly rely on God. For Egypt too, being a "low kingdom" is the primary condition for her new existence. If she is to survive as a kingdom in the future, it will depend on how she maintains herself as a low kingdom. This relates to her basic character as a restored land.

In contrast to the proud claim of Pharaoh to be the creator and master of the Niles, Egypt's new existence and status as a low kingdom points to God's particular action, which he announces in Ezek 21,31, signalling a order:

> Thus says the Lord GOD:
> Take off the turban, remove the crown. It will not be as it was;
> The lowly will be exalted and the exalted will be brought low.

To exalt the lowly and make the exalted low is typical of God's judgment. He reverses fortunes and turns a previous condition or status upside down. To the proud and arrogant crocodile (cf. Ezek 29,3.9; 32,2), His judgment comes as a warning about the futility of keeping such an attitude and resisting submission to

---

[141] The event refers to the first batch of exiles who were carried to Babylon in 597 BC [16/3/597 in Babylonian Chronology]; cf. 2Kgs 24,10-17//2Chr 36,10; see VOGELS, *God's Universal Covenant*, 63.

[142] TSEVAT wrongly transposes "vassal states" to מַמְלָכָה שְׁפָלָה in Ezek 29,14 on the basis of 17,14, and fails to notice its basic meaning, "low kingdom" which relates to the first oracle of judgment against Egypt, making the first part of the oracles (29,1-16), a highly structured unit. See his "Neo-Assyria Vassal Oaths," in *JBL* 78, 199-204.

His plan (compare Mt. 25,31ff.). By this God shows His uncontested sovereign power in creation. Therefore, God makes Israel low by His judgment on account of her unfaithfulness, and Egypt also will be made low because of her pride, so that she too will learn to accept His sovereignty in His creation.

מַמְלָכָה שְׁפָלָה "low kingdom" expresses Egypt's new status and reveals God's sovereign power and judgment. Here, שְׁפָלָה modifies the nature of מַמְלָכָה and gives specific character to Egypt as a kingdom. It is God Himself who through His own action judges to humble the proud and to raise the lowly, giving them new status and dignity.[143] This becomes clear from the last two verses (vv.15-16).

The Hebrew root שָׁפֵל (*qal*) means "to be/become low" or "abased," and its causative sense (*hiphil*) means "to make/bring low" whereas שֵׁפֶל (n. m.) means a "low state/condition"; שִׁפְלָה (n. f.) means "humiliation" or "lowliness"; שְׁפֵלָה (n. f.) "low-land," and שָׁפָל (adj.) means "low," "lowly" or "modest," "not ambitious" and "humiliated".[144] Fifty occurrences of this root are attested in the Old Testament and 30 occurrences appear in verbal forms.[145] It is obvious that salvation to Egypt (29,1-16) guarantees her new existence as a humble and low kingdom. It removes her pride (cf. 3bβ.9bβ), and this is God's judgment.

The usage of מַמְלָכָה שְׁפָלָה in vv.14-15 does not connote any treaty relationship between Israel and Egypt although vv.6-7 refer to some kind of political alliance between the house of Israel and Egypt. Even though 17,13 refers to Zediakiah being put under oath and vv.13-14 refer to the term בְּרִית and mention Israel as מַמְלָכָה שְׁפָלָה (v.14), this does not necessarily lead to the status of a "vassal kingdom," as Tsevat suggests is indicated in 17,14 and 29,14.15.[146]

וְהָיוּ שָׁם מַמְלָכָה שְׁפָלָה in 29,14 is similar to Ex 19,6 in construction: וְאַתֶּם תִּהְיוּ לִי מַמְלֶכֶת כֹּהֲנִים "You will be a kingdom of priests to me". These two texts refer to God's promises to Egypt and to Israel, respectively. But the similarity between 29,14 and Ex 19,6 should not be overstated beyond the reasonable meaning of the literary construction (מַמְלֶכֶת כֹּהֲנִים // מַמְלָכָה שְׁפָלָה in Ex 19,6 and Ezek 29,14, respectively). Although Ex 19,6 refers to Israel's new status and existence, it depends on the condition that she will abide by the covenant; moreover, מַמְלֶכֶת כֹּהֲנִים "kingdom of priests" as a new privileged status for Israel is not comparable with מַמְלָכָה שְׁפָלָה "low kingdom," which is the new status of Egypt. מַמְלֶכֶת כֹּהֲנִים in Ex 19,6 expresses a covenant reality for Israel that bestows upon her a dignity as God's chosen people. On the other hand, Egypt's new status refers to a humbled state compared to her previously, self-exalted position. In no

---

[143] Ps 18,28; 75,8; 147,6; Prov 29,23; Isa 2,11.17; 5,15; 10,33; 13,11; 26,5; 40,4.

[144] *BDB*, 1050a.

[145] The Hebrew root שׁפל occurs 69 times (28 verbs) in the OT: Pentateuch 5x; Prophets 33x; Historical books 15x; Wisdom 16x; see ENGELKEN, שָׁפֵל", in *ThWAT* VIII, 439-400.

[146] TSEVAT, "Neo-Assyrians Vassal Oaths," 201.

case does it denote a position of greatness and yet, her existence as a kingdom is a favour coming from the LORD himself.

The preposition מִן in 15a could be taken as a comparative,[147] thus rendering מִן־הַמַּמְלָכוֹת "than all other kingdoms" as attested in Ex 19,5: מִכָּל־הָעַמִּים "out of all the nations." In Deut 7,7, Moses explains the reason for God's preference for Israel. It is not because Israel is numerous, but because she is the "fewest," the "smallest" (הַמְעַט) of all peoples. All the same, מִן־הַמַּמְלָכוֹת תִּהְיֶה שְׁפָלָה (15a) could be best rendered in the superlative: "It shall be the lowest of all the kingdoms".[148] This change in degree also shows the contrast and the progression in comparison to 14c.

The verb מָעַט means "to be/become small," "diminished" or "few". In *hiphil* (13 occurrences), it means "to make small or few" or "to diminish". Its noun form means "a little," "fewness" or "a few." Its substantive הַמְעַט (הַ interr. +adj. m. sg. abs.) occurs 11 times in the Old Testament,[149] but except for Num 13,18 (cf. Num 35,8), all other occurrences mean "Is it not enough?" or, "Is it too little?" In Num 13,18 הַמְעַט denotes the number or the size of people (cf. Deut 7,7).[150] However, שְׁפָלָה in Ezek 29,15a does not signify the size of Egypt's population, but her attitude, i.e., "lowly". Thus, שְׁפָלָה implies primarily the result of God's action: God reduces Egypt in power, size (population), and territory, even relocating her, but more significantly, he makes her lowly in her disposition, and, on the other hand מעט denotes her externally existing condition. He makes Egypt "small" and so she becomes the lowest of all the kingdoms.

4.5.3. New implications of the restoration of Egypt (15b-16c)

Egypt's new existence as the low, even as the lowest kingdom, has implications for herself and her neighbours (15b-16b) and they concentrate on three points:

1) What Egypt will not/be able to do;
2) How the LORD is going to deal with Egypt; and
3) The implications for the nations and for the house of Israel.

Egypt, the low kingdom, is viewed not so much from a political as a theological viewpoint, i.e., from the perspective of Egypt's disposition and attitude toward God; this is brought into focus in 15b.15c. וְלֹא־תִתְנַשֵּׂא עוֹד "she will not exalt

---

[147] WALTKE and O'CONNOR, *Biblical Hebrew Syntax*, 214.264.

[148] NEWCOME, *A Metrical Arrangement*, 109.

[149] Gen 30,15; Num 13,18; 16,9.13; 35,8; Deut 7,7; Jos 22,17; Job 15,11; Isa 7,13; Ezek 16,20; 34,18.

[150] In other places הַמְעַט signifies an attitude, e.g., jealousy (Gen 30,15); anger (Num 16,9.13); frustration (Num 35,8).

herself again" (15b) and וְהִמְעַטְתִּים לְבִלְתִּי רְדוֹת "and I will make them small never to rule" (15c), which both explain its significance and extent. Re-establishing Egypt in a state lower than her former political, territorial and geographical conditions highlights her new status as a lowly kingdom, and explains its significance. In a negative sense, Egypt will not longer possess the potential to threaten, and to dominate (cf. תִתְנַשֵּׂא) and rule (cf. רְדוֹת) over other nations.

The Hebrew verb נשׂא means to "lift," "carry," or "take."[151] Its meaning "to raise" is frequently used in prayer and lament, and the reflexive (cf. *niphal*) "to be raised" contrasts with "to be lowly,"[152] which could point to the new character of Egypt. In *hithpael*, it usually means "to raise oneself" or "raise one's head".[153] Raising oneself over others expresses a sense of superiority over others. In this sense, נשׂא is just another and perhaps, more direct expression of the crocodile's pride that is spoken of metaphorically in 29,3. Its context and usage in Ezek 17,14 is similar to its context and usage in 29,14c-15b. In 15b וְלֹא־תִתְנַשֵּׂא has been used negatively to denote Egypt's humbled political status so that she can no longer manoeuvre and influence her neighbours, and certainly no longer threaten or dominate them. Because of her small numbers, she will never rule over others again (לְבִלְתִּי רְדוֹת 15c). In this context וְהִמְעַטְתִּים "and I will make them small" signifies not only making Egypt fewer in number, but also reducing her source of power-base. Concretely, it refers to her hordes (cf. 29,19; 30,4.10), the army, and her supporters (cf. 30,5-6). Thus, "never to rule over the nations" points to a permanent feature of restored Egypt.

Two underlying factors involved in the restoration of Egypt show a close relationship between making "few" or "small" (15c) and becoming a "low kingdom" (14c):

> 1) The changed attitude of the returnees: that they are humble
>   and are willing to submit themselves to the LORD; and
> 2) They are reduced in number (i.e., population) and in territory.

The former refers to the new disposition of Egypt. The latter makes the former concretely visible, i.e., in the size of Egypt's population and territory, including her geo-physical location. Both these aspects determine Egypt's new political stature: The LORD will diminish Egypt; He will make her small and as a result, she will not be in a position to rule over others. In political terms, this means Egypt will lose its

---

[151] נשׂא occurs 650 times in the OT including 68 occurrences in Ezek; cf. Farby, „נשׂא", in *ThWAT* V, 629. On its meaning, see DRIVER, "Studies in the vocabulary," in *JTS* 34 (1933) 375-385.

[152] STOLZ, "נשׂא *nś'* to lift, bear," in *TLOT* II, 771-773.

[153] נשׂא (*hithpael*) occurs in Num 16,3; 23,34; 24,7; 1Kgs 1,5; 1Chr 29,11; 2Chr 32,23; Prov 30,32; Ezek 17,14; 29,15; Dan 11,24.

capability to manoeuvre. Her political influence would be reduced to such an extent that it would not be a threat to other nations and her pride extinguished. Behind this political frame of her restoration, there is heavy emphasis on her inner attitude.

The Hebrew verb רדה means to "have domination," "rule" or "dominate" and it occurs 27 times ([I] 24x "to rule"; [II] 3x "to take", "scrape out") in the OT.[154] In practically all the occurrences (except Judg 14,9), it means to "dominate," "rule," "subdue" or "lead" (e.g. Ps 68,28). In Gen 1,28; Lev 25,43.46.53; 26,17; 1Kgs 5,4; Ps 49,15; 68,28; 110,2; Isa 14,6; Ezek 34,4, it means "to rule". In Isa 14,6 it refers to Israel subduing the nations or, as Ps 110,2 says, "Israel will rule in the midst of her enemies"; and Lev 26,17 (also Neh 9,28) speaks about Israel being ruled by her enemies. The verb רדה also seems to have a negative connotation, i.e., an oppressive rule or domination and subjugation. In Gen 1,26.28, however, it has a positive sense: to harness and further life. It occurs twice in Ezekiel in 29,15 and 34,4. In Ezek 29,15c רְדוֹת denotes cessation of oppressive domination due to the reduced population and size of Egypt (as well as her location in the southern region). Egypt's reduced political power and stature prevent her from dominating other nations.

Two direct consequences of Egypt's new status relate to the house of Israel: 1) לְמִבְטָח a "source of reliance" (16a); and 2) מַזְכִּיר עָוֹן a "reminder of sin" (16b). Both these aspects reflect Egypt's past role in the politics of Israel (cf. 6b-7). The *first* is formulated as a negative statement וְלֹא יִהְיֶה־עוֹד...לְמִבְטָח "and it will not be a source of reliance," while the *second* is an acknowledgement of Israel's tendency in the past to form a political alliance with Egypt. The expression וְלֹא יִהְיֶה־עוֹד לְבֵית יִשְׂרָאֵל "It will no more be for the house of Israel," appears also in 28,24 with a similar literary structure as 29,16:[155]

<table>
<tr><td align="center">Ezek 28, 24:</td><td align="center">Ezek 29, 16:</td></tr>
<tr><td align="right" dir="rtl">וְלֹא־יִהְיֶה עוֹד לְבֵית יִשְׂרָאֵל סִלּוֹן מַמְאִיר אוֹתָם</td><td align="right" dir="rtl">וְלֹא יִהְיֶה־עוֹד לְבֵית יִשְׂרָאֵל לְמִבְטָח</td></tr>
<tr><td align="right" dir="rtl">וְקוֹץ מַכְאִב מִכֹּל סְבִיבֹתָם הַשָּׁאטִים</td><td align="right" dir="rtl">מַזְכִּיר עָוֹן בִּפְנוֹתָם אַחֲרֵיהֶם</td></tr>
<tr><td align="right" dir="rtl">וְיָדְעוּ כִּי אֲנִי אֲדֹנָי יְהוִה</td><td align="right" dir="rtl">וְיָדְעוּ כִּי אֲנִי אֲדֹנָי יְהוִה</td></tr>
<tr><td>And it shall no more be a brier</td><td>And It shall no more be confidence</td></tr>
<tr><td>for the house of Israel, causing pain and</td><td>for the house of Israel,   /them;</td></tr>
<tr><td>a thorn causing pain from all those around,</td><td>a reminder of sin when they turned to</td></tr>
<tr><td>the ones treating them with malice;</td><td>/GOD.</td></tr>
<tr><td>Then they will know that I am the Lord GOD.</td><td>Then they will know that I am the Lord</td></tr>
</table>

These two texts display marked similarities, but 28,24 is a negative statement whereas 29,16 is positive in its interpretation. The form of 28,14 is longer than 29,16, which is short and precise. The meaning of this concluding clause signifies

---

[154] ZOBEL, „רָדָה", in *ThWAT* VII , 351.

[155] BLOCK, *Ezekiel 25-48*, 144.

that the end result of God's intervention will be the restoration of Egypt as a low kingdom, as ultimately seen in connection with her relationship to Israel. By removing those factors that tempted Israel to turn to Egypt for help and security, God restores Israel's faithful relationship with him and assures her lasting peace and security.

The Hebrew stative verb בָּטַח (118 occurrences) means "to trust".[156] It occurs mostly in the Psalms (45x) and describes "secure circumstances or secure frame of mind."[157] Its noun-derivative בֶּטַח (42x) means "security" (adj. "securely"), and מִבְטָח (n. m.) means "confidence" or "source of confidence."[158] בֶּטַח occurs 11 times in Ezekiel but מִבְטָח occurs only once in 29,16. The use of מִבְטָח in reference to the house of Israel begs inquiry into why Ezekiel makes such a charge against Egypt. Apart from Ezekiel, the prophets Isaiah and Jeremiah repeatedly denounce Israel's attempt to seek an alliance with Egypt to protect herself against the threats of invasion from Assyria and Babylon (cf. Isa 20,5; 30,2-7; 31,1; 36,6; Jer 37,5-10, cf. 7-8; 43,8-10; 44,29-30; 46,25-26).[159] The texts from Isaiah and Jeremiah affirm that any reliance on Egypt is useless because, like king Zedekiah of Judah, Pharaoh Hophra is also under the same judgment of the LORD, i.e., invasion and capture by Nebuchadnezzar, the king of Babylon. Given this situation, Egypt cannot guarantee security to Israel. Theologically, it is not because Egypt has betrayed or failed to keep her alliance with Israel, but because her attempt to prevent Babylon from capturing Jerusalem is seen as acting directly against God's plan. Therefore, the futility of reliance on Egypt comes not from Egypt's incapability or unreliability in helping Israel, but from the fact that her action threatens to jeopardise God's own plan for Israel.[160]

In 16a, לְמִבְטָח refers to the political alliance that Israel formed with Egypt in an attempt to prevent the siege and capture of Jerusalem by Nebuchadnezzar. Thus, מִבְטָח envisages reliance or security, a "basis" or an "object of confidence,"[161] which here denotes some kind of military assistance to thwart any attempt by Nebuchadnezzar to lay siege to the city, as Jer 37,5-10 makes plain. This manoeuvre for an alliance to avert the national disaster is not new in the history of Israel. In a similar situation at an earlier time, the prophet Hosea denounced

---

[156] GERSTENBERGER, "בטח *bṭḥ* to trust," in *TLOT* I, 227. LISOWSKY (*Konkordanz*, 209-210) gives 116 occurrences.

[157] GERSTENBERGER, "בטח *bṭḥ* to trust," in *TLOT* I, 228.

[158] בֶּטַח (n.m.) occurs 42 times in the OT: Pentateuch 7x; Historical Books 4x; Wisdom Writings 9x; Prophets 22x; and מִבְטָח (n. m.) occurs 19 times: Historical Books 1x; Prophets 5x; Wisdom Writings 13x.

[159] BLOCK, *Ezekiel 25-48*, 144; see also, BOADT, *Ezekiel's Oracles*, 48

[160] BLOCK, *Ezekiel 25-48*, 145.

[161] GERSTENBERGER, "בטח *bṭḥ* to trust," in *TLOT* I, 229; see also JEPSEN, „בָּטַח", in *ThWAT* I, 608-615, cf. 610.

Israel's diplomatic shuttling between Assyria and Egypt to seek to avoid such disaster (cf. Am 8,9; 12,1ff.).

The expression מַזְכִּיר עָוֹן "a reminder of guilt" serves as an apposition to לְמִבְטָח. "Reminder" (מַזְכִּיר[162] *hiphil* ptc.) is a neutral term and its reference is to Egypt[163] but as a complement of עָוֹן ("guilt" or "inquity")[164] it refers to Israel (dat. object), i.e., to her earlier attempts to form an alliance with Egypt.[165] This situation is illustrated in Jer 37,5-10 and 46,25-26.[166]

The idea of covenant does not seem to be a major theme in the book of Ezekiel and the text does not speak about any explicit treaty between Israel and Egypt. All the same, Ezekiel does speak about the LORD's covenant with the house of Israel in relation to her failure to keep it. He does not disguise his disapproval of any alliance between Israel and Egypt (cf. 17,11-21). Seeking military help through political alliance with others is against Israel's covenant-relation with the LORD (cf. 21,23-29). מַזְכִּיר עָוֹן "a reminder of guilt" in relation to לְמִבְטָח ("reliance" or "security" 16a) points to the political perjury of Israel.

There is a clear shift in the subject of the verb from the feminine singular in 15b to the masculine singular in 16a. In 15b מַמְלָכָה שְׁפָלָה is the implied subject, but in 15c the LORD is the proper subject. In 16a יִהְיֶה has an impersonal subject, "it" which does not correspond with the preceding subjects. This calls for syntactical clarification to determine the impersonal subject of יִהְיֶה in 16a. The land of Egypt or the kingdom (both 3f. sg.) cannot be the subject of יִהְיֶה here; neither can the

---

[162] The Hebrew root זכר occurs 161 times in the Old Testament; cf. as verb "bring to memory" 31x; and "remembrance" (זִכָּרוֹן) 24x; see EISING, „זָכַר", in *ThWAT* II, 571-593, esp. 571.

[163] DRIVER, "Linguistic and Textual Problems," in *Biblica* 35, 300.

[164] עָוֹן is mostly used in the exilic and post-exilic period with maximum usages in Ezekiel (31 out of 44 occurrences); see JEPSEN, „בָּטַח", in *ThWAT* I, 608-615; also KOCH, „עָוֹן", in *ThWAT* V, 1160-1177.

[165] מַזְכִּיר refers to the king's messenger or spokesperson who reminded the addressee(s) of many benevolent deeds undertaken by the king in favour of his subjects, so that the subjects in turn would pay attention to their own obligations to the king and his commands. Thus, מַזְכִּיר was a kind of reminder of the 'failed' obligations of the subjects. See BOADT, *Ezekiel's Oracles*, 48. In 29,16 מַזְכִּיר עָוֹן may also refer to Zediakiah's act of sending an ambassador to Pharaoh Hophra (588-568) of Egypt for a military aid against Nebuchadnezzar of Babylon, who had deployed his army against Jerusalem (cf. Ezek 17,15). Jeremiah and Ezekiel regard this move as a rebellion not just against Nebuchadnezzar, but also against the LORD himself.

[166] Jer 37,5-10 (//2Kgs 24,17-20) refers to the siege of Jerusalem by Nebuchadnezzar in 588, B.C., which was temporarily lifted when Hophra marched out to relieve Jerusalem. Jer 46,25-26 may refers to Nebuchadnezzar's campaign to punish Egypt for her league with Jerusalem following its siege in 589 (cf. Ezek 30,20-31,18). See HAYES and HOOKERS, *A New Chronology*, 97; see also MALAMAT, "The Last Kings of Judah," in *IEJ* 18/3, 151.

captivity of Egypt (3f. sg.) or אַחֲרֵיהֶם (suff. 3m. pl., i.e., the Egyptians) be its subject. Therefore, יִהְיֶ֑ can properly refer to Egypt as a nation.[167]

4.6. Conclusion:

The omission of the usual temporal indicator וַיְהִי and the use of בְּ + date formula in 29,1 instead, sounds a word of caution. The date formula records the earliest possible date of Ezekiel's oracles against Egypt. Although the doubling of the divine name, אֲדֹנָי יְהוִה occurs frequently in Ezekiel, it is absent in the word event formula. The use of יְהוָה in these places indicates an older form. Change in the normal usage of the preposition from אֶל to עַל (and *vice versa*) in certain places points to Aramization, but at the same time it also intends to lay special emphasis on the object against whom the oracle of judgment is directed (but cf. 29,14). The use of דַּבֵּר וְאָמַרְתָּ "imperative + indicative" with the force of an imperative may have been intended to serve the same purpose.

The first oracle of judgment against Egypt is spoken in a metaphor. The metaphor of the "big crocodile" lying in its Niles is used to denote Pharaoh, king of Egypt. The motive for accusation lies in the crocodile's "hubris", i.e., its claim that the Nile belongs to him and he is its maker. This claim is the basis for judgment against him and against all Egypt.

As the life-line of Egypt, the Nile symbolises the land of Egypt. The big crocodile, while symbolising Pharaoh also represents the primeval mythical dragon of chaos, which tries to disrupt God's order at the beginning of creation. The crocodile's proud claim implicitly ascribes to himself the dignity of a god. This is a defiance of God's order and rule, and invites his intervention. The problem underlying this metaphor is not political but Theological. It touches upon God's role in creation, his order and purpose in creation and history. The humbling of the crocodile's pride and that of his hordes, helpers and supporters is a prerequisite to maintaining peace and order among the nations. This throws some light on God's power and control over His creation.

The metaphor of the "unreliable staff of reed" in the second oracle of judgment is apparently a depiction of Egypt as a land or kingdom,[168] especially in its relation to the house of Israel. The context is here political-historical, and it refers to Zedekiah's military alliance with Hophra against a possible invasion from Nebuchadnezzar of Babylon. By this political alliance, Egypt and Israel both defy God's plan, which constitutes the reason for accusation against Egypt. Here the problem shifts from the question of God's role in creation to his guidance of political history. It focuses on those who defy His plan. Here, the judgment against

---

[167] KEIL, *Ezekiel*, COT 9, 248.
[168] KEIL, *Ezekiel*, COT 9, 246.

Egypt underlines a theological-political motif that is symbolised by the sword that causes desolation of the land.

The third oracle does not have any new motive for judgment, but again takes up the motif of the hubris of the crocodile and establishes a direct link with the first oracle. Here God's judgment envisages desolation of the land of Egypt. A new element in the announcement of judgment is the reference to the geographical boundaries of Egypt and to the period of "forty years" of her desolation. Forty years of desolation reminds us of the Israelite's forty years of wanderings in the desert following her exodus from Egypt.

The fourth oracle is an oracle of salvation of Egypt, and it draws a parallel between God's dealing with Israel's history and His action toward Egypt. His dealing with Israel, includes not only His choice of her as His own people, but also His judgment, exile and restoration of her, and all these factors are also present in God's handling with Egypt. Through forty years of wandering in the wilderness, God trains Israel to be faithful and dedicated to him. He judges the Israelites for their unholy practices in the land and exiles them to Babylon. Yet He promises to bring them back to their own land after forty years of exile. Similarly, after the Egyptians have been dispersed through the countries for forty years, God will gather and bring them back and cause them to dwell in their native land. Egypt will receive a new identity in accordance with God's order for the nations and for Israel.

Theologically, something quite significant is being said here: Egypt has sought to exalt herself contrary to the fact that true greatness comes not by the self-exaltation of a person, people, or a nation. Such wilful pride and self-grandeur provokes God's judgment. He is the One who raises those who are humble, to a high place of honour. On the other hand, He also brings low those who raise themselves above others. This is His order of justice. It is His prerogative that the high and the mighty, the proud and the haughty are humbled so that they may see God's deed, for He alone makes people truly great. Unless the LORD makes them low and humble through judgment and gathers them together, bringing them back and causing them to dwell in their own land, they cannot rise, nor can they achieve any greatness.

This reflects God's prerogative in dealing with Egypt, which is set as precedent primarily for his dealing with Israel, but ultimately also for other nations. It affirms God's sovereignty in creation and His control over chaos. It means that He humbles defiant Egypt and reshapes it in such a way that Israel and the nations may live in reliance on God's security and acknowledge Him.

CHAPTER FIVE
THE USAGE OF קבץ "TO GATHER"
TO DESCRIBE GOD'S SAVING ACTION FOR EGYPT

The oracle of hope in 29,13-16 looks beyond God's judgment and focuses on His promise of salvation. It constitutes the core of the oracles against Egypt, for it displays God's judgement against Egypt combined with the purpose of her restoration and salvation. Its vocabulary and style display significant similarities to the oracles of salvation for Israel. Indeed, it presents a paradigm of God's salvation for Israel.

"Gathering," "bringing back the captivity," and "settling them," constitute three key-concepts of the oracle of salvation. Therefore, before explaining the oracle of salvation in 29,13-16 and incorporating the results gained from the preceding chapters, it is expedient to discuss and inquire into these key concepts so as to understand their implications for the oracle. We here limit our inquiry mainly to the first two concepts.

The present chapter takes up the first fundamental concept, "to gather" (קבץ), and inquires into its meaning and usage in the Old Testament, particularly in denoting the action of God's judgment and salvation for Israel and for the nations.

5.1. The usage of the verb קבץ

There are 40 occurrences of קבץ in the Old Testament describing God's action of gathering his people, Israel, and the other nations.[1] Out of these, 35 occurrences relate to God's direct address, announcing His action in the first person singular: "I will gather."[2] Only 5 times does it describe this action in a reported speech: "He

---

[1] MANDELKERN gives 127 occurrences of the verb forms of קבץ besides the two noun forms קְבֻצָה "assemblage" in Ezek 22,20 and קִבּוּצַיִךְ "gathering" in Isa 57,13. There are 38 usages in *qal*, 32 in *niphal*, 49 in *piel*, 1 in *pual* and 8 in *hithpael*. There are 83 usages in active, 30 usages in middle and 14 usages in passive. See his *Concordantiae*, 1007-1008; MOMMER, "קבץ", in *ThWAT* VII, 1144-1149; on its meaning, see JASTROW (Compiler), *Dictionary of the Targumim* II, 1312.a; and ZORELL, *Lexicon*, 706.b.

[2] The basic meaning of קבץ is "to gather," "collect," "assemble." In *niphal* (intrans.), it means "to assemble," "gather" and (passive) "be gathered"; in *piel* it means to "gather together," and in *hithpael* to "gather together" (intrans.), or "be gathered." Its participle usually denotes "gathering" as in Ezek 29,13: "gathering the dispersed Egyptians," while its noun קִבּוּץ (m. sg.) means "assemblage," and קְבֻצַת (f. sg. cstr. of קְבֻצָה) means "gathering" (cf. Ezek 22,20) or its plural with suffix 2f. קִבּוּצַיִךְ (cf. Isa 57,13 קִבּוּצַיִם). cf. JASTROW, (Compiler) *Dictionary of the Targumim* II, 1312.

will gather/He who gathers". A fairly large group (19x) of the objects of the verb describing God's action are pronouns: "you"/"your" and "they", all referring to Israel. There are 4 other occurrences where the pronouns "you" and "they" function as the objects of God's action. In 6 occurrences, "nations" and "kingdoms" are the recipient objects of His action, and Egypt is mentioned by name (cf. Ezek 29,13). In the remaining 10 occurrences, Israel is the object of God's action and is referred with various expressions: "house of Israel," "outcast of Israel," "remnant of Israel," "remnant of my flock," "dispersed of Judah," "all of Jacob," "those driven away," and "the outcast". One reference to a recipient object of God's action (Is 40,11: "the lambs") probably carries a general sense without specifically referring to Israel or to the nations. Moreover, in 6 occurrences, God's action of gathering Israel, the nations and the kingdoms relates to his judgment against them (3x against Israel and 3x against the nations). Leaving this aside, the majority of the occurrences (33x) of the verb קבץ refer to God's "saving" action.

Aside from Isa 40,11 and 66,18, קבץ is used mostly (31x) to denote God's saving action for the people of Israel. Interestingly, it is used once in Ezek 29,13 to describe His saving action for Egypt. In 7 occurrences where it denotes "to gather the nations"/"kingdoms," Egypt is mentioned explicitly (e.g., Ezek 29,13). There are two more occurrences in Isa 56,8 and 66,18 where קבץ relates to God's saving action for the nations. Otherwise, He usually gathers them for judgment.

קבץ occurs twice in Ezek 29 (vv 5.13). In v.5, "You will not be gathered," expresses God's judgment, while in v.13, "I will gather the Egyptians from the nations where they are dispersed," refers to His saving action. Like Isa 40,11, Jer 23,3 and Ezek 34,13, Ezek 29,13 reveals God's protection and care as a good shepherd who gathers together his dispersed flock.[3] It is typical of his saving action for Israel: despite punishing them for their unfaithfulness, by scattering them among the nations, He promises to gather them together and bring them back to their own land. In Ezek 29,13 He promises to do the same for Egypt. This shows God's new prerogative for the nations, as revealed in His promise of salvation to Egypt.

God's gathering takes into account his prior judgment. It is He who punitively scatters the people and the nations. So both scattering and gathering are God's own action. The first oracle of judgment against Egypt (29,1-12) relates to God's judgment against Egypt, which reaches its climax in the announcement of their "scattering" and "dispersion" throughout the countries (cf. v.12).[4] Ezekiel uses

---

[3] FREEDMAN, *Hosea*, 506.

[4] Scattering the Egyptians among the peoples and dispersing them through the countries is the climax of the judgment against Egypt in 29,1-12, which is immediately followed by the oracle of salvation to Egypt in vv.13-16. The last oracle of judgment (29,17-30,19) which follows it, announces God's judgment against Egypt in terms of "carrying away her hordes, and plunder and pillage of her wealth" (29,19).

various metaphors in 29,1-12 to describe the crime of Pharaoh/Egypt; this use of metaphoric language to announce God's judgment against her shows a close parallel to His dealing with Israel:[5]

Table 1:

Egypt (Ezek 29)	Israel (in Ezekiel)
v.5: beasts of the field and the birds of the air	5,17; cf. 14,15.21; 33,27: I will send famine and wild beasts against you
v.8: I will bring sword against you	5,17; cf. 5,2.12; 6,3. 11.12; 7,15; 11,8. 10; 14,4.17; 33,2; 39,23: I will bring the sword upon you
vv.9.10: the land will become desolation and waste	5,14; cf. 5,35, 4; 36,4,10.33; 38,8.12: I will make you a desolation and an object of reproach
vv.9.10.12: wastes and waste of desolation	6,14; cf. 12,20; 14,15.16; 15,8; 33,28.29; 35,3.4.7.9.14.15: and I will make the land desolate and waste
v.5: not collected, not gathered	35,8; chap. 37. on your hills and in your valleys and in all your ravines those slain with the sword shall fall.
v.11: no foot will pass through it	14,15; cf. 5,14; 33,28; 36,34 (cf., Jer 9,9.11): and it be made desolate, so that no one may pass through because of the beasts.
v.12 (cf. 30,23.26; 32,9): I will scatter the Egyptians among the nations and disperse them through the countries	12,15; cf. 5,10; 11,17; 20,34; 22,35; 36,19: when I disperse them among the nations and scatter them through the countries.

This table illustrates how the oracles of judgment against Egypt use various metaphors that highlight the breadth of the judgment covering the land, its ruler and its people. It shows the increasingly severe and all-encompassing nature of God's judgment. This makes the oracle of salvation (29,13-16), given to Egypt at the end of the first oracle of judgment, a great surprise. There are few oracles of salvation for the nations in the Old Testament, and it is unique in Ezekiel because it reflects God's promise of salvation for His people Israel.

God's unique action of saving Egypt by completely reversing his judgment at the end of forty years (vv.11.13) implies a gathering of the Egyptians from their dispersion (v.13), bringing them back from their captivity, and establishing them in Pathros, their homeland (v.14). Thus, God's judgment against Egypt and His salvation for her present close parallel to his judgment and salvation of Israel, as He "scattered them among the nations and dispersed them through the countries" (cf. Ezek 11,16; 12,15; 20,23; 22,15; 36,19) for forty years, because they neglected

---

[5] VOGELS finds a similarity in the use of these expressions in the judgment against Egypt and Israel; see his *God's Universal Covenant*, 88.

to keep his "statutes and ordinances" (cf. 5,6; 11,12.20; 18,9.17; 20,11.13.18.19. 21.24.25; 36,27; 37,24).[6]

קבץ plays a fundamental role in God's salvation because bringing back Israel and Egypt, each to their own land, is a consequence of this primary action of gathering them. Thus, it expresses God's care and concern for His people. Though He punishes them, He also looks after them. As such, קבץ expresses God's prerogative both for Israel and for Egypt, revealing a heart that is full of compassion for them.

In the following pages, we have classified these 40 occurrences of קבץ in the Old Testament, and describe God's action of gathering the house of Israel and the nations in eight different groups that highlight His purpose and way of dealing with the people and the nations. It should be noted that this is one way of classifying them, and it may not always present a clear-cut distinction among the different groups. Another descriptive schema could have been to categorize them chronologically, following the order in which they appear in the prophetic books. A significant advantage of the former schema is that it focuses more on God's action, i.e., His salvation.

5.2. God's saving action for His people Israel
5.2.1. "I will gather you" (Israel)

In the first category, the verb קבץ relates to God's direct address to his people Israel. It expresses his personal appeal to them, giving them an assurance of salvation. He will gather them from the nations and bring them back to their own homeland. This direct address reveals his concern for them:

Isa 43,5:

אַל־תִּירָא כִּי אִתְּךָ־אָנִי מִמִּזְרָח אָבִיא זַרְעֶךָ וּמִמַּעֲרָב אֲקַבְּצֶךָ׃

Fear not, for I am with you; I will bring your offspring from the east,
and from the west I will gather you.

Isa 54,7:

בְּרֶגַע קָטֹן עֲזַבְתִּיךְ וּבְרַחֲמִים גְּדֹלִים אֲקַבְּצֵךְ׃

For a brief moment I forsook you, but with great compassion I will gather you.

God comforts His people by promising to gather them from their captivity[7] and bring them back to their own land. This gathering extends beyond those who live in Babylonian captivity to include also those who are scattered in other countries,

---

[6] VOGELS, *God's Universal Covenant*, 89.
[7] ELLIGER, *Deuterojesaja 1*, 300.

namely, those who fled to Egypt for fear of repression from Nebuchadnezzar.[8] The reference to offspring (זַרְעֶךָ) indicates a whole new generation who were born in captivity and in the dispersion. It reveals an extraordinary saving action of God, who takes a new initiative to gather them from their dispersion to bring them back from their captivity. This action reflects the concern of a good shepherd who takes personal care of his sheep (Isa 40,11). Thus, קבץ reveals God's compassion, goodness and kindness that surpasses even His righteous judgment (cf. Isa 54,7-8).

Jer 29,14:

וְנִמְצֵאתִי לָכֶם נְאֻם־יְהוָה וְשַׁבְתִּי אֶת־שְׁבִיתְכֶם **וְקִבַּצְתִּי אֶתְכֶם
מִכָּל־הַגּוֹיִם וּמִכָּל־הַמְּקוֹמוֹת אֲשֶׁר הִדַּחְתִּי אֶתְכֶם שָׁם נְאֻם־יְהוָה
וַהֲשִׁבֹתִי אֶתְכֶם אֶל־הַמָּקוֹם אֲשֶׁר־הִגְלֵיתִי אֶתְכֶם מִשָּׁם:

I will be found by you, says the LORD, and I will restore your fortunes
and gather you from all the nations and all the places where I have driven you,
says the LORD; and I will bring you back to the place from which I sent you into exile.

Many commentators[9] think that the Greek Text of Jer 29,14 is better than the MT. Against this view, following Thiel's explanation, W. Mckane maintains that the longer form in the MT does not necessarily mean that it is a late addition (exilic or post-exilic) only because it is absent in the Septuagint.[10] The verse serves as a conclusion to Jer 29,12-13[11] and it speaks about God's action of gathering the people of Israel from their dispersion. Its context (Jer 29,10-13) makes clear that at the end of Israel's seventy years of exile to Babylon, God will gather them from all the nations and from all the places to which he drove them and bring them back to the place of their dwelling.

H.-J. Stipp observes that the promise to bring them back from dispersion is lacking in the Alexandrian Text.[12] He argues that the text describes a scattering of the Jews world-wide, whereas the context refers only to the exiles in a city, i.e., to Babylon; moreover, the expression, "among all the nations"[13] where the Jews would be dispersed, is attested only in the Pre-masoretic modification.[14]

---

[8] ELLIGER, *Deuterojesaja 1*, 300.

[9] Here MCKANE names GIESEBRECHT, CORNILL, STRENEM, PEAKE, SCHMIDT, RUDOLF, WEISER, and NICHOLSON; see his *Jeremiah XXVI-LII*, Vol. II, 729.

[10] MCKANE, *Jeremiah XXVI-LII*, Vol. II, 729-730.

[11] VOLZ, *Der Prophet Jeremia*, 270; see also RUDOLF, *Jeremia*, 169.

[12] STIPP, *Sondergut des Jeremiabuches*, 70.

[13] Cf. "from all the countries" (מִן־הָאֲרָצוֹת) in Jer 16,15 = 23,8; 23,3; 32,37; "from all the places" (מִכָּל־הַמְּקוֹמוֹת) in Jer 8,3; 24,9; 29,14; 40,12; and "from all the nations" (מִכָּל־הַגּוֹיִם) in Jer 29,14.18; 30,11; 43, 3; 46,26.28; cf. 9,15. See STIPP, *Sondergut des Jeremiabuches*, 79.

[14] STIPP, *Sondergut des Jeremiabuches*, 70.

Ezek 11,17:

לָכֵן אֱמֹר כֹּה־אָמַר אֲדֹנָי יְהוִה וְקִבַּצְתִּי אֶתְכֶם מִן־הָעַמִּים וְאָסַפְתִּי אֶתְכֶם
מִן־הָאֲרָצוֹת אֲשֶׁר נְפֹצוֹתֶם בָּהֶם וְנָתַתִּי לָכֶם אֶת־אַדְמַת יִשְׂרָאֵל:

Therefore say, thus says Lord GOD: I will gather you from the peoples,
and assemble you out of the countries where you have been scattered,
and I will give you the land of Israel.

The first occurrence in Ezekiel of God's promise to gather the people of Israel is attested in 11,17. It touches upon the theme already popularised by Jeremiah[15] and enshrined in the final instruction of Moses to the people of Israel in Deut 30,3-4. In Ezek 11,17 God's promise to gather His people signals their restoration, which begins with His action of gathering them back from dispersion among the countries. This promise carries a message of "hope and encouragement,"[16] which is closely linked to the guarantee that Moses gives to the people (cf. Deut 30,5), on condition that they "return" to him (cf. Deut 30,2), and it looks forward to their renewal, reflected in their "undivided heart" and the "new spirit" (Ezek 11,19).[17]

Ezek 20,34:

וְהוֹצֵאתִי אֶתְכֶם מִן־הָעַמִּים וְקִבַּצְתִּי אֶתְכֶם מִן־הָאֲרָצוֹת אֲשֶׁר נְפוֹצֹתֶם בָּם
בְּיָד חֲזָקָה וּבִזְרוֹעַ נְטוּיָה וּבְחֵמָה שְׁפוּכָה:

I will bring you out from the peoples and gather you out of the countries where you are
scattered with a mighty hand and an outstretched arm, and with wrath poured out.

Ezek 20,41:

בְּרֵיחַ נִיחֹחַ אֶרְצֶה אֶתְכֶם בְּהוֹצִיאִי אֶתְכֶם מִן־הָעַמִּים וְקִבַּצְתִּי אֶתְכֶם מִן־הָאֲרָצוֹת
אֲשֶׁר נְפֹצֹתֶם בָּם וְנִקְדַּשְׁתִּי בָכֶם לְעֵינֵי הַגּוֹיִם:

As a pleasing odour I will accept you, when I bring you out from the peoples
and gather you from the countries where you have been scattered
and I will be hallowed among you in the sight of the nations.

The motif of God's action to gather (cf. Ezek 20,34.41) continues the message of hope and encouragement,[18] revealing Him as the shepherd who gathers the dispersed of Israel from the nations and from the countries, as He previously did

---

[15] In the parable of the "two baskets of Figs" (Jer 24), Jeremiah prophesises the exile of Judah to Babylon but he also assures them of God's care in exile, and the promise that He will bring them back, and build and settle them in the land so that they will know Him. It is a necessary action for Israel's return to Him. For this reason, Zedekiah and those who remain in Jerusalem as well as those who escaped to Egypt are seen as an abhorrence (זַוֲעָה) and as an offence (רָעָה) before the kingdoms. The exile is part of God's saving action. In other words, the scattering is not the ultimate aim, but rather their "return," and "knowledge of God." In Jer 42,7ff., the prophet reveals God's plan for the survivors. See STIPP, *Jeremia im Parteienstreit*, 36.

[16] COOKE, *Ezekiel*, 223; BERTHOLET, *Hesekiel*, HAT 13, 41; FOHRER, *Ezechiel*, 62.

[17] FOHRER, *Ezechiel*, 62; see also POHLMANN, *Hesekiel*, 167.

[18] COOKE, *Ezekiel*, 125.

with their fathers when He took them out of Egypt. However, He will not bring them back immediately to their land, but, as He led their fathers through the desert after their exodus from Egypt, so also in this new exodus from the nations, will He take them through a desert-path (cf. v.35f.).[19]

Although the desert or wilderness frequently symbolizes God's judgment, it also must be viewed as a period of their return through personal conversion to Him. As such, this does not necessarily signify a punishment.[20] The expression, "out of the countries where you are scattered" (v.34), presupposes exile as their punishment (cf. "pouring of His wrath" at the end of v.34). Nonetheless, in v.34 קבץ does not stress God's action of judgment but the bestowal of His generous and everlasting love. V.41 adds another point, namely, that His action of gathering the people of Israel will have a positive effect on the nations. When He gathers His people from the countries, this will reveal His holiness to them; in other words, He will prove himself as the Faithful and the holy God (cf. 28,22.25; 36,23; 38,16.23; 39,27).[21]

Ezek 22,19:

לָכֵן כֹּה אָמַר אֲדֹנָי יְהוִֹה יַעַן הֱיוֹת כֻּלְּכֶם לְסִגִים
לָכֵן הִנְנִי קֹבֵץ אֶתְכֶם אֶל־תּוֹךְ יְרוּשָׁלָ‍ִם׃

Therefore thus says Lord GOD: Because you have all become dross;
therefore, behold, I will gather you into the midst of Jerusalem.

Israel has become base and worthless because of her bloodguilt and idolatry, just does a metal, when mixed with base material that needs to be separated by smelting, become worthless before it can be put to any use (cf. 20,1-5). But God will gather Israel back to Jerusalem so that He may refine her and make her once again precious to Himself.[22] The purging and refining of Israel that makes her once again precious and acceptable will take place through punishment. The text hints at the imminent fall of Jerusalem and the captivity of her people. Here, Ezekiel visualizes the destruction of Jerusalem and the exile of her people as God's way of purifying Israel.

Ezek 36,24:

וְלָקַחְתִּי אֶתְכֶם מִן־הַגּוֹיִם וְקִבַּצְתִּי אֶתְכֶם מִכָּל־הָאֲרָצוֹת
וְהֵבֵאתִי אֶתְכֶם אֶל־אַדְמַתְכֶם׃

For, I will take you from the nations, and gather you from all the countries,
and I will bring you into your own land.

---

[19] FOHRER, *Ezechiel*, 116.

[20] FOHRER, *Ezechiel*, 116.

[21] COOKE, *Ezekiel*, 125.

[22] FOHRER, *Ezechiel*, 130.

Ezek 36,24 is related to Ezek 20,41; 28,25; 39,27. God's promise to gather His people from the peoples and from the countries in these texts refer to His future saving action by bringing back His people from their exile and dispersion to their own homeland. The reason for this new initiative is God's holiness (cf. 36,22). Ezekiel interprets Israel's conduct and deeds, by which she defiled the land and God's holiness, as a reason for her punishment through dispersion and exile (cf. 36,16ff.). But God turns the period of her dispersion and exile into a time of her purification, so that when He gathers her at the end of that period, it will reveal His holiness to them and to the nations. Thus, God's holiness and the sanctification of His people becomes a basis of His promise[23] for giving them a new heart and a new spirit (v.25).[24] Gathering the people from their exile and dispersion is impossible by any human effort,[25] thus requiring God's unique saving action, which makes the nations acknowledge Him as God.[26]

Zeph 3,20:

בָּעֵת הַהִיא אָבִיא אֶתְכֶם וּבָעֵת קַבְּצִי אֶתְכֶם כִּי־אֶתֵּן אֶתְכֶם לְשֵׁם וְלִתְהִלָּה
בְּכֹל עַמֵּי הָאָרֶץ בְּשׁוּבִי אֶת־שְׁבוּתֵיכֶם לְעֵינֵיכֶם אָמַר יְהוָה:

At that time I will bring you, at the time I will gather you;
I will give you fame and praise among all the peoples of the earth,
when I bring back your captives before your eyes, says the LORD.

Zeph 3,20 is considered to be a repetition of v.19, but it could also be its continuation. Barthélemy gives another rendering of בָּעֵת הַהִיא "<it will be> the time (when)" and points to a small variation, וּבָעֵת הַהִיא ("and at that time").[27] There is an emphasis on the indication of "time" here, which testifies God's future saving action marked by a parallelism of קבץ (*piel*) and בוא (*hiphil*).[28] This exilic or post-exilic text speaks about God's action of gathering his people from their captivity, which will make them "an object of envy and renown" among the nations.[29] Here קבץ indicates the beginning of salvation and restoration of the exiles of Israel, when God will bring them back, and the final signatory formula affirms it to be solely His action.[30]

---

[23] KEIL, *Ezekiel*, COT 9, 301.

[24] POHLMANN, *Hesekiel*, 488.

[25] FOHRER, *Ezechiel*, 204.

[26] BERTHOLET, *Hesekiel*, 125.

[27] BARTHÉLEMY (ed.), *Preliminary and interim report* 5, 387.

[28] IRSIGLER, *Zefanja*, 433.

[29] SMITH, WARD, and BEWAR, *Micah, Zephaniah*, 260.

[30] IRSIGLER, *Zefanja*, 433.

5.2.2. Conclusion:

The above-mentioned texts are addressed directly to the people of Israel, revealing the promise of God's salvation to them. God will "gather" them from the nations and from the countries where they were scattered and dispersed.[31] In the exilic period and especially in the exilic theology, קבץ acquires a great significance in view of God's promise of gathering (קבץ) the dispersed (פוץ) of His people.[32] It reveals His primary care and concern for them. Although He judges them and punishes them, He still comforts them and shows them His love and "great compassion" (בְּרַחֲמִים גְדֹלִים). This is very significant in view of undoing His "furious anger and great wrath" (בְּאַף וּבְחֵמָה וּקֶצֶף גָּדוֹל cf. Deut 29,27), which caused Him to scatter (פוץ) them.[33] On the other hand, קבץ indicates God's new initiative, i.e., reversal of His judgment.

God's act of gathering (קבץ) reveals that dispersion of the people among the nations as punishment for their apostasy, bloodguilt, and idolatry is not His ultimate purpose. His prerogative is to show to them His compassion and His holiness. For this reason, He promises to gather them from all peoples, nations and countries and to save them. To gather them together is an enormous, unprecedented saving action on His part.

The duration of their exile to Babylon and dispersion among the nations is viewed as a time for Israel's return (conversion) to Him. Therefore, at the end of her punishment, God takes a new initiative and announces: "I will gather you." Here, the pronoun "you" refers directly to the people of Israel whom He has scattered among the nations. They realise that their scattering among the nations was God's judgment, but that their future gathering from the nations will prove His unique saving action. Dispersion and exile as judgment is not the final event in God's action. The people of Israel can always rely on His watchful care and compassion, for He seeks them out and promises to gather and bring them back to their own homeland.

5.2.3. "I will gather them" (Israel)

This section deals with the texts relating to God's promise to gather and save His people. God does not address this message directly to the people, but discloses it through His prophets. It reveals the role of the prophets in God's plan of salvation for His people. Although God punishes them by scattering them in the farthest lands, gathering and saving them remains His highest aim. The prophets to whom He reveals His purpose become His instruments through whom He works out the

---

[31] Its sense relates to the exile of the people; cf. הִגְלֵיתִי אֶתְכֶם "I exiled them" (Jer 29,4).

[32] KOOLE, *Isaiah 40-48*, 295; and *Isaiah 49-55*, 367

[33] KOOLE, *Isaiah 49-55*, 367.

conversion of His people and their return to Him in faithful observance of His laws and decrees. This process of punishment, conversion and return to God, is characterized by His new initiative, namely, to gather them together and bring them back to their own land.

Jer 31,8:

הִנְנִי מֵבִיא אוֹתָם מֵאֶרֶץ צָפוֹן וְקִבַּצְתִּים מִיַּרְכְּתֵי־אָרֶץ בָּם עִוֵּר וּפִסֵּחַ הָרָה
וְיֹלֶדֶת יַחְדָּו קָהָל גָּדוֹל יָשׁוּבוּ הֵנָּה:

Behold, I will bring them from the north and gather them from the farthest ends of the earth,
among them the blind and the lame, the woman with child and the one in labour, together,
a great company shall return here.

BHS suggests reading final הֵנָּה with v.9, but there is no need of joining it with v.9 because it denotes the Land (cf. 40,11). LXX reads MT בָּם עִוֵּר וּפִסֵּחַ ("among them blind and the lame") as ἐν ἑορτῇ φασεκ = בְּמוֹעֵד פֶּסַח ("on the feast of the Passover"), with a view that בָּם עִוֵּר may be a corruption of בְּמוֹעֵד.[34]

Jer 31,8 refers to God's promise of bringing the dispersed of Israel "from the north country and gathering them from the farthest ends of the earth." It is the reversal of the earlier prophecy of Jeremiah concerning the imminent catastrophe that was coming upon them "from the land of the north…from the ends of the earth" (6,22). This reversal is interesting because "the north country" (cf. 6,22; 25,32) denoted Israel's "enemy-lands" whereas God's promise of gathering them from those territories denotes their salvation.[35] The picturesque description of God's saving action for His people highlights His tremendous activity of gathering them from all places, even from the remotest ends on the globe. The overwhelming nature of His action is further affirmed by the description of the people whom He gathers together: the blind, the lame (cf. Isa 35,5-6), and the woman with child and in labour (cf. Isa 7,14).[36] Gathering and bringing them back in a procession subtly recalls the catastrophe Jerusalem suffered, as well as God's tender love for His people[37] and depicts a reversal of His previous judgment (cf. Jer 6,21). It also expresses their consolation[38] and jubilation, as well as the grace and power of their God.[39]

Jer 32,37:

הִנְנִי מְקַבְּצָם מִכָּל־הָאֲרָצוֹת אֲשֶׁר הִדַּחְתִּים שָׁם בְּאַפִּי וּבַחֲמָתִי וּבְקֶצֶף גָּדוֹל
וַהֲשִׁבֹתִים אֶל־הַמָּקוֹם הַזֶּה וְהֹשַׁבְתִּים לָבֶטַח:

---

[34] MCKANE, *Jeremiah XXVI-LII*, Vol. II, 790.

[35] HOLLADAY, *Jeremiah 2*, 184.

[36] HOLLADAY, *Jeremiah 2*, 184.

[37] Note the list of people mentioned here; see HOLLADAY, *Jeremiah 2*, 184.

[38] VOLZ, *Jeremia*, 292.

[39] RUDOLF, *Jeremia*, 177.

> Behold, I will gather them from all the countries to which I drove them in my anger and my wrath and in great indignation;
> I will bring them back to this place and I will make them dwell in safety.

Chapter 32 of Jeremiah continues the motif of God's promise of salvation to Israel. V.32 speaks about his promise of salvation by gathering his people from the countries where he scattered them. He will bring them back to their own land where they will live in security. He will make them His own people and He will be their God (v.38). LXX attests אֲרָצוֹת as singular, possibly referring to exile in Babylon, whereas MT (pl.) suggests "dispersion" through the countries.

The *mem*-ending suffix (pron. 3m. pl.) in אֶל־הַמָּקוֹם הַזֶּה ("to this place") refers to הָעִיר (Jerusalem[40]) in v.36, while vv.38-40 make it clear that God's salvation of Judah (Israel) aims at making a permanent covenant with them, assuring them of His unfailing protection.[41] Thus, His action to "gather" them reveals His special choice for them, which is also a prerequisite for re-establishing them, far exceeding their judgment.

Ezek 34,13:

וְהוֹצֵאתִים מִן־הָעַמִּים וְקִבַּצְתִּים מִן־הָאֲרָצוֹת וַהֲבִיאֹתִים אֶל־אַדְמָתָם
וּרְעִיתִים אֶל־הָרֵי יִשְׂרָאֵל בָּאֲפִיקִים וּבְכֹל מוֹשְׁבֵי הָאָרֶץ׃

And I will bring them out from the peoples, and gather them from the countries,
and will bring them into their own land; and I will feed them on the mountains of Israel,
by the fountains and in all the inhabited places of the country.

Ezekiel 34 speaks about God's saving action for Israel mainly through the figure of a good shepherd. It shows His saving action, reflecting the care and concern of a good shepherd, and in this sense it resembles Jer 23,1-6. All the same, there are some significant differences in Ezekiel, which appear in v.13. In Jer 23,3 "to bring back to their pasture" is not very specific, whereas "to pasture them on the mountains of Israel, in the ravines and in all the settlements" in Ezek 34,13 is more specific. Jeremiah speaks about God placing shepherds over His flock (23,4), but in Ezek 34 it is God himself who will watch over the flock, find the lost and bring them back (v.15).

Ezek 34,13 emphasizes the promise of Israel's restoration,[42] which also means their re-settlement in their own land and pasturing them on the mountains of Israel. The meaning of קבץ comes out quite strongly in describing the shepherd's task of gathering the flock together, including seeking out the lost and gathering the scattered "on the day of clouds and darkness" (cf. v.12). While it makes an obvious

---

[40] KEIL, *Jeremiah. Lamentations*, COT 8, 294.

[41] CARROLL, *Jeremiah*, 629.

[42] COOKE, *Ezekiel*, 375.

reference to God's judgment against Israel/Judah, it also signals a new Exodus of his people and thus points to His new saving action in gathering them together.[43]

Ezek 37,21:

וְדַבֵּר אֲלֵיהֶם כֹּה־אָמַר אֲדֹנָי יְהוִה הִנֵּה אֲנִי לֹקֵחַ אֶת־בְּנֵי יִשְׂרָאֵל מִבֵּין הַגּוֹיִם
אֲשֶׁר הָלְכוּ־שָׁם וְקִבַּצְתִּי אֹתָם מִסָּבִיב וְהֵבֵאתִי אוֹתָם אֶל־אַדְמָתָם:

And say to them: Thus says Lord GOD:
Behold, I will take the people of Israel from the nations among which they have gone,
and will gather them from all sides and bring them to their own land.

Ezek 37,21 (cf. vv.20-24) is most likely a late addition.[44] It is a reformulation of v.19 "I will take the wood of Joseph" to denote "I will take the Israelites out of the nations where they have gone" (v.21), whereby it implies the countries where they are scattered.[45] Gathering the dispersed of Israel is seen as a real problem here. Nevertheless, the historical concern of re-uniting the divided kingdoms of Israel and Judah receives a new impetus and perspective in God's saving action, who will gather them together and bring them back to their own land.[46]

This new perspective of uniting the divided kingdoms of Israel and Judah does not mean their future political unity under one Davidic king,[47] even though God's action of gathering and bringing them back to their own land and re-uniting all the scattered people of Israel could be viewed as a reconciliation of the divided kingdoms (cf. v.22f.). God's saving action in 37,21 does not imply any political sense; instead, it views re-uniting the broken house of Israel (i.e., of Israel and Judah) as "one people" (v.22) once he has purified them from their idolatry (גִּלּוּלִים 22,3), abominations (שִׁקּוּצִים 5,11) and rebellion (פֶּשַׁע 14,11), making His saving action known to them by gathering them together.[48]

Ezek 39,27:

בְּשׁוֹבְבִי אוֹתָם מִן־הָעַמִּים וְקִבַּצְתִּי אֹתָם מֵאַרְצוֹת אֹיְבֵיהֶם
וְנִקְדַּשְׁתִּי בָם לְעֵינֵי הַגּוֹיִם רַבִּים:

When I have brought them back from the peoples,
and have gathered them from the lands of their enemies,
and I am hallowed in them in the sight of many nations.

---

[43] FUHS, *Ezechiel II*, 155-156.

[44] ZIMMERLI, *Ezechiel 25-48*, 866; see also POHLMANN, *Hesekiel 20-48*, 502.

[45] ZIMMERLI, *Ezechiel 25-48*, 866.

[46] ZIMMERLI, *Ezechiel 25-48*, 866.

[47] POHLMANN, *Hesekiel*, 503.

[48] ZIMMERLI, *Ezechiel 25-48*, 867.

Ezek 39,27 is an expansion of v.26b[49] which continues the theme of the promise of salvation to Israel (cf. 34,13; 34,24; 37,21), by gathering them from the lands of their enemies and bringing them back from the nations by which God intends to show his holiness in the sight of many[50] nations (cf. 36,23.24; 20,41). Against the background of the defeat of Gog and its burial in Israel, in the valley of Hamon-Gog, God's saving action for His people marks an astounding victory against the enemies of His people. However, it is not primarily because He destroys Gog but because He gathers His people and brings them back from the pagan lands that He will be hallowed in their sight and they will come to acknowledge Him as their holy God.[51] Thus, God's mercy and compassion for the house of Israel manifests itself in His holiness, which is the ultimate motive of gathering Israel from her dispersion.

Zech 10,8:

אֶשְׁרְקָה לָהֶם וַאֲקַבְּצֵם כִּי פְּדִיתִים וְרָבוּ כְּמוֹ רָבוּ׃

I will hoot to them and gather them in, for I have redeemed them,
and they shall be as many as of old.

Zech 10,10:

וַהֲשִׁיבוֹתִים מֵאֶרֶץ מִצְרַיִם וּמֵאַשּׁוּר אֲקַבְּצֵם וְאֶל־אֶרֶץ גִּלְעָד וּלְבָנוֹן אֲבִיאֵם וְלֹא יִמָּצֵא לָהֶם׃

I will bring them home from the land of Egypt, and gather them from Assyria;
and I will bring them to the land of Gilead and to Lebanon, till there is no room for them.

God's promise to give a call to gather his people, just as a shepherd hoots to gather his flock together, signals a new era of increase in Israel's number as indicated by Zech 10,8. "I will hoot" (אֶשְׁרְקָה v.8) basically means "to entice" (cf. Isa 5,26; 7,18), while the use of the prophetic perfect in פְּדִיתִים "I have redeemed them" assures the guarantee of salvation.[52] V.10 outlines Israel's restoration anew and marks out two countries, Egypt and Assyria specifically, where the people have been scattered.[53] It may reflect the campaigns of Tiglath-pileser and Shalmaneser of Assyria, when many from the northern kingdom took refuge in Egypt,[54] but it

---

[49] KEIL, *Ezekiel*, COT 9, 341. Compare the formulation of Ezek 39,27 with 28,25; cf. ZIMMERLI, *Ezechiel 25-48*, 870.

[50] LXX omits רַבִּים ("many") but it is attested in the MT.

[51] KRAETZSCHMAR, *Ezechiel*, 261.

[52] KEIL, *Minor Prophets*, COT 10, 586.

[53] MITCHELL, SMITTH, and BEWAR, *Haggai, Zechariah, Malachi*, 291.

[54] Against this opinion of KOEHLER and others, KEIL argues that there is not very convincing historical evidence of a large number of the Ephraimites having fled to Egypt; even Hos 9,3 does not mean it so, rather than a literary device to refer to Egypt as "the land of bondage." See KEIL, *Minor Prophets*, COT 10, 587.

may also be a reminder of the invasion of Shishak I (1Kgs 14,25ff.) and Necho II's routing of Josiah at Megiddo (2Kgs 23,29f.).[55]

Neh 1,9:

וְשַׁבְתֶּם אֵלַי וּשְׁמַרְתֶּם מִצְוֹתַי וַעֲשִׂיתֶם אֹתָם אִם־יִהְיֶה נִדַּחֲכֶם בִּקְצֵה הַשָּׁמָיִם
מִשָּׁם אֲקַבְּצֵם *וַהֲבִיאֹתִים **וַ**הֲבִיאוֹתִים אֶל־הַמָּקוֹם אֲשֶׁר בָּחַרְתִּי לְשַׁכֵּן

But if you return to me and keep my commandments and do them,
though your dispersed be under the farthest skies, I will gather them from there
and bring them to the place which I have chosen, to make my name dwell there.

Neh 1,9 constitutes a part of Nehemiah's prayer (Neh 1,5-11), which represents a people's "lamentation."[56] It recalls Moses' declaration of God's promise of salvation for Israel if they would "return" to him while the preceding v.8 speaks about Israel's unfaithfulness as a reason for their being scattered among the nations. It views exile as punishment for their rebellion and disobedience (cf. Deut 30,1-4; also 28,64; Lev 26,33.40-45).[57] The very fact that God has evicted Israel from their land on account of their rebellion and transgression and has scattered them among the nations has proved His righteousness and faithfulness to his covenant, which gives a boost to Nehemiah's supplication that since God is faithful to His promise, He will gather them and bring them back to Jerusalem[58] when the people turn to Him and learn to keep His laws and observe His decrees.[59] It simply means their return to Him in obedience and faithfulness. So, just as "scattering" them among the nations because of their unfaithfulness is seen as God's punishment to them, "gathering" them and bringing them back to their own land is seen as His own initiative to save them.

5.2.4. Conclusion:

As in the previous group, so also here, God declares His intention to save His people by "gathering" them from the nations. But unlike in the first group, which shows God's direct address to Israel, here He announces His promise of salvation to them indirectly through His prophets. The prophets receive the revelation of His plan of salvation for Israel, and they announce it to the people on God's behalf. Their announcement of God's saving action explains that the scattering and

---

[55] MITCHELL, SMITTH, and BEWAR, *Zechariah*, 292.

[56] RUDOLF, *Ezra und Nehmia*, 105. Nehemiah's prayer of lament touches upon significant motifs in the book of Deuteronomy: Neh 1,5 = Deut 7,9.21 cf. 9,4; Neh 1,8ff. = Deut 30,1-4; Neh 1,10 = Deut 9,29; see RUDOLF, in the same place.

[57] LORING, *Ezra-Nehemiah*, 186-187; see also BECKER, *Esra Nehemia*, 62.

[58] Jerusalem as God's chosen place; see Deut 12,11; 14,12; 16,6.11; 26,2, etc. See LORING, *Ezra-Nehemiah*, 187.

[59] KEIL, *Ezra Nehemiah*, COT 4, 103.

dispersion of the people of Israel among the nations was God's punishment for their unfaithfulness to His laws and decrees, in other words, God did it because of their rebellions and transgressions.

God's plan to gather them and to return them to their own land is not due to their new faithfulness per se, even though this is how Neh 1,9 seems to interpret God's new initiative. Neh 1,9 and Deut 30,1-4 underline faithful adherence to God's commands and statutes as the only way to remain God's people. Thus, by linking God's action of "gathering" the people of Israel with their "return", i.e., their conversion to him, Nehemiah (cf. Deut 30,1-4) gives a theological basis for their return from dispersion and from exile. It should be admitted that although conversion of the people and their return to God is necessary, ultimately it is God's own choice and prerogative to gather them from the nations and to bring them back to their own land because He has compassion and He cares for them. So, if scattering the people of Israel among other nations is characteristic of His judgment, gathering them together and bringing them back to their homeland reveals a love and compassion that far exceeds His judgment. It brings into focus that God never forgets His people.

5.2.5. "I will gather the remnant of my flock"

The texts placed in this group compare God's care for His people with the shepherd's care for His flock and relate to his promise to gather them from the nations into which He drove them. He reveals it first to his prophets, who in turn declare it to the people, giving them hope of their salvation. God addresses to the people of Israel with different and sometimes with endearing expressions, e.g., "remnant of my flock," "house of Israel," "remnant of Israel," those who are "driven away," and "the outcast," indicating his special relationship with them. It also reveals Israel's own experience of His watchful care even if He has exiled and dispersed them in the pagan countries.

Jer 23,3:

וַאֲנִי אֲקַבֵּץ אֶת־שְׁאֵרִית צֹאנִי מִכֹּל הָאֲרָצוֹת אֲשֶׁר־הִדַּחְתִּי אֹתָם שָׁם

וַהֲשִׁבֹתִי אֶתְהֶן עַל־נְוֵהֶן וּפָרוּ וְרָבוּ:

Then I will gather the remnant of my flock out of all the countries where I have driven them; and I will bring them back to their fold, and they shall be fruitful and multiply.

The pronoun וַאֲנִי is attested in MT, but it is considered to be an addition. W. L. Holladay renders it in the emphatic sense, "I on my part," which makes good sense in the context. He observes that the usage of קבץ in the *piel* is the standard verb-form to denote God's action of gathering His scattered people, which is primarily applied to a shepherd's function of gathering his flock together.[60] The word שְׁאֵרִית "remnant" evokes the kingdom and is a critique of the role of the Israelite kings who have not taken care of his people (cf. Mic 2,12).[61] LXX renders מִכֹּל הָאֲרָצוֹת ("from all the countries") in the singular (but see ἀπο γῆς φαρρά in Jer 16,15; 23,8).[62] The next clause אֲשֶׁר־הִדַּחְתִּי אֹתָם שָׁם ("where I have driven them") seems to contradict God's charge against the shepherds, who are blamed for "scattering" His sheep in v.1.[63] Jeremiah perceives the scattering of his people among the nations as punishment. Seen from this perspective, God's action of gathering His flock indicates His abundant love for them, in the constant pastoral care He has for them even when they are being punished.[64] It points to the beginning of a new era for Judah (Israel).[65]

Ezek 28,25:

כֹּה־אָמַר אֲדֹנָי יְהוִֹה בְּקַבְּצִי אֶת־בֵּית יִשְׂרָאֵל מִן־הָעַמִּים אֲשֶׁר נָפֹצוּ בָם
וְנִקְדַּשְׁתִּי בָם לְעֵינֵי הַגּוֹיִם וְיָשְׁבוּ עַל־אַדְמָתָם אֲשֶׁר נָתַתִּי לְעַבְדִּי לְיַעֲקֹב

Thus says Lord GOD: When I gather the house of Israel from the peoples
among whom they are scattered, and manifest my holiness in them in the sight of the nations,
then they shall dwell in their own land which I gave to my servant Jacob.

The verse speaks about God's revelation of His holiness in the eyes of the nations by gathering the people of Israel from their dispersion among the peoples so that they may truly possess the land that was promised to their father Jacob and become one people. It reflects God's promise of giving the Land to Israel and securing its possession. In exilic theology, God's punishment of Israel through exile and dispersion is understood to be temporary, while His gathering and restoring them to their own land is a guarantee of His faithfulness.[66]

Mic 2,12:

אָסֹף אֶאֱסֹף יַעֲקֹב כֻּלָּךְ קַבֵּץ אֲקַבֵּץ שְׁאֵרִית יִשְׂרָאֵל יַחַד אֲשִׂימֶנּוּ כְּצֹאן בָּצְרָה
כְּעֵדֶר בְּתוֹךְ הַדָּבְרוֹ תְּהִימֶנָה מֵאָדָם׃

I will surely gather all of you, O Jacob, I will gather the remnant of Israel; I will set them
together like sheep in a fold, like a flock in its pasture, a noisy multitude of men.

This text of Micah witnesses several text-critical difficulties. MT attests כֻּלָּךְ ("all of you" 2m. sg.), but LXX reads it σὺν πᾶσιν ("with all" adj. indef. dat. m. pl.) and

---

[60] HOLLADAY, *Jeremiah 1*, 614-615.

[61] HOLLADAY, *Jeremiah 1*, 615; see also SMITTH, WARD, and BEWAR, *Micah, Zephaniah*, 67.

[62] STIPP, *Sondergut des Jeremiabuches*, 54.

[63] HOLLADAY, *Jeremiah 1*, 615.

[64] This may reflect an exilic concern and possibly a later interpolation. See MCKANE, *Jeremiah, I-XXV*, Vol. I, 556.

[65] HOLLADAY, *Jeremiah I-XXV*, Vol. I, 615.

[66] FUHS, *Ezechiel II*, 157.

makes "Jacob" the passive object of אָסֹף (*qal* inf. abs. + impf. 1sg.), while MT emphasizes God's action through an inf. + impf. construction, addressing Jacob directly. Vulgate reads בְּצָרָה (I) "enclosure" (MT בְּצְרָה "fold"), whereas BHS suggests reading הַדְּבְרוֹ ("their pasture") instead of MT הַדֹּבֵר as attested also in Symmachus, Theodotion, Targum and Vulgate, while in place of תְּהִימֶנָה (< הום *hiphil* impf. 3f. pl. "be noisy"[67]) BHS conjectures reading MT תְּהִימֶנָה (*qal* impf. 3f. pl.) as תֶּהֱמֶה.[68]

It is the first oracle of salvation in the book of Micah, but in the older structure of Mic 1-3, it is viewed as secondary.[69] The expression שְׁאֵרִית יִשְׂרָאֵל "the remnant[70] of Israel" (cf. Jer 23,3) is put in parallel with "all of you, Jacob"[71] thus, it probably refers to "the survivors of the northern kingdom." The metaphoric description of God's saving action of gathering His flock in a sheepfold points to their present existence in exile. God's action of gathering all of Jacob and the remnants of Israel, like a shepherd who gathers his scattered flock together, visualizes a re-uniting of the divided kingdoms of Israel and Judah as one people.[72] God's action of gathering His people promises the increase of their multitude which further sets off a whole series of consequent actions signaling their restoration.

Mic 4,6:

בַּיּוֹם הַהוּא נְאֻם־יְהוָה אֹסְפָה הַצֹּלֵעָה וְהַנִּדָּחָה אֲקַבֵּצָה וַאֲשֶׁר הֲרֵעֹתִי׃

In that day, says the LORD, I will assemble the lame and gather those
who have been driven away, and those whom I have afflicted.

Mic 4,6 (cf. v.7) describes the promise of God's saving action in metaphoric terms, depicting His care and concern for His people as that of a good shepherd for his flock and it thus relates closely to Mic 2,12. However, despite the thematic similarity of "gathering" between Mic 4,6 and 2,12, the two formulaic expressions, namely, בַּיּוֹם הַהוּא (introductory formula)[73] and נְאֻם־יְהוָה (God's saying formula)[74] in 4,6, display a distinction from Mic 2,12. The indication of time, "on that day," in the introductory formula refers to the time of God's direct

---

[67] KAUTZSCH, *GESENIUS' Hebrew Grammar*, 196-197, §72i.k
[68] KESSLER, *Micha*, 136-137.
[69] KESSLER, *Micha*, 137.
[70] The term "remnant" is rooted in the oracles of disasters, thereby denoting the survivors of a catastrophe, e.g., "no remnant" (Jer 11,23; 50,26; Am 1,8) or "a remnant" (2Kgs 19,4 = Isa 37,4; Jer 8,3; 40,11; etc.), or "rejection of the remnant" (2Kgs 21,14; Isa 14,30; 15,9; etc.); see KESSLER, *Micha*, 139.
[71] KESSLER, *Micha*, 139.
[72] SMITTH, WARD, and BEWAR, *Micah*, 67-68.
[73] KESSLER, *Micha*, 192.
[74] HOSSFELD, *Untersuchungen*, 46-47.

intervention, signalling the end of the period of Israel's punishment (cf. וַאֲשֶׁר
הֲרֵעֹתִי "and those whom I have afflicted" 6bβ). Thus, dispersion of Israel is
viewed as God's own act of judgment against His people, a judgment that He
reverses at the time of His new intervention that brings salvation. This means that
He is going to gather them together from the countries where He dispersed them
and bring them back to Zion (cf. Mic 4,7), a name synonymous with His rule and
security.

Zeph 3,19:

הִנְנִי עֹשֶׂה אֶת־כָּל־מְעַנַּיִךְ בָּעֵת הַהִיא וְהוֹשַׁעְתִּי אֶת־הַצֹּלֵעָה וְהַנִּדָּחָה אֲקַבֵּץ
וְשַׂמְתִּים לִתְהִלָּה וּלְשֵׁם בְּכָל־הָאָרֶץ בָּשְׁתָּם:

Behold, at that time I will deal with all your oppressors and I will save the lame
and gather the outcast and I will change their shame into praise and renown in all the earth.

This text contains some textual critical problems. In place of MT עֹשֶׂה אֶת־כָּל ("I
will deal with"), BHS suggests to insert כָּלָה after עֹשֶׂה ("to make an end with") as
attested in the Targum, and it seems to make better sense.[75] MT בָּעֵת הַהִיא is
supposed to be an addition, while BHS proposes בְּשׁוּבִי אֶת־שְׁבוּתָם ("when I bring
back their captivity") in place of בָּשְׁתָּם ("their shame").

Banished through God's judgment, the exiles enjoy no comfort and blessing in
their dispersion.[76] Yet God promises to gather them (cf. Mic 4,6; Ezek 34,16; Zech
11,16). The exiles are aware that their exile is God's judgment against the land and
its people. Zeph 3,19 depicts God's saving action, which is comparable to a
shepherd's care for his limping and scattered sheep.[77] His promise of salvation for
them opens a wider horizon and recalls Deut 26,17-19, which relates to God's
covenant with His chosen people.[78] Israel's fame and glory above all the nations
(cf. Deut 26,19) will be the result of His blessing for them in the Deuteronomic
promises, referring to His covenant-faithfulness with them. Although God created
all nations and they all equally belong to Him, still, because of His covenant
relationship with Israel, His salvation gives her new dignity, making her "the
object of envy and renown" throughout the earth.[79]

5.2.6. Conclusion:

The preceding texts make it clear that God knows the suffering and oppression of
His people in the countries where He scattered them as punishment, but in His

---

[75] Irsigler, *Zefanja*, 426.

[76] Smitth, Ward, and Bewar, *Zephaniah*, 259.

[77] Vlaardingerbroek, *Zephaniah*, 218.

[78] Irsigler, *Zefanja*, 432.

[79] Smitth, Ward, and Bewar, *Zephaniah*, 259.

compassion He also promises to gather them together. In their dispersion, the people of Israel recognize that this is God's act of judgment upon them. However, their punishment through hardships and misery in alien lands is not God's ultimate motive. He takes a new initiative to gather them and bring them back to their own land. Ezek 28,25 gives another motive in addition to God's compassion for His people, namely, He manifests His holiness to them and to the nations by gathering them together from dispersion. Thus, God's action of gathering Israel together both displays His compassion, care and concern for His people, and reveals his holiness to all.

5.2.7. "He will gather you" (Israel)

In the final address to the people of Israel in Deut 30, Moses reminds them of God's faithfulness to his covenants with them. Although God will punish their disobedience and transgression, scattering them through the countries (cf. Deut 28,36-37),[80] He will still be there to watch over them and will never forget to gather them when they return to Him.[81] Making God's covenantal faithfulness a motive, Moses exhorts them to remain faithful in keeping His laws and observing His decrees.

Deut 30,3:

וְשָׁב יְהוָה אֱלֹהֶיךָ אֶת־שְׁבוּתְךָ וְרִחֲמֶךָ וְשָׁב וְקִבֶּצְךָ מִכָּל־הָעַמִּים
אֲשֶׁר הֱפִיצְךָ, יְהוָה אֱלֹהֶיךָ שָׁמָּה:

Then Lord your GOD will return your captivity, and have compassion upon you,
and he will gather you again from all the peoples where Lord your GOD has scattered you.

Deut 30,4:

אִם־יִהְיֶה נִדַּחֲךָ בִּקְצֵה הַשָּׁמָיִם מִשָּׁם יְקַבֶּצְךָ יְהוָה אֱלֹהֶיךָ וּמִשָּׁם יִקָּחֶךָ:

If your outcasts are in the uttermost parts of heaven,
from there Lord your GOD will gather you, and from there he will bring you.

A few text critical observations seem appropriate, here. LXX renders MT וְשָׁב (שׁוּב qal waw-consec. "he will return") in Deut 30,3 as καὶ ἰάσεται ("and he will heal") and omits second אֱלֹהֶיךָ in יְהוָה אֱלֹהֶיךָ, but the Vulgate omits double divine names. Further, LXX adds κύριος ὁ θεός σου ("the Lord your GOD") to יִקָּחֶךָ ("he will fetch you") in v.4.

---

[80] The people of Israel and Judah were exiled to different lands by their enemies (Assyria and Babylon, respectively) from where they migrated to still other countries, e.g., Phoenicia, Ammon, Moab, Edom, Syria, Assyria, Babylonia, Media, Persia, Elam, Asia Minor, Egypt, Nubia, and elsewhere (cf. 2Kgs 16,17; 25,11; Isa 11,11; Jer 40,11; 41,16; chap. 44; Obad 20; Esth 3,8); see TIGAY, *Deuteronomy*, 266.
[81] Deut 30,1 looks back on Deut 29 (curses) and Deut 28 (blessings).

Deut 30,3-4[82] is a part of the larger unit (30,1-14) in which the exile of the people of Israel overshadows (cf. Deut 29,21ff.) and which emphasizes on God's covenant-faithfulness as the basis for Israel's salvation and restoration. Theologically, it is closely related with the theme of the "new covenant" (cf. Jer 30).[83] Moses reminds the people of Israel of God's blessing and curse upon them. If they listen to his voice and keep his commandments, he will gather the remnant and the outcast (שְׁאֵרִית / הַנִּדָּחָה cf. Mi 2,12; 4,6; Zeph 3,9) and those who are driven away, i.e., scattered (פּוּץ cf. Ezek 11,17; 20,34.41)[84] among the nations, but he will bring them back to their own land from all parts of the earth.[85]

These verses offer the main reason for the exile of Israel and the possibility of their return. Even though they will be punished for their disobedience and be exiled and be dispersed in the countries, when they return to him and commit themselves to "keep his laws and observe his decrees," the LORD their God, being faithful to his covenant-promises, will gather them together and bring them back to their homeland. Here their "return to the LORD" (Deut 30,2 cf. 4,30)[86] denotes a "change of heart" and "inner renewal" (cf. Jer 31,33; 32,39-41; Ezek 36,24.27),[87] which is seen as a condition for His saving action for them. Moses reminds the people of God's faithfulness to his covenant-promises if the people are willing to keep his laws and observe his decrees faithfully (compare v.6; cf. vv.16.20; 6,5).[88] When they show true conversion, God will show His compassion and love and gather them from the nations where He scattered them and bring them back to their own land. The Deuteronomist deals succinctly with the theme of blessing and curse here and reveals His theology of exile and return.

---

[82] Cf. Neh 1,9; Zech 8,7-8.

[83] BRAULIK, *Deuteronomium II*, 216.

[84] NIELSEN, *Deuteronomium*, 271.

[85] From "utmost parts of heaven" denotes from any part of the world. It shows unlimited power and control of God over the world; cf. NIELSEN, *Deuteronomium*, 271.

[86] "Return to the LORD" (Deut 30,2) is a prerequisite condition for God's saving action (Deut 30,3-4). Unlike the prophets, Torah's understanding of the concept of "return" is different. It is something that happens after a punishment. When people disobey, God will punish them, but when they return to Him, He will reverse their punishment and restore and save them. Developing this idea further, the prophets (and the classical Judaism) called upon the people to return to the LORD before it was too late. Thus, they go far beyond this, even to the point of averting the punishment itself (see TIGAY, *Deuteronomy*, 54). Deut 30,3-4 looks back to Deut 4,30-31 which exhorts the Israelites to return to the LORD and obey Him; thus, both their return and their obedience rest on the nature of the compassionate God (Deut 4,30). It underlines this state of affairs that Israel's failure and the resultant judgment of the impassionate God (cf. Deut 4,24) is always an open possibility, but it does not close an access to His mercy (Deut 4,30). So, "return" necessarily also includes "restoration."

[87] BRAULIK, *Deuteronomium II*, 218.

[88] Here, God's compassion and love for Israel is directly linked with her obedience to him; see BRAULIK, *Deuteronomium II*, 218.

5.2.8. He will gather the dispersed of Judah

There are five texts that refer to the dispersion of Israel/Judah as God's act of judgment against them, and also reveal His promise to gather them together because of His compassion for them. These promises of God's salvation to Israel reflect keen observations of the prophets on how God executes His judgment against His people and shows His care and compassion for them.

Isa 11,12:

וְנָשָׂא נֵס לַגּוֹיִם וְאָסַף נִדְחֵי יִשְׂרָאֵל וּנְפֻצוֹת יְהוּדָה יְקַבֵּץ מֵאַרְבַּע כַּנְפוֹת הָאָרֶץ׃

He will raise an ensign for the nations, and will assemble the outcasts of Israel,
And gather the dispersed of Judah from the four corners of the earth.

It was almost impossible for the people of Judah and Israel, those who were exiled, to think that they would return to their homeland. This is what Isa 11,12 displays when it describes the role of the coming Messiah, who will assemble the outcasts of Israel, gather the dispersed of Judah, and bring them back to their homeland. Indeed, God will signal to the far off nations (cf. Is 5,26; 11,10) and they will heed it, but the call is not for Israel.[89] However, through their prayers, the home-coming of His people will be possible; in other words, the nations will cooperate in God's action of gathering Israel and be helpful in her return to their homeland.[90]

God's saving action of gathering the dispersed of Israel is similar to a shepherd's action of gathering his scattered sheep in the fold.[91] Isaiah uses this metaphor as a technical term to describe God's action of gathering the exiled,[92] which will become a remarkable sign for the nations (Isa 5,26; 11,10 cf. 49,22). The word פוּץ refers to the dispersed of Judah (cf. Jer 40,15). It shows that to be cut off and separated from one's own place and people and living in a foreign land, under a foreign ruler is a great burden and pain.[93] By placing the "outcasts of Israel" and the "dispersed of Judah" in a parallel, Isaiah focuses on the future reunion and reconciliation of the two broken kingdoms of Israel and Judah as one people (v.13), which will be the result of Messiah's action of gathering them

---

[89] WILDBERGER, *Jesaja 1-12*, 469.
[90] WILDBERGER, *Jesaja 1-12*, 469. Against the background of the preceding context (stump of Jesse 11,1-9), which speaks of his peaceful and just kingdom, the powerful nations will give up their arms and aggression which will create an amenable atmosphere for the exiled and dispersed of Israel to return to their homeland from distant lands. See BEUKEN, *Jesaja 1-12*, 319.
[91] Isa 13,14; 40,11; Jer 23,3; 49,5
[92] Cf. outcasts of Israel/dispersed of Judah (נדח) in Deut 30,3; Isa 27,13; 56,8; Jer 40,12; 43,5; 49,5.36; Zeph 3,19; Ps 147,2; Neh 1,9; Sir 51,12; (פוּץ): Jer 40,15; Ezek 11,17; 20,34.41; 28,25; 34,6.12); see BEUKEN, *Jesaja 1-12*, 319; see also WILDBERGER, *Jesaja 1-12*, 469-470.
[93] WILDBERGER, *Jesaja 1-12*, 470.

together. Here, gathering them together from all four corners of the earth signifies the completeness of His action as well as a remarkable increase in their number.[94]

The gathering of the dispersed of Israel/Judah is not understood merely in a geo-political sense, namely, their gathering from the lands of their exile and from the farthest countries where they have been dispersed. It is also interpreted in a religious sense that highlights God's concern to gather them and bring them back to Him. Here קבץ (= אסף "to gather together") carries not only a geo-political sense (i.e., gathering from exile) but also a theological one, namely, conversion of heart and return to God. In this sense, the dispersion of the people denotes their estrangement from the LORD and their distancing themselves from Him. So, a geo-political condition (dispersions/exile) of his people becomes a symbol for the prophet to announce Theo-centric action (conversion/salvation) of the Messiah. Lack of any clear reference to their homeland in relation to his gathering and bringing back, suggests truly spiritual nature of his action.

Isa 40,11:

כְּרֹעֶה עֶדְרוֹ יִרְעֶה בִּזְרֹעוֹ יְקַבֵּץ טְלָאִים וּבְחֵיקוֹ יִשָּׂא עָלוֹת יְנַהֵל׃

He will feed his flock like a shepherd; he will gather the lambs in his arm,
He will carry them in his bosom, and gently lead those that are with young.

From a text-critical point of view, BHS suggests reading וּבְחֵיקוֹ ("in his bosom") without *waw*-conjunctive.[95] A logical sequence of the four strophes of Isa 40,11 is usually considered to consist of independent clauses.[96] It describes God's care for His people, comparable to a shepherd's care and concern for his flock, especially toward those who are weak and need help. Among the various aspects of His care for the sheep, His activity of gathering the lambs is emphasised in particular.[97] It reflects the concern of the Second Isaiah regarding Israel's future, which faced the danger of exile.[98] In view of the threat to exile, the prophet assures them of God's promise to gather them and provide them security in His great kindness and mercy, and to lead them back to their homeland,[99] eliciting joy and hope for them. It

---

[94] WILDBERGER, *Jesaja 1-12*, 470-471.

[95] LXX attests *waw*-conjunctive but KJV, NIV and RSV render it without it.

[96] KOOLE, *Isaiah 40-48*, 77.

[97] "Gathering the lambs in the arms" is not a usual expression, and "to carry in the arms" would be more appropriate expression. Therefore, in the context, the use of קבץ to express, "he will gather the lambs in his arms," is a peculiar expression that nicely parallels with the next clause, "He will carry them in his bosom." It points to the significance of this particular action that God performs for His people to protect them and to give them security.

[98] KOOLE, *Isaiah 40-48*, 77.

[99] God's promise of leading His people back home reflects the description of Jacob's home-coming in Gen 33, see ELLIGER, *DeuteroJesaja 1*, 38.

emphasizes the goodness and power of God, who is both the ruler and the shepherd.[100]

Isa 56,8:

נְאֻם אֲדֹנָי יְהוִה מְקַבֵּץ נִדְחֵי יִשְׂרָאֵל עוֹד אֲקַבֵּץ עָלָיו לְנִקְבָּצָיו׃

Thus says Lord GOD, who gathers the outcasts of Israel,
I will gather yet others to him besides those already gathered.

The oracle begins with a signatory formula נְאֻם אֲדֹנָי יְהוִה, that points to the significance of God's message. נִדְחֵי יִשְׂרָאֵל ("the outcasts of Israel" cf. Isa 11,12; 16,3; 27,13 cf. Ezek 34,16) refers to the captives of Israel, who seeking refuge from fear and the panic of war, were carried into exile in addition to those who were dispersed to other countries. The imagery of a shepherd's care for his flock lies in the background to describe God's action of gathering the Dispersed (Isa 66,20) of Israel.[101] The prepositional phrase עָלָיו ("to it") refers to Israel and the preposition לְ in לְנִקְבָּצָיו is explicative, which is equivalent to עַל־נִקְבָּצָיו and points to the abundant action of God's salvation.[102] God's gathering of the outcasts of Israel goes beyond the dispersed of the house of Israel to include also the non-Israelites together with God's people (cf. Jn 10,16). This phenomenon will swell the number of the gathered significantly.[103] It shows that although God's saving action concerns primarily the dispersed of Israel, it does not rule out gathering other nations who share in His saving action (cf. Eph 2,11f.).

Jer 31,10:

שִׁמְעוּ דְבַר־יְהוָה גּוֹיִם וְהַגִּידוּ בָאִיִּים מִמֶּרְחָק וְאִמְרוּ מְזָרֵה יִשְׂרָאֵל
יְקַבְּצֶנּוּ וּשְׁמָרוֹ כְּרֹעֶה עֶדְרוֹ׃

Hear the word of the LORD, O nations, and declare it in the coastlands afar off; Say,
He who scattered Israel will gather him, and will keep him as a shepherd keeps his flock.

MT וְאִמְרוּ is considered to be an addition, here. God's action of gathering the scattered people of Israel is compared to a shepherd's care and protection for his sheep, making it known even to far-off shores. The imperative nature of this verse in addressing the nations signifies that God's saving action is not restricted to the scattered people of Israel alone, although it is His primary focus. It supposes to gather also the non-Israelites. They will also share in His salvation. Thus, Jer 31,10 shows its affinity with the Second Isaiah (cf. 56,8,).[104] Jer 31,10 distinguishes

---

[100] ELLIGER, *DeuteroJesaja 1*, 38.

[101] KOOLE, *Isaiah*, Part 3, Vol. 3, Isaiah 56-66, (2001), 28. MARTI (*Jesaja*, 365) thinks that "dispersion" of Israel in this place also includes the Proselytes.

[102] DELITZSCH, *Isaiah*, COT 7, 539.

[103] DELITZSCH, *Isaiah*, COT 7, 539.

[104] HOLLADAY, *Jeremiah 2*, 162.

מְזָרֵה יִשְׂרָאֵל ("the one who scattered Israel") as referring to God's action and implies that it was He who punished Israel. Nevertheless, His action of gathering them together and taking care of them far exceeds His punishment and opens a new perspective for Israel and for the nations.

Ps 107,3:

וּמֵאֲרָצוֹת קִבְּצָם מִמִּזְרָח וּמִמַּעֲרָב מִצָּפוֹן וּמִיָּם׃

And those he gathered in from the lands, from the east and from the west,
from the north and from the south.

MT וּמֵאֲרָצוֹת ("from the lands") is omitted in LXX and Syriac adds וּמִכָּל to it, and MSS, LXX and Syriac add *waw*-conjunctive to מִצָּפוֹן ("from the north") and BHS proposes וּמִיָּמִין ("from the south") instead of MT וּמִיָּם ("from the sea") which seems to be a better reading of the text.[105] But Allen thinks that there is no need for this emendation.[106]

Psalm 107,1-32 reflects a personal thanksgiving of the redeemed of the LORD at cultic liturgy (cf. Isa 62,12; compare 35,9f.; 51,10; 56,8; 63,4; also 49,12).[107] On account of the reference to all four corners of the earth, C. A. Briggs and E. G. Briggs maintain that v.3 does not specifically speak about the deliverance of the people of Israel from their enemies and that too, not necessarily their restoration from the exile but in a very general sense.[108] Gunkel is of the opinion that v.3 speaks about the Jews whom God has gathered together from all directions to offer thanksgiving worship to him.[109] In any case, the song of the thanksgiving to God for his deliverance affirms his Lordship and his rule over the entire universe.[110]

5.2.9. Conclusion:

The above texts from Isaiah, Jeremiah and Psalm 107 show God's saving action in gathering the exiled and the dispersed of Israel which is compared with a shepherd's care in gathering his flock together and husbanding them. The gathering of the dispersed reveals God's goodness, i.e., His mercy and love for them. Despite punishing them by exile, God creates a favourable condition in the countries of exile so as to allow their gathering and return to their land. He lets other people join them and share in His salvation when He brings them back as well. His gathering together opens a new perspective, in which other nations also

---

[105] KRAUS, *Psalmen 60-150*, 909.

[106] ALLEN, *Psalms 101-150*, 58.

[107] KRAUS, *Psalmen 60-150*, 911; ALLEN, *Psalms, 101-150*, 60; see also KITTEL, *Die Psalmen*, 392; DELITZSCH, *Die Psalmen*, 664.

[108] BRIGGS and BRIGGS, *Psalms*, 358.

[109] GUNKEL, *Die Psalmen*, 471.

[110] ALLEN, *Psalms 101-150*, 62.

partake. God's concern for those in need of help reflects His true pastoral care; He gathers them together, leads them from all parts of the globe, and other nations join them. This becomes a reason for giving thanks to God, which also attests to His goodness and Lordship over the nations.

5.3. God's action toward the nations
5.3.1. "I will gather yet others" (the nations)

The previous section described how God's action of gathering His people from dispersion also includes other peoples. However, these texts do not address the nations directly. God's promise of gathering them together is articulated clearly only in the following texts. There are three texts that describe His action of gathering the nations. In view of God's special choice of Israel (cf. Deut 4,34), whom He made His own people and possession (cf. Ex 19,5; Deut 7,6; 14,2; 26,18), and whom He promises to gather together and bring them back to their own home land, his announcement to gather also other nations, who are considered to be Israel's oppressors and enemies, is quite surprising. Nevertheless, it belongs to His plan of salvation for all peoples and nations.

Isa 56,8:

נְאֻם אֲדֹנָי יְהוִֹה מְקַבֵּץ נִדְחֵי יִשְׂרָאֵל עוֹד אֲקַבֵּץ עָלָיו לְנִקְבָּצָיו׃

Thus says the Lord GOD, who gathers the outcasts of Israel,
I will gather yet others to him besides those already gathered.

The Third-Isaiah begins with the assurance of God's salvation, and the repetition of the verb קבץ is noteworthy (cf. 56,8). Here מְקַבֵּץ (*piel* ptc. m. sg.) relates to God's action of gathering together the outcasts of Israel (cf. 11,12), לְנִקְבָּצָיו (3rd occurrence) refers to fulfillment of this action of gathering, and עוֹד אֲקַבֵּץ ("I will gather yet others," 2nd occurrence) refers to his action of gathering other nations, even the eunuchs and the Proselytes,[111] giving them a hope of salvation as promised in vv.1-9.[112] So, עוֹד אֲקַבֵּץ in 56,8 relates to God's motive to "gather", which concerns not only the exiles of Israel but also the non-Israelites, who eventually increase the number of His people (cf. 49,29).[113] In this way, God salvation reaches out beyond the confines of His people Israel to include other peoples and nations, across geo-political boundaries of Israel (66,19-20). By this, He proves the faithfulness of His promises (cf. vv.1-7). In this plan to gather other nations in addition to Israel, God reveals something new, namely, He includes

---

[111] MARTI, *Das Buch Jesaja*, 364.
[112] KOOKE, *Isaiah 56-66*, 25
[113] MARTI, *Das Buch Jesaja*, 364.

other nations in His salvation promised for his chosen people, Israel. Thus, gathering "yet others" denotes God's choice for the nations in addition to Israel.

Isa 66,18:

וְאָנֹכִ֗י מַעֲשֵׂיהֶם֙ וּמַחְשְׁבֹֽתֵיהֶ֔ם בָּאָ֕ה לְקַבֵּ֥ץ אֶת־כָּל־הַגּוֹיִ֖ם וְהַלְּשֹׁנ֑וֹת
וּבָ֖אוּ וְרָא֥וּ אֶת־כְּבוֹדִֽי׃

For I (know) their works and their thoughts, and I am going to gather all nations
and tongues and they shall come and shall see my glory.

The syntax of this verse is complex and, as Delitzsch argues, the meaning and relation of וְאָנֹכִי ("and/but I") to כְּבוֹדִי ("my glory") is not easy to establish.[114] Targum, Syriac, Sahidic and some other versions add יָדַעְתִּי and translate וְאָנֹכִי יָדַעְתִּי ("and I know").[115] BHS suggests deleting MT מַעֲשֵׂיהֶם וּמַחְשְׁבֹתֵיהֶם ("their deeds and thoughts"). LXX (including Syriac and Vulgate) reads MT וּבָאוּ as ἔρχομαι ("I am going") and BHS suggests to read בָּא but Delitzsch argues that there is no need to amend it because it can still be taken in a neuter sense.[116]

Isa 66,18 is the beginning of the concluding section of the Third Isaiah and it speaks about the end-time. V.18 begins with a note on the return or the conversion of the nations and their list is given in v.19. God is going to gather the nations and languages of peoples (cf. Dan 3,4.7 also Gen 10,5.20.31). This gathering the nations denotes their conversion and return to him. In this sense, "I am coming to gather all nations" signals participation of the nations in God's future salvation.[117] Although some commentators see this action as the nations' being gathered for judgment (vv.15-17; cf. Joel 4,16), beginning from v.19f., it is clear that the purpose is not judgment but a pilgrimage of the nations to His holy mountain, Jerusalem, which is a sign of their salvation (Joel 4,18; Zech 14,4-10; Isa 7,11).[118]

Ezek 29,13:

כִּ֣י כֹּ֤ה אָמַר֙ אֲדֹנָ֣י יְהוִ֔ה מִקֵּ֖ץ אַרְבָּעִ֣ים שָׁנָ֑ה אֲקַבֵּ֖ץ אֶת־מִצְרַ֔יִם
מִן־הָעַמִּ֖ים אֲשֶׁר־נָפֹ֥צוּ שָֽׁמָּה׃

For thus says the Lord GOD: At the end of forty years I will gather the Egyptians
from the peoples among whom they were scattered.

Ezek 29,13 is the only passage in the book of Ezekiel in which God's promise to gather Egypt is mentioned explicitly. His declaration to gather the Egyptians, at the end of forty years of judgment, from their dispersion among the other countries gives an impetus to Egypt's future restoration, making it a lower kingdom.

---

[114] DELITZSCH, *Isaiah*, COT 7, 635.

[115] DELITZSCH, *Isaiah*, COT 7, 635; BARTHÉLEMY (ed.), *Preliminary and Interim Report*, 171.

[116] DELITZSCH, *Isaiah*, COT 7, 635.

[117] KOOKE, *Isaiah 56-66*, 518.

[118] KOOKE, *Isaiah 56-66*, 518; MARTI, *Das Buch Jesaja*, 412.

The expression מִקֵּץ אַרְבָּעִים שָׁנָה "at the end of forty years," denoting the period of Egypt's punishment, recalls the forty years of Israel's wandering in the desert (cf. Ex 16,35; Deut 8,2.4, etc.). It is consciously applied here (compare 4,4)[119] as a prelude to God's announcement of salvation for Egypt. Israel's forty years of wandering in the wilderness was not a punishment, but rather a time of probation when God tested Israel's fidelity and rendered her obedient to Him. It was a time of her "return" to Him and a place of her "knowledge" of Him. Its usage to describe the period of Egypt's dispersion serves a similar purpose.

God's promise to restore Israel, i.e., to gather her people from the nations where He dispersed them, and bring them back to their own land (Ezek 11,17; 20,34.41; 28,25), is here applied directly to the restoration and salvation of Egypt.[120] God reveals His saving action for Israel by promising to gather her from the nations with a "mighty arm" (Ezek 20,33.34; cf. Deut 26,8), bringing the dispersed into the "desert" (= exile) of the nations to execute His judgment upon them (Ezek 20,35f.), as He did with their ancestors when He brought them out of Egypt into the desert (Ezek 20,36). In the same way, God judges Egypt and punishes her people by dispersing them among the nations for forty years; nevertheless, He promises to gather them together and bring them back to Pathros, their homeland (Ezek 29,14). This shows a close similarity between God's dealing with Israel and with her archenemy, Egypt.

5.4. God gathers Israel and the Nations for judgment

The texts discussed so far, have used קבץ, denoting God's action to gather and save both Israel and the nations, Egypt in particular. The following passages relate to his action of gathering Israel and the nations for judgment. Here, there are equal numbers of occurrences relating to Israel and to the nations.

5.4.1. Israel

Ezek 16,37:

לָכֵן הִנְנִי מְקַבֵּץ אֶת־כָּל־מְאַהֲבַיִךְ אֲשֶׁר עָרַבְתְּ עֲלֵיהֶם
וְאֵת כָּל־אֲשֶׁר אָהַבְתְּ עַל כָּל־אֲשֶׁר שָׂנֵאת
וְקִבַּצְתִּי אֹתָם עָלַיִךְ מִסָּבִיב וְגִלֵּיתִי עֶרְוָתֵךְ אֲלֵהֶם

Therefore, behold, I will gather all your lovers, with whom you took pleasure,
All those you loved and all those you loathed;
I will gather them against you from every side,
And I will uncover your nakedness to them, that they may see all your nakedness.

---

[119] ZIMMERLI, *Ezechiel 25-48*, 712-713.
[120] ZIMMERLI, *Ezechiel 25-48*, 713.

Ezek 16 is a metaphor, describing Israel's relation to God. On the one hand, it depicts God's love and fidelity for Israel, and on the other hand it illustrates Israel's infidelity and sin because of her enchantment to the gods of Egypt and other nations. It presents a picture of a wife that is unfaithful to her spouse (God), as she persisted in playing the whore with other lords (cf. Hos 1,2) and foreign powers (cf. Ezek 16,15-34)[121] instead of relying on the Lord GOD. She has defiled herself by her arrogance, ingratitude and lack of faith, despite all that the Lord GOD did for her (Ezek 20; 23; cf. 20,22).

Both Israel's worship of other gods and her foreign policy reveal her whoring-attitude. But God will gather her so-called "lovers"[122] in judgment against her (cf. vv.35-43). Ezek 16,37 speaks about this judgment against her. He will gather all nations with whom she indulged in whoring, i.e., seeking friendship and alliance, while betraying her loyalty to Him. These nations will not only witness her humiliation, but they will actively take part in plundering her (16,39f.).[123] Ezekiel does not specifically speak about the national catastrophe of 587 B.C. in this oracle; therefore, it may only be presumed that he is speaking about her punishment in a general sense. Pohlmann is of the opinion that "your lovers" in the text denotes the Babylonians, who hem in Jerusalem from all sides, loot and destroy her, and carry her population into exile to Babylon.[124]

Ezek 22,20:

קְבֻצַת כֶּסֶף וּנְחֹשֶׁת וּבַרְזֶל וְעוֹפֶרֶת וּבְדִיל אֶל־תּוֹךְ כּוּר לָפַחַת־עָלָיו אֵשׁ לְהַנְתִּיךְ
כֵּן אֶקְבֹּץ בְּאַפִּי וּבַחֲמָתִי וְהִנַּחְתִּי וְהִתַּכְתִּי אֶתְכֶם:

As men gather silver and bronze and iron and lead and tin into a furnace,
to blow the fire upon it in order to melt it;
So I will gather you in my anger and in my wrath, and I will put you in and melt you.

Ezek 22 describes the present sins of Jerusalem, namely, bloodshed and idolatry (vv.1-5), oppression by her rulers (vv.6-12), and desecration (vv.13-16), all of which makes Israel a fitting case for refinement by the fire of judgment.[125] Thematically, it is related to Ezek 16 and 23 (cf. v.22), but while Ezek 16 describes

---

[121] POHLMANN, *Hesekiel 1-19*, 227. Against the dangers of foreign invasion, especially from Assyria and Babylon, Israel's diplomatic relations with Egypt, reflects what the book of Deuteronomy and the Prophets term as Israel's reliance on Egypt's horses and chariots, cf. Deut 17,16; 20,1; Isa 30,16; Jer 51,21; Hos 15,4; see also Zech 12,4; Ezek 39,20.

[122] It is a reference to the nations around Israel with which she entered into alliance, rejecting her reliance on the Lord GOD. ZIMMERLI (*Ezechiel 1-24*, 360) thinks that מְאַהֲבַיִךְ "your lovers" does not denote peoples/nation with whom Israel is in league, but rather refers indirectly to her effort to build a community in defiance of God's will.

[123] ZIMMERLI, *Ezechiel 1-24*, 360.

[124] POHLMANN, *Hesekiel 1-19*, 229.

[125] KEIL, *Ezekiel*, Vol. 9, 178-180.

Israel's sin in metaphors, Ezek 22 is more explicit, and describes them without metaphor or symbolism.

יַ֫עַן הֱיוֹת כֻּלְּכֶם לְסִגִים ("because all of you have become dross" v.19) gives a motive for gathering the house of Israel in Jerusalem. The house of Israel has become dross, a worthless metal, and therefore God will gather her in Jerusalem and refine her in the fire of His judgment.[126] The text hints at the imminent siege of Jerusalem by Nebuchadnezzar of Babylon and the plunder, destruction, and burning of the city by his army that takes place in 587 B.C.

Hos 8,10:

גַּם כִּי־יִתְנוּ בַגּוֹיִם עַתָּה אֲקַבְּצֵם וַיָּחֵלּוּ מְּעָט מִמַּשָּׂא מֶלֶךְ שָׂרִים:

Though they hire allies among the nations, I will soon gather them up
And they shall cease for a little while from anointing king and princes.

Hos 8,8-10 describes Israel's attempt to acquire political alliances with other nations. It poses a serious threat to her covenant relationship with the LORD because it undermines Israel's faith on allegiance to Him, just as her idolatry violates her singular relationship with Him. Shuttling diplomatic activity in order to strike a political alliance with other nations (Hos 8,9.10), e.g., Assyria and Egypt (Hos 8,9.13, respectively; cf. 12,1), has reduced the king and princes of Israel to the level of the pagans, because their activity amounts to political prostitution.[127] Israel has paid tributes to her ally to win support, and thus she has freely sold herself,[128] seriously endangering the monarchy.[129]

In times when war was threatened, political alliances with the neighbouring nations became a constant temptation for Israel, seeking help from powerful nations instead of relying on the LORD (cf. Hos 14,4). God will gather the people of Israel for judgment because they breached this trust and fidelity to Him (cf. Zeph 3,8; Joel 4,2).[130] That is, Israel will be diminished under the oppression[131] of the same ally (Assyria) in whom she sought her security, and will suffer loss of political sovereignty and her monarchy.[132] Her political alliances will not be able to avert the impending catastrophe and to keep her sovereignty intact.

---

[126] FUHS, *Ezechiel 1*, 119.

[127] FREEDMAN, *Hosea*, 482; see also DIESSLER, *Zwölf Propheten*, 39

[128] This is a reference to the tribute that Israel paid to Assyria; see FREEDMAN, *Hosea*, 506.

[129] ROBINSON, *Die kleinen Propheten*, 33.

[130] WOLFF, *Dodeka Propheten 1, Hosea*, 184.

[131] MACHINTOSH, *Hosea*, 320-321.

[132] MACHINTOSH favours the rendering, "the king of princes," for מֶלֶךְ שָׂרִים denotes the ruler of Assyria, see his *Hosea*, 321. The RSV translates it, "king and princes" although שָׂרִים is not joined by any conjunction. A rendering "king and princes," makes it refer to the 'house of Israel,' which seems to make better sense in the context because it speaks about its consequence, i.e., the loss of her king and princes due to her political subjugation.

5.4.2. The Nations

Joel 4,2:

וְקִבַּצְתִּי אֶת־כָּל־הַגּוֹיִם וְהוֹרַדְתִּים אֶל־עֵמֶק יְהוֹשָׁפָט וְנִשְׁפַּטְתִּי עִמָּם שָׁם עַל־עַמִּי
וְנַחֲלָתִי יִשְׂרָאֵל אֲשֶׁר פִּזְּרוּ בַגּוֹיִם וְאֶת־אַרְצִי חִלֵּקוּ:

I will gather all the nations and bring them down to the valley of Jehoshaphat;
there I will enter into judgment against them concerning my inheritance, my people Israel;
For they scattered my people among the nations and divided up my land.

Joel 4,2 reveals God's goodness to His people (cf. 4,1) by announcing His intention to gather all nations for judgment when he appears as the judge who brings charges against and judges them.[133] Here God's salvation for His people is closely linked with His judgment against the nations. His promise is to gather all the foreign nations (cf. Ezek 38; Zeph 3,8; Hos 8,10; 9,6) in the valley of Jehoshaphat. Because of its narrowness, this location is more of a rivulet than a valley.[134] Wolff observes that except for Joel 4,2, the Old Testament does not contain knowledge of the "valley of Jehoshaphat," which came to be known as the "Kedron Valley" (cf. Jn 18,1) only beginning in the 4th century A.D. Jehoshaphat is translated as "God judges" or "God has judged" so, symbolically, it denotes His judgment.[135] The "valley of Jehoshaphat" is used as a rhetorical device by the prophet to emphasize God's judgment against the nations because of their role in the dispersion of Israel. Joel 4,2 is also an allusion to the siege, capture, plunder and destruction of Jerusalem by Nebuchadnezzar, as well as the deportation of her inhabitants into exile, including those who fled to other lands, especially to Egypt, after the murder of Gedaliah in 586 B.C. (cf. Ezek 11,17; 12,15; 20,34; 28,25; 36,19). However, the text does not clearly indicate whether the deportation of northern Israel is also meant to be included in this reference. All the same, the final clause "and divided up my land" apparently refers to occupations of some of the territories of Judah by Ammon, Edom, and Philistia after 586 B.C., and to the settlements in northern Israel after the fall of Samaria in 722 B.C.[136]

Mic 4,12:

וְהֵמָּה לֹא יָדְעוּ מַחְשְׁבוֹת יְהוָה וְלֹא הֵבִינוּ עֲצָתוֹ כִּי קִבְּצָם כֶּעָמִיר גֹּרְנָה:

But they do not know the thoughts of God, they do not understand his plan,
That he has gathered them as sheaves to the threshing floor.

Mic 4,12 continues the motif of "God's dealing with the nations," touched upon by the preceding v.11, which speaks about the nations who are gathered (אָסַף) against

---

[133] DIESSLER, *Joël*, 83. See also CRENSHAW, *Joel*, 174.

[134] WOLFF, *Dodekapropheten 2*, 91.

[135] SMITTH, WARD, and BEWAR, *Joel*, 127.

[136] SMITTH, WARD, and BEWAR, *Joel*, 129.

Israel. Mic 4,14 declares that the nations are unaware of God's thought (מַחְשְׁבוֹת) that in gathering (קְבִּץ) them together against Israel, as well as in their dealings with her, they accomplish His own plan (עֵצָה) for both for Israel and themselves.[137] Although they are unaware of it, God's plan is clear. He is concerned about the salvation of the oppressed who, at the same time, stand in judgment against the oppressors (cf. Mic 2,3). On the other hand, Mic 4,12 seems to indicate indirectly that at the destruction of Jerusalem the nations rejoiced. However, although Jerusalem stands judged by this event, the nations are guilty of taking advantage of her weakness. Therefore, they are equally guilty (cf. Mic 1,2; also 5,14).[138] The significant point is this, that even if they gather against Zion, it is God who gathers them to judgment.

Zeph 3,8:

לָכֵן חַכּוּ־לִי נְאֻם־יְהוָה לְיוֹם קוּמִי לְעַד כִּי מִשְׁפָּטִי לֶאֱסֹף גּוֹיִם לְקָבְצִי
מַמְלָכוֹת לִשְׁפֹּךְ עֲלֵיהֶם זַעְמִי כֹּל חֲרוֹן אַפִּי כִּי בְּאֵשׁ קִנְאָתִי תֵּאָכֵל כָּל־הָאָרֶץ:

Therefore wait for me, says the LORD, for the day when I arise as a witness.
For, my decision is to assemble nations, to gather kingdoms,
To pour out upon them my indignation, all the heat of my anger;
For in the fire of my jealous wrath all the earth shall be consumed.

LXX and Vulgate render MT חַכּוּ (Wait! impv. pl.) as ὑπόμεινόν (= חַכִּי (impv. sg.), which is addressed to Jerusalem (cf. לָכֵן). Further, LXX (and Syriac) reads MT לְעַד as εἰς μαρτύριον ("as a witness"), but BHS suggests לְעֵד ("as witness"). Furthermore, instead of MT לְקָבְצִי (qal inf.) LXX, Syriac and Targum attest τοῦ εἰσδέξασθαι (= לְקָבֵּץ (qal ptc. m. sg.). On the other hand, BHS suggests reading עֲלֵיכֶם (2m. sg.) in the place of MT עֲלֵיהֶם (3m. pl.). Thus, God's indignation, which He is going to pour out upon nations and kingdoms (MT), is to be poured upon Jerusalem. But God's judgment does refer to the nations and kingdoms.

Zeph 3,8 is an announcement of judgment against the nations and kingdoms, consequent upon vv.6-7 (cf. לָכֵן). "On the day"[139] God will stand up for their judgment; He will attest "witnesses" against them in order "to judge" them (cf. vv.6-7; also see Lev 5,1). It means that God will pour out His indignation and anger upon the nations (cf. Hos 5, 1; Jer 10,25; Isa 42,25; Ps 69,25; 79,6). Thus, the underlying motive to assemble (אָסֹף) the nations and gather (קְבִּץ) the

---

[137] KESSLER, Micha, 209.
[138] KESSLER, Micha, 212.
[139] It may be referring to the "day of Jerusalem" when Nebuchadnezzar of Babylon laid siege on Jerusalem and plundered it during the reign of Zedekiah (597-586 BC); see IRSIGLER, Zefanja, 353.

kingdoms[140] is to judge them (cf. Hos 8,10; Ezek 20,34; 22,19f.) because they gathered together against a weak city and instead of coming to her aid, they stood aloof and took pleasure when she was devastated and plundered by the most terrible nation.[141] Here, God's action of gathering the nations and kingdoms points to His judgment of Judah and all the nations (cf. Hos 10,10) when He pours out His anger on her (Ezek 21,36; 22,31).[142] But while His judgment will bring salvation to Judah, He will hold all nations and kingdoms (cf. Jer 1,15-16) responsible for their dealing with her. The universal and eschatological nature of His judgment seems to be the reason for not specifically mentioning the gathering of the nations and the kingdoms against Jerusalem or against Israel in one particular place in this text.[143]

5.4.3. Conclusion:

In these texts, God's action of gathering the nations indicates His motive for judging them. They are guilty of scattering His people among the nations (cf. Joel 4,2). It is a clear reference to Nebuchadnezzar of Babylon, who carried away Judah's population into exile (cf. Ezek 21,23-37; 25; Obad 11-14; Nah 3,10) while her neighbours stood by and enjoyed watching her disaster without coming to her aid. One aspect of judging these nations is that God will punish them in the same manner as they treated her (cf. Mic 4,12).[144] In the last instance (cf. Zeph 3,8), the text speaks of God's conclusive decision to gather the nations to face the anger of His judgment, symbolised by 'fire'.

God gathers Israel to judgment because of her unfaithfulness that is manifest in her utter disregard of His laws and ordinances. She perpetrated bloodshed, violence, and oppression, as well as desecrating worship and relying on the nations rather than on the LORD. He gathers the nations as well to face His judgment because they have fully disregarded the weak and vulnerable condition of Jerusalem in acting against His people. His judgment shows no partiality either against Israel or against the nations.

---

[140] There is an interesting parallelism in the usage of אסף / קבץ (assemble/gather together) here cf. Isa 43,9; Joel 2,16; Mic 2,12; Hab 2,5. See IRSIGLER, *Zefanja*, 354.

[141] The war of the nations against Jerusalem as a means of judgment against the nations in Zeph 3, 8 goes back to exilic and post-exilic times cf. Isa 29,1-8; Ezek 38-39; Zech 12,2-6.9; 14,2-3 (cf. 1.19) so also judgment against the nations as announcement of the Day of the LORD as found in Obad 15a.16; Joel 4,1-3.9-14; Mic 4,12. See IRSIGLER, *Zefanja*, 357.

[142] IRSIGLER, *Zefanja*, 356.

[143] SMITTH, WARD, and BEWAR, *Zephaniah*, 247.

[144] This may be a reference to the tributes paid by Edom, Moab, and Ammon, to Sennacherib, and his capture of Sidon and all the Philistine cities on the coastal plain in 701 B.C., cf. 2Kgs 18,13-16.

5.5. Conclusion of the preceding sections

The result of our survey on the usage of the verb קבץ in relation to God's action in the Old Testament shows that it is used mostly in a positive sense to denote His saving action in favour of Israel. In three cases it has been used in favour of the nations. There are only 6 cases where it has been used with reference to His judgment of Israel and the nations. Except for these 6 uses (Ezek 16,37; 22,20; Hos 8,11, Joel 4,2; Mic 4,12; Zeph 3,8), it is used with reference to His judgment against the nations alone, by scattering (פוץ) them through the countries.

The basic lexical meaning of קבץ is "to gather", and its use in the Old Testament denotes God's action of gathering, and action that is rich in nuances, which are best expressed through comparison to the action of a shepherd gathering his flock (Isa 40,11; Jer 23,3). Here, קבץ reveals God's action and explains His inner attributes. In upholding His goodness and holiness, He condemns injustice, oppression, violence, bloodshed, unfaithfulness, disobedience and hypocrisy (cf. desecration) in worship, but always judges with compassion for His people, as He never forgets to take constant care of them ("to gather them"), even when He banishes them from their homeland.

5.6. God's new prerogative
5.6.1. God makes the Nations on a par with Israel

A survey of the usage of קבץ to describe God's action shows that only in three texts, in Isa 56,8; 66,18 and Ezek 29,13, is it used to denote God's saving action for the nations. Isa 56,8 describes how He has chosen to place other nations alongside Israel, while Isa 66,18 reveals His motivation in gathering them together, namely, that they also may see His glory. God is going to gather not only the house of Israel, but also other nations and tongues, so that they also will come and gather together on His holy mountain to offer Him worship. Israel remains God's chosen people; nonetheless, He extends the privilege of worshiping Him also to other nations, bringing them on a par with Israel.

Hos 8,8-10:

נִבְלַע יִשְׂרָאֵל עַתָּה הָיוּ בַגּוֹיִם כִּכְלִי אֵין־חֵפֶץ בּוֹ׃
כִּי־הֵמָּה עָלוּ אַשּׁוּר פֶּרֶא בּוֹדֵד לוֹ אֶפְרַיִם הִתְנוּ אֲהָבִים׃
גַּם כִּי־יִתְנוּ בַגּוֹיִם עַתָּה אֲקַבְּצֵם וַיָּחֵלּוּ מְּעָט מִמַּשָּׂא מֶלֶךְ שָׂרִים׃

Israel is swallowed up; already they are among the nations like a useless vessel.
For they have gone up to Assyria like a wild donkey wandering alone;
Ephraim has hired lovers. Although they have given themselves among the nations,
now I will gather them up; and in a little while they will tarry
from the burden of the king of princes.

MT פֶּרֶא בּוֹדֵד לוֹ ("a wild donkey wandering alone") in v.9 is frequently transposed after יִשְׂרָאֵל in v.8. BHS proposes reading MT אֲקַבְּצֵם ("I will gather them") as נָתְנוּ ("they gave"), and many MSS, LXX, Syriac, Targum and Vulgate attest וְשָׂרִים ("and princes") instead of MT שָׂרִים ("princes").

Hos 8,8-10 expresses God's complaint against the house of Israel that she has broken her covenant with Him. The theme of Israel's breaking of the covenant runs throughout the whole chapter. Israel's guilt consists in her wrong religious conduct, namely, her going after Baal (Hos 2,4ff.; 2,18ff.; 5,3f.), but she is also guilty of erring in her foreign relations, as she has run to Assyria (and Egypt) for military help (8,8.13).[145] On the one hand, Ephraim wants to maintain Israel's independence, and on the other hand it also looks for alliance with other nations that are not "compatible with its vocation."[146] Both actions amount to religious and political prostitution. In the first case, she has gone after other gods (= religious prostitution, i.e., idolatry, cf. v.11), and in the second case, she has sought out the favours of powerful nations by paying tributes to them (= political prostitution: "hired lovers" cf. Ezek 16,33).[147] Thus, Israel is guilty of a double crime.

Israel is "swallowed up" because the "foreigners have eaten away her strength" (cf. Hos 7,9, Isa 1,7).[148] She has lost her independence as a political entity, but much more seriously, she has lost her covenant relationship with the LORD, making her "worthless" (cf. Jer 22,28; 48,38). By subordinating herself to Assyria, Israel has exhausted herself with political manoeuvrings and has placed her own survival in peril.[149] This has placed her on the brink of political bankruptcy, by putting her on the verge of losing her own sovereignty. Because she has proven herself unfaithful to the LORD religiously and politically, she has lost her own freedom and the special privilege of being called "His people". On account of her own conduct, she has become like any other nation. Her diplomatic efforts to obtain help and protection from Assyria has exposed her arrogance and pride,[150] while her initiative to offer tributes to Assyria amounts to a "self-seeking"[151] (cf. 8,9; Hos 5,5; 7,10) that has earned her false security. These errors are referred to as Israel's infidelity and her love-affair.[152]

---

[145] DIESSLER, *zwölf Propheten*, 38; see also FREEDMAN, *Hosea*, 482; MACHINTOSH, *Hosea*, 314; JEREMIAS, *Hosea*, 109; and WOLFF, *Dodeka Propheton I*, 183

[146] KEIL, *Minor Prophets*, COT 10, 76.

[147] JEREMIAS, *Prophet Hosea*, 109.

[148] FREEDMAN, *Hosea*, 500.

[149] MACHINTOSH, *Hosea*, 315. Manahem paid a huge tribute to Tiglath-pileser in 738 B.C. But it was unnecessary except that it highlighted Israel's futility and proved her political bankruptcy. See MACHINTOSH, *Hosea*, 318.

[150] I.e., Israel played a role with the foreign powers. See ROBINSON, *Kleinen Propheten*, 33.

[151] ROBINSON, *Kleinen Propheten*, 33.

[152] The prophet Hosea considers Hoshea's tribute to Assyria in 732 B.C. a kind of prostitution. The difference lies in this that instead of receiving a price for her husband, Israel herself pays

Although Israel feels satisfied and secure by winning allies through her freely paid tributes, it will prove a nightmare for her because God is going to gather Israel for "indictment and punishment".[153] The combination of two conjunctive particles כִּי and גַם ("indeed" 10a) here, is a rare phenomenon in which גַם serves as a normal conjunction and כִּי lays greater emphasis on the verb יִתְנוּ ("they will recount").[154] It indicates God's intervention, serving a key to interpretation, and shows a link between "although they hire allies," in v.10 and "Ephraim has hired allies" in v.9.

Many commentators[155] prefer to render מֶלֶךְ שָׂרִים as "king of kings" or "king of princes" to denote the great king of Assyria (cf. Hos 5,12; 10,6). It means that despite Israel's own initiative to pay heavy tributes to win her allies and her false sense of security from their power, she will be diminished soon and burdened under the weight of Assyria. It implies that she will suffer loss of political sovereignty, proving the futility of her seeking out Assyria as guardian.

Isa 19,23-25:

בַּיּוֹם הַהוּא תִּהְיֶה מְסִלָּה מִמִּצְרַיִם אַשּׁוּרָה וּבָא־אַשּׁוּר בְּמִצְרַיִם וּמִצְרַיִם בְּאַשּׁוּר וְעָבְדוּ מִצְרַיִם אֶת־אַשּׁוּר:
בַּיּוֹם הַהוּא יִהְיֶה יִשְׂרָאֵל שְׁלִישִׁיָּה לְמִצְרַיִם וּלְאַשּׁוּר בְּרָכָה בְּקֶרֶב הָאָרֶץ:
אֲשֶׁר בֵּרֲכוֹ יְהוָה צְבָאוֹת לֵאמֹר בָּרוּךְ עַמִּי מִצְרַיִם וּמַעֲשֵׂה יָדַי אַשּׁוּר וְנַחֲלָתִי יִשְׂרָאֵל:

In that day there will be a highway from Egypt to Assyria.
The Assyrians will come into Egypt and the Egyptians come into Assyria
And the Egyptians will worship with the Assyrians.
In that day, Israel will be the third with Egypt and Assyria, a blessing
in the midst of the earth, whom the God of hosts has blessed:
"Blessed be Egypt, my people, Assyria, work of my hands, and Israel my inheritance."

In v.25 MT attests אֲשֶׁר בֵּרֲכוֹ ("whom He blesses"), but LXX reads ἣν εὐλόγησεν ("whom the LORD Almighty blessed") and BHS suggests בֵּרֲכָהּ (suff. 3f. sg.).

Geographically, Egypt and Assyria lie on the two extremities of Israel. This north-south geographical position presents a kind of totality that includes everything falling between the two poles.[156] The fact that there will be a highway (מְסִלָּה) between Egypt and Assyria bringing two disparate geographical regions and political powers in direct relation with each other, shows Isaiah's

---

gifts for her "lover". See MACHINTOSH, *Hosea*, 318; see also JEREMIAS, *Hosea*, 109; WOLFF, *Hosea*, 183-184; ROBINSON, *Kleinen Porpheten*, 33.

[153] MACHINTOSH, *Hosea*, 320. FREEDMAN (*Hosea*, 507) and MACHINTOSH (*Hosea*, 320) think that 8,18b may refer to Manahem's tribute to Tiglath-pileser in 738 B.C. All the same, it did not prevent Assyria from invading Israel and annexing her northern territories.

[154] FREEDMAN, *Hosea*, 508.

[155] E.g., FREEDMAN, *Hosea*, 508; JEREMIAS, *Hosea*, 108; MACHINTOSH, *Hosea*, 321; WOLFF, *Hosea*, 184;

[156] KILIAN, *Jesaja II*, 125.

eschatological vision that one day (cf. "in that day"[157]), the conflicting and warring nations will understand each other and come to know God and will be able to offer Him worship (cf. עבד) together[158] and the Lord GOD will become king over all nations (cf. Ps 47,9f.).[159]

Egypt and Assyria, two powerful nations between whom Israel shuttled, seeking diplomatic alliances, will finally submit to God (cf. Zeph 3,9). Both of these powerful nations lived in hostility against each other in the past, but in God's future salvation of the nations they will be linked by a highway, signalling that He will bridge the previously existing gap and remove enmity among the nations. The term "highway" (מְסִלָּה) is used here as a metaphor to denote the removing any kind of alienation and separation between the peoples and the nations (cf. 11,16; 33,8; 35,8; 40,3; 49,11; 62,10).[160]

Isaiah envisages something very unique here: Israel will be third with Egypt and Assyria. This does not mean reduction of Israel in relation to Egypt and Assyria, but she will be at a par[161] with them; so much so, that she will be a blessing in the midst of the earth, a motif that goes back to Gen 12,2f., concerning God's blessing to Abram, making him a blessing for the people and the nations. This motif of blessing is developed further in v.25, where Egypt and Assyria are seen as representatives of the peoples and the nations. They are gathered by the God of Abraham and receive His blessing through Israel, concretely from Jerusalem, His holy sanctuary.[162] Thus, Egypt and Assyria become a testimony of God's blessing for the nations, being called God's people (Egypt: cf. Ex 3,7 also Isa 10,24; 43,6.7), and his handiwork (Assyria: cf. Isa 60,21; 64,7; Ps 119,73; 138,8).

It reveals Israel's role among the nations, which is not to be a great power at the cost of others and in league with the powerful nations. The political role does not enter into the picture here; instead, it is her spiritual role by which other nations will partake in God's salvation (blessing) and come to know and acknowledge Him as their God.[163] The nations are placed on a par with Israel, His people (cf. Ex 3,7),

---

[157] I.e., the fulfilment of YHWH's judgment against Egypt in relation to Zion; see GROSS, "Israel und die Völker", in Zenger (ed.), *Der Neue Bund im Alten*, 152f.

[158] KILIAN, *Jesaja II*, 125.

[159] WILDBERGER, *Jesaja 13-27*, 745.

[160] OSWALT, *Isaiah 1-39*, 380.

[161] From a literary-structural point of view, Israel is placed third with Egypt and Assyria, but the discussion here regards neither a partnership with Egypt and Assyria as three great powers nor it relates to her rank among them; rather, it regards their relationship among them because all three will be called God's people and the LORD will be their God. See WILDBERGER, *Jesaja 13-27*, 745.

[162] WILDBERGER, *Jesaja 13-27*, 745.

[163] KAISER, *Jesaja 13-39*, 90.

and His possession (סְגֻלָּה cf. Ex 19,5) and inheritance (נַחֲלָה cf. Deut 32,8f.; Joel 4,2).

The titles, "God's people," "God's possession," and "God's inheritance" were exclusively used to denote God's special relation with Israel, but are now used in a way that also includes other nations (cf. "Egypt, my people"). Israel was God's heritage and He had a special prerogative for her all along, but now He makes himself known to Egypt and Assyria by blessing them through Israel and making them also His people. Thus, God reveals Himself as the universal saviour and God of all peoples, whereby Egypt and Assyria can take their proper places beside Israel.[164] Wildberger observes that although the nations stand side by side with Israel, because God "created" (ברא cf. Isa 43,1.15), "formed" (יצר cf. Isa 44,2.24; 45,11) and "made" (עשׂה cf. Isa 44,2) Israel, Israel maintains her primacy among the blessed nations; her position remains above all the others. Even if God calls Egypt "my people," and Assyria as "my handiwork," he calls Israel alone "my inheritance" (נַחֲלָה cf. Deut 32,8f.; Joel 4,2).[165]

5.6.2. A synthesis

In Hos 8,8-10 and Is 19,23-25, we discover something extraordinary about God's dealing with Israel and the nations. Hos 8,8-10 shows that Israel has forfeited her privileged status as God's people because of her disloyal political conduct.[166] By both her religious and political conducts, she has made herself like any other nation. Consequently, she forfeits her political sovereignty when God gathers her allies against her. He lets her suffer under the burden (of tribute) of the great king (Assyria). Yet despite her infidelity to the LORD, she remains His chosen people and the LORD turns the judgment pronounced against her into an opportunity for the nations also to become His people. Isa 19,23-25 articulates God's universal declaration by which He calls Egypt "my people" (עַמִּי מִצְרַיִם), just as he called Israel "my people" (Ex 3,7; Joel 4,2). There is a remarkable change in God's dealing with Israel and the nations here, for He reveals His new prerogative toward Egypt, bringing her on a par with Israel. The status of special privilege bestowed on Israel is not abrogated, but rather now it has also been extended to Egypt. Israel's covenant infidelity makes her no different from other nation around her. This gives a new perspective to the understanding of God's overall plan of

---

[164] KILIAN, *Jesaja II*, 125.

[165] WILDBERGER, *Jesaja 13-27*, 745-746; see also WATTS, *Isaiah 1-33*, 260-261; GRAY, *Isaiah, 1-39*, 331-332.

[166] Hos 8,8-10 speaks mainly about Israel's political conduct, i.e., courting Egypt and Assyria to win allies, and of her own initiative of paying tributes to Assyria. This is a sign of her arrogance. This conduct shows her refusal to put her reliance in God. The religious aspect of her conduct, i.e., her practice of Baal-cult, is an open rebellion against God, who entered into a special relationship with her (cf. Hos 2,4.18; 5,3).

salvation for the nations, by which He reveals His plan of salvation also for Egypt, bestowing on her privileges similar to those given to Israel, whom he called "my people." It reveals His goodness and universal justice, which knows no favourites (cf. Sir 35,12) and makes no difference between Israel and Egypt, but places Israel's arch-rival, on par with her.

Israel's failure to keep her covenant faithfully and God's new initiative to allow the nations experience His salvation, thereby partaking in the privilege previously reserved for Israel, highlights his special intervention on behalf of the nations, including Egypt which has been given the hope of restoration when the period of her judgment is over. Thus, God's dealing with Israel becomes a paradigm for His dealing with Egypt, now called "His people." God judges Egypt as He judges Israel, but he also promises to gather her people from the countries where they were dispersed, bringing them back out of their captivity and settling them in their own homeland, exactly as is promised Israel. In His dealing with Egypt, God reveals His new plan for the nations. God's judgment against Egypt on account of her pride and her obstruction of His plan for Israel are superseded by this prerogative that reverses the former judgment (cf. Ezek 29,5), making Egypt see His salvation. Egypt will be gathered and this is God's privileged action for her.

Thus Egypt comes to resemble Israel, and becomes God's people like Israel (cf. Isa 19,23-25). Like Israel, Egypt receives a promise of restoration, in terms of "gathering," "bringing back their captivity," and "establishing them in their homeland." The "land-giving" formula, which was a prominent motif in Israel's exodus from the slavery of Egypt, comes out forcefully in this context.[167] It is God who has apportioned the nations and the peoples their land (cf. Deut 32,8; also Gen 10). Thus, He reveals His sovereign power over both Israel and the other nations; He shows His universal care and concern for them when He gathers them together that they may see His salvation and recognise Him as their God.

5.7. General Conclusion

In concluding the discussion presented in this chapter, what comes to the fore is that God reveals the place of the nations, vis-à-vis Israel. Israel is His own people, His preferred possession. Despite Israel's failure and the resulting judgment that comes upon her through the Israelites' exile from their own land, and their scattering among other nations, it remains God's prerogative to gather them and to bring them back to their own land. Thus, gathering, bringing back, and restoring them in their own land are concrete actions by which He reveals His pastoral care and concern for His people. Although the verb קבץ primarily means "to gather," its specific nuances are reflected in the pastoral activities of a shepherd, especially

---

[167] VOGELS, *God's Universal Covenant*, 93; also WIJNGAARDS, *Deuteronomic Creed*, 22-27.

in his care and concern for his flock. His primary concern is to gather the flock together by going in search of them and by hooting to them (cf., Lk 15,1f.; Jn 10,14f., cf. Ps 23). The nations find their place next to Israel not because Israel forfeits her privileged status on account of her false (religious and political) conduct, but because it is God's own will to make Himself known to the nations through their salvation. Egypt, which constantly reminds Israel of her slavery, and which consistently tempted her fidelity to the LORD by her political power, is cleared when God chooses to call Egypt "my people" and promises to gather the dispersed of Egypt. This unique action towards Egypt as His people, together with His actions towards Israel, signal God's new prerogative for Egypt and for the nations. Thus, while His plan for Israel remains a paradigm for the nations, His prerogative for Egypt becomes a paradigm for other nations, and His plans to gather all of them.

CHAPTER SIX
THE USAGE OF שׁוּב שְׁבוּת "BRING BACK [FROM] CAPTIVITY"
TO DENOTE GOD'S SAVING ACTION FOR EGYPT

Chapter Six takes up an inquiry into the meaning and usage of another key concept, שׁוּב שְׁבוּת, of the oracle of salvation. Its verb-root and basic meaning is discussed in the beginning. This chronological survey studies its exilic and post-exilic usage and meaning in the Old Testament, where it occurs mostly in the books of the prophets.

6.1. The root and meaning of שׁוּב שְׁבוּת

This treatment of the study of the expression שׁוּב שְׁבוּת will relate mainly to two points: the "root" of שְׁבוּת and its "meaning". There are two opinions concerning its root, namely, שׁוּב ("to turn", "return") and שׁבה ("to take captive"). The meaning and the usage of שׁוּב is generally intransitive, so questions arise mainly due to its uncertain transitive sense. Another aspect of the discussion relates to the variant readings of שְׁבוּת/שְׁבִית as encountered in the Biblical text. The Masorets have not always been consistent on this point, which becomes clear from the statistics.[1]

With regard to the usage of the verb (שׁוּב/שׁבה) Borger remarks that *Qere*-reading of the verbs in the citations have hardly been noted; moreover, the Masorets paid little attention to the *matres lectionis waw* and *yodh*, thus they frequently replaced one for the other as in the case of the *qal/hiphil* forms.[2] Another useful observation on שׁוּב שְׁבוּת relates to its usage in the texts where it takes different objects of action according to their context:[3]

    1) An individual as object: Job 42,10
    2) A collective group as object:
        a) *City*: Samaria, Sodom: Ezek 16,53; the tent of Jacob: Jer 30,18;
            Jerusalem: Lam 2,14; Zion: Ps 126,1.4
        b) *Country*: dynasty of David: Jer 33,26
        c) *Land*: Jer 32,44; 33,11

---

[1] שְׁבוּת without *Qere* 17x, cf. Zeph 3,20 with emendation; שְׁבִית without *Qere* 2x (Ezek 16,53 and Ps 126,1 with emendation); שְׁבוּת in *Kethib* but שְׁבִית in *Qere* 4x; שְׁבִית in *Kethib* but שְׁבוּת in *Qere* 7x. Cf. BORGER, „Zu שׁוּב/ית", in *ZAW* 66 (1954), 315-316.

[2] BORGER, „Zu שׁוּב/ית", in *ZAW* 66, 316.

[3] DIETRICH, שׁוּב שְׁבוּת, 12; see also BAUMANN, „שׁוּב שְׁבוּת", in *ZAW* 73 (1929), 25-26.

> d) *People*: the Egyptians: Ezek 29,14; Moab: Jer 48,47; Ammon: Jer 49,6; Elam: Jer 49,39; the exiles: Jer 29,14; the remnant of the house of Judah: Zeph 2,7; Judah and Israel: Jer 33,7; Jerusalem: Joel 4,1ff., Jer 31,23; Israel: Am 9,14; Judah: Jer 30,3; Jacob: Ps 85,2; Jacob and house of Israel: Ezek 39,25; people in general: Hos 6,11; Ps 14,7 (53, 7); Deut 30,3; Zeph 3,20.

The categories given above distribute the occurrences of this expression on a socio-political basis. It is one of the ways that the various occurrences of this expression can be examined. But this model fails to show a semantic development of its usage. Another way to look at its usage could be simply to list its occurrences as they appear in different books in the Old Testament. This, however, poses difficulty regarding some texts that are considered to be late additions. This study prefers to take a chronological approach as a criterion for examining its usage in the prophetic books of the Old Testament. Such an approach will allow us to see the development of semantic meaning through the centuries of Israelite history, including the pre-exilic, exilic and post-exilic periods, such as:[4]

> 1) "to turn someone's captivity" (Pre-exilic): Am 9,14; Hos 6,11; Zeph 2,7; 3,20;
> 2) "to turn (round) fortune" or "restore someone," i.e., "bring back captivity" (exilic):
>   a) in Jeremiah: 29,14; 30,3.18; 31, 23; 32,44; 33,7.11.26; 48,47; 49,6.39.
>   b) in Ezekiel: 16,53; 29, 14; 39,25.
> 3) "to bring back captivity" (post-exilic): Deut 30,3; Joel 4,1; Ps 14,7 = 53,7; 85,2; 126,(1) 4; Lam 2,14; Job 42,10 (cf. "restore fortune").

Preuschen thinks that שְׁבוּת (שְׁבִיָה, שְׁבִי [n. f. sg.] = "captivity") comes from the root שבה and means "to take captive," thus שׁוּב שְׁבוּת means "to return" or "bring back captives." However, this proposed meaning causes some difficulty in translating the expression in some texts like Job 42,10. Dietrich says that שְׁבוּת originally derived from שׁוּב, but was later mixed up with the noun (שׁב׳ת) and was wrongly translated as "captivity" until it was changed to שְׁבוּת. Therefore, he says that where the noun clearly derived from שׁוּב, the MT wrote שְׁבִית (cf. Lam 2,14), but where it denoted "captivity," they wrote שְׁבוּת (cf. Jer 48,47). He argues further that שְׁבוּת originally meant "to restore" and only later, due to the exilic influence, came to denote "to return captivity."[5] Bracke asserts that it's meaning is eschatological and carries prophetic significance, implying "return" or "restoration to an earlier prosperity".[6] Schwally argues that morphologically שְׁבִית, and certainly not שְׁבִית (n. cf. Num 21,29), is the only possible form of the root שׁוּב and that שְׁבוּת is clearly an incorrect pronunciation of שְׁבִית from שׁוּב that was taken up

---

[4] PREUSCHEN, „Die Bedeutung von שׁוּב שבות", in *ZAW* 15 (1895), 22-64.

[5] DIETRICH, שׁוּב שְׁבוּת, 28-36.

[6] BRACKE, "šûb šᵉbût," in *ZAW* 97 (1985), 234; see also DIETRICH, שׁוּב שבות, 27-28.

in the tradition.[7] Baumann thinks that שְׁבוּת derives from שׁבה and that the expression שׁוּב שְׁבוּת carries an ethical-juridical sense. On the one hand it implies sin, guilt, anger and revenge but on the other hand it also implies grace, forgiveness, justification and freeing.[8]

Preuschen and Dietrich (as well as Baumann) dealt with the problem through grammatical-etymological analyses and tried to verify their results by exegetically examining the texts wherever this expression occurs. However, J. M. Bracke contends that they failed to note the literary contexts in which the expression occurs. He thinks that the expression points to a model of restoration whose primary characteristic is God's reversal of His judgment. He examines the literary contexts in which the expression occurs to arrive at a correct meaning.[9] Outside the Old Testament, the earliest usage of this expression is witnessed in Aramaic in the inscriptions of Sefire (Tablet III 24th line) from the 8th cent. B.C., where it denotes "render a restoration."[10]

6.2. The usage of שׁוּב שְׁבוּת in the Old Testament
6.2.1. In the pre-exilic texts

Preuschen argues that שׁוּב שְׁבוּת was used to denote "to turn"/"change someone's captivity."[11] This expression is not frequently used in the pre-exilic writings in the OT. It appears only in the books of Amos, Hosea, and Zephaniah. Although its use is comparatively rare, these texts do throw some light on its meaning.

Am 9,14:

וְשַׁבְתִּי אֶת־שְׁבוּת עַמִּי יִשְׂרָאֵל וּבָנוּ עָרִים נְשַׁמּוֹת וְיָשָׁבוּ
וְנָטְעוּ כְרָמִים וְשָׁתוּ אֶת־יֵינָם וְעָשׂוּ גַנּוֹת וְאָכְלוּ אֶת־פְּרִיהֶם׃

I will bring back the captives of my people Israel and they shall build the waste cities and inhabit them; they shall plant vineyards and drink their wine and they shall make gardens and eat their fruit.

The concluding unit of the book of Amos 9,13-15 is an oracle of restoration that speaks about a new abundance of land and peace. F. I. Anderson and D. N. Freedman show how this expression is used in the midst of God's activity of

---

[7] SCHWALLY, „Die Reden des Buches Jeremiah", in *ZAW* 8 (1888), 200.

[8] BAUMANN, „שׁוּב שְׁבוּת", in *ZAW* 73, 24.

[9] BRACKE, "šûb š°bût," in *ZAW* 97 (1985), 235-236. See also BARR, *Semantics of Biblical Language*, 109, esp. Chap. 6.

[10] WOLFF, *Dodekapropheten 2*, 91; see also FITZMYER, "Aramaic Suzerainty Treaty," in *CBQ* 20, (1958), 463-464.

[11] PREUSCHEN, „Die Bedeutung von שׁוּב שְׁבוּת", in *ZAW* 15, 22.

building and planting.[12] His promise to restore His people, Israel (14b),[13] is placed within the oracle of overall restoration of the Land. However, the authenticity of this unit (Am 9,11-15) is seriously doubted and regarded as late.[14] It seems unlikely that Amos created or imagined an exilic or post-exilic situation in his oracles, which comes from 7th century.[15] S. Paul argues that the "last verses come from an exilic or post-exilic theologian-redactor who, from his own point of view, bore tidings of consolation and salvation of his people."[16] The oracle presumes an understanding of exile, but speaks about restoration in general terms, without specifically referring either to the "Babylonian captivity" or to the "Persian restoration," and its language is "hyperbolic". On the other hand, the reference to David seems to indicate the fall of the Davidic dynasty, and this reference is understood as evidence that the text came from the 6th cent. B.C.[17] Am 9,14 definitely presupposes a different situation than the time of the prophet, probably referring to the troubled years of the northern kingdom prior to its fall which may suggest that it is late (cf. Hos 6,11), composed during the exile.[18]

God judges (= exiles) Israel for her failure to repent even though He gave her several chances to return to Him (4,6.8.9.10.11., cf. 6,8; 5,11.16f.).[19] In view of this, שׁוּב שְׁבוּת denotes a reversal of Israel's fortune, which means that God will annul His judgment against His people and show His mercy to them.[20] Concretely, it signifies "restoration of captives to their homeland".[21] Dietrich thinks that it indicates an eschatological promise - renewal of the Davidic dynasty - signifying the political and material restoration of Israel.[22] Thus, it would indicate an oracle of salvation, for which he refers to the parallel pointed by Preuschen in v.15b: "They shall never be rooted out of the land."[23] Baumann, however, interprets its meaning in the sense of being freed from sin.[24]

---

[12] ANDERSON and FREEDMAN, *Amos*, 886-887; see also MAYS, *Amos*, 165-166.

[13] This expression is found also in Jer 30,3 and Ezek 29,14.

[14] PAUL, *Amos*, 288.

[15] ANDERSON and FREEDMAN, *Amos*, 893.

[16] PAUL, *Amos*, 288. PAUL suggests two generally held arguments for its late date, i.e., *linguistic*: "such as many affinities to late biblical Hebrew in this section" and *ideological* although there isn't any substantial basis to argue except to take note of the "abrupt transition." However, Amos focuses on the restoration of the Davidic dynasty which is found also in Hosea (2,2; 3,5) and revived in Ezekiel 37,16ff.; see in the same, 289.

[17] ANDERSON and FREEDMAN, *Amos*, 893.

[18] DRIVER and GRAY, *Job*, 349; see also MAYS, *Amos*, 166.

[19] ANDERSON and FREEDMAN, *Amos*, 924; also BRACKE, "šûb šᵉbût," in *ZAW* 97, 241.

[20] MAYS, *Amos*, 167; see also ANDERSON and FREEDMAN, *Amos*, 924.

[21] ANDERSON and FREEDMAN, *Amos*, 923.

[22] DIETRICH, שׁוּב שְׁבוּת, 24.

[23] DIETRICH, שׁוּב שְׁבוּת, 25; PREUSCHEN, „Die Bedeutung von שְׁבוּת שׁוּב", in *ZAW* 15, 31.

[24] BAUMANN, „שׁוּב שְׁבוּת", in *ZAW* 73, 33.

Hos 6,11:

גַּם־יְהוּדָה שָׁת קָצִיר לָךְ בְּשׁוּבִי שְׁבוּת עַמִּי:

Also, O Judah, a harvest is appointed for you when I return the captives of my people.

Hos 6,11 is an oracle of judgment that describes thematically a range of wickedness committed by Israel's priesthood (6,7-9; 7,1b) and set forth the nation's crime (7,10-7,1a).[25] F. I. Anderson and D. N. Freedman agree that it is difficult to find traditional poetry in Hos 6,7-7,2, and thus it is difficult to ascertain any close-knit structure of the unit. Still, within this broad structure, Hos 6,11-7,1 is the only sub unit that may be said to resemble "classical norms."[26] It mentions Israel and Judah, although the latter may be a gloss. The final clause of the sub-unit (cf. 11b) constitutes an oracle of restoration,[27] but it may be late.[28] Preuschen admits that it is not easy to determine the meaning of שׁוּב שְׁבוּת[29] in this context, and Dietriech understands it in the sense of "restoration" of the people.[30] On the other hand, Baumann thinks that it expresses "removal" of sinfulness,[31] while Bracke interprets it as God's refusal to restore His people because of their obstinacy.[32] Bracke's rendering, "to restore," is correct but his interpretation, "Yahweh's refusal to "restore" (šûb šᵉbût) his people," does not seem correct because God's action is positive and He does act to restore His people Israel.

Zeph 2,7:

וְהָיָה חֶבֶל לִשְׁאֵרִית בֵּית יְהוּדָה עֲלֵיהֶם יִרְעוּן בְּבָתֵּי אַשְׁקְלוֹן בָּעֶרֶב יִרְבָּצוּן
כִּי יִפְקְדֵם יְהוָה אֱלֹהֵיהֶם וְשָׁב *שְׁבוּתָם **שְׁבִיתָם:

The seacoast shall be for the remnant of the house of Judah; they shall feed their flocks there; in the houses of Ashkelon they shall lie down at evening; for the LORD their God will intervene for them, and return their captives.

Zephaniah's prophecies coincide with the reign of king Josiah of Judah (c. 640-625 BC cf. 1,1) and may have lasted only a few weeks or months, and he delivered his oracles mostly in the context of the temple liturgy.[33] Zeph 1 begins with a warning on the coming destruction and judgment against Judah, and describes the coming Day of the LORD. Zeph 2 speaks about God's judgment against the foreign nations:

---

[25] ANDERSON and FREEDMAN, *Hosea*, 432-435.

[26] ANDERSON and FREEDMAN, *Hosea*, 434.

[27] ANDERSON and FREEDMAN, *Hosea*, 443-444; see also WOLFF, *Dodekapropheten 1. Hosea*, 157. WOLFF considers שׁוּב שְׁבוּת as parallel to רפא (*qal* "healing") in 5,13 and 6,1, i.e., as the restoration of the people who are afflicted; see in the same place.

[28] DRIVER and GRAY, *Job*, 349.

[29] PREUSCHEN, „Die Bedeutung von שׁוּב שְׁבוּת", in *ZAW* 15, 31.

[30] DIETRICH, שׁוּב שְׁבוּת, 28.

[31] BAUMANN, „שׁוּב שְׁבוּת", in *ZAW* 73, 32.

[32] BRACKE, "šûb šᵉbût," in *ZAW* 97, 242.

[33] BOADT, *Reading the Old Testament*, 340.

Philistia (vv. 4-7), Moab and Ammon (vv.8-11), Cush (v.12), Assyria and Nineveh (vv.13-15), and his oracles against the nations seem to lie in the background of Josiah's claim that the land occupied by Israel's neighbours belonged to Israel. However, Josiah saw Assyria and Egypt as threats to his efforts to expand Israel's territories.[34]

Zephaniah's oracle of judgment against Philistia[35] announces a destruction of Philistia that will leave it uninhabited, so that it will belong to the remnant of Judah to pasture their flocks there. Nevertheless, even though such a pattern may be arguably discernable, Philistia's doom here is not seen as a salvation for Judah. Zephaniah maintains that God certainly does not exterminate a people to raise His own people, Israel.

The oracle of salvation to Judah: "For the LORD their God will intervene for them, and return their captives" appears at the end of the oracle of judgment against Philistia (2,7). The MT has שְׁבוּתָם, but *Qere* read שְׁבִיתָם; nevertheless, this variation between *Kethib* and *Qere* does not affect the meaning of the expression. Preuschen puts Zeph 2,7 along with Am 9,14; Hos 6,11 and Zeph 3,20 in the same category where שׁוּב שְׁבוּת denotes, "to reverse the captivity of someone." He also points to Wellhausen's observation that the presence of וְשָׁב שְׁבוּתָם ("He will return their captivity") in the verse raises a suspicion against כִּי יִפְקְדֵם ("for the [LORD] will intervene for them") because both judgment and exile seem to be presupposed here.[36] The text is pre-exilic and it denotes "to restore the fortune," but most likely due to interpolation, it is interpreted as "to reverse captivity."[37]

Zeph 3,20:

בָּעֵת הַהִיא אָבִיא אֶתְכֶם וּבָעֵת קַבְּצִי אֶתְכֶם כִּי־אֶתֵּן אֶתְכֶם לְשֵׁם וְלִתְהִלָּה
בְּכֹל עַמֵּי הָאָרֶץ בְּשׁוּבִי אֶת־שְׁבוּתֵיכֶם לְעֵינֵיכֶם אָמַר יְהוָה:

At that time I will bring you back even at the time I gather you;
for I will give you fame and praise among all the peoples of the earth
when I return your captives before your eyes, says the LORD.

Zeph 3 begins by expressing woe on the wickedness of Jerusalem (vv.1-8) and God's promises of salvation to her (vv.9-20). The last sub-unit of this chapter (vv.18-20), which is supposed to be an exilic text (cf. NJB, p.1027), is an oracle of hope for Jerusalem that shows how God will change Judah's disaster into her glory. The promise of restoration of Jerusalem in Zeph 3,20 is seen as a variation of v.19.[38] There is some textual variation in 20c. LXX, Syriac and the Vulgate read

---

[34] VLAARDINGERBROEK, *Zephaniah*, 125-134.

[35] Philistia, i.e., Gaza, Ashkelon, Asdod and Ekron. Gath is missing from the list. See VLAARDINGERBROEK, *Zephaniah*, 126-129; 133.

[36] PREUSCHEN, „Die Bedeutung von שׁוּב שְׁבוּת", 22-32.

[37] PREUSCHEN, „Die Bedeutung von שׁוּב שְׁבוּת", 34; see also DIETRICH, שׁוּב שְׁבוּת, 23.

[38] SMITH, WARD, and BEWAR, *Micah, Zephaniah, Nahum*, 258-260.

MT שְׁבוּתֵיכֶם as שְׁבוּתְכֶם, but according to the explanation in Joüon-Muraoka (§94j: suffixes of singular and plural nouns), a variant reading doesn't seem necessary here, since it does not affect its meaning,[39] "to turn the captivity."[40] Bracke, however, claims that in 2,7 and 3,20 the expression denotes a reversal of God's judgment.[41]

6.2.2. Conclusion

The above examples show that the expression שׁוּב שְׁבוּת in used relatively seldom in the pre-exilic texts. The dates of Am 9,14 and Hos 6,11 are considered late[42] and are probably added by a later redactor. Even so, they are thought to be exilic. The reference to David (cf. Am 9,14) suggests its date as 6th cent. B.C. Still, it is presumed that "the oracle of restoration, return, and revival could have come from almost any period from the middle of the eight century on when the invasion, conquest, and exile was thrust on the consciousness of Israel and Judah by the prophets from both north and south."[43] Though Amos and Hosea stood farther away from exile than Zephaniah, if Israel's relationship with Yahweh and among themselves was any indication, it was not very difficult for these prophets to foresee a possible disaster awaiting God's people. In view of such a prospect of defeat and captivity, they used the expression to instill hope in God's promises of salvation to Israel despite her failures, and the prophets meant this in a concrete sense. Thus, even in these pre-exilic oracles, שׁוּב שְׁבוּת is aptly translated to denote "return"/"bring back captives."

6.3. The usage of שׁוּב שְׁבוּת in the exilic texts
6.3.1. In Jeremiah

A large number of occurrences of שׁוּב שְׁבוּת appear in the Book of Jeremiah. The prophet Jeremiah lived during the reign of Josiah (cf. Jeremiah's ministry: 627-622 B.C.) and saw the most turbulent days of the kingdom of Judah until it fell to the Babylonians (587 B.C.). After Josiah's death, the kings of Judah, Johoiakim (cf. Jeremiah's ministry: 609-598 B.C.) and Zedekiah (cf. Jeremiah's ministry: 598-587 B.C.) totally disregarded God's will by refusing to listen to the prophet and adamantly pursued their own policies of political manoeuvrings in their efforts to

---

[39] VLAARDINGERBROEK, *Zephaniah*, 219.

[40] SMITH, WARD, and BEWAR, *Micah, Zephaniah, Nahum*, 260.

[41] BRACKE, "šûb šᵉbût," in *ZAW* 97, 242.

[42] DRIVER and GRAY, *Job*, 349.

[43] ANDERSON and FREEDMAN, *Amos*, 893.

avert Jerusalem's imminent catastrophe.[44] In view of this national disaster, Jeremiah's oracles of salvation to Judah/Jerusalem/Israel reveal God's wonderful deed for his people.

Jer 29, 14:

וְנִמְצֵאתִי לָכֶם נְאֻם־יְהוָה וְשַׁבְתִּי אֶת־שְׁבִיתְכֶם **שְׁבוּתְכֶם** וְקִבַּצְתִּי אֶתְכֶם
מִכָּל־הַגּוֹיִם וּמִכָּל־הַמְּקוֹמוֹת אֲשֶׁר הִדַּחְתִּי אֶתְכֶם שָׁם נְאֻם־יְהוָה
וַהֲשִׁבֹתִי אֶתְכֶם אֶל־הַמָּקוֹם אֲשֶׁר־הִגְלֵיתִי אֶתְכֶם מִשָּׁם:

I will be found by you, says the LORD, and I will bring you back from your captivity;
I will gather you from all the nations and from all the places where I have driven you,
says the LORD; and I will bring you to the place from which I cause you to be carried away
into exile.

Jer 29,14 speaks about God's promise of gathering the Israelites and bringing them back into their homeland.[45] During the exile the well being of the exiles was very closely related to the well being of Babylon.[46] When the period[47] of their exile comes to an end, however, God reveals His new plan for their future (אַחֲרִית).[48] Jer 29,10-14 speaks about this plan (מַחֲשָׁבוֹת) for the exiles in Babylon. He affirms the fulfilment of God's gracious promise to bring them back (לְשִׁיב) to their land. He assures them that God will listen (שָׁמַע) to them when they call upon (קְרָא) Him and pray (פָּלַל hithpael v.12 cf. v.7) to Him. In comforting assurance God tells them through the prophet: "You will seek me and find me when you seek me with all your heart." (cf. v.13).

Verses 13-14 are very closely linked to each other and present a type of *protasis* (v.13) and *apodosis* (v.14),[49] where the second sub-verse of v.13 is linked with the first sub-verse of v. 14. The original text in vv.12-14 seems to have been shorter. Taking note of this, D. B. Duhm remarks that the text has been very much enlarged.[50] God's action to bring back his people especially refers in v.10 to their Babylonian captivity whereas v.14 refers to their captivity in general: "from all the nations and from all the places where I have driven you."[51] Duhm thinks that the

---

[44] BOADT, *Reading the Old Testament*, 360-361.

[45] BRAULIK, *Deuteronomium II*, 216.

[46] HOLLADAY, *Jeremiah 2*, 141.

[47] The period of exile is indicated as being "seventy years" in 25,11-12 and in 29,10 with different dating (605 and 597 B.C., respectively); the latter seems to be secondary, a correction of the understanding that the Babylonian exile was permanent. See CARROLL, *Jeremiah*, 553.

[48] HOLLADAY, *Jeremiah 2*, 141.

[49] MCKANE, *Jeremiah*, Vol. II, 729.

[50] DUHM, *Jeremia*, 230; see also HOLLADAY, *Jeremiah 2*, 134. Many scholars favour post-exilic composition of these verses. See KEWON, SCALISE, and SMOTHERS, *Jeremiah 26-52*, 67.

[51] MCKANE, *Jeremiah*, Vol. II, 729; see also CARROLL, *Jeremiah*, 553.

expression שׁוּב שְׁבוּת (*lit.* "to turn the turning") in this text means to "turn someone's fortune."[52]

The relation between God's action of gathering (קבץ) the captives (14b) and bringing them back seems to have been overlooked in most interpretations. When both of these actions are taken together as a whole, it becomes clear that שׁוּב שְׁבוּת cannot be translated as merely "to restore the fortunes," but must more concretely mean "to bring back from captivity" those whom the LORD has gathered from the nations as a mark of His new initiative, which enables the exiles to return to their homeland again.

Jer 30,3:

כִּי הִנֵּה יָמִים בָּאִים נְאֻם־יְהוָה וְשַׁבְתִּי אֶת־שְׁבוּת עַמִּי יִשְׂרָאֵל וִיהוּדָה אָמַר יְהוָה וַהֲשִׁבֹתִים אֶל־הָאָרֶץ אֲשֶׁר־נָתַתִּי לַאֲבוֹתָם וִירֵשׁוּהָ׃

For behold, the days are coming, says the LORD, when I will bring back from captivity
my people Israel and Judah, says the LORD, and I will cause them to return to the land
which I gave to their fathers, and they shall possess it.

Jer 30,1-31,40 speaks about the restoration of Israel.[53] The much larger portion of the text (cf. 30,1-31,22) may have been written during Josiah's Reforms (615 B.C.) and his tragic death in Megiddo (609 B.C.).[54] Jer 30,1-4 forms an introductory unit with a superscription in vv.1-2 and an oracle of salvation in v.3, concluding with the affirmation of God's word formula in v.4. The oracle of salvation begins with a typical prophetic formula "for behold the days are coming,"[55] which makes God's saving intervention definite. BHS suggests that וִיהוּדָה ("and Judah")[56] in 3b (cf. v.4), which is an addition, while the subject of וִירֵשׁוּהָ in the final clause, is not very clear.[57]

Jer 30,3 seems to be redactional; it is reworked and apparently related to 31,27.31.38.[58] The expression שׁוּב שְׁבוּת in the sense of "to restore the fortunes" may be applied only in a general sense, but the second part of the verse, "I will

---

[52] DUHM, *Jeremia,* 230; see also HOLLADAY, *Jeremiah 2,* 135.142 ("restore one's fortunes"); DIETRICH (שׁוּב שְׁבוּת, 36-37) took it as cognate accusative and translated, "render a restoration."

[53] CARROLL, *Jeremiah,* 571.

[54] HOLLADAY, *Jeremiah 2,* 18.

[55] Its usage in the prose section of the book is characteristic of Jeremiah's style: 7,32; 9,25; 16,14; 19,6; 23,5.7; 31,27.38; 33,14; 48,12; 49,2; 51,47.52 and elsewhere, Am 4,2; 8,11; 9,13; 1Sam 2,31; 2Kgs 20,17. See JONES, *Jeremiah,* 376.

[56] According to HOLLADAY, "Israel and Judah" points to the presence of the early northern recension (Israel) in the southern recension (Judah). See his *Jeremiah 2,* 171.

[57] KEWON, SCALISE, and SMOTHERS, *Jeremiah 26-52,* 88. In the translations "their fathers" is usually made its subject, see in the same place.

[58] JONES, *Jeremiah,* 377; see also CARROLL, *Jeremiah,* 571.

cause them to return to the land" and again, "which I gave to their fathers[59] and they shall possess it"[60] make it amply clear that the expression denotes the return of the dispersed of Israel (cf. 721 B.C.) and the exiles of Judah (587 B.C.).[61] The text does not speak about the people converting or repenting. This is astounding in that it exhibits God's wholly gracious intervention.[62]

Jer 30,18:

כֹּה אָמַר יְהוָה הִנְנִי־שָׁב שְׁבוּת אָהֳלֵי יַעֲקוֹב וּמִשְׁכְּנֹתָיו אֲרַחֵם
וְנִבְנְתָה עִיר עַל־תִּלָּהּ וְאַרְמוֹן עַל־מִשְׁפָּטוֹ יֵשֵׁב׃

Thus says the LORD: Behold, I will bring back the captivity of Jacob's tents,
and have mercy on his dwelling places; the city shall be built upon its own mound,
and the palace shall remain according to its own plan.

Jer 30,18 which properly belongs to 30,18-22,[63] speaks about a "general form of proclamation of salvation,"[64] but more concretely it speaks about "God's promise of restoration to Jacob's rural, urban and political life and of the covenant relationship."[65] There are two textual points that deserve our attention in v.18, where אָהֳלֵי "his tents" is missing in LXX[B] and instead of וּמִשְׁכְּנֹתָיו ("and his dwelling places"), LXX refers directly to καὶ αἰχμλωσίαν (וּשְׁבִיתוֹ "his captivity").[66] W. L. Holladay noted that the occurrences of assonance *miš-b* (thrice) and *miš* (twice) are a characteristic feature of this verse.[67]

In the book of Jeremiah, אָהֳלֵי "tents" (= "curtain" cf. 4,20; 10,20) refers to the temple in Jerusalem, but מִשְׁכְּנֹתָיו "his dwellings" usually refers in a poetic manner to urban residential buildings, although it may also refer to the LORD's sanctuary.[68]

---

[59] "The land which I gave to their fathers" is a deuteronomic expression which appears in Jer 7,7.14; 14,5.10; 10,23; 23,39; 24,5; 31,32; 32,22; 34,13; 35,15; see JONES, *Jeremiah*, 377. According to HOLLADAY the term "fathers" is associated with the covenant in Deut, cf. 5,3; 7,12; 8,18; so also "to bring out of Egypt by (the LORD's) hand" Deut 5,15; 6,21; 7,8; 9,26, 26,8. See his *Jeremiah 2*, 165.

[60] The verb יָרֵשׁ ("to take possession of") is a "key word" in the book of Joshua, see KEWON, SCALISE, and SMOTHERS, *Jeremiah 26-52*, 89.

[61] The exiles of Israel (i.e., the northern kingdom) are never mentioned in the re-building of Jerusalem in Ezra-Nehemiah, cf. KEWON, SCALISE, and SMOTHERS, *Jeremiah 26-52*, 89.

[62] KEWON, SCALISE, and SMOTHERS, *Jeremiah 26-52*, 89.

[63] KEWON, SCALISE, and SMOTHERS, *Jeremiah 26-52*, 103. HOLLADAY gives slightly different composition of this unit: 30,18-21+31,1aβb, see HOLLADAY, *Jeremiah 2*, 168.

[64] HOLLADAY, *Jeremiah 2*, 168.

[65] KEWON, SCALISE, and SMOTHERS, *Jeremiah 26-52*, 103.

[66] KEWON, SCALISE, and SMOTHERS, *Jeremiah 26-52*, 102.

[67] HOLLADAY, *Jeremiah 2*, 176.

[68] HOLLADAY, *Jeremiah 2*, 176. KEWON, SCALISE, and SMOTHERS (*Jeremiah 26-52*, 103) take it to represent the "rural" and the "city-buildings"/"royal palaces" (tent and dwellings, respectively), while CARROLL (*Jeremiah*, 583) interprets "his tents" as reflecting a "pastoral image."

Cultic terminology, e.g., "tent" (v.18), "congregation" (v.20), "thanksgiving" (v.19), and a reference to monarchy (cf. v.21) appears in the text.[69] The parallel drawn through the use of these terms may have been intended to point to the cultic reunion under Josiah's reform (cf. 3,14; 31,6), as indicated in Balaam's oracle in reference to "tents" and "encampments" (Num 24,5).[70]

This act of restoration flows from God's promise to bring back from captivity (שׁוּב שְׁבוּת) the tents of Jacob. In a general sense, the expression may mean "to restore fortunes," but more concretely it means to "return the captives/exiles" who will take up the re-building of the temple, signalling not just a cultic unification, but also a political reconciliation of the divided kingdoms.

Jer 31,23:

כֹּה־אָמַר יְהוָה צְבָאוֹת אֱלֹהֵי יִשְׂרָאֵל עוֹד יֹאמְרוּ אֶת־הַדָּבָר הַזֶּה בְּאֶרֶץ יְהוּדָה וּבְעָרָיו
בְּשׁוּבִי אֶת־שְׁבוּתָם יְבָרֶכְךָ יְהוָה נְוֵה־צֶדֶק הַר הַקֹּדֶשׁ:

Thus says the LORD of hosts, the God of Israel: They shall again use this speech
in the land of Judah and in its cities, when I bring back their captivity:
The LORD bless you, O home of justice, and mountain of holiness!

The introductory formula, "Thus says the LORD of hosts, the God of Israel" appears frequently in the "prose tradition."[71] One of the difficulties of relating to this verse is whether it should be taken as a part of 31,24-25 or as a separate unit.[72] LXX's rendering of the final clause εὐλογημένος κύριος ἐπὶ δίκαιον ὄρος τὸ ἅγιον αὐτοῦ ("blessed be the LORD on his righteous holy mountain"), presents a difficulty because of its different interpretation. While the "restored holy mountain"[73] is the object of God's blessing in MT, in the LXX God himself becomes the object of praise.

בְּשׁוּבִי אֶת־שְׁבוּתָם "When I bring them back from their captivity" refers to people's experience of God's deeds of restoring Judah and Israel, which evokes a prayer of blessing for His "holy mountain"[74] and the "home of justice" (cf. Isa

---

[69] HOLLADAY, *Jeremiah 2*, 157.

[70] HOLLADAY, *Jeremiah 2*, 176.

[71] JONES, *Jeremiah*, 396.

[72] HOLLADAY, *Jeremiah 2*, 195. HOLLADAY thinks that from a form-critical point of view, v.23 is distinct from vv.24-25, although both "come from the same period" (cf. Isa 56,7; 65,26; 66,20); see in the same place. CARROLL places v.23 under the first of the five additions in Jer 31, i.e., vv.23-26;27-30; 31-34; 35-37; 38-40; see CARROLL, *Jeremiah*, 605; see also KEWON, SCALISE, and SMOTHERS, *Jeremiah 26-52*, 126.

[73] I.e., the city with its temple; cf. Isa 56,7; 65,26, 66,20; also HOLLADAY, *Jeremiah 2*, 166.

[74] The phrase "holy mountain" occurs 23 times in the prophets, including six times in Isa 40-66 and the Psalms; see HOLLADAY, *Jeremiah 2*, 196. In Ex 13,15 it refers to the land of Canaan, see HOLLADAY, in the same place. Likewise, in Isa 11,9 it denotes the entire land. See RUDOLF, *Jeremia*, 182;

50,7) from the returning captives who fill the land of Judah again.[75] So, the meaning of שׁוּב שְׁבוּת "to restore the fortunes" is inadequate in expressing this astonishing deed of God. Therefore, it should be rendered "to bring back captives."

Jer 32,44:

שָׂד֞וֹת בַּכֶּ֣סֶף יִקְנ֗וּ וְכָת֤וֹב בַּסֵּ֙פֶר֙ וְחָת֔וֹם וְהָעֵ֖ד עֵדִ֑ים בְּאֶ֤רֶץ בִּנְיָמִן֙ וּבִסְבִיבֵ֣י יְרוּשָׁלַ֔ם
וּבְעָרֵ֣י יְהוּדָה֩ וּבְעָרֵ֨י הָהָ֜ר וּבְעָרֵ֤י הַשְּׁפֵלָה֙ וּבְעָרֵ֣י הַנֶּ֔גֶב כִּֽי־אָשִׁ֥יב אֶת־שְׁבוּתָ֖ם נְאֻם־יְהוָֽה׃

Men will buy fields for money, sign deeds and seal them, and take witnesses,
in the land of Benjamin, in the places around Jerusalem, in the cities of Judah,
in the cities of the mountains, in the cities of the lowland, and in the cities of the South;
for I will cause their captives to return, says the LORD.

Jer 32 is seen as an extension of the oracles of consolations in Jer 30,1-31,40.[76] In the face of the imminent catastrophe of Jerusalem,[77] Zedekiah put all his efforts into averting the danger threatening himself, personally. Against this background, the concluding unit of Jer 42-44[78] reflects God's own care for the land,[79] as the text announces the reversal of His judgment. The exact date of these oracles is difficult to ascertain because different scholars give different dates for the tumultuous days of Zedekiah's reign, before Jerusalem fell to the Babylonians.[80]

V.42 begins with a declaration from God, who promises to bestow prosperity on the people even as He makes them bear the punishment of His judgment. The land that bore the deserted look[81] of destruction and deportation will be populated again when the returnees buy fields (cf. v.10; 33,12-13)[82] and settle there. The surrounding countryside around Jerusalem[83] will be populated when the LORD

---

[75] CARROLL, *Jeremiah*, 606.

[76] KEWON, SCALISE, and SMOTHERS, *Jeremiah 26-52*, 149.

[77] RUDOLF considers the historical information in vv.1-5 significant because it clarifies the situation of the prophet; see his *Jeremiah*, 189.

[78] KEOWN, SCALISE, and SMOTHERS, *Jeremiah 26-52*, 145; see also JONES, *Jermiah*, 418-419. HOLLADAY (*Jeremiah 2*, 208) argues that vv.41-44 belong to the original text of the book.

[79] KEOWN, SCALISE, and SMOTHERS, *Jeremiah 26-52*, 147.

[80] "HOLLADAY (2:34) dates the siege from January 588 to July 587, whereas HAYES and HOOKER (*New Chronology*, 97-98) put it one year later, i.e., from January 587 to July 586. MALAMAT ("The Twilight of Judah," in VT.Suppl. 28, 145) calculates the length of the siege as thirty months, i.e., from January 588 to July 586. The Babylonians lifted the siege temporarily (37:5-11), apparently due to the threatening approach of an Egyptian army under Pharaoh Hophra (HOLLADAY, *Jeremiah*, 2, 34, in the summer of 588; and MALAMAT, in *IEJ* 18, 152: in winter-spring 587)." See KEOWN, SCALISE, and SMOTHERS, *Jeremiah 26-52*, 150.

[81] This (שְׁמָמָה 4,23-28; cf. 12,4) is caused by the absence of humans, birds and beasts, cf. HOLLADAY, *Jeremiah 2*, 218.

[82] HOLLADAY, *Jeremiah 2*, 218.

[83] I.e., fields and landed property will be purchased in the Jerusalem countryside, the hill-country, the Shephala and the Negev, and thus the whole country of Judah will witness the registration of records and the conveyance of deeds, a sign of God's act of restoration of the land. See MCKANE, *Jeremiah*, Vol. II, 851.

brings back the captives (from Babylon). This description reflects the significance of Jeremiah's purchase of a piece of property in Anathoth (cf. 32,1-15.24f.,43f.).[84]

Since v.43 concludes Jeremiah's prayer in vv.16-25, v.44 seems to further elaborate upon it.[85] It mentions politically significant places: "the land of Benjamin," "the surroundings of Jerusalem" and "the cities of Judah," and mentions topographical regions of Judah: "the cities of the mountains," and "the lowland and of the south" (cf. Ps 126,4).[86] God's restoration of all these places, cities and regions will take place when he brings the captives back (שׁוּב שְׁבוּת) who were carried away to Babylon, which means that the Babylonians will not occupy the land for ever.[87]

Jer 33,7:

וַהֲשִׁבֹתִי אֶת־שְׁבוּת יְהוּדָה וְאֵת שְׁבוּת יִשְׂרָאֵל וּבְנִתִים כְּבָרִאשֹׁנָה:

I will bring Judah and Israel back from captivity and will rebuild them as they were before.

Jer 33 is broken into two parts: vv.1-13 and vv.14-26; where vv.1-13 speaks about God's revelation to Jeremiah concerning the restoration of Jerusalem and Judah.[88] The expression שׁוּב שְׁבוּת occurs in vv.7 and 11. Many Greek versions read "Jerusalem" in place of "Israel" in v.7. Rudolf thinks that "Jerusalem" is probably correct in the context because there is no reference to Israel (Samaria) in this section and its appearance in the second part of the verse is a secondary addition. Even though Jerusalem will lie under siege and be destroyed by the sword because of God's wrath (v.5), He promises to bring healing, peace and security to His people because of His goodness and mercy (v.6).[89] The description of the horror (v.5) and God's initiative to restore them (v.6) indicate that the restoration of Jerusalem is impossible without God's special intervention.

In the background of vv.5-6, God's announcement to "bring back the captives of Judah and Jerusalem" (with emendation) in v.7[90] reveals His saving intervention for His people and enlarges the scope of restoration spoken in v.6 so that His restoration and well-being are not limited to Jerusalem alone, but extended to the whole of Judah.[91] The usage of the verb בנה ("to build" cf. 30,18; 31,4 also 1,10) originally relates to building houses.[92] Theologically speaking, the rebuilding of Jerusalem and Judah presuppose certain condition: "only with the forgiveness of

---

[84] CARROLL, *Jeremiah*, 631.

[85] JONES, *Jeremiah*, 418-419; see also MCKANE, *Jeremiah*, Vol. II, 851.

[86] KEOWN, SCALISE, and SMOTHERS, *Jeremiah 26-52*, 162, see also CARROLL, *Jeremiah*, 631.

[87] CARROLL, *Jeremiah*, 631.

[88] HOLLADAY, *Jeremiah 2*, 222. See also CARROLL, *Jeremiah*, 631; RUDLOF, *Jeremiah*, 197.

[89] RUDLOF, *Jeremiah*, 196-197.

[90] Here שׁוּב שְׁבוּת is considered to be secondary; see HOLLADAY, *Jeremiah 2*, 230.

[91] RUDLOF, *Jeremiah*, 197-198.

[92] RUDLOF, *Jeremiah*, 198; see also KEOWN, SCALISE, and SMOTHERS, *Jeremiah 26-52*, 171.

the past and the cleansing of guilt and rebellion could the renewed city and temple
become again a place which would yield joy, praise and glory to Yahweh."[93]

Jer 33,11:

קוֹל שָׂשׂוֹן וְקוֹל שִׂמְחָה קוֹל חָתָן וְקוֹל כַּלָּה קוֹל אֹמְרִים הוֹדוּ אֶת־יְהוָה צְבָאוֹת

כִּי־טוֹב יְהוָה כִּי־לְעוֹלָם חַסְדּוֹ מְבִאִים תּוֹדָה בֵּית יְהוָה

כִּי־אָשִׁיב אֶת־שְׁבוּת־הָאָרֶץ כְּבָרִאשֹׁנָה אָמַר יְהוָה:

The voice of joy and the voice of gladness, the voice of the bridegroom
and the voice of the bride, the voice of those who will say: Praise the LORD of hosts,
for the LORD is good, for his mercy endures forever and of those who will bring
the sacrifice of praise into the house of the LORD.
For, I will cause the captives of the land to return as at the first, says the LORD.

Jer 33,11 belongs to the second sub-unit (vv.10-11 cf. 33,1-13),[94] where we come
across a new announcement of salvation.[95] This small passage assures that the land
that has become a waste (חָרֵב) for lack of man and beast will again sing the praises
of God (v.10). עוֹד ("once again") is here characteristic of this sub-unit,[96] which
points to the result of God's act of restoration.

The expression of thanksgiving in v.11 is reminiscent of the thanksgiving Psalm
136.[97] It expresses a joyful gratitude of the captives whom God has brought back to
the land; thus שׁוּב שְׁבוּת occurs a second time in this chapter. Although its
secondary meaning denotes "restoration of their fortunes," the joyful thanksgiving
is a result of the prime cause, namely, of God's bringing the captives back to their
own land. "The voice of the bridegroom and the voice of the bride" is imagery of
marriage,[98] and it gives an indication of "hope for the future" and "the survival of
God's people," which is guaranteed by "bringing back captives" to the land.[99]

Jer 33,26:

גַּם־זֶרַע יַעֲקוֹב וְדָוִד עַבְדִּי אֶמְאַס מִקַּחַת מִזַּרְעוֹ מֹשְׁלִים אֶל־זֶרַע בְּרָהָם יִשְׂחָק וְיַעֲקֹב

כִּי־אָשׁוּב **אָשִׁיב** אֶת־שְׁבוּתָם וְרִחַמְתִּים:

Then I will cast away the descendants of Jacob and David my servant,
so that I will not take any of his descendants to be rulers
over the descendants of Abraham, Isaac, and Jacob.
For, I will cause their captives to return, and will have mercy on them.

---

[93] CARROLL, *Jeremiah*, 635.

[94] CARROLL thinks that 33,10-11 are variations of 32,36.43; cf. CARROLL, *Jeremiah*, 635.

[95] HOLLADAY, *Jeremiah 2*, 224.

[96] KEOWN, SCALISE, and SMOTHERS, *Jeremiah 26-52*, 172.

[97] JONES, *Jeremiah*, 422.

[98] McKANE, *Jeremiah*, Vol. II, 859.

[99] KEOWN, SCALISE, and SMOTHERS, *Jeremiah 26-52*, 172;

Jer 33,26 belongs to the concluding sub-unit 33,23-26 (cf. Jer 33,13-26). Vv.23-26 speaks about the divine guarantee of the permanence of God's covenant, which is reaffirmed in v.26. The expression שְׁבוּת שׁוּב occurs in vv.7.11.26 and serves as a link between 33,1-13 and 33,14-26.[100] The use of שְׁבוּת שׁוּב in v.26 shows textual variation. *Kethib* has אָשׁוּב (*qal* impf.), but many versions prefer to read אָשִׁיב (*hiphil* impf.) as in *Qere*.

The first part of Jer 33,26 partly reflects a thinking of one group of people who thought that the fall of Jerusalem and the captivity of its people was an indication of God's rejection of the house of Judah and therefore, of the house of David.[101] The rejection of any ruler (MT מֹשְׁלִים pl.)[102] of Davidic descent is a subtle criticism of kingship itself, which was viewed as largely responsible for the catastrophe of Jerusalem. Nevertheless, a direct link of שְׁבוּת שׁוּב with רָחַם ("to have/show mercy") in the final clause, together with a reference to "causing the captives to return" to their homeland in the preceding clause, gives a motive for God's restoration of His people.[103]

Jer 48,47:

וְשַׁבְתִּי שְׁבוּת־מוֹאָב בְּאַחֲרִית הַיָּמִים נְאֻם־יְהוָה עַד־הֵנָּה מִשְׁפַּט מוֹאָב:
Yet I will bring back the captives of Moab in the latter days, says the LORD.
Thus far is the judgment of Moab.

Jer 48,47 belongs to the fourth poem on Moab (vv.29-47) in Jer 48.[104] It is missing in LXX[105] and its first part (47a) has the same sense as in 46,26b while its second part (47b) is the author's own addition.[106]

This oracle is a reversal of judgment against Moab. After its destruction, time will come when God will restore the fortunes of Moab, thereby revealing His sovereignty over it. The usage of שְׁבוּת שׁוּב to denote "bring back captives" does not make proper sense here; therefore the phrase should be rendered to denote a more general sense of "restoration of fortunes." Carroll notes that it reflects a Judean perspective of the people who survived the catastrophe of 587 BC.[107] The

---

[100] HOLLADAY, *Jeremiah 2*, 230.

[101] CARROLL, *Jeremiah*, 639.

[102] HOLLADAY, *Jeremiah 2*, 228.

[103] CARROLL, *Jeremiah*, 639; see also KEOWN, SCALISE, and SMOTHERS, *Jeremiah 26-52*, 175.

[104] JONES, *Jeremiah*, 505. CARROLL (*Jeremiah*, 795) makes a smaller unit: Jer 48,40-47 and argues that the poem ends effectively in v.42, with vv.43-47 depicting the ruin of Moab are secondary additions. See also HOLLADAY, *Jeremiah 2*, 353.

[105] Jer 48,45-47 are missing in LXX, see MCKANE, *Jeremiah*, Vol. II, 1198.

[106] RUDOLF, *Jeremiah*, 263.

[107] CARROLL, *Jeremiah*, 796.

announcement of salvation to Moab (cf. 30,6) is similar to the salvation to Ammon (49,6), Elam (49,39) and – more remotely - to the salvation of Egypt (46,26b).[108]

Jer 49,6:

וְאַחֲרֵי־כֵן אָשִׁיב אֶת־שְׁבוּת בְּנֵי־עַמּוֹן נְאֻם־יְהוָה׃

But afterward I will bring back the captives of the people of Ammon, says the LORD.

Jer 49,6 (cf. 49,1-6) is an oracle of judgment against Ammon.[109] It announces destruction and desolation of the land of Ammon and defeat and exile of its deity and of its officials. It also denounces her pride and false trust, and establishes the sovereignty of the LORD. The general situation of Ammon's judgment is similar to that against Moab, although Ammon was found guilty of rebellion (594 B.C.) and disloyalty to Babylon (Jer 27,3) in the latter's campaign against Jerusalem in 589-587 (cf. Ezek 21,23-37).[110] Holladay maintains that there are two oracles here (vv.1-2 & vv.3-5), which may come from 587 and 598 B.C., respectively.[111]

The opening prepositional phrase וְאַחֲרֵי־כֵן (v.6) is lacking in LXX.[112] Although some exegetes propose its date in the time of Josiah, we do not know the exact date of this oracle, even though Jer 27 refers to the gathering of the officials from Tyre, Sidon, Ammon and Moab in Jerusalem in 594 B.C.[113] Here שׁוּב שְׁבוּת denotes "to bring back the captives" of Ammon who were driven out because of their pride.[114]

Jer 49,39:

וְהָיָה בְּאַחֲרִית הַיָּמִים *אָשׁוּב *אָשִׁיב אֶת־*שְׁבִית *שְׁבוּת עֵילָם נְאֻם־יְהוָה׃

But it shall come to pass in the latter days I will bring back the captives of Elam,
says the LORD.

Jer 49,34-39 (in LXX 25,14-19) is an oracle of judgment against Elam.[115] The historical date of this oracle, according to v.34, is the beginning of Zedekiah's reign (cf. 2Kgs 24,18). Accordingly, the oracle concerning the destruction of Elam[116] by the Persians is placed in 597 B.C. However, this date comes into

---

[108] HOLLADAY, *Jeremiah 2*, 353.

[109] Other oracles concerning Ammon: Am 1,13-15; Zeph 2,8-11; Ezek 21,20; 28-32; 25,1-7; see KEOWN, SCALISE, and SMOTHERS, *Jeremiah 26-52*, 322.

[110] BRIGHT, *Jeremiah*, 326.

[111] HOLLADAY, *Jeremiah 2*, 367.

[112] KEOWN, SCALISE, and SMOTHERS, *Jeremiah 26-52*, 322.

[113] KEOWN, SCALISE, and SMOTHERS, *Jeremiah 26-52*, 325.

[114] HÖFFKEN considers the oracles of salvation to Moab and Ammon as restoration of the East Jordan land. See his „Zu den Heilszusätzen", in *VT* 27, 402.

[115] RUDOLF, *Jeremia*, 273; HOLLADAY, *Jeremiah 2*, 387; KEOWN, SCALISE, and SMOTHERS, *Jeremiah 26-52*, 340; MCKANE, *Jeremiah*, Vol. II, 1144-1145; CARROLL excludes v.34 from this unit, see CARROLL, *Jeremiah*, 813.

[116] Elam, the land of the Parthians (cf. HÖFFKEN, „Zu den Heilszusätzen", in *VT* 27, 404), once a very rich kingdom, was situated to the east of Babylon and north of the Persian Gulf (southwest

conflict with Jer 46,2ff., which refers to the battle of Carchemish between Neco II of Egypt and Nebuchadnezzar of Babylon[117] as being in the 4th year of Jehoiakim's reign.[118] Jer 25,25 describes Nebuchadnezzar's campaign against Elam, which probably took place in 596/595.[119]

The MT shows a variant reading in v.39: *Kethib* has אָשׁוּב אֶת שְׁבִית (*qal* impf. + n. fem. sg. cstr.), whereas *Qere* reads אָשִׁיב אֶת־שְׁבוּת (*hiphil* impf. + n. fem. sg. cstr.). The prepositional phrase בְּאַחֲרִית הַיָּמִים ("in the later days") at the beginning, does not have an eschatological sense, but merely refers to the end of the period of punishment of Elam. שׁוּב שְׁבוּת denotes "to bring back the captives" of Elam, which gives hope also for the captives of Judah.

Although the oracle of salvation to Elam is an addition,[120] in the larger perspective of Jeremiah's call to be a prophet to the nations (cf. 1,5), God's promise to bring back her captives clearly establishes His sovereignty over the nations.[121] Holladay maintains that it is difficult to find a motive for this addition other than that it traces a note of universalism.[122] Rudolf thinks that the oracle of restoration to Elam gives strong hope that the captives of Judah will also be brought back.[123]

6.3.2. Conclusion

The meaning of שׁוּב שְׁבוּת in Jeremiah is very clear. In view of the exile of the people of Jerusalem/Judah to Babylon in 598 and 587 B.C., Jeremiah used the expression in its basic sense, "to bring back out of captivity" Jerusalem/Judah. However, its general sense, "to restore the fortunes" is also not completely ruled out, for restoration of the devastated city and country was equally significant. In

---

of Iran), had Susa as its capital city (cf. RUDOLF, *Jeremia*, 273). It fell to the powers of Assyria in 645 and when Assyria itself fell to the Medes in 612 B.C., Elam "became a protectorate" and remained so until it became part of the Persian rule in 550. See HOLLADAY, *Jeremiah 2*, 388; see also DRESDEN, "Elam," in *IDB* 2, 70-71.

[117] The battle of Carchemish took place in May-June 605 BC. See WISEMANN, *Chronicles of the Chaldean Kings*, 25; HAYES and HOOKER, *A new Chronology*, 89; MALAMAT, "The Last King of Judah," in *IEJ* 18, 139; DONNER, *Geschichte des Volkes Israel* 2, 402.

[118] According to Jer 46,1ff., the 4th year of Jehoiakim's reign is attributed to 1st Nisan 597 B.C., (upon the death of Josiah, the elders of Judah put Jehoahaz [Josiah's second son] on the throne, ignoring Eliakim [Jehoiakim] his eldest son, but on his retreat, Neco II removed Jehoahaz and made Jehoiakim as king of Judah). See HAYES and HOOKER, *A new Chronology*, 89-90; see also RUDOLF, *Jeremiah*, 273.

[119] HAYES and HOOKER, *A new Chronology*, 36; see also HOLLADAY, *Jeremiah 2*, 388.

[120] HOLLADAY, *Jeremiah 2*, 389. RUDOLF considers this verse to be original and an affirmation of 9,15. See his *Jeremia*, 273.

[121] HOLLADAY, *Jeremiah 2*, 389.

[122] HOLLADAY, *Jeremiah 2*, 389; see also CARROLL, *Jeremiah*, 814.

[123] RUDOLF, *Jeremia*, 273.

fact, this was the first concern of the returning people. All the same, "to restore the fortunes" or simply the "restoration" of Jerusalem was conditioned upon first returning of the people from their captivity.

6.4. In Ezekiel

Ezekiel was among the first group of people from Judah who were carried in 597 B.C. into exile by Nebuchadnezzar along with king Jehoiachin, the queen-mother, and the courtiers. As an exile, Ezekiel lived far away from Jerusalem/Judah (cf. 1,1), but still received information on the events taking place in the homeland. For him and his companions exile became a reality and they began to concentrate on how to return to their land. In this context שׁוּב שְׁבוּת in Ezek 16,53 and 39,25 speak about the salvation to Israel, while 29,14 speaks about the salvation of Egypt.

> Ezek 16,53:
>
> וְשַׁבְתִּי אֶת־שְׁבִיתְהֶן אֶת־שְׁבִית ‏שְׁבוּת סְדֹם וּבְנוֹתֶיהָ
> וְאֶת־שְׁבִית־שְׁבוּת שֹׁמְרוֹן וּבְנוֹתֶיהָ וּשְׁבִית ‏וּשְׁבוּת שְׁבִיתַיִךְ בְּתוֹכֶהְנָה:
>
> When I bring back their captives, the captives of Sodom and her daughters,
> and the captives of Samaria and her daughters,
> then I will bring back the captives of your captivity among them.

Ezekiel 16 is basically an allegory of unfaithful Jerusalem (cf. 16,1-43), which is carried further in the allegory of the two sisters (16,44-58)[124] and concludes by referring to God's enduring covenant (16,59-63). Unlike 16,1-43, which looks forward to the disaster of Jerusalem, the second part of the allegory (16,44-63) comes from a different time and place because it (vv.43bβ-58) looks back at the catastrophe that has befallen her.[125] It speaks about her two sisters, Samaria and Sodom. A preference for her Hittite mother over her Amorite father (v.45) is a subtle indication of her broken relationship with her LORD. Jerusalem's relationship with Samaria and Sodom as her sisters is reflected in the terms that all three have despised their "husbands".[126] Jerusalem is compared to Samaria through her numerous sins (v.51) which amount to her religious disqualification, while

---

[124] COOKE, *Ezekiel*, 176. W. JÜNGLING (lectures [WS 2002/03] on *Das Buch Ezekiel*, 124-160 cf. 148) includes 43b in Ezek 16,44-58. See also M. MARK, „Ewiger Bund", in SEDLEMIER (ed.), *Gottes Wege suchend*, 203-252; SWANEPOEL, "Ezekiel 16: Abandoned Child...Wife," in DAVIES and CLINES (eds.), *Among the Prophets*, JSOT.Suppl. 144, 84-104.

[125] BROWNLEE, *Ezekiel 1-19*, 243.

[126] By deserting God, Samaria, Sodom and Jerusalem have become like three sisters. The figurative term "husbands" is used here more as a completing metaphor to show the "infidelity" of Jerusalem and her "two sisters," than to insist on their actual sexual moral character. See WEVERS, *Ezekiel*, 130.

corresponding also to the guilt (v.49) of Sodom.[127] Beyond sexual immorality and lewdness (v.58), the sin of Sodom and Samaria is primarily their pride and haughtiness. But Israel has become more depraved than Samaria and Sodom because her evils are worse, making her sisters look comparatively righteous (v. 52).[128]

V.53 (cf. vv.52-58) is marked by the verb נָשָׂא ("to raise," "carry" cf. vv.54.58). Three aspects of Jerusalem's shame (cf. vv.52.54.56-58) are interwoven with two aspects of God's grace to her (cf. vv.53.55), which is the motive both for God's judgment against the three sisters and also His restoration of their fortunes. Here, Mark renders שׁוּב (qal) "to change" the fortunes of Sodom, Samaria, and Jerusalem (cf. v.53), and שׁוּב (hiphil) "to return" or "restore" their fortunes to the condition of times past (קַדְמָה Ezek 36,11; Isa 23,7). This has great theological significance because it means that Sodom and Samaria will share in the covenant when God renews it.[129]

When Jeroboam became king in place of his father Solomon, ten tribes of Israel rebelled and broke away from Judah (cf. 1Kgs 11,29-12,19). Samaria became the capital city of Israel under Omri (1Kgs 16,23-24). Israel's evil deeds multiplied during Hoshea's reign. When Shalmanaser defeated Hoshea, Israel became a vassal-state of Assyria; however, Hoshea did not pay tribute to Assyria but quietly sent an emissary to Egypt for help. This led the king of Assyria to attack Samaria in 721 B.C. Samaria was destroyed and the population of Israel was scattered in the Assyrian provinces (cf. 2Kgs 17).[130] Israel's worship of other gods and her practice of seeking support from other nations were interpreted as the motives of her judgment.

The city of Sodom existed in the Patriarchal period, but was no longer extant at the time of the settlement in the Land. Still, it was a reminder of wickedness especially of her homosexuality (Gen 19,4-9),[131] for which God destroyed it with fire (v.50; cf. Gen 18,20-21; 19,23). In the allegory, Ezekiel does not insist on Sodom's lasciviousness, but on her failure to help the needy in her prosperity. Brownlee maintains that Ezekiel knew a tradition concerning Sodom other than Gen 19. In this regards, he refers to Zimmerli, who goes so far to argue that Ezekiel was thinking of Jerusalem when he spoke of Sodom.[132]

---

[127] MARK, „Ewiger Bund", in SEDLMEIER (ed.), *Gottes Wege suchend*, 229. See also KOCK, „חָטָא", in *ThWAT* II, 859.

[128] This reflects Jerusalem's "abominations" (vv.2.22.26), "prostituting" (vv.2.21.22.26.27), and "licentiousness" (v.27). See ALLEN, *Ezekiel 1-19*, 243, also, GALAMBUSH, *Jerusalem in the Book of Ezekiel*, SBL Diss. Series 130, 107.

[129] MARK, „Ewiger Bund", in SEDLMEIER (ed.), *Gottes Wege suchend*, 231-233; 245.251.

[130] BROWNLEE, *Ezekiel 1-19*, 247.

[131] COOKE, *Ezekiel*, 177. Concerning Sodom's homosexuality, GREENBERG refers to Lev 18,22; 20,13; see his *Ezekiel 1-20*, 289.

[132] BROWNLEE, *Ezekiel 1-19*, 247.

Jerusalem surpassed Samaria and Sodom in doing evil, even though both were guilty of reproachable behaviour.[133] This heavy guilt of Jerusalem made Sodom and Samaria appear more righteous, giving them an opportunity to receive a promise of restoration of their fortunes[134] and of their villages (v.53)[135] to their former prosperity (v.55) before God restores the fortunes of Jerusalem.[136] Their restoration forces Jerusalem to bear (v.54) her reproachful sin and be ashamed of her pride (v.56) and empty righteousness. Yet, in his great mercy, God will cause her return to Him (vv.53.55; cf. v.60), and not through restoring her to former covenant relationship, but by establishing an everlasting covenant.[137] The restoration of Jerusalem is not stressed in v.53, but is almost passed over in silence. Still, it is remarkable that the promise of salvation of Jerusalem is interspersed with the promise of salvation to Sodom and Samaria, without granting her a place of priority.[138]

From external observation of Sodom's destruction (with fire) what follows is the consequent destruction of Samaria and Jerusalem.[139] Here, the meaning of the term שְׁבוּת[140] as "captivity" makes no sense; instead, הָפַךְ ("to overturn" cf. Gen 19,29), denoting destruction and reversal of the place and of its people, becomes prominent. Thus, the meaning of שְׁבוּת stands between the condition of death, which is the power of the Underworld and God's punishment.[141]

---

[133] Vv.47.48.51f.; and 5,6; 23,11; see also Jer 3,11; 23,14; 2Kgs 21,9 = 2Chr 33,9; see COOKE, *Ezekiel*, 177.

[134] LXX renders וְשַׁבְתִּי אֶת־שְׁבִיתְהֶן (v.53) καὶ ἀποστρέψω τὰς ἀποστροφὰς αὐτῶν ("and I shall turn their fortune") although it generally translates שְׁבוּת as αἰχμαλωσία ("captivity"), but following the tradition it questionably rendered the term here differently which is doubtful. The Vulgate renders it *convertam restituens eas conversione Sodomorum*. See PREUSCHEN, „Die Bedeutung von שׁוּב שְׁבוּת", in *ZAW* 15, 4-6, see also SEDLMEIER, *Das Buch Ezekiel 1-24*, 218.

[135] וּבְנוֹתֶיהָ "and her daughters" refers to the villages and towns around Sodom and Samaria (cf. Num 21,25; Judg 1,27; Ps 48,12); see ALLEN, *Ezekiel 1-19*, 244; WEVERS, *Ezekiel*, 130.

[136] It is the bitterest irony of God's judgment that the godlessness of Jerusalem will be a cause of comfort for others, all the more for Samaria and Sodom whom she hated and disdained. See BERTHOLET, *Hesekiel*, KHAT 12, 88-89.

[137] MARK, „Ewiger Bund", in *Gottes Wege suchend*, 245.

[138] The reverse order, Samaria-Sodom/Sodom-Samaria in their judgment/salvation (v.46 and v.53.55, respectively) is remarkable. The geographical orientation North-South/South-North here is definitely not accidental. Compare with Ps 126,4: אֲפִיקִים בַּנֶּגֶב ("streams in Negev").

[139] BAUMANN, „שׁוּב שְׁבוּת", in *ZAW* 73, 23.

[140] Ezek 16,53 attests שְׁבִית (*Kethib*) and שְׁבוּת (*Qere*) in all the three occurrences. In the last occurrence, BHS suggests the reading וְשַׁבְתִּי. Similarly, one would expect שְׁבוּתֵךְ instead of MT שְׁבִיתַיִךְ. ALLEN remarks that here the Masorets have frequently confused the וֹתֵךְ and וֹתַיִךְ endings; see his *Ezekiel 1-19*, 231.

[141] BAUMANN, „שׁוּב שְׁבוּת", in *ZAW* 73, 23.

Baumann points to two aspects of this: namely, realisation of sin and forgiveness, and the recognition of grace and the removal of punishment. Thus, שְׁבוּת is an expression that is required to establish the necessity of judgment and punishment. He concludes further that the object of the verb שבה denotes a collective term or a unity and from the perspective of an external event, the "change or transference of place" is not perceived by the term שְׁבוּת. Thus, it carries a transcendent rather than an historical-geographical meaning. For this reason, Baumann maintains that שְׁבוּת belongs to the religious sphere and that God is the subject of both שבה and שׁוּב. Therefore, by highlighting the sinfulness of the three sisters, שְׁבוּת shows that it also belongs to the ethical-juridical sphere.[142]

Ezek 29,14:

וְשַׁבְתִּי אֶת־שְׁבוּת מִצְרַיִם וַהֲשִׁבֹתִי אֹתָם אֶרֶץ פַּתְרוֹס
עַל־אֶרֶץ מְכוּרָתָם וְהָיוּ שָׁם מַמְלָכָה שְׁפָלָה:

I will bring back the captives of Egypt and cause them to return to the land of Pathros,
to the land of their origin, and there they shall be a lowly kingdom.

The oracle of salvation to Egypt (29,13-16)[143] follows the oracles of judgment against her (29,1-12). The punishment following judgment refers to acts that "cut off man and beast" (v.8) by the "sword" (v.8) and make "desolation and waste" (v.9.10; cf. 30,6) of the land of Egypt, and this is highly dramatised by the expression, "no foot of man...will pass through it" (v.11).[144] God will "scatter the Egyptians among the nations" and "disperse them through the countries" (v.12). The whole of Egypt "from Migdol to Syene, till the border of Cush" (v.10; cf. Judg 20,1; 1Sam 3,20) will bear this punishment, which will last for "forty years" (v.12).

The beginning of the oracle of salvation is characterized by the verb קָבַץ (v.13). God announces that he will gather the Egyptians from the peoples where he scattered them, which leads to his subsequent action, namely, "to bring back the captives of Egypt" (v.14). Here שׁוּב שְׁבוּת denotes "to return" or to "bring back from captivity." Here שׁוּב שְׁבוּת could be rendered "restoration", but it lacks the powerful sense that qualifies God's extraordinary saving intervention, previously known only in favour of Israel, when he brought them out of Egypt with a mighty hand (cf. Ex 20,2; Deut 4,37; 5,6; 6,21; 9,26; 26,8; Ps 80,9; 81,10). This is precisely the point that שׁוּב שְׁבוּת in 29,14 makes, i.e., "to bring back from captivity" because it also aims at giving hope to the exiles of Judah.

The two points that support translating שׁוּב שְׁבוּת as "to return/bring back from captivity" in 29,14 are: 1) waste and desolation of the land due to the devastation

---

[142] BAUMANN, „שׁוּב שְׁבוּת", in *ZAW* 73, 24.

[143] BERTHOLET calls it the relative restoration; see his *Hesekiel*, KHAT 12, 153.

[144] Other texts: Ezek 5,14; 14,15; 33,28; 36,34; see also Jer 9,9.11

caused by war; and 2) the dispersion of the Egyptians among the nations. These aspects have been described in 29,8-12 and elaborated further in 30,13-19. Therefore, the restoration of Egypt is possible only when her scattered inhabitants are brought back and settled[145] in the land of Pathros. It is not a restoration to the former place or state.

Ezek 39,25:

לָכֵן כֹּה אָמַר אֲדֹנָי יְהוִה עַתָּה אָשִׁיב אֶת־שְׁבִית ["שְׁבוּת] יַעֲקֹב
וְרִחַמְתִּי כָּל־בֵּית יִשְׂרָאֵל וְקִנֵּאתִי לְשֵׁם קָדְשִׁי:

Therefore thus says the Lord GOD: Now I will bring back the captives of Jacob,
and have mercy on the whole house of Israel; and I will be jealous for my Holy Name.

Ezek 39,25 is a part of the conclusion (39,21-29) of the Gog-unit (Ezek 38-39), which integrates the latter with Ezek 33-37.[146] In this way, the promise to return the captives to the land (cf. Ezek 33-37) is not obscured, but is constantly kept in mind.[147] The destruction of Gog is important both for the enemy nations and also for Israel; the nations require so, that they may come to recognize the LORD, and Israel requires it because the LORD wants to be her only God.[148] Thus, Ezek 39,25 is a promise of salvation for Jerusalem. It looks back at Israel's failure, (vv.23-24) and at the same time it also looks forward to the future restoration of Israel (vv.25-29).[149]

When God has destroyed Gog, He will bring the captives of Jacob back in safety and show His mercy to Israel. The parallel between אָשִׁיב אֶת־שְׁבִית / שְׁבוּת ("I will bring back the captives") and וְרִחַמְתִּי ("I will have mercy") stresses God's unique role in the restoration of Israel.[150] Here שׁוּב שְׁבוּת clearly means "to bring back captives,"[151] and this meaning is appropriate in view of the safe return of the exiles from Babylon and their peaceful re-settlement in the land.

6.4.1. Conclusion

The use of שׁוּב שְׁבוּת in the oracles of salvation to Israel (16,53; 39,25) and to Egypt (29,14) shows that it denotes "to return/bring back captives." The context of

---

[145] LXX, (Syriac as well as the Vulgate) renders וַהֲשִׁבֹתִי in Ezek 29,14 as καὶ κατοικίσω; BHS also suggests to read וְהוֹשַׁבְתִּי (< ישׁב hiphil "cause to dwell," "settle," cf. Ezek 36,11.33).

[146] ALLEN, *Ezekiel 20-48*, 204.

[147] ALLEN, *Ezekiel 20-48*, 208.

[148] BERTHOLET, *Hesekiel*, 194. BLOCK points to similar motive in God's promise to bring back captives; see his *Ezekiel 25-48*; 486.

[149] ALLEN, *Ezekiel 20-48*, 209.

[150] DEISSLER, *Joël*, 83.

[151] COOKE, *Ezekiel*, 422. DIETRICH (שׁוּב שְׁבוּת, 26) takes it as "restoration" and BRACKE ("šûb šᵉbût," in *ZAW* 97, 240) considers it a correction of previous judgment, i.e., its reversal.

all three occurrences provides sufficient reason to support this interpretation. It is true that the salvation of Jerusalem is not explicitly expressed or highlighted as the salvation of Sodom and Samaria in 16,53. The most striking feature of Ezekiel's oracle of salvation for Egypt is that it is presented as a paradigm for the salvation of Israel. God's return of the captives of Egypt, which mirrors His promise for the captives of Israel, places her archrival, Egypt beside Israel. God's prerogative in dealing with Egypt, both in her judgment and her restoration, through reflecting His action toward Israel, reveals His larger plan for Egypt as a nation, namely, He brings Egypt closer to Israel, and places her side by side with Israel.

6.5. The usage of שׁוּב שְׁבוּת in the post-exilic texts

The usage of שׁוּב שְׁבוּת in the post-exilic texts accounts for the second largest group: it appears in the books of Deuteronomy, Lamentations, Joel, the Psalms and Job. Although the book of Deuteronomy is thought to have been written before the exile,[152] Deut 30,3 where שׁוּב שְׁבוּת occurs, is considered to be a deuteronomistic revision.

Deut 30,3:

מִכָּל־הָעַמִּים אֲשֶׁר הֱפִיצְךָ יְהוָה אֱלֹהֶיךָ שָׁמָּה׃ וְשָׁב יְהוָה אֱלֹהֶיךָ אֶת־שְׁבוּתְךָ וְרִחֲמֶךָ וְשָׁב וְקִבֶּצְךָ

That the LORD your God will bring you back from captivity,
and have compassion on you, and gather you again from all the nations
where the LORD your God has scattered you.

According to Preuschen, Deut 30,2 offers a basic background for the usage of the expression שׁוּב שְׁבוּת in the Old Testament.[153] Deut 30,1-10 deals with the theme of Israel's "return"[154] to the LORD (v.3) and the LORD's turning to them (vv.3.9), His bringing them back from their exile (v.3), and gathering them from the nations where He scattered them (v.3). A chiasmus[155] holds the unit together, and a careful

---

[152] Scholars generally agree that the deuteronomic tradition originated in the north, but after the collapse of the northern kingdom (Israel), those who were responsible for it, such as the prophets and the Levites, brought it to the south, and introduced it in Judah. Hezekiah took these ideas and tried to implement them in Judah between 722-700 B.C.; cf. BOADT, *Reading the Old Testament*, 354-356.

[153] PREUSCHEN, „Die Bedeutung von שׁוּב שְׁבוּת", in *ZAW* 15, 7. See also HEGENSTENBERG, *Beiträge zur Einleitung*, 104ff.

[154] The Hebrew verb שׁוּב, is the key term of this section; see TIGAY, *Deuteronomy*, 282.

[155] TIGAY, *Deuteronomy*, 284.

observation of the unit shows two concentric structures.[156] Deut 30,2 follows Deut 28 rather than Deut 29[157] and presents the possibility of Israel's return to the LORD.

By stating God's "blessing and curse" (cf. Deut 28) as a motive for Israel's willingness to "return" (שׁוּב v.2)[158] and to "listen/obey" (v.2) to his voice (v.2), Deut 30,1-10 speaks about God's saving action for Israel in terms of "bringing them back from their captivity" (שׁוּב שְׁבוּת v.3) and showing his mercy on them (v.3). It implies to bring them back (שׁוּב v.3.9) at the end (v.4) of their banishment (v.4), by gathering (קבּץ *hiphil* v.3) them from the nations (v.3) where He scattered (פּוּץ v.3) them as punishment (v.1) and bring (v.5) them back to the land (v.5) that their forefathers (v.5) possessed (v.5); so that they will take possession (v.5) of it. There they will prosper (v.9) by obeying (שָׁמַע v.10) Him and by keeping (v.10) His commands (v.10) and His decrees (v.10).

Banishing (נדח *hiphil* cf. v.1) the people of Israel among the nations is seen as God's judgment against them for their disregard of his covenant, and it echoes the curses spoken in Deut 28, whereas His blessing means the reversal of judgment by bringing them back, returning them from captivity to their own land, the land promised to their fathers.[159] The curse in Deut 28 gave their forefathers no chance of return, but Deut 30,1-10 did offer every generation of Israel a possibility to return.[160] It reveals the *kerygma* as preached in 2Kgs 17ff., i.e., a chance to return to the LORD is recurring initiative of God embodied in His faithfulness to His promise.[161] It reveals the Deuteronomic theology of grace which was developing during the experience of exile.[162] Thus, while the older tradition meant שׁוּב שְׁבוּת as "restoration,"[163] the younger text (cf. 4,1-10) views שׁוּב שְׁבוּת as repentance in exile and returning to God, whereas 30,1-10 interprets שׁוּב שְׁבוּת also as the return to their homeland.[164] In other words, 30,1-10 announces a post-exilic restoration conditioned upon Israel's repentance and a future prosperity conditioned upon her obedience.[165] Israel's "return" to the LORD becomes the central motive of later

---

[156] NELSON, *Deuteronomy*, 347; WRIGHT, *Deuteronomy*, 289; CHRISTENSEN, *Deuteronomy 21:10-34:12*, 736.

[157] REIMER (ed.), *Deuteronomy*, 194-195.

[158] The verb שׁוּב ("to return," "repent," "restore") occurs in vv.1.2.3.8.9.10. NELSON presents a concentric structure of Deut 30,1-10; see his *Deuteronomy*, 347; see also BRAULIK, *Deuteronomium II*, 219, and CHRISTENSEN, *Deuteronomy*, 736.

[159] DIETRICH, שׁוּב שְׁבוּת, 27.

[160] OTTO, *Das Deuteronomium im Pentateuch*, FzAT 30, 153-155.

[161] PERLITT, *Deuteronomium-Studien*, FzAT 8, 28.

[162] OTTO, „Deuteronomium 4", in VEIJOLA (ed.), *Das Deuteronomium*, SFEG 62, 205-208.

[163] DIETRICH, שׁוּב שְׁבוּת, 27.

[164] LOHFINK, „Fortschreibung?", in VEIJOLA (ed.), *Das Deuteronomium*, SFEG 62, 136.

[165] NELSON, *Deuteronomy*, 347.

deuteronomistic theology[166] which relates to a "new covenant."[167] According to S. R. Driver, since the text mainly deals with Israel's disobedience, a description as "blessing" is not appropriate, and the author's aim should be understood as Israel's future as a whole.[168] As such, שׁוּב שְׁבוּת does not necessarily mean to bring back captives, and points to Jer 29,14; 30,3 and Ezek 29,14, where "restoring fortune" and "bringing back"/"to return from captivity" are mentioned separately.[169] It was a pet theme of exilic and post-exilic prophecy and it refers to gathering the outcast and the dispersed.[170]

The root שׁוּב was often translated as "to return", indicating its goal in the accusative, where שְׁבוּת expressed the "status," i.e., a state of captivity, and thus שׁוּב שְׁבוּת was rendered "to bring someone or somebody from captivity." As Preuschen points out, however, this meaning does not hold true for all the occurrences in the OT although they do all look back to this foundational text in Deut 30,3 for usage and meaning. One may conclude that there are occurrences where שׁוּב שְׁבוּת specifically means "to restore fortune," as in Job 42,10 (in a transferred sense). In this sense, its background (cf. Deut 30,3) fails to offer the clarification that שׁוּב does not always carry a transitive sense.[171]

Joel 4,1:

כִּי הִנֵּה בַּיָּמִים הָהֵמָּה וּבָעֵת הַהִיא

אֲשֶׁר *אָשׁוּב **אָשִׁיב אֶת־שְׁבוּת יְהוּדָה וִירוּשָׁלָם:

For behold, in those days and at that time, when I bring back the captives of Judah
and Jerusalem.

Joel, 4,1 is an "editor's connecting link,"[172] and it speaks about the salvation of Jerusalem when God will bring back the captives of Judah and Jerusalem.[173] Thus, Joel maintains the prophetic tradition of handling the theme of "Israel and the

---

[166] BRAULIK, *Deuteronomium II*, 217. Here BRAULIK points out the basis for Jer 31,16-22 and its closeness with Jer 31,31-34.

[167] BRAULIK, *Deuteronomium II*, 216; see also his „Das Buch Deuteronomium", in ZENGER (ed.) *Einleigtung in das Alte Testament*, 155.

[168] DRIVER, *Deuteronomy*, 329.

[169] DRIVER points to Ewald's comment on Jer 48,47 (in *Jahrb. bibl. Wiss. v.* [1841], 216f. cf. Lehrbuch der Hebr. Srpache [⁸1870], 430, No.3), that by grammatical analogy of לְזוּת from לוּז, the expression שׁוּב שְׁבוּת means "to turn a turning." See his *Deuteronomy*, 329.

[170] NIELSEN, *Deuteronomium*, 271.

[171] PREUSCHEN, „Die Bedeutung von שׁוּב שְׁבוּת", in *ZAW* 15, 7-8.

[172] SMITH, WARD, and BEWAR, *Micah, Zephaniah, Nahum*, 127.

[173] DEISSLER, *Joël*, 83; DIETRICH considers it an eschatological presentation of God's judgment; see DIETRICH, שׁוּב שְׁבוּת, 24. In PREUSCHEN's view, the expression does not mean to return from the captivity, because Joel cannot be placed in the pre-exilic times. It has another intention, i.e., it points to the "end of time" when the Day of the LORD approaches. See his „Die Bedeutung von שׁוּב שְׁבוּת", in *ZAW* 15, 65.

nations."[174] אָשׁוּב אֶת־שְׁבוּת ("I will bring back the captives") is preceded by אֲשֶׁר, which is lacking in some manuscripts.[175] It defines the indicated time, "in those days and at that time" (4,1a; cf. Jer 33,15; 50,4.20),[176] and shows a parallelism in which the second part of the parallel narrows down the longer time into a single moment. In this way, it makes God's promise of his saving action definite and imminent. J. L. Crenshaw thinks that the main idea of שׁוּב שְׁבוּת in Joel 4,1, as also in Am 9,14, is "restoration" from captivity or calamity.[177]

Ps 14,7 (= 53,7):

מִי יִתֵּן מִצִּיּוֹן יְשׁוּעַת יִשְׂרָאֵל בְּשׁוּב יְהוָה שְׁבוּת עַמּוֹ
יָגֵל יַעֲקֹב יִשְׂמַח יִשְׂרָאֵל:

Oh, that the salvation of Israel would come out of Zion when the LORD brings back
the captivity of his people. Let Jacob rejoice and Israel be glad.

Ps 14 appears also in Ps 54 with some variations, which supposes that Ps 14 was found in two different collections from where it has come into the book of Psalms.[178] According to F.–L. Hossfeld and E. Zenger, Ps 14 and Ps 54 are both text variations[179] of an older text. The difference lies in their contemporary literary context, but there is hardly any theological difference.[180] As such, the readings of Ps 53 are understood to be secondary.[181] Ps 53 presents a peculiarity found in the second group of Davidic Psalms (cf. the first group, which is Pss 1-41) and it contains a wisdom element that is common to Pss 52; 54; 55.[182] Explaining the background of Ps 53, K. Budde[183] says that it touches on Sennacherib's siege of Jerusalem in 701 B.C. Ps 14 recalls the past experience that God has proven His faithfulness and remains powerful for His people. This aspect closely binds it to the prophets Haggai, Zechariah, and Malachi.[184] It speaks about the opposite attitude of the Godless who live in the midst of God's people, yet who expect help and salvation from Him.

Ps 14,7 is a prayer for deliverance of God's people. The Psalm accepts the existence of evil, but not that it has taken hold of the world. V.7 reflects an old

---

[174] WOLFF, *Dodekapropheten 2*, 91.

[175] CRENSHAW, *Joel*, 173.

[176] SMITH, WARD, and BEWAR, *Micah, Zephaniah, Nahum*, 127; see also PREUSCHEN, *Joel*, 173.

[177] PREUSCHEN, *Joel*, 173.

[178] KRAUS, *Psalmen 1-59*, 246.

[179] E.g., Ps 14 uses יהוה whereas Ps 53 uses אלהים; see HOSSFELD and ZENGER, *Die Psalmen 51-100*, 75-76.

[180] HOSSFELD and ZENGER, *Psalmen 51-100*, 75.

[181] KRAUS, *Psalmen 1-59*, 246.

[182] HOSSFELD and ZENGER, *Psalmen 51-100*, 75.

[183] BUDDE, „Psalm 14 und 53", in *JBL* 47, 160-183; see also HOSSFELD and ZENGER, *Psalmen 51-100*, 76.

[184] HOSSFELD and ZENGER, *Psalmen 51-100*, 77.

tradition, namely, God's salvation will come from Zion where He makes himself present for His people and for the nations.[185] H.-J. Kraus agrees with J. Jeremias (115) that it may have been added later[186] and reflects Zion's perspective.[187] V.7b indicates that God renews everything and brings salvation to his people:[188] בְּשׁוּב יְהוָה שְׁבוּת עַמּוֹ ("When the LORD brings back the captives of His people"). Dietrich thinks that "to return from the captivity" and "to restore" both find a basis in the expression.[189] But as Bracke remarks, the Psalm does not elaborate the promise of the LORD.[190]

Ps 85,2:

רָצִיתָ יְהוָה אַרְצֶךָ שַׁבְתָּ *שְׁבוּת **שְׁבִית יַעֲקֹב׃

LORD, you have been favourable to your land,
You have brought back the captivity of Jacob.

Ps 85 is a prayer of the whole community for peace and justice. H. Gunkel considers it to be a prophetic liturgy[191] that turns around the conventional explanation of God's previous saving deeds in vv.2-4[192] and concludes with a lament over God's present wrath against His people and an appeal for peace (present need of the land cf. vv.5-8). Both these elements, recall Ps 80,9-13, which speaks of God's great saving deeds for Israel, namely, His wonderful action of taking them out of Egypt and giving them the Land promised to their forefathers (cf. Ps 77,12). In this sense, Ps 126 parallels Ps 85.[193] Kraus recalls Gunkel's

---

[185] HOSSFELD and ZENGER, *Psalmen 51-100*, 85.

[186] KRAUS, *Psalmen 1-59*, 247; see also HOSSFELD and ZENGER, *Psalmen 51-100*, 79.

[187] HOSSFELD and ZENGER, *Psalmen 51-100*, 79.

[188] KRAUS, *Psalmen 1-59*, 250.

[189] DIETRICH, שׁוּב שְׁבוּת, 26. Against the view of DIETRICH, PREUSCHEN asserts that due to chronological doubts, the translation of שׁוּב שְׁבוּת, "to turn the captivity" is not possible. See his „Die Bedeutung von שׁוּב שְׁבוּת", in *ZAW* 15, 65.

[190] BRACKE, "šûb šᵉbût," *ZAW* 97 (1985), 242.

[191] HOSSFELD and ZENGER (*Psalmen 51-100*, 527) suggest that it is a liturgy of repentance in a concrete situation of need.

[192] KRAUS, *Psalmen 60-150*, 754. According to HOSSFELD and ZENGER (*Psalmen 51-100*, 527) vv.2-4 recall the end of the Babylonian exile, which was, in accordance with the prophecies of Deutero-Isaiah (40-55), hailed as a great turning point in the salvation of Israel; though in reality, it proved to be a disappointment for Israel, because though the exile was officially ended by the Persian emperor Cyrus, Israel did not achieve her political freedom, but remained under the foreign rule of the Persians. Further, even though the temple was rebuilt, the expected kingship of the LORD and His universal peace among the nations of the world was far from established. This discrepancy between great promises and disappointing fulfilment becomes the theme of prayer in vv.5-8.

[193] In Ps 126 שׁוּב שְׁבוּת refers to agricultural prosperity, see CROW, *The Songs of Ascent*, 63.

observation that the introductory verse deals with realized salvation and the first part of the Psalm is an announcement of the future (prophetic perfect).[194]

In v.2, *Kethib* has שְׁבוּת, in but *Qere* reads שְׁבִית (cf. Ps 126,4). Hossfeld and Zenger remark that שִׁיבַת (in Ps 126) derives from שבה which means "to lead into captivity" but the occurrence of "captivity" in Num 21,21 derives from שׁוב which means "to return," "bring back," "turn" or "turn back."[195] The meaning of שׁוב שְׁבוּת is not to "restore the fortunes" but to "re-establish former state," i.e., doing again as in the former times. Therefore, the expression does not mean to "restore the fortunes of the exiled" since it does not speak about returning to the first beginning.[196]

The reference to "your land" (אַרְצֶךָ) points to the Land that God entrusted to Israel (cf. בְּאַרְצֵנוּ in vv.10.13). It suggests Israel's first beginning, and relates to Israel's exodus-experience, which is closely linked with her status as a "people" and the "land-giving." Therefore, the petition seems to restore His former relationship in dealing with Israel in the present situation and shows His salvation and faithfulness to her.[197] The reference to land, people and sin in vv.2-4 suggests that it is a *prolepsis*, a view of the future spoken in prophetic perfect.[198] From this it may be concluded that it is a prayer not of the people who are in exile or in captivity, but of those who are in their own land. Therefore, the translation of the expression may not mean an end of exile or to return the captives, but rather to restore peace in the land by removing the iniquity of those who are in the land.[199] The prayer also seems to ask for the restoration of the land as in the days of peace and prosperity, which it has witnessed.

Ps 126,4:

שׁוּבָה יְהוָה אֶת־שְׁבוּתֵנוּ **שְׁבִיתֵנוּ כַּאֲפִיקִים בַּנֶּגֶב׃

Bring back our captivity, O LORD, as the streams in the south.

Ps 126 is a song of a holy pilgrimage that recalls God's deed of bringing back the exiled to their homeland. It expresses wonder and jubilation over His act of salvation for His people (vv.1-3) and a prayer for further fulfilment of His saving action for them (v.4). The Psalm concludes with words of consolation for the same pilgrims at prayer (vv.5-6). The fulfilment of his saving action (cf. v.4) bears great significance in light of Neh 5, because those who return from captivity have to

---

[194] KRAUS, *Psalmen 60-150*, 754

[195] HOSSFELD and ZENGER, *Psalmen 51-100*, 524; see also SOGGIN, „שׁוב šub zurückkehren", in *THAT* II (1976), 885.

[196] HOSSFELD and ZENGER, *Psalmen 51-100*, 527.

[197] HOSSFELD and ZENGER, *Psalmen 51-100*, 530-531.

[198] HOSSFELD and ZENGER, *Psalmen 51-100*, 527.

[199] BAUMANN, „שׁוב שְׁבוּת", in *ZAW* 73 (1929), 20.

begin anew, rebuilding the temple, which becomes a sign of the coming of the messianic age.

    L. C. Allen observes that M. Dahood (*Psalms III*, 217-18), on the basis of the Aramaic parallel of שְׁבוּת (v.4) to שְׁבִית (v.1) and its "archaic forms," considers this Psalm as pre-exilic[200] although many agree on its post-exilic origin.[201] In any case, vv.1 and 4 seem to refer to two different events. V.1 is a "retrospection" of a past event while v.4 suggests that the nation lies under severe judgment. In this case, the use of שׁוּב שְׁבוּת in the Psalm is not "exclusively prophetic."[202]

    שִׁיבַת צִיּוֹן ("captives of Zion") in v.2 indicates that it is a past event because God has already brought them back to the land. As such, in v.4 שׁוּב שְׁבוּת may not mean "to return the captives," but "to restore fortunes" or simply "restoration."[203] Here restoration is related to אֲפִיקִים "winter-streams" (cf. LXX and Pesitha) in the Negev. Etymologically, אֲפִיקִים means "wadi," "stream," "water bed," "river" or "sea."[204] According to Baumann, אֲפִיקִים ("streams") and שְׁבוּת ("captivity") stand as objects of שׁוּב, and thus שְׁבוּת is brought into comparison with אֲפִיקִים. Therefore, שְׁבוּת is not an abstract noun but a concrete expression of a collective term (i.e., אֲפִיקִים). Further, שְׁבוּתֵנוּ ("our fortunes") is the direct object of שׁוּבָה ("restore"). It is a question of syntax whether to take אֲפִיקִים as a direct object or as a complement noun phrase of שְׁבוּתֵנוּ.[205] As it is, two dissimilar ideas, שִׁיבַת צִיּוֹן (v.2) and אֲפִיקִים בַּנֶּגֶב (v.4),[206] are brought together in the Psalm to denote an end of sadness and welling up of new joy.[207]

    The underlying idea is that the LORD will change the captivity (cf. iniquity) of the remnant, just as He restores the captivity of the winter-streams of Negev. The sterility and un-productivity of the land is visualized as a kind of captivity and as punishment of God's anger to which the prayer is directed that He may restore

---

[200] ALLEN, *Psalms 101-150*, 172.

[201] KRAUS, *Psalmen*, 247; see also ANDERSON, *Psalms*, 131.

[202] ALLEN, *Psalms 101-151*, 173.

[203] DIETRICH, שׁוּב שְׁבוּת, 25.

[204] In Job 40,18 אֲפִיקִים is translated "tubes"; 41,7 ("rows"); 6,15 ("stream"); Ezek 6,3 ("ravines"); 35,8 ("ravines"); Joel 4,18 ("ravines"); cf. 1,20 ("streams"); Ps 18,16 ("valleys"); 42,2 ("streams").

[205] BAUMANN, „שׁוּב שְׁבוּת", in *ZAW* 73, 20.

[206] The streams of Negev remained dry and empty for the long part of summer but suddenly swelled with the coming of the winter rain. Y. AHARONI remarks that "most of these floods swept into the Mediterranean and were useless in antiquity; however, along these river beds are located most of the springs and wells of Negev which were essential for permanent habitation." See his *The Land of the Bible*, 24. See also ALLEN, *Psalms 101-150*, 171.

[207] BAUMANN, „שׁוּב שְׁבוּת", in *ZAW* 73, 20.

them. So, שְׁבוּת in Ps 126,4 does not refer to "exile" but to the fortunes of the southern land that here represents the entire land.[208]

Lam 2,14:

נְבִיאַיִךְ חָזוּ לָךְ שָׁוְא וְתָפֵל וְלֹא־גִלּוּ עַל־עֲוֹנֵךְ לְהָשִׁיב ׳שְׁבִיתֵךְ ׳׳שְׁבוּתֵךְ
וַיֶּחֱזוּ לָךְ מַשְׂאוֹת שָׁוְא וּמַדּוּחִים:

Your prophets have seen for you false and deceptive visions;
they have not uncovered your iniquity, to bring back your captives,
but have envisioned for you false prophecies and delusions.

Lam 2,14 belongs to a recognised literary sub-unit 2,11-17 in which the second (vv.14-15) and the third (vv.16-17) canticles are closely linked by internal parallelisms (v.14//v.17; and v.15//v.16).[209] Its date is dependent on Ezekiel 13 (cf. שָׁוְא "emptiness" or "worthless" cf. vv.6.7.8.9.23 and תָּפֵל "whitewash" cf. vv.10.11.14.15.28). Accordingly J. Renkema supposes that it may have been composed c. 470 B.C. He argues that their external antithetical parallelism is theologically quite unusual. He points out that 2,14 draws a contrast between the "empty words of Jerusalem's prophets" on the one hand and the true prophetic words of the LORD on the other hand (2,17). Thus, the fate of the children of Jerusalem (2,11-13) and the downfall of Jerusalem (2,16-17) are God's own action, causing joy to her enemies, and bringing out the weight and significance of 2,14-15 in the centre of the structure.[210]

Lam 2,14 focuses on the prophets who were responsible for the catastrophe of Jerusalem.[211] They see deceit (שָׁוְא) and emptiness (= worthless, cf. תָּפֵל II). Their words are false and untruthful because they do not discern the iniquities. Because they have failed to uncover Jerusalem's iniquities, they fail to make her turn back to God so that He may forgive her sins. The people are in this way deceived about their actual state before God.[212] Lam 2,14 reads it in the background of the fall of Jerusalem, and condemns their prophecies.[213] Instead of relying on false security, a true prophecy of God's word could have provided an opportunity for a conversion that would have allowed her to avoid the misfortune[214] that came in the form of

---

[208] BAUMANN, „שׁוּב שְׁבוּת", in ZAW 73, 22.

[209] RENEKMA, *Lamentations*, 280-281. MÜLLER, KAISER, and LOADER present 2,13-19 as a unit which gives reasons for the fall of Jerusalem; see their *Das Hohelied/Klagelieder*, 143.

[210] RENEKMA, *Lamentations*, 280-281.

[211] RENEKMA, *Lamentations*, 281; MÜLLER, KAISER, and LOADER point to the sin of Jerusalem in v.14; see in their *Klagelieder*, 144.

[212] MÜLLER, KAISER, and LOADER, *Klagelieder*, 144.

[213] RENEKMA, *Lamentations*, 282-284.

[214] MÜLLER, KAISER, and LOADER, *Klagelieder*, 144.

exile.[215] Here שׁוּב שְׁבוּת means to "turn around" the impending "fate" or "restoration of fortunes."[216]

Job 42,10:

וַיהוָה שָׁב אֶת־שְׁבִית ‫**‬שְׁבוּת אִיּוֹב בְּהִתְפַּלְלוֹ בְּעַד רֵעֵהוּ
וַיֹּסֶף יְהוָה אֶת־כָּל־אֲשֶׁר לְאִיּוֹב לְמִשְׁנֶה:

And the LORD restored Job's losses when he prayed for his friends;
indeed the LORD gave Job twice as much as he had before.

Job 42,7-17 is the author's conclusion of Job's story. Job 42,10 speaks about what God does for Job, namely, He restores his previous prosperity (שׁוּב שְׁבוּת). Here שׁוּב שְׁבוּת is used in relation to an individual.[217] שְׁבִית appears in *Kethib* but *Qere* (שְׁבוּת) is to be preferred here. Aquila, Symmachus and Theodotion render it ἀποστρέφειν (ἐπιστρέφειν) τὴν ἀποστροφήν (ἐπιστροφήν) "to restore the fortunes" (cf. Deut 30,3; Jer 37,3; 39, 44; cf. Ezek 16,53).[218]

In the overall context, the rendering of שׁוּב שְׁבוּת in the sense of "return/bring back captives" (from שׁבה) does not make much sense in Job 42,10. According to Ewald, it should be rendered "to turn the turning" or simply, to "change" or "to return"/"restore fortune."[219] According to Preuschen it means "to return"/"bring back captives," which cannot be applied here.[220] Driver and Gray are of the opinion that in some of the texts in the prophetic literature, Psalms, and Lam 2,14, שְׁבוּת was used to denote captivity, which LXX frequently rendered αἰχμαλωσία ("captivity" *or* "band of prisoners").[221]

6.5.1. Conclusion

The exegesis of these texts show that the meaning of שׁוּב שְׁבוּת denotes "to bring back captives." However, taking into consideration that the new reality, i.e., the return of the exiles, has already taken place, which has struck the returning exiles

---

[215] RENEKMA, *Lamentations*, 286-287.

[216] RENEKMA, *Lamentations*, 287. Since it concentrates on Jerusalem's sin, BAUMANN thinks that the tradition took it as the acceptance of conversion; see BAUMANN, „שׁוּב שְׁבוּת", in *ZAW* 73, 32. On the other hand, DIETRICH thinks that שׁוּב שְׁבוּת is less used as a technical term here than to denote an eschatological restoration. See DIETRICH, שׁוּב שְׁבוּת, 17.

[217] DRIVER and GRAY, *Job*, 349; see also DIETRICH, שׁוּב שְׁבוּת, 12-13. DIETRICH divides its usage into two groups according to the objects referred in them. See on p.141, No. 6.1. above.

[218] PREUSCHEN, „Die Bedeutung von שׁוּב שְׁבוּת", in *ZAW* 15, 6; DIETRICH, שׁוּב שְׁבוּת, 13.

[219] As referred in DRIVER and GRAY, *Job*, 349; see also DUHM, *Hiob*, 205; BEN-YASHAR/ZIPOR, „שׁוּב שְׁבוּת/שְׁבִית", in *ThWAT* VII, 958-965; also STRAUSS, *Hiob* 2, 308-309.

[220] PREUSCHEN, „Die Bedeutung von שׁוּב שְׁבוּת", in *ZAW* 15, 73.

[221] DRIVER and GRAY, *Job*, 349.

with wonder, the expression is now taken to mean "to restore the fortunes." After the return of the exiles, the next exigency is the restoration of the land and the living conditions on it, so that those who have returned from the exile and have settled in the land can hope for security, peace, and prosperity. Its usage in Job 42,10 has taken this same meaning of restoration in a general sense.

6.6. The meaning of שבה outside שׁוּב שְׁבוּת

The root of שבה occurs also outside this traditional expression of שׁוּב שְׁבוּת. In trying to verify its meaning and its derivatives outside this customary usage of the expression, Baumann examines other occurrences of שבה, where the terminology denotes "to carry someone or somebody into captivity."[222] Still another meaning that comes under consideration is "deportation," but it does not come directly from שבה, and is related only as its accident.[223] Since the scope of our study is limited mainly to those texts where the expression שׁוּב שְׁבוּת occurs, we will not go into further details regarding these other texts.

6.7. Conclusion:

At the end of this discussion, we can see that the root, morphology and the meaning of שׁוּב שְׁבוּת have all witnessed a long tradition, particularly in the translation in the LXX. Its translation by Aquila, Symmachus and Theodotion had bearings on its interpretation. The exegetes have tried to grapple with its exact meaning and its possible root. Still, the different approaches and methods adopted by the exegetes[224] have not changed its basic meaning: "to bring back captives."

The primary meaning of שׁוּב שְׁבוּת from the root שבה means "to return" "to bring back the captives." Its secondary meaning denotes "to restore fortunes." Exegetes hold different opinions, some saying that שׁוּב שְׁבוּת originally meant "to restore fortunes," and that only in the context of the exile was it interpreted to denote "to bring back captivity/captives." Others, who argue that originally it derived from the root שׁוּב, claim that שׁוּב שְׁבוּת denotes "to turn to previous prosperous time" and in this sense it means "to restore fortunes."

The debate regarding the root derives from the difficulty connected with its vowel-pointing. From the root שׁוּב, שְׁבִית is the only logical morphological form

---

[222] BAUMANN, „שׁוּב שְׁבוּת", in *ZAW* 73, 36-38.

[223] BAUMANN, „שׁוּב שְׁבוּת", in *ZAW* 73, 39.

[224] The etymological, grammatical and exegetical approaches used by PREUSCHEN, DIETRICH and BAUMANN.

possible and not שְׁבוּת. In the tradition, שְׁבוּת (from שׁוּב) was wrongly articulated as שְׁבוּת. These are, of course, hypothetical explanations. In addition to questions regarding its root, the main difficulty centers on the determination of its meaning. "To bring back [from] captivity" can be appropriately applied in most, but not all of the occurrences. For this reason, the observation of Bracke seems quite valid that its interpretation should earnestly take into account its context.[225]

In interpreting שׁוּב שְׁבוּת in Jeremiah where most occurrences are found, as also in Ezekiel, the meaning "to bring back [from] captivity" is preferable. Following the events of 597 B.C., and the catastrophe that befell Jerusalem in 587 B.C. and the consequent exile of the inhabitants of Judah, the return of the exiles became a primary concern of the exiled and the prophets. In these texts, the secondary or general meaning of "restoration of fortunes" seems to be weak and insufficient. Bringing the captives back to their own homeland is viewed as God's wonderful saving intervention that comes from His own initiative and reveals His power and control over world history. Not only in the pre-exilic texts of Amos(?), Hosea(?) and Zephaniah, but also in the book of Deuteronomy, is "bring back [from] captivity" an exegetically correct interpretation of שׁוּב שְׁבוּת. The only place where it specifically means to "restore fortunes" is in Job 42,10.

Finally, beyond its basic and general meaning, theologically שׁוּב שְׁבוּת refers to God's action that causes His people (and the nations) to return to Him. His saving action of bringing them back (= causing them to return) is not dependent on human initiative; it is purely God's own initiative that comes forth because of His great mercy. In bringing the captives back, He shows his command over the entire world and His full control over his creation. Despite the utterly hopeless situation of the people and the nations, which was caused by war (sword), devastation, desolation and exile, which are also interpreted as God's conventional means of judgment, it ultimately belongs to His saving intervention to restore His people to their former state. Even so, He alone can cause the captives to return to their homeland and guarantee a new future for them. By this He makes his power and sovereignty known, which ultimately leads all people to recognize Him as God and the LORD.

---

[225] BRACKE considers שׁוּב שְׁבוּת as a model of restoration and interprets it as a "reversal" of judgments. See his "šûb šᵉbût," in *ZAW* 97, 243-244.

CHAPTER SEVEN
RESTORATION OF EGYPT: EZEKIEL 29,13-16
FURTHER EXPLANATION OF THE ORACLE OF SALVATION

Following the analysis of the root, usage and significance of the fundamental concepts of the oracle of salvation in the previous two chapters, and the text-critical, structural and semantic analyses of the first oracle of judgment against Egypt (29,1-12) presented through Chapters 2 through 4, this chapter now undertakes an exegetical explanation of the oracle of salvation for Egypt. Here each verse will be explained so as further to bring out the significance of this oracle for Egypt and for the house of Israel.

7.1 The End of the Punishment of Judgment: Ezek 29,13

The first oracle of judgment against Egypt establishes two main motifs for judgment against her: 1) Egypt's pride (3b), and 2) her unreliability or unfaithfulness to Israel (6b). Deeper analysis of these motifs points to her attitude towards God's creation and her interference in his plan for Israel. God's judgment against Egypt becomes increasingly severe in the successive oracles, reaching its climax in the third oracle (9b-12), which dwells mainly on three aspects: 1) cutting off man and beast from the land, 2) devastating the land, and 3) dispersing her inhabitants through the countries.

God fixes the punishment of Egypt for "forty years," at the end of which he promises her salvation. He will take a new initiative to restore her and the salvation He bestows will surpass His judgment when He gathers the dispersed Egyptians, bringing them back from captivity, and establishes them in their native land, Pathros, where they will exist as a low kingdom. The nations will not fear Egypt any more because she will not raise herself or rule over them again. Israel also will live in faithfulness to the LORD because Egypt will no more lead her astray.

7.1.1. "At the end of forty years" (13a)

The basic meaning of קֵץ[1] denotes "end," "limit," "boundary" or "farthest", and מִקֵּץ, a compound of a noun and preposition (קֵץ + מִ), means "at the end" of a specific time. It occurs 23 times in the Old Testament and except in one case (Jer 50,26: בֹּאוּ לָהּ מִקֵּץ "they come against her from afar"), it consistently refers to the

---

[1] קֵץ occurs 67 times in the OT: in Pentateuch 10x; Deuteronomic History 8x; Prophets 20x, Writings 31x. See TALMON, „קֵץ", in *ThWAT* VII, 85.

end of a specific time. Thus, מִקֵּץ indicates an enclosure or a point of time and, with reference to a time span, the end of a period, while its construct (with number of days, years, etc.), indicates the end of a given time.[2]

The adjective אַרְבָּעִים ("forty") occurs 93 times in the OT. In 30 occurrences it relates to an indication of time or to the age of a person, and 14 of these recall Israel's wandering in the wilderness after the Israelites came out of Egypt.[3] When the people of Israel settle down in the Land, this numerical figure is used to describe Israel's peaceful existence in the land (cf. Judg 3,11.30; 5,31; 8,28) after they were delivered from their enemies. Originally, the number "forty" denotes the period of 40 years that the people of Israel wandered in the desert. Similarly, in Judg 13,1 the number "forty" is used to signify the length of time the Philistines ruled the land (cf. 1Sam 4,18; 2Sam 5,4; 1Kgs 2,11; 11,42).

Biblical tradition attributes to the number "forty" a significantly long period of time. It implies completion or end of a given period of time, and it also symbolizes a period of a generation.[4] The formulation מִקֵּץ אַרְבָּעִים שָׁנָה ("at the end of forty years") occurs only in Ezek 29,13 and in 2Sam 15,7. Although LXX, Syriac, and the Vulgate read "four" instead of "forty" (cf. MT in 2Sam 15,7), the number "forty" in this place might refer to David's age when Absalom made a move to usurp his father's throne. Thus here the number "forty" denotes a full ripe age of man, which means that the passage of such period would bring about a change in the people who were active in handling public responsibility.[5]

In three occurrences where Ezekiel intentionally uses the term אַרְבָּעִים in combination with שָׁנָה,[6] he calls to mind Israel's "forty years" of wandering in the wilderness. This is emphasized in Num 14,33-34, which recalls 40 years of wandering in the desert and relates it to another situation of "forty days" spent spying the land of Canaan, for which God swears to punish the children of Israel for "forty years" until the last one who grumbled against the LORD dies in the desert. In his symbolic oracle concerning the siege of Jerusalem in Ezek 4,1f., Ezekiel warns that God will bring the people of Israel into the desert of the nations for judgment against them (cf. Ezek 20,35). On the one hand, he compares Israel's wandering in the desert for 40 years with her judgment in the "desert of the nations" (i.e., exile) for 40 years, and on the other hand, he refers to the desolation of the land of Egypt and the dispersion of her inhabitants for 40 years (29,11.12), thereby establishing a link between God's dealings with Israel and Egypt. Thus, Ezekiel puts Egypt beside Israel. He also presents the salvation of Egypt as a paradigm for the salvation of Israel and as a model for a new Israel.

---

[2] TALMON, „קֵץ", in *ThWAT* VII, 87-88.

[3] STENDEBACH, „שָׁנָה", in *ThWAT* VIII, 332.

[4] VOGELS, *God's Universal Covenant*, 92.

[5] STENDEBACH, „שָׁנָה", in *ThWAT*, VIII, 332.

[6] שָׁנָה occurs thrice in 29,1-16; cf. vv.11.12.13.

At another level, by referring to "forty years", Ezekiel seems to recall Israel's "forty years" of wandering in the desert, following her Exodus and liberation from Egypt, the "land of slavery" (Ex 20,1; cf., 13,14), although Israel could not totally deny that Egypt occupied a significant role for her, not simply as a place of refuge in times of famine and hunger (Gen 42-44), but even more so as a place of her own origin as a people of God (cf. Hos 11,1). In other words, Egypt was the place where God multiplied and preserved Israel, and where she came to know Him as her liberator, following which she became His chosen people. Thus, Israel's experience of God's liberation is intimately related to the contact she established with Egypt during the more than 430 years she lived there (cf. Ex 12,40-41).

Israel's 40 years of wandering in the desert also denotes her formative years when God tested her in different ways to convert and transform her from within.[7] The same deeper significance is present in "I will return the captives of Egypt" (29,14), for it implies Egypt's conversion to Him. In this respect, 40 years refer to the testing and transformation of Egypt, and her return to the LORD. Ezekiel deals with this motive in a metaphorical story in Ezek 16,1-63, where he describes Jerusalem (Israel) as an unfaithful wife.[8] Thus, "At the end of forty years I will gather the Egyptians..." (29,13), refers not merely to the 40 years of her punishment, but also to the period of her transformation, through which He "humbles" her pride and causes her to "return" to Him (cf. 29,3.9). While reference to the "forty years" makes the punishment of Egypt relative by announcing God's "promise" of salvation at the end of this period, it does not state that change and conversion are integral to his restoration.

Forty years' journey through the desert to the Promised Land also saw the death of the whole generation that came out of Egypt and of those who grumbled against the LORD (Num 14,26f.), so that only a new generation would cross over Jordan to occupy the Land (cf. Num 32,13).[9] Also in the case of Egypt does, the 40 years of exile through the countries mean the death of a proud generation, so that God will bring back only a new and humble generation of Egypt to their homeland.

7.1.2. "I will gather the Egyptians"[10] (13b)

The oracle of salvation to Egypt begins with God's announcement to "gather" the Egyptians. This marks the beginning of His great saving deeds for Egypt. Other consequent actions follow, until God's saving deeds for her come to fulfilment and

---

[7] I.e. "conversion" in Ex 24,18; 34,28; Deut 8,2-6; 9,9.11.18; and "renewal" in 1Kgs 19,8; see VOGELS, *God's Universal Covenant,* 92.

[8] Ezek 20 and 22 refer to Israel's "unfaithfulness;" cf. Hos 12.

[9] VOGELS, *God's Universal Covenant,* 92-93.

[10] קבץ as God's saving action is used only once for any foreign nation; see MOMMER, „קבץ", in *ThWAT* VII, 1149; see also PREMSTELLER, *Fremdvölkersprüche,* 149;

the ultimate purpose of His action is achieved, i.e., the Egyptians come to recognise Yahweh as their Lord and GOD. God's action of "gathering" the dispersed of Egypt is reminiscent of how a shepherd takes care of His flock by gathering the scattered sheep together in one place. One of the main concerns of the shepherd is to provide his sheep with security.

God's announcement that He will gather the Egyptians displays a similar concern and care, and exhibits a reversal of His previous action, namely, when He destroyed the land and devastated her wealth by His judgment, dispersing her inhabitants among the nations and scattering them through the countries. God's action of "gathering" them from the people occurs at His own initiative, and without this intervention it would be impossible for the dispersed (29,12) and the exiled (30,17.18) of Egypt to think about a return to their homeland. Thus, the action of gathering together begins one of God's great saving activities, preparing the ground for his next action, i.e., the great exodus from the countries when He will cause them to return to their land.

7.2. The Restoration of Egypt: Ezek 29,14

Gathering the dispersed of Egypt from the countries where God scattered them, is a great metamorphic action for the nation that is made possible through God's own initiative and action. However, it is only the beginning of His saving activity, and a prelude to further action. The next series of God's saving deeds build upon this fundamental action of "gathering". Each of them, however, is a new act of God's salvation that will continue until Egypt has been re-established according to His plan, which unfolds itself in the following verses.

7.2.1. "I will return the captives of Egypt" (14a)

שׁוּב שְׁבוּת/שְׁבִית is used for the first time in the oracle of salvation of Egypt in 14a and it is translated as "to return"/"bring back the captives"[11] (cf. Vulgate, LXX,

---

[11] שָׁבָה ("to take captive") is traditionally supposed to be the root of the substantive שְׁבוּת/שְׁבִית (n. f. sg.), meaning, "captivity" or "exile" (*BDB*, 986). This view is supported by the analogy to constructions of לְזוּת from לְזוּת; of פְּדוּת from פְּדוּת; of דְמוּת from דְמוּת; and of כְּסוּת from כָּסוּת. However, on the basis of the changes in the vowel-pointing that appears in different groups of related weak verbs, E. L. DIETRICH (שׁוּב שְׁבוּת, 30) points to שׁוּב as an alternative root of שְׁבוּת. E. BAUMANN („שׁוּב שְׁבוּת. Eine Untersuchung", in *ZAW* 47, 19) thinks that שְׁבוּת could derive from שׁוּב through its meaning "to make a return," but not a "new turn" (e.g., return from evil to salvation). H. CAZELLES suggests יָשַׁב as a possible root of שְׁבוּת and with the meaning "to return"/"bring back" someone or somebody to one's homeland. (cf. BEN-YASHAR and ZIPOR, „ שׁוּב שְׁבוּת/שְׁבִית", in *ThWAT* VII, 959; see also CAZELLES, "L'expression šubh šebhut

NKJ, NIB), but Boadt (cf. RSV, ESV, EIN) renders it in a general sense, "to restore the fortunes,"[12] which is an equally possible meaning in this context. The expression שְׁבוּת/שְׁבִית שׁוּב occurs 32 times in the Old Testament,[13] but the exact expression (שׁוּב שְׁבוּת) "to turn back," "return") occurs only 18 times.[14] In all of these 18 occurrences, with the exception of Job 42,10 where the expression clearly means "to return"/"restore prosperity," the expression could very well mean "to return" or "to bring back captivity," and the exceptions to this meaning point to the post-exilic interpolations.[15] Whether the expression means "to restore fortune" or "bring back [from] captivity," it is the LORD himself who is the principle agent of this action. In 14a, it is this unique role of God's action that is being emphasized through the use of שׁוּב שְׁבוּת. It is God who takes precedence in the restoration of Egypt. Just as the gathering of Egyptians from the countries where they were dispersed (v.13) was God's prerogative, so also is bringing them back from captivity his priority. Human aspirations and pride have no role in this act. It happens only by way of God's sovereign will, and man can only wait on His divine initiative. This also reveals God's sovereign power over human history, placing Him above all powers and claims, and guiding their destiny.

7.2.2. "And I shall establish them on the land of Pathros" (14b)

The use of verb שׁוּב appears once again in 14b וַהֲשִׁבֹתִי, carrying a causative sense of "cause to return." Rendering it in the active sense as "to bring back," however, lays greater emphasis on the significance of God's action of bringing back the Egyptian captives to a new location, Pathros. Here וַהֲשִׁבֹתִי (14b) relates to God's action of bringing back the captives of Egypt to the land of Pathros (14b). The use of שׁוּב in *hiphil* with the complement noun phrase, "to the land of Pathros" is intentional and it is meant to place special emphasis on His concrete action related to this goal and destination. Here God's act of bringing back the captives of Egypt is viewed as possible *only* thanks to His intervention. There is absolutely no human

---

viendrait-elle del'accadien d'Asarhaddon?" *GLECS* 9, 57-60). It is no wonder that this root and meaning has witnessed much discussion. See also E. PREUSCHEN, „Die Bedeutung von שְׁבוּת שׁוּב", in *ZAW* 15, 1-22; and HENGSTENBERG, *Beiträge zur Einleitung*, 104ff.

[12] BOADT, *Ezekiel's Oracles*, 45-46.

[13] BEN-YASHAR and ZIPOR, „שׁוּב שְׁבוּת/שְׁבִית ", in *ThWAT* VII, 959; see also HOLLADAY, *Hebrew and Aramaic Lexicon*, 358; BRACKE, sûb šᵉbût," in *ZAW* 97, 235; VLAARDINGERBROEK, *Zephaniah*, 134-135; BORGER, „Zu שְׁבוּת/ית", in *ZAW* 66, 316.

[14] Besides 18 occurrences of the exact expression, eight other occurrences appear with pronominal suffixes; see also BEN-YASHAR and ZIPOR, „שׁוּב שְׁבוּת/שְׁבִית ", in *ThWAT* VII, 959. LISOWSKY'S *Konkordaz* considers שְׁבוּת deriving from שָׁבָה and gives 24 occurrences while BRACKE gives 27 occurrences; see his "šûb šᵉbût," in *ZAW* 97, 236.

[15] BRACKE, "šûb šᵉbût," in *ZAW* 97, 223.

person or agent who could take credit for bringing them back from captivity to their land.

שׁוּב is generally understood as the root of MT וַהֲשִׁבֹתִי ("I will restore"), and means "to return" "to restore."[16] Ezekiel uses repetition as a literary device, whereby "to restore" is repeated in both the colons (cf. 14a.14b). But LXX, Vulgate, Syriac, Targum and Latin *fragmentorum Sangallenseium* read MT וַהֲשִׁבֹתִי καὶ κατοικίσω ("and I will cause them to dwell"), which is preferable. The context, describing God's saving action, requires a progressive sense and the repetition fails to bring out this sense in this context. Therefore, וַהֲשִׁבֹתִי (from שׁוּב) needs to be amended to read וְהוֹשַׁבְתִּי ("I will establish" from יָשַׁב) in order to show this dynamic development of God's saving action that is clear from the context (13b-15a):

> 13b: I will gather the Egyptians from the peoples where they were dispersed;
> 14a: And I will bring back the captivity of Egypt;
> 14b: And I will cause them to dwell in the land of Pathros;
> 14c: And they will be there a low kingdom;
> 15a: She will be the lowest of all the kingdoms.

God does not gather the dispersed in order to bring the captives of Egypt back to any, arbitrary place, which would make God's saving action less significant and disguise the very purpose of gathering them and bringing them back.[17] In fact, God's action of bringing back the captives of Egypt does not remain inconclusive, but reaches its immediate goal in His second action of causing them to "dwell"/"settle" in the land of Pathros. For the Egyptians who were dispersed among the nations and lived in captivity, there could be nothing better than returning to their roots, to their own homeland, and being settled there.

Pathros (cf. 30,14 also Isa 11,11; Jer 44,1.15) is not a name of a city or a locality, but refers to a geographical region - Upper Egypt or "the southern land." It comprises "the apex of the Nile to the First Cataract at modern Aswan,"[18] i.e., the region south of Cairo extending till Aswan (Syene).[19] Ezek 30,13-19 describes how the strongholds and military garrisons are not able to stop the destruction of the cities in the Nile Delta. From political and military points of view, Lower Egypt will lose its importance. Instead, Pathros (Upper Egypt) which played a

---

[16] ALLEN, *Ezekiel 20-48*, 102; BLOCK, *Ezekiel 25-48*, 141; COOKE, *Ezekiel*, 328; EICHRODT, *Hesekiel 19-48*, 277; GREENBERG, *Ezekiel 21-37*, 601; ZIMMERLI, *Ezekiel 25-48*, 703; BOADT, *Ezekiel's Oracles*, 45-46.

[17] Compare this with the event when the Israelites come out of Egypt and murmur against Moses at the hardships in the desert, only to face the pursuing army of Pharaoh (Ex 14,11.12); similarly, when they lack water to drink (Ex 15,23f.) and suffer hunger (Ex 16,2ff.).

[18] BLOCK, *Ezekiel 25-48*, 169.

[19] BOADT, *Ezekiel's Oracles*, 46-47.

pivotal role in bringing the whole land under one king (Menes) in the 29th cent. B.C.,[20] once again gains importance.

The Asiatic Hyksos of the 15th Dynasty of Pharaohs (c.1785-1570 B.C.) established their administrative capital in Zoan (Avaris) in the eastern Nile Delta and ruled Egypt for over 100 years, but their hold on Upper Egypt was only indirect. Ahmosis I of the 18th Theban Dynasty (1552-1527 B.C.) drove the Hyksos from Avaris c.1540 B.C. and brought the capital to Noph (Memphis).[21]

Noph, the capital of the Early Kingdom, was also the capital of the Old Kingdom and the New Kingdom.[22] Noph and No both were important cities in southern Egypt and they symbolized Egypt's power and prosperity. Ezekiel's oracles of judgment against Egypt predict its destruction (Ezek 30,13-19). Against this background, bringing the captives of Egypt back and settling them in the land of Pathros, the place of their birth (Upper Egypt), takes on a new significance. It signifies that God has the power to restore the desolated land, restore its past prosperity, and lay a new foundation for Egypt as a kingdom by bringing its captives back to the place from where they derived their origin and name. It has two main significances, namely, it relates to: 1) the origin of Egypt as a people and as a kingdom; and 2) its farthest southern location. Both these aspects have positive significance for Israel and for the nations.

To settle the captives of Egypt in their native place of Pathros is God's special favour for Egypt. It reveals a close similarity between His dealing with Egypt and with His people, Israel, whom He took out of Egypt with a mighty arm (Deut 6,21; 7,8) and brought into the land of Canaan, which He had promised to give to their fathers (cf. Gen 12,7).[23] It is interesting to note that Egypt is mentioned in this promise of "land-giving" to Israel by specifying the river of Egypt as the land's southern boundary and stating that its north-eastern boundary will expand up to the Euphrates (Gen 15,18). The latter denotes Babylon, by whose king God judges Egypt.

---

[20] PARKER (ed.), *Atlas of World History*, 58; and BRIGHT, *A History of Israel*, 38f.

[21] BRIGHT, *History of Israel*, 61; see also HARRISON, *Introduction to the Old Testament*, 102-124; MAY (ed.), *Oxford Bible Atlas*, 54-55; PARKER (ed.), *Atlas of World History*, 59.

[22] N. GOTTWALD assigns the 1st-3rd Dynasties (3000-2700 B.C.E.) to the Early Kingdom; the 4th-8th Dynasties (2700-2200 B.C.E.) to the Old Kingdom; the 9th-11th Dynasties (2200-2000 B.C.E.) to the First Intermediate Period when the central administration of Egypt was dissolved, spreading chaos in the land; the 12th-13th Dynasties (2000-1750 B.C.E.) to the Middle Kingdom, which was responsible for the second unification of Egypt; the 14th-17th Dynasties (1750-1550 B.C.E.) to the Second Intermediate Period when Asiatic Hyksos ruled Egypt from Avaris in the Delta but were never able completely to overthrow the Theben Dynasties in the South. See his *Politics of Ancient Israel*, 129-140.

[23] It concerns the promise of salvation that God makes to Egypt (29,13-16), as He does also for Israel; compare 11,17-20; cf. VOGELS, *God's Universal Covenant*, 97; see also EICHRODT, *Hesekiel 19-48*, 227.

Establishing the captives of Egypt in Pathros, the farthest region from Israel, may have a symbolic significance. As the place of origin, Pathros will always remind Egypt as her renewed existence, which depends now on God's purpose. This location in the distant south will also reduce Egypt's political significance, since her geographical extremity will not allow easy access to major trade-routes and neighbours. More significant is, however, that Egypt's new geo-political and territorial location creates a new situation. Her confinement to a small territory in the farthest south will reduce her importance greatly, making her a low and a humble kingdom, not having the power to dominate other nations.[24] But beyond the "historical-geographical-political-territorial" view, there lies a deeper "theological-political" perspective in her re-location to Pathros. This is discussed in the following sections.

In the judgment against the individual cities of Egypt in 30,13-19, three cities from Upper Egypt: Noph (Memphis), No (Thebes), and Syene (Elephantine), and five cities from Lower Egypt: Sin (Pelusium), Zoan (Tanis), Migdol, Pi-Beseth (Bubastis), and On/Awen (Heliopolis), are mentioned.[25] Although the list mentions comparatively more cities from Lower Egypt in God's judgment, it is Pathros (Upper Egypt), which gains prominence in the oracle of salvation.

The choice of Pathros in the oracle of salvation to Egypt may not be by chance. Just as God promises to gather the people of Israel from the countries where He dispersed them and bring them back to their own land, the land He had promised their forefathers,[26] He promises to gather the Egyptians from the countries where He dispersed them and bring them back to their own land. The Egyptians will be brought back and settled not just anywhere in the vast region of the Nile valley, such as the Nile Delta, which is easily accessible to foreign incursions, but they will be brought to a secure geographical region called Pathros, which is associated with the history and origin of the Egyptians. It affirms God's sovereignty as Creator of the world who apportions the land to the nations. His saving action for Egypt restores the original order in relation to her. It also reminds the Egyptians of their humble origin and their place among the nations.[27] Despite being banished from their land, they can inherit it again as a gift from God but only as a low

---

[24] The "southern region" may also denote a place that enjoys God's blessing of peace and security; cf. Ps 126,4 (remotely).

[25] COOKE, *Ezekiel*, 333.

[26] God's promise to Abraham to give the land of Canaan to his descendents (Gen 17,8) is fundamentally related to the fulfilment of His promises and to Israel's existence as God's people.

[27] The twin-motifs of Exodus, i.e., Israel's "return" to the LORD and the "land-giving," reflect the fundamental relationship between God and Israel. So, possession of the Land becomes primary motive after they come out of Egypt (cf. Deut 1,8.21.39; 2,31; also Isa 57,13; 60,21; 65,9; cf. GNILKA, *Matthäusevangelium 1,1-13, 58*, 123). Their identity as a people and their existence comprises not only the Promised Land but also their actual relation to God, who alone gives it to them. Thus, as Deut 32,8 understands it, God apportions His created earth, and thus it is His "gift" that plays a decisive role in their relationship with Him.

kingdom. Thus, there is a heavy stress on God's saving action for Egypt that surpasses her punishment.

7.2.3. "On the land of their origin" (14b)

The Hebrew word מְכוֹרָה / מְכֹרָה means "origin" and its supposed verb-root כָּרָה (I)[28] means "to dig" (cf. Gen 26,25; 50,5; Ex 21,33; Num 21,18; Jer 18,20.22Q (a pit); Ps 40,7 ("piercing"); 7,16; 57,7; 119,85 ("pitfalls"); Prov 16,27; 26,27 ("pit as a trap"); 2Chr 16,14 ("to dig"/"hew a grave"). Its two other derivatives כָּרָה meaning "cistern" or "well," and מִכְרֶה denoting "pit [of salt]" (cf., Zech 2,9) carry a similar sense. Two other places where Ezekiel uses the word מְכוֹרָה are 16,3 and 21,35 (pl.). There is no other occurrence of this term in the Old Testament.

Ezek 16,3:

וְאָמַרְתָּ כֹּה־אָמַר אֲדֹנָי יְהוִה לִירוּשָׁלַם מְכֹרֹתַיִךְ וּמֹלְדֹתַיִךְ מֵאֶרֶץ הַכְּנַעֲנִי אָבִיךְ הָאֱמֹרִי וְאִמֵּךְ חִתִּית:

And say: Thus says the Lord GOD to Jerusalem: Your ancestries and your birth were
in the land of Canaan; your father was an Amorite and your mother a Hittite.

In Ezek 16,3 the prophet Ezekiel is told to speak to Jerusalem about her origin[29] (cf. "your ancestry" [מְכֹרֹתַיִךְ, LXX ῥίζα "root"] which is elaborated by the next noun phrase "and your birth [is] of the land of Canaan" [הַכְּנַעֲנִי וּמֹלְדֹתַיִךְ מֵאֶרֶץ]). Since Israel's sacred traditions[30] as a nation are closely bound up with Jerusalem, she stands for the whole of Israel. Therefore, when Ezekiel speaks about her origin, he indirectly speaks about Israel's own origin as well. He uses it as a rhetorical device with certain amount of polemic. By referring to Jerusalem's Canaanite origin Ezekiel deflates the pride of Israel's sacred traditions concerning her origin, associated with Abraham and with Exodus, both of which are viewed as enshrined in Jerusalem, the city/place that the LORD has chosen for his dwelling (cf. Ps 132,13-14).[31]

---

[28] BOADT, *Ezekiel's Oracles*, 46.

[29] Jerusalem was originally a Canaanite city whose existence dates back to the19[th]-18th c. B.C. See PRITCHARD, *ANET*, 329.

[30] Israel's sacred traditions as a nation trace her roots to the call of Abraham (cf. Gen 11,31: "Ur of the Chaldaeans") and to Exodus (cf. Ex 19,4); see BLOCK, *Ezekiel 1-24*, 474.

[31] A wrong place and a wrong parentage are attributed to Israel's origin, here (see BLOCK, *Ezekiel 1-24*, 475), which is a polemic against Israel's claim to the sacred traditions that trace back to Abraham and the Exodus as her descent (parentage), and election as God's people. Contrary to Israel's claim to such sacred traditions about her origin, she is down to earth "gentile" by her very birth, which she has proved by her constantly rebellious attitude against her LORD.

Before the conquest of the land of Canaan, the Canaaites, Hittites, Hivites, Perizzites, Girgashites, Amorites, and Jebusites lived in the land[32] (cf. Ex 23,20-33; Jos 3,10) and Jerusalem was a city of the Jebusites, who lived there until David conquered it and made it his capital (2 Sam 5,6ff.). The origin of Jerusalem as a city goes back to 19th-18th cent. B.C.[33] By stressing Jerusalem's relation to the land of Canaan,[34] and by linking her parentage to "an Amorite father and a Hittite mother" (cf. Ex 23,23 and Deut 7,1), Ezekiel apparently emphasizes Jerusalem's Canaanite origin. Jerusalem perfectly represents Israel's thoroughly "pagan" origin, especially in her relation (i.e., unfaithfulness[35]) to the LORD.[36] There is nothing good that Jerusalem (Israel) now stands for before God. In this way, she has proved herself true to her "origin"[37] in that she is thoroughly pagan in her attitude.

מְכֹרֹתַיִךְ ("your ancestry") in this verse is best explained by the noun phrase וּמֹלְדֹתַיִךְ מֵאֶרֶץ that follows it, literally means, "and your birth [are] the land of" (cf. ילד "to give birth"). The Hebrew word מְכוּרָה / מְכֹרָה ("origin," כָּרָה [I] "to dig") relates primarily to a "place of birth". Since it is tied to a birthplace, it implies the right of inheritance to the place/land. From this point of view, God's promise to bring back the captives of Egypt and to settle them in the land of Pathros, the place of their birth, has great significance because it is bound up with the inheritance of the land that belongs to them by virtue of their birth, their patrimony. Thus, this new initiative of the LORD for the captives of Egypt is nothing less than the restoration of their ancestral homeland. We must give some attention to whether מְכֹרָה / מְכוּרָה means merely that the expression denotes "place of origin" or a "native place" or also carries a secondary meaning. It is presumed that the term implies the "former" or "initial" stage of their humble

---

[32] "In Egyptian texts, Canaan is used as a designation for Egypt's Asiatic Provinces. In the Bible, Canaan could refer to the whole Palestine west of Jordan, the ideal inheritance of the Hebrews; but it could also refer to more restricted areas, especially the coastland of Palestine." See MILLER and HAYES, *History of Ancient Israel*, 38. A. NIBBI (*Canaan*, 17-19) notes that the earliest reference to "Canaanite" is found in a Mari letter of the 18th cent. B.C. and the earliest reference to Canaan is found "on the statue of Idrimi from Alalakha." NIBBI argues that etymologically it is difficult to hold Canaan as a Semitic word; even Biblical evidence shows Canaan as son of Ham who was not of Semitic origin (cf. Gen 10,6ff.).

[33] PRITCHARD, *ANET*, 329.

[34] Canaan's reference in relation to Jerusalem, points to latter's character, namely, her rebelliousness and unfaithfulness (= Canaanite origin), which she acquired from her birth.

[35] COOKE, *Ezekiel*, 160.

[36] BLOCK, *Ezekiel 1-24*, 474.

[37] SEDLMEIER (*Ezekiel 1-24*, 206) observes that Israel's (Jerusalem's) imperfect or mixed origin, notwithstanding her smallest and insignificant status among the nations (Deut 7,7) and her rebelliousness, which is depicted from the beginning, as in Ezek 16,3b-5, opens up a universal horizon, giving an equal opportunity of God's salvation to the "elected" as well as to the "pagans."

beginning and small existence as a people. It relates to Egypt's emergence as a people and as a nation, without having such power as yet, by which she could dominate others or become a threat to them. On the contrary, the pride and arrogance of the Nile-crocodile stand in opposition to this.

Ezek 21,35

הָשֵׁב אֶל־תַּעְרֶהּ בִּמְקוֹם אֲשֶׁר־נִבְרֵאת בְּאֶרֶץ מְכֻרוֹתַיִךְ אֶשְׁפֹּט אֹתָךְ

Return it (the sword) to its scabbard; in the place where you were created,
in the land of your origin, I will judge you.

Sword is a special means of the LORD for executing His judgment against His people and against the nations. He brings the sword against Jerusalem and her temple as judgment against her (Ezek 21).[38] However, vv.33-37 show that the LORD turns His sword (i.e., the sword of Nebuchadnezzar) also against the Ammonites (cf. 21,23-25; 25,1-5.6-7).[39] The sword, however, is not the last word in His judgment, for v.35 indicates that when the period of His judgment is over, He causes it to return to its scabbard. Here the phrases "in the place where you were created" (35b) and "in the land of your origin" (35c) form a parallel, in which "in the land of your birth" elucidates the preceding relative clause. "Scabbard" in the first part of the verse (35a) carries a similar sense, a particular "place" where the sword properly belongs (cf. MT 26,52). Thus, causing the sword to return to its own place also belongs to God's judgment. It means His judgment is limited by a definite period of time; at the same time, he who wields the sword to execute God's judgment will be brought back to his own place from where he had marched to execute God's judgment against Jerusalem, and will there face God's judgment.

The parallelism בְּאֶרֶץ מְכֻרוֹתַיִךְ // בִּמְקוֹם אֲשֶׁר־נִבְרֵאת ("in the place where you were created"//"in the land of your origin") and their juxtaposition indicate that מְכֻרָה ("origin") and נִבְרֵאת ("created") are closely related to a "place" or "land." Even without the use of a noun construct בְּאֶרֶץ, מְכֻרָה assumes the sense "place of origin," thereby implying a "native place." The reference to the scabbard in relation to a native place in the parallelism highlights not only the meaning of the term (מְכֻרָה) but also its significance. It is ultimately in one's "native place" where God's decisive action takes place, prompting the people to acknowledge him. Just as God causes the sword to return to its scabbard where it belongs, he causes Nebuchadnezzar to return to his "native place" to face his judgment even though he served Him as His servant. Likewise, God will return the captivity of Egypt to Pathros, to the land of their origin, where they properly belong.

Digging a "cistern" or a "well" is derived from the same root כָּרָה (II), but apparently with a different meaning, and it is not specifically related to the place of

---

[38] SEDLMEIER, *Ezekiel 1-24*, 302; see also SCHÖPFLIN, *Theologie als Biographie*, 51-52.
[39] SEDLMEIER, *Ezekiel 1-24*, 309.

birth, although this action is closely related with dwelling in the land or in a place, as we find in Gen 26,25 and Num 21,18; (cf. 50,5: "dig a grave"; Ex 21,33: "dig a pit"; Jer 18,20: "dig a pit"; 2Chr 16,14: "to dig a grave"). All the same, they do not denote "place of birth."

7.2.4. Conclusion:

The Hebrew root word מְכוּרָה / מְכֵרָה means "place of birth"/"origin" and the use of the construct עַל־אֶרֶץ מְכוּרָתָם in 14b does not just emphasize a close relationship of "birth"/"origin" with the "place"/"land" but it also qualifies it. It denotes not just any place or land but a place or land that is intimately connected with one's birth or origin. Beyond the emotional or psychological relationship attached to this term, it gives the people dignity as a people and as a nation. God promises to settle the captives of Egypt not anywhere in the land of former Egypt, but in a definite region that was always known as their original birthplace, the region of the First Kingdom of Egypt, and that from where it spread out to become a mighty kingdom and a world power (cf. Ezek 31). Therefore, much is at stake here when God promises to bring back the captives of Egypt and settle them in the land of Pathros. It is a very decisive step, a foundational point that makes His judgment righteous both for His people Israel as well as for the nations, and particularly, for Egypt. By doing this God shows that it is His prerogative to bring back the captives and to settle them in the place of their birth, where they naturally belong. By this, He restores their dignity and identity as a people and as a nation.

It is a matter of special favour and status that Egypt receives from the LORD who is God of Israel, and this idea comes out very forcefully here. What God does (or promises to do) for Egypt finds no other parallel in Biblical history except in that which He does also for Israel when He gathers the dispersed of Israel and Judah from the nations and brings them back from their captivity to their own land, and settles them there. This becomes clear from the comparison of Ezek 29,13-16 with Ezek 11,17-20, concerning the promise of salvation to Israel:[40]

---

[40] VOGELS, *God's Universal Covenant*, 97.

Table 2:

EGYPT: (Ezek 29,13-16)	ISRAEL. (Ezek 11,17-20)
I will gather the Egyptians from the peoples among whom they were scattered	I will gather you from the peoples
I will bring back the captives of Egypt	I will assemble you out of the countries where you have been scattered.
I will settle them in the land of Pathros	I will give the land of Israel[41]

This close similarity between the oracles of salvation for Egypt and Israel shows that God deals with Egypt in the same way as with Israel. This places Egypt in a privileged place on par with Israel.

7.3. Egypt – The lower kingdom
7.3.1 "There they will be a low kingdom" (14c)

The first kingdom of Egypt originated in the southern region.[42] Now the Egyptians are promised that they will be a "low kingdom." In view of God's judgment against Egypt, this new status as a "low kingdom" is more than what they could have hoped for.[43] It is a complete reversal of their judgment: bringing back their captives and establishing them in the place of their origin and making them a low kingdom; this could not come about without God's special favour to them. He puts Egypt on the map of the nations again and gives her a place among other nations. The land destroyed by His sword is restored and reinstated by His own favour and granted the dignity of a "kingdom" and people of God.

The expression מַמְלָכָה שְׁפָלָה ("low kingdom") occurs only in Ezek 17,14; 29,14.15. In all the three occurrences it uses the verb הִיה to express the concept. Ezek 29,14 indicates Egypt's future existence, which is stated in the superlative in

---

[41] BALTZAR refers to 17 occurrences of the "land of Israel" (genitive construction) noted by ZIMMERLI (*Ezechiel 1-24*, 169), but none outside Ezekiel. See his „literarkritische und Literarhistorische Anmerkungen" in LUST (ed.), *Ezekiel and his book* (BEThL 74), 169.

[42] Pre-dynastic Egypt, known as the "Two Lands", was brought under a unified Kingdom in the 29th cent. B.C. by King Menes of Upper Egypt. The Hyksos (17th Dynasty), who ruled Egypt from Avaris (Lower Egypt), controlled Upper Egypt only indirectly. Sekenenre, a Theban ruler began the liberation of Egypt from the Hyksos, whose son Ahmosis I (18th Dynasty) began the New Kingdom. Pathros as the birthplace of the Egyptians may relate to these significant events (ascribed to the 18th Dynasty) in Egyptian history. Cf. BRIGHT, *History of Israel*, 38-61. See also HARRISON, *Introduction to the Old Testament*, 102-124; MAY (ed.), *Oxford Bible Atlas*, 54-55; and PARKER (ed.), *Atlas of World History*, 58-59.

[43] Egypt's new status as a "low kingdom" need not be interpreted in a geographical-political sense, but rather in theological-political sense. It means a condition different from her former pride and ambition, a changed effect through God's judgment, a becoming humble to acknowledge God.

v.15. The significance of its new existence is expressed in two respects: 1) in relation to other nations (v.15), and 2) in relation to Israel (v.16). Ezek 17,14 indicates a similar status for Israel, but views its significance in her relation to the covenant by which she is bound to the LORD:

Ezek 17,14:

לִהְיוֹת֙ מַמְלָכָ֣ה שְׁפָלָ֔ה לְבִלְתִּ֖י הִתְנַשֵּׂ֑א לִשְׁמֹ֥ר אֶת־בְּרִית֖וֹ לְעָמְדָֽהּ

That the kingdom might be humble and not lift itself up,
and that by keeping his covenant it might stand.

Ezek 29,14:
   And there they will be a low kingdom.

וְהָי֥וּ שָׁ֖ם מַמְלָכָ֥ה שְׁפָלָֽה

Ezek 29,15:

מִן־הַמַּמְלָכוֹת֙ תִּהְיֶ֣ה שְׁפָלָ֔ה וְלֹֽא־תִתְנַשֵּׂ֥א ע֖וֹד עַל־הַגּוֹיִ֑ם
וְהִ֨מְעַטְתִּ֔ים לְבִלְתִּ֖י רְד֥וֹת בַּגּוֹיִֽם

Lowest of the kingdoms she will be;
She will not raise herself again over the nations;
And I will make them small never to rule over the nations.

The Hebrew root שפל ("to humble," "make low," "be/bring low") is attested 69 times in the Old Testament; 28 occurrences are verb-forms (שָׁפֵל *qal* 10x and *hiphil* 18x), 18 times שָׁפָל ("low") is used as an adjective, and the noun שְׁפֵלָה ("low region") occurs 19 times. In most cases, whether as a verb, an adjective or a noun, it denotes God's action in respect to the people concerned.[44] Its adjectival use, cf. Lev 13-14; cf. 13,20; 14,37, relate to declaring someone or something clean/unclean when any mark in the skin [deeper than] or on the wall is detected. שְׁפָלַת ("low of height") occurs in Ezek 17,6 while הַשְּׁפֵלָה ("lowland," "foothills") refers to a geographical region, cf. Jos 11,16; 2Chr 28,18; Jer 17,26; 32,44; 33,13. In 2Sam 6,22 שפל is used to state David's disposition: "I will be low in my own eyes." But in a few other occurrences, like Ezek 17,24 ("I make the low tree grow tall"), Job 5,11 ("the lowly He sets on high"), and Isa 57,15 ("[I live in a high and holy place, but also with him] who is contrite and lowly of spirit"; cf. 5,15), it denotes God's action regarding the people concerned.[45]

The latter texts (above) highlight the motive for God's action, which Prov 16,19 lays down as a norm for a good life: "Better to be of a humble spirit with the lowly, than to divide the spoil with the proud."[46] Thus, "humble spirit" or "being

---

[44] ENGELKEN, „שָׁפֵל", in *ThWAT* VIII, 439-440.

[45] Isa 2,11, 5,15; 25,12; Jer 13,18; Ezek 21,31; Job 22,29.

[46] "Humble spirit" is placed parallel to "proud" while the "lowly" to "divide the spoil" which makes a sharp contrast. See WHYBRAY, *Proverbs*, 247.

lowly" relates to a basic attitude of someone in relation to God.[47] The same attitude is expected also in relation to one's neighbour. When this basic attitude is lacking, God acts to humble a person's ambition and pride so that they may have an attitude that is more open to God and neighbour. Vertically, it touches upon one's relationship to God and horizontally, to one's neighbour. As long as one is proud and arrogant, one lacks the attitude that God desires and this hinders both God's saving action and fellowship with others.

The Magnificat of Mary (Lk 1,46-55) begins with bursts of joyful praise of God and is followed by providing reasons for God's action with regard to two distinct groups of people who make a "lowly state" a fundamental basis for a true relationship with him:[48] "God looks down on the lowly" (v.48). His actions towards the two groups of people are diametrically opposed: He scatters the proud of heart but exalts the lowly; He puts down the mighty but exalts the lowly (vv.51-52 = 1Sam 2,6-8; cf., Ezek 21,31).[49] It alludes to God's saving activity for His people Israel (cf. Ex 6,6; also Ps 88,11 in LXX),[50] but its application can be extended to cover others as well.

Jesus preaches humility as one of the basic tenets of God's Kingdom (MT 5,5 cf., Ps 37,11): μακάριοι οἱ πραεῖς, ὅτι αὐτοὶ κληρονομήσουσιν τὴν γῆν ("Blessed are the meek, for they shall inherit the earth").[51] Jesus brings "meekness" and "inheriting the land" together and places the former as a prerequisite for possession of the land. Although πραΰς is intended to highlight the religious dimension of being poor, it does not alter its basic meaning.[52] In this regard Davies and Allison take note of Schweizer's suggestion that the "powerless" indicates an existential condition of the addressed, which is a more appropriate translation of πραεῖς.[53]

---

[47] The relation of שָׁפֵל ("be humble," "low") with עֲנִיִּים ("poor," "afflicted," "humble") in this verse recalls the "poor of Yahweh," who are God's favourites. HITZIG rightly points that the root "עני may truly take the sense of ענו" ("sufferer"), therefore, there is no need to change עֲנִיִּים (*Kethib*) to עֲנָוִים (*Qere*); see DELITZSCH, *Proverbs*, COT 6, 249.

[48] MARSHALL, *Gospel of Luke*, 82; see also GREEN, *Gospel of Luke*, 103. Johnson (*Gospel of Luke*, 42) sees salvation being tied to lowliness of His servant whereas the arrogant attitude "blocks the perception of God's visitation."

[49] It shows God's dealing with Mary. It refers to God's mighty works of salvation that He has done for His people in the past to which the OT bears testimony. It also means God's judgment against those who are opposed to His basic demand (i.e., to be humble and low). See MARSHALL, *Gospel of Luke*, 83-84. H. SCHÜRMANN thinks that more than a description of God's saving action in the past, the second part of the Magnificat needs to be taken as a description of his future action. He maintains that vv.51-53 contain an ethical-religious qualification; see his *Lukasevangelium*, 1,1-9,50, 75.

[50] JOHNSON, *Gospel of Luke*, 42.

[51] This verse resembles Ps 37,11, but it is lacking in Luke and is understood to be an addition by Q[mt] to explain the first beatitude. See DAVIES and ALLISON, *Gospel Matthew I*, 449.

[52] DAVIES and ALLISON, *Matthew I*, 449.

[53] DAVIES and ALLISON, *Matthew I*, 449.

Here, "For they shall inherit the earth" reflects the conditional promise concerning the possession of the Land in Deut 4,1 (cf. Num 14,26f.); in other words, only the "meek" and the "humble" stand a chance to possess the Land.[54] In Judaism, it becomes a picture of an eschatological promise.[55] Those who are humble and meek can inherit the land, but not those who are proud or wicked.[56]

The existence of Egypt as a low kingdom implies that God humbles her pride through His judgment for forty years so she will learn to submit to Him. Only when she is cleansed of her ambition and pride and transformed by Him, can she have new identity as a kingdom. Her status as a "low kingdom" is the result of God's salvation, which gives impetus to new consequences (vv.15-16).

7.3.2. Conclusion

God's promise about future existence of Egypt as a "low kingdom" makes it clear that God has a plan for her. Her future existence in not altogether doomed by His judgment, like was Sodom and Gomorrah (Gen 19). Her new existence as a "low kingdom" forecasts Israel's hope of salvation that God will bring back her captives as well and establish her in the land promised to the fathers. Above all, transformed by his action, she will exist and live as His people.

The restoration of the Egyptians to Pathros as a "low kingdom" indicates a geographically relocated and territorially reduced size of Egypt. It will have consequences for her, for the nations and for Israel (vv.15-16). Beyond Egypt's new geographical-political establishment as a "low kingdom," lies a deeper theological significance: Egypt becomes humble before God.

The earth belongs to God and He apportions it to the nations. He brings back Egypt to the land of her birthplace where she can exist as a low kingdom. The gifts of land and salvation come entirely from God, but their effectiveness also depends on the nations to have an attitude that He expects the people and the nations to have. The maxim is clear: Only the meek will inherit the land. Egypt as a low kingdom indirectly points to Israel's messianic hope and eschatological salvation.

---

[54] I.e., if Israel will obey God's laws and keep His statutes, in other words, if she does not become arrogant and proud, she can expect to inherit the Promised Land. See DAVIES and ALLISON, *Matthew I*, 449.

[55] GNILKA, *Matthäusevangelium*, 1/1, 123.

[56] KRAUS, *Psalmen 1-59*, 441.

7.4. God brings back the captives of Egypt
and Settles them in Pathros (Excursus)

God's gathering of the Egyptians from their dispersion among the nations, bringing back their captives and settling them in the land of Pathros, the place of their origin, makes them a low kingdom there. Her new existence as the lowest kingdom, no more ruling or raising herself over other nations and persuading the house of Israel to be disloyal to the LORD, heralds a new era of God's salvation. It guarantees Egypt a new existence and anticipates Israel's future restoration.

According to Bertholet, One could always imagine well for a nation like Tyre, which, though small in size, had much potential because of its maritime location, but the restoration of a big country like Egypt seems quite impossible. It would be enough if it did not pose any threat to Israel in the future and for this reason, the great world power must be broken; instead, it should become a low kingdom. Further developments concerning her restoration are described in 29,14f. This announcement of salvation of Egypt affirms the whole opinion on Ezekiel's oracles of judgment against the foreign nations from this point of view that it is indispensable for his oracle of salvation for Israel. Ezekiel perceives that the future guarantees for Israel's secure and undisturbed dwelling in the Land needs to be established (cf. v.16). To this purpose belongs also the future restoration of Egypt for which her captives should be brought back and settled in the place of their origin in Pathros, in the southern region.[57]

It is clear that Ezekiel does not look at Egypt as an enemy of Israel, but seeks to establish a parallel between Israel and Egypt.[58] His oracles of judgment against Israel and Egypt (and of their salvation) should be seen from this perspective. The oracles of judgment against Israel and Egypt are both similar in that both face destruction and exile from their land. Their judgments are expressed metaphorically: sword, famine, wild beasts, and plague, signifying war, exile, draught and devastation (Ezek 14,21). Ezekiel draws a similarity also in the oracles of their salvation (cf., Ezek 11 [Israel] = Ezek 29 [Egypt]).

Israel's origin lies in the desert (Ezek 16) and the LORD's choice of Israel from among the nations made her His own people and her covenant-relation with the LORD is rooted in her exodus from Egypt. Israel's peaceful existence in the Promised Land and her covenantal fidelity, i.e., faithfully belonging to the LORD, are both connected with the fate of Egypt, from where He took Israel out with a

---

[57] BERTHOLET, *Hesekiel*, KHAT 12, 153.

[58] The parallel between Israel and Egypt in their judgment and restoration is striking: forty years of punishment of Judah/Israel (Ezek 4,6) and of Egypt (29,11), dispersion of Israel among the nations (Ezek 22,15) and of Egypt (Ezek 29,12; 30,23.26); still, God remains Israel's sanctuary in her dispersion (Ezek 11,16), and promises restoration of Israel (11,17f.; 20,41f.; 28,25f., 34,13f.; 39,27) and of Egypt (29,13-16). See ZIMMERLI, *Ezekiel 25-48*, 712-713; EICHRODT, *Hesekiel 19-48*, 277).

mighty arm. If God disperses the Egyptians in the countries for forty years, like He did Israel, when He brought her out of Egypt, He promises also to give Egypt a similar hope of salvation as he does for Israel.[59] In this respect, gathering the Egyptians, bringing back their captives, and settling them in their native place, gives hope to Israel in its exile. The new prospect of life for Egypt in Pathros as a low kingdom brightens hope for a secure and peaceful dwelling for the captives of Judah-Israel because Egypt will no longer interfere in God's plan for Israel.

If Israel's relation with Egypt in the past proved a constant temptation to her fidelity to the LORD, Egypt herself indulged freely in manipulating and persuading Israel to rely on her (= Israel's apostasy).[60] Israel and Egypt both have rejected LORD by taking recourse to such behaviour. Israel's harlotry and Egypt's hubris are two different facets of their deviant and estranged relationship with the LORD. Israel and Egypt both have forgotten their God, to whom alone belongs honour and power. Thus, the restoration of Egypt by gathering and bringing her back to Pathros and making her a low kingdom means that Egypt recognises her proper place in God's plan for the nations and His sovereignty.

The restoration of Egypt as a low kingdom reflects God's sovereign power and goodness, which will lead her to recognise His greatness, and Israel will see a guarantee of future restoration. Just as God revives the winter streams in the Negev region year after year, streams that would otherwise remain dry for the major part of the year (cf. Ps 126,4), so also do Egypt and Israel come to know of God's wonderful creative power for them when He brings the period of their judgment to an end. Egypt's farthest southern location upstream the Nile and Israel's experience of the revival of the winter streams in the Negev, point not merely to a new geographical orientation and location, but also raise a new hope for Israel's restoration and her loyalty to God, leading her to the song of praise on His holy mountain (Ps 126,2).

In Ezekiel's view, Judah's foreign policy, i.e., her friendly relations with the foreign nations, is a "sin" and "guilt" (cf. Ezek 16). In his view, Egypt stands as a reminder of Israel's guilt (מַזְכִּיר עָוֹן Ezek 29,16 also see 21,28), of her constant infidelity to the LORD. The fact that Israel sought Egypt's help more than relying on God has made her like the godless nations. Thus, God's judgment against Egypt becomes a measure for the godless nations, including Israel. Precisely this constituted the guilt of Egypt - her godlessness.[61]

The parallel that Ezekiel draws between the announcement of judgment against Israel and Egypt uses traditional images like, the sword, wild beasts, dryness/desolation of the land, no burial/tomb (for the slain) and depopulation/no

---

[59] God's salvation of Egypt gives a hope of salvation to Israel. If God does it for Egypt, Israel's arch enemy, He would surely also bring back the captives of Israel and restore them.

[60] By boasting of her wealth and power, Egypt constantly tempted Judah to seek her help instead of putting her faith in God thus, putting herself in a serious danger. See HEINISCH, *Ezechiel*, 143.

[61] BERTHOLET, *Hesekiel*, KHAT 12, 154.

passers-by, which are employed frequently in the announcements of judgment in the Old Testament. W. Vogels calls attention to this close similarity in God's judgment against them:[62]

Table 3:

	Egypt	Israel	
Elements:	Ezek 29,1-12	Ezek 29,1-12	Lev 26
sword	v.8	5,2.12.17; 6,3.11.12; 7,15; 11,8.10; 14,17; 33,2; 39,23	vv.25.33.36.37
wild beasts	v.5	5,17; 14,15.21; 33,27	22
desolation of the land	vv.9.10	5,14; 35, 4;36,4.10.33	31.33
and desert	vv.9.10.11	6,14; 12,20; 14,15.16; 15,8; 33,28.29; 35,3.4.7.9.14.15	33
no burial/ tomb	v.5	35,8; 37 (the story of the bones); 39,11ff.	30,30; cf. Deut 28,26
no passers-by	v.11 cf. 32, 13	5,14; 14,15; 33,38; 36,34; cf., Jer 9,9.11	

7.5. Egypt's New Existence: Ezek 29,15

After her restoration in Pathros, Egypt may have lost her relevance as a world-power, especially with respect to her hold in the Nile Delta, the gateway to Egypt, but her history is not at all lost because in becoming a low kingdom she is promised also a new status. Egypt will be the lowest of the kingdoms. This is going to be her new status. Historians note that the once mighty kingdom of Egypt - which had experienced two major periods of breakup over a history of many centuries,[63] but survived through re-unification of the kingdom, and commanded one of the largest territorial boundaries, effectively influencing politics in the ancient world as far as Syria-Palestine at one point – took on a situation greatly different from its glorious past with its new existence as the lowest kingdom. In God's plan, it is the beginning of a new era for Egypt, one that becomes a model and a hope for others. Her new existence, that is referred to in vv.14c-15b, bears further consequences for the nations, for Israel and for Egypt herself (v.16).

---

[62] VOGELS, *God's Universal Covenant,* 87-90, cf. 88.
[63] GOTTWALD, *Politics of Ancient Israel,* 129.

7.5. 1. "She will be the lowest of the kingdoms" (v.15a)

Egypt's future existence is described using a superlative term: "She will be the lowest of the kingdoms." This displays a significant difference from the previous statement about her existence which was: וְהָיוּ שָׁם מַמְלָכָה שְׁפָלָה ("And there they will be a lowly kingdom" v.14c). In comparison to a simple description of her existence, which indicates her inner characteristic (14c), the superlative statement in 15a relates to the implications of her new existence in relation to others, especially with respect to her relation to Israel and the nations. Notwithstanding its implication for others, it bears a special significance also for Egypt herself.

Beyond Egypt's future guarantee of being a "low kingdom" (v.14c), the superlative statement (v.15a) that "she will be the lowest of the kingdoms" re-affirms her new status and states her transformed nature, qualifying her new character in relation to God and to her neighbours. It concerns her humble submission to the plan of He who promised to "gather" her from the peoples, "bring back" her captives[64] and "settle" them in the land of Pathros, the land of their origin. Now, He takes His action further and makes her the "lowliest of all the kingdoms." By becoming the lowest of all kingdoms, Egypt possesses the guarantee of God's saving deeds for her, as God is He who overthrows the mighty and exalts those of low degree (cf. Lk 1,52). Egypt's new status - the lowest kingdom - is a position of God's favour and exaltation for her by which He unfolds his plan for Israel (cf. Ex 19 6).[65]

7.5.2. Egypt's new relationship with the nations

As the lowest kingdom, Egypt plays a different role in her relationship with the other nations. As a world power, she dominated and ruled over them and her enormous wealth and power attracted mercenaries and different groups of people to serve in her army including the people of the covenant land (30,5). This role has been turned upside down. She is no longer a threat to the nations nor does she attract mercenaries. Her foreign politics have been slashed, together with her army, the size of her territory and her geographical location. All this has a significant bearing on the nations.

7.5.2.1. "She will not raise herself again above the nations" (15b)

The first impact of Egypt's new status is seen in her relation to other nations: "She will not raise herself again above the nations." This recalls Egypt's ambition for

---

[64] In a theological-political sense, it implies their conversion; see VOGELS, *God's Universal Covenant*, 91.

[65] VOGELS, *God's Universal Covenant*, 95.

power and domination in her own land, in the northwest African regions, and in Syria-Palestine.[66] The struggle for supremacy among different Pharaohs over the centuries over control of Egypt highlights this desire for power that goes back to the end of the pre-dynastic era, when Menes (Upper Egypt) united the two kingdoms of the Upper and the Lower Egypt c. 3100 B.C. and established the first unified kingdom (Early Kingdom) with its capital in Memphis.[67]

V.15b is a negative statement but it is not a new announcement of judgment; rather, it is an affirmation of Egypt's new character. As a negative statement, it indicates her past character, amply proved in her involvement in the politics of Syria-Palestine and in the African lands (cf. Nubia[68] and Libya[69]). She has pursued the ambition of her greatness, seeking to dominate other nations through her wealth and power. The usage of the Hebrew verb נָשָׂא[70] (*qal* "to lift high," "carry," "take;" *hithpael* "to raise oneself," "arise") in 15b describes this attitude.[71] It can be illustrated by two other texts, Num 16,3 and Prov 30,31 (cf. Ezek 32,2), where it occurs in a similar construction (with עַל):

Num 16,3:

רַב־לָכֶם כִּי כָל־הָעֵדָה כֻּלָּם קְדֹשִׁים וּבְתוֹכָם יְהוָה
וּמַדּוּעַ תִּתְנַשְּׂאוּ עַל־קְהַל יְהוָה:

You have gone too far! The whole community is holy, every one of them,
and the LORD is with them;
Why then do you set yourselves above the LORD's assembly?

---

[66] REDFORD, *Egypt, Canaan, and Israel*, 148-160; ALING, *Egypt and Bible History*, 111-117. VAN DE MIEROOP, *History of the Ancient Near East*, 154-156.

[67] From Menes to the conquest of Alexander the Great in 333 B.C., Egypt was ruled by 31 dynasties of Pharaohs. See PARKER, "The Calendars and Chronology," in HARRIS (ed.), *Legacy of Egypt*, 21.25; see also BRIGHT, *History of Israel*, 38-39.

[68] The first three kings of the 18th Dynasty made a very concerted effort to establish Egyptian hegemony in Nubia, which meant that they had to fight the Kushites of Nubia and destroy them. For this purpose, they built strongholds (garrisons) in the region. Thutmose I was responsible for the final overthrow of "the Kushite Kingdom of the Second Intermediate Period." See REDFORD, *Egypt, Canaan, and Israel*, 149-153.

[69] Thutmose attacked Ullaza and Ardata (6 km. south of modern Tripoli) in the 29th year of his reign (1476 B.C.), and held control over Libya, and made the northern coast secure for Egypt. See REDFORD, *Egypt, Canaan, and Israel*, 158.

[70] נָשָׂא occurs more than 650x in the OT, of which 68 occurrences are found in Ezekiel. Cf. FARBY, "נָשָׂא", in *ThWAT* V, 626-643. נָשָׂא (*Hithpael*) with עַל occurs in Num 16,3; Ezek 29,15; Prov 30,31 (cf. Ezek 32,2) and its Aramaized substantive, cf. LXX[L] ἔπαρσις (= *prominence*) points to the antithetical change taking place in Egypt's attitude in respect to other nations. Its derivative נָשִׂיא I ("leader," "prince") occurs 37 times in Ezek (cf. twice in the Oracles against Egypt in 30,13; 32,29). See KOEHLER and BAUMGARTNER, *Hebrerw and Aramic Lexicon,* Study Edition, Vol. I, 727.

[71] Cf. Lk 1,51-52 ; also Is 2,11; 5,15; 25,12; Ezek 21,31.

Num 16,3 relates to the privileged position of Moses and Aaron, which the LORD gave to them above all Israel. It becomes a point of jealousy among the rest and they contend against this "privileged position" of the two on the ground, that, since the whole community of Israel was made holy by the LORD and He was with every one of them, Moses and Aaron could not claim themselves to be more privileged before the LORD, that He should not speak and reveal His plan for Israel only through them, excluding the rest from this privilege.

Prov 30,31:

זַרְזִיר מָתְנַיִם אוֹ־תָיִשׁ וּמֶלֶךְ אַלְקוּם עִמּוֹ׃

A strutting rooster, a he-goat, and a king with his army around him.

The saying of the Prov 30,31 (זַרְזִיר מִתְנַשֵּׂא וְתַיִשׁ וּמֶלֶךְ לָקוּם עִמּוֹ cf. the proposed reading of the probably corrupted MT) focuses on just one simple fact, namely, one's delight in raising or making oneself higher than others. It implies a certain sense of privilege and self-importance, even a touch of pride that a person gains by adopting such a posture in relation to others.

The meaning of עַל + נָשָׂא (hithpael) in these texts makes it clear that it relates to a "privileged position" over the rest. In the case of Moses and Aaron, their superior position is never meant for their own boasting or domination over the rest of Israel, but for service of the community. Prov 30,31 seems to denote both a "privileged position" and also "lordship" or "domination" over the rest. A sense of pride is not ruled out here. This may explain further implication of Egypt's latest condition that she will not raise herself again above the nations. By making Egypt the "lowest of all the kingdoms," God offers an opportunity to other nations around her to live in a new atmosphere of equanimity, respect, and brotherhood. Egypt's changed existence becomes a parameter for the nations to follow in their own right relation with God and with others.

In the pursuit of her greatness over other nations, Egypt failed to realize that such behaviour provoked God's judgment against herself. But through forty years of judgment (cf. Num 14,33-34), God transforms Egypt by making her the lowest of all the kingdoms, so that she may pose no threat to others. Positively, her status as the "lowest kingdom" becomes a sign and a model also for stability and peaceful co-existence of other nations and, above all, in their relation to God.

7.5.2.2. "I will make them small" (15c)

God's announcement, "I will make them few" (15c) reveals yet another detail of His plan for Egypt. God plans to make the Egyptians few. Apparently, וְהִמְעַטְתִּים refers to the population of Egypt (cf. "hordes"). It was the main supply and stay of her army, and served as labour for her construction projects and agriculture. Therefore, the size of the population played a significant role in Egypt's sense of greatness and ability to exercise dominion over others. There were, of course, mercenaries, other ethnic groups, even Hebrews (cf. 30,5) who served in the army of Egypt at the side of Pharaoh's regular Egyptian army.

Ezekiel does not in vain mention "carrying her hordes away" (29,19; 30,4; cf. hordes of Egypt: 30,10; 32,20; of No: 30,15; of Pharaoh: 32,12) while announcing God's judgment against Egypt. The Hebrew word הָמוֹן generally means "turmoil," "multitude" or "crowd." In the present context, it is not ruled out that the statement in 15c indirectly refers to the hordes of Egypt, in reference to her population and not strictly to her armies and hordes of mercenaries.

Populating the land was important for the country's agriculture in addition to the completion of her various construction works (cf. Ex 1,11f.) and for commerce. In view of its material role in supporting and sustaining the troops, and the nation as a whole, the role of agriculture cannot be overlooked. In fact, the annual flooding of the Nile brought rich silt that made the Nile valley very fertile, but to till and cultivate it, a sizable supply of agricultural labour, and thus a large population, was needed. Therefore, devastation and drying of the land of Egypt in the announcement of judgment (cf. 29,9-10) could not be a mere metaphorical expression. The scattering and dispersion of the Egyptians (29,12) renders the land desert (29,11), turning it into a haunting place, disrupting the lifeline of support for the huge Egyptian army, both in terms of food and the supply of young men.

Therefore, it is the population of Egypt (= inhabitants), which provided the basis and support of Egypt's power, that is ultimately trimmed to size. It is made small so that it won't allow any thought of future conquest. This new picture of Egypt should not be viewed as punishment. On the contrary, it should be taken as a special status and a privilege that God himself plans for her and unfolds for her good and for the good of her neighbours.

The Hebrew verb מעט (*qal* "be few," "become few," "be small;" *hiphil* "to gather little," "to diminish, reduce," "make the number few")[72] occurs 22 times[73] and its noun ("little," "small," "few") occurs 94 times (+ 3 derivatives) in the OT.[74] Its basic meaning is best expressed in 1Kgs 17,12:[75]

מָעוֹג כִּי אִם־מְלֹא כַף־קֶמַח בַּכַּד וּמְעַט־שֶׁמֶן בַּצַּפָּחַת

I don't have any bread, only a handful of flour in a jar and a little oil in a jug.

This half verse narrates what the widow of Zarephath has to say to the prophet Elijah when the former asks her to fetch him a little water and a piece of bread. It reveals the widow's actual existential condition, namely, she has only "a handful

---

[72] HOLLADAY, *Hebrew and Aramaic Lexicon*, 205-206.

[73] HOLLADAY, *Hebrew and Aramaic Lexicon*, 843; ZOBEL, „מָעַט", in *ThWAT* VI, 1030-1036.

[74] LISOWSKY, *Konkordanz*, 838.

[75] ZOBEL, „מָעַט", in *ThWAT* VI, 1030.

of flour in a jar and a little oil in a jug." It implies that what she has is the only and the very last means of subsistence left with her and, indeed, it is too little to share it with another with dignity. She has just "a little" and nothing more to hope for, for her further sustenance and for existence thereafter. On the other hand, its parallel הָמוֹן ("abundance") is found in Ps 37,16 which again helps to explain its meaning:[76]

טוֹב־מְעַט לַצַּדִּיק מֵהֲמוֹן רְשָׁעִים רַבִּים:
Better the little that the righteous have than the wealth of many wicked.

This saying of the Psalm (cf. Prov 15,16; 16,8) draws a sharp contrast between the attitudes of the righteous and of the wicked in respect to how many earthly possessions they have. Compared to the wicked, who usually have more earthly possessions, the righteous have but *little*. Indeed, this "little" possession of the righteous denotes their lowly and humble attitude. Here הָמוֹן (usually a "noisy multitude") denotes "earthly possessions."[77]

Both of these texts show that "a little" (of a thing or possession) does not necessarily mean deprivation, and certainly does not mean a negative or punitive judgment. Instead, it helps to identify two types of people who are associated with such state of affairs, namely, the poor, e.g., the widow of Zarephath, and the righteous; both of them have only "a little." However, more than what they have or possess from a material point of view, it reflects their basic attitude, namely, their good and just behaviour. Implicitly, "goodness" and "justice" are attributed to them. So, by making Egypt "little," "few" or "small" in number, God intends to instil the attitude of goodness in her, an attitude that is counter to her previous nature of domination.

As a noun מעט relates to any material possession, a thing or, an amount,[78] but its usage as a verb (*hiphil*) refers to God's action,[79] as He means to "make few" in number. In Ezek 29,15 it refers to the inhabitants of Egypt, whom God reduces in number. Making the population of Egypt small does not mean she is being punished for even though demographically reduced in number, she will cease to inspire awe and fear of the nations and politically she will no longer have any significant influence to maneuver or to dominate others. Her small population means other nations will also have a better prospect of peace and security. More than any direct impact on Egypt's political power, "making them small in number" relates to her new and fundamental attitude, namely, of being humble, good and just towards others, as the meaning of מעט in 1Kgs 17,12; Ps 37,16 shows.

---

[76] ZOBEL, „מָעַט", in *ThWAT* VI, 1031.

[77] DELITZSCH, *Psalms*, COT 5, 284.

[78] ZOBEL, „מָעַט", in *ThWAT* VI, 1031.

[79] Cf. three occurrences of "to make few" (people): Jer 10,24 & Ezek 29,15; (cattle): Ps 107,38.

7.5.2.3. "That they will never rule over the nations" (15c)

The second part 15c reveals God's motive for making Egypt small in number: לְבִלְתִּי רְדוֹת בַּגּוֹיִם "never to rule over the nations." It explains Egypt's new existence as the lowest of all the kingdoms and is here clarified by מעט. Making Egypt small relates directly to "never to rule over the nations." As a result of reduced population, Egypt's army is automatically cut to size so that it loses its power to rule and dominate others. The history of the Ancient Near East bears witness to the fact that a large and powerful army was required to undertake campaigns and to control other nations. When the army of a nation became small and weak, that nation stood the risk of losing its independence and often came under the vassalage of a more powerful nation.

The Hebrew root I רָדָה ("become powerful") occurs 27 times in the OT[80] and in *qal* has two specific meanings: (1) to "tread" the winepress (cf. Joel 4,1), and (2) to "rule" (with the associated meaning of oppression and its opposite משל cf. Ps 110, 2).[81] Its rendering in LXX varies frequently, which creates difficulty for its interpretation.[82] Often a person is its grammatical subject,[83] but a person or a people can also be its object.[84] Its meaning and usage in the OT texts suggests that רָדָה in v.15 refers to Egypt's oppressive domination of other nations, a negative characteristic that God removes from her by making her "few" in number.

7.5.3. Conclusion:

Ezek 29,15 gives a picture of Egypt that is completely different than what was previously known to be, namely, proud and unreliable (29,3b-9), arrogant and self-indulgent (32,2). New Egypt has no trace of her past character. She is a low kingdom, and among the kingdoms she is the lowest, she is small and humble, and does not dominate others. These new characteristics are purely the result of God's action, and not of her own achievement. It reveals God's prerogative in the restoration of Egypt, for He chooses to act in favour of one, out of the seven nations that find a place in the oracles against the nations in the book of Ezekiel. In

---

[80] ZOBEL, „רָדָה", in *ThWAT*, Vol. VII, 351-358

[81] KOEHLER and BAUMGARTNER, *Hebrew & Aramaic Lexicon*, Vol. II, Study Edition, 1191.

[82] ZOBEL, „רָדָה", in *ThWAT* VII, 351-352.

[83] Cf. "the priests" (Jer 5,31); "a foreigner," "an Israelite," or "the whole Israel" (Lev 25,43.46.53; Deut 20,20; Isa 14,2); "a supervisor" (1Kgs 5,30; 2Chr 8,10; or "Egypt" [Ezek 29,15], or "shepherds" (Ezek 34,4). See ZOBEL, „רָדָה", in *ThWAT* VII, 352.

[84] Cf. "the nations" (Isa 14,2.6; 45,1; Ezek 29,15; Ps 144,2); "their kings" (Isa 41,2); "enemies" (Ps 110,2 compare Num 24,19;), "Israel" (Lev 26,17; 1Kgs 5,30; 9,23; 2Chr 8,10); "tribes" (Ps 68,28); see ZOBEL, „רָדָה", in *ThWAT* VII, 352.

so far as God's dealing with Israel is concerned, His dealing with Egypt makes her like Israel. Although God never calls Egypt "my people," in Ezekiel's oracles as He does Israel,[85] or His own possession, as Israel (Ex 19,5; Deut 7,6; Mal 3,17), still, God's salvation for Egypt not only resembles His salvation for Israel, but it also places Egypt beside her. Egypt's new and changed character is what God seeks also from Israel. This places Egypt next to Israel and gives her the privilege to become God's people.

7.6. Egypt's New Relationship with the House of Israel: Ezek 29,16

God's restoration of Egypt has positive implications not only for other nations but also for Israel. Egypt was accused of being unreliable (cf. 29,6b-7) and giving false hope of reliance to her ally, the house of Israel (29,16). By making Egypt the lowest of all the kingdoms and her stature small, God has thus removed her past character as a temptress of Israel, making a new relationship possible. For Israel, Egypt is neither a source of reliance nor she is a tempter to her faith in the LORD. This is a positive development in God's plan of salvation for the house of Israel, with whom He deals following the Egyptian paradigm. With her guilt of infidelity removed, Israel will also return to the LORD.

7.6.1. "She will no more be a source of confidence for the house of Israel" (16a)

Ezek 29,6-7 refers to Israel's reliance on Egypt. In the ensuing political events of 588-587 B.C., Judah was involved in an alliance with Egypt to get her support for the security of Jerusalem against the danger from Nebuchadnezzar of Babylon.[86] But Israel's alliance with Egypt for her national security was utterly useless because it was against God's plan for Israel, as well as against her covenant-relationship with the LORD. The new situation of Egypt, i.e., low and small, removes her ambition and pride and she ceases to be a power to coerce or persuade Israel to any negative behaviour. "She will no more be a source of confidence for the house of Israel." Its political implication is clear, in that Egypt loses her relevance as world-power, but much more than this is its theological implication which touches directly on Israel's fundamental relationship to God. The birth of Israel as a people is related to her covenant relationship with the LORD. Therefore, her existence is dependent on this fundamental relationship with Him, which she has violated in the past by her enchantment for Egypt (cf. Ex 19,4-6).

---

[85] E.g., Ex 3,7; Isa 1,3; 5,13; 19,25; 52,4; Jer 2,11.13; 2,31.32; 5,31; 18,15; Ezek 46,18
[86] 2Kgs 18,20-21 (Judah against Babylon), and 2Kgs 17,4 (Israel against Assyria).

The Hebrew verb root בטח means "to feel secure," "be secure" or "to rely on something or someone."[87] But often it carries a negative sense in that it denotes deception or a false trust; it is also used equally to refer to absolute reliance on God. Thus, it is an ambivalent term. LXX usually translates בטח as ἐλπίζειν and it refers to reliance on God, whereas in Isaiah and Jeremiah it renders בטח as πεποιθέναι to refer to false security.[88] Its verb form occurs 116 times,[89] its noun variants[90] occur 48 times[91] and its substantive מִבְטָח ("confidence," "trust") occurs 15 times[92] (cf. Ezek 20,16) in the Old Testament.

Against Egypt's negative description of her relationship with Israel in 29,6b-7, the new situation of Egypt described in 29,14c-15c leads subsequently to enumerate the result of this new situation with regard to Israel. Its result is positive but expressed through a negative statement (16a): "It (Egypt) shall no more be reliance for the house of Israel." God is sovereign over His entire creation, and has bound Israel to Himself through a covenant. But Egypt had in the past succeeded in persuading Israel to betray His trust through her boasting, and Israel, seeking her security in the army of Egypt, has relied on the latter rather than trusting in the LORD, who alone can be relied upon absolutely. Egypt's action of persuading Israel is deception, usurping God's role, and thereby leading the house of Israel to apostasy. In the texts, where מִבְטָח (בטח) is used to describe man's security, this becomes quite clear.[93]

In a face of national crisis, Israel was persuaded to rely on Egypt for support instead of turning to the LORD. Egypt played a dubious political role in this scenario, swaying Israel's trust although it was a known fact that she was no longer a mighty power in comparision to the Babylonians. Therefore, Israel's reliance on Egypt was the result of a deception, cf. Isa 31,1 (also Isa 36,4.5.6):

Isa 31,1 (remotely):

הֹוֹי הַיֹּרְדִים מִצְרַיִם לְעֶזְרָה עַל־סוּסִים יִשָּׁעֵנוּ וַיִּבְטְחוּ עַל־רֶכֶב כִּי רָב וְעַל פָּרָשִׁים
כִּי־עָצְמוּ מְאֹד וְלֹא שָׁעוּ עַל־קְדֹושׁ יִשְׂרָאֵל וְאֶת־יְהוָה לֹא דָרָשׁוּ׃

---

[87] JEPSEN, „בטח", in *ThWAT* I, 608-615; cf. its meaning in *qal* "trust," "feel safe," "be full of confidence," "be unsuspecting," *hiphil* "direct somebody's trust to someone or to something," "inspire trust," see HOLLADAY, *Hebrew and Aramaic Lexicon,* 37; and "to be reliant," "to trust", see LISOWSKY, *Konkordanz,* 209.

[88] JEPSEN, „בטח", in *ThWAT* I, 610.

[89] LISOWSKY, *Konkordanz,* 209-210.

[90] "Security," "securely" (cf. LISOWSKY, *Konkordanz,* 210), and "trust," "safety"; see HOLLADAY, *Hebrew and Aramaic Lexicon,* 37.

[91] I.e., Pentateuch 7x; Deuteronomic History 6x; Writings 11x; Prophets 24x.

[92] LISOWSKY, *Konkordanz,* 746.

[93] JEPSEN, „בטח", in *ThWAT* I, 610-612.

Woe to those who go down to Egypt for help and rely on horses;
Who trust in chariots because they are many and in horsemen because they are very strong,
but do not look to the Holy One of Israel or consult the LORD!

Isa 36,9:

וְאֵיךְ תָּשִׁיב אֵת פְּנֵי פַחַת אַחַד עַבְדֵי אֲדֹנִי הַקְּטַנִּים
וַתִּבְטַח לְךָ עַל־מִצְרַיִם לְרֶכֶב וּלְפָרָשִׁים:

How then can you repulse a single captain among the least of my master's servants,
When you rely on Egypt for chariots and for horsemen?

The above texts sufficiently intimate Isaiah's opposition to Israel's reliance on any outside help other than on God himself. Isaiah questioned Israel's alliance with Egypt[94] repeatedly because he was aware of its consequences for Israel's future. During the Syro-Ephraimite crisis (i.e., Hoshea's alliance with Damascus against Judah in 734 B.C.) and later during the imminent threat of Sennacherib against Jerusalem (701 B.C.), Isaiah strongly warned Ahaz (2Kgs 15,29-30.37; 16,5-6) and Hezekiah (2Kgs 18,13-16; also see 2Chr 32,10) against seeking help from Egypt.[95] The end of Israel's northern kingdom in 722-721 B.C. by Tiglath-Pileser III of Assyria[96] (2Kgs 17,5-6) is interpreted as God's judgment against Israel for not heeding this message of the prophet.

Jer 2,37 (indirectly):

גַּם מֵאֵת זֶה תֵּצְאִי וְיָדַיִךְ עַל־רֹאשֵׁךְ כִּי־מָאַס יְהֹוָה בְּמִבְטַחַיִךְ
וְלֹא תַצְלִיחִי לָהֶם:

From it too you will come away with your hands upon your head;
For, the LORD has rejected those in whom you trust, and you will not prosper by them.

Jer 46, 25:

אָמַר יְהֹוָה צְבָאוֹת אֱלֹהֵי יִשְׂרָאֵל הִנְנִי פוֹקֵד אֶל־אָמוֹן מִנֹּא וְעַל־פַּרְעֹה
וְעַל־מִצְרַיִם וְעַל־אֱלֹהֶיהָ וְעַל־מְלָכֶיהָ וְעַל־פַּרְעֹה וְעַל הַבֹּטְחִים בּוֹ:

The LORD of hosts, the God of Israel, said: Behold, I am bringing punishment
upon Amon of Thebes and Pharaoh, and Egypt and her gods and her kings,
upon Pharaoh and those who trust in him.

Judah takes pride in the strong and secure walls of Jerusalem, still, she seeks an alliance with Egypt against the threat from Nebuchadnezzar of Babylon, even though Jeremiah views Egypt as "rejected by God," implying that reliance on Egypt will mean the self-destruction of Jerusalem. He also predicts destruction of Egypt, a punishment for assuring such help to Judah. Thus, any political alliance of Judah with Egypt is seen as rejecting God, which will bring judgment down upon both Judah and Egypt. All the same, Egypt does not seem to be unfaithful to her

---

[94] DELITZSCH, *Isaiah*, COT 7, 328.
[95] BOADT, *Reading the Old Testament*, 325-329; also JAGERSMA, *History of Israel I*, 157-158.
[96] The Assyrians attribute it to Sargon II (721-705 BC); see JAGERSMA, *History of Israel I*, 162.

ally. Neco II did come to aid Assyria against the rising power of Babylon (cf. 2Kgs, 23,31f.).[97] Israel's dependence on Egypt does not mean that her alliance with Egypt was without effect, but rather was a sign of Israel's failure to see what God expected and to prevent what God had planed for them, both.

The above texts (cf. Ezek 29,6b-7) are self-explanatory and depict Israel's compulsion to put her confidence in Egypt, on the one hand, and on the other hand, it shows the emptiness of Egypt's boasting - even though Egypt's army did force Nabuchadnezzar to lift the siege of Jerusalem temporarily in 587 B.C. However, when Jerusalem most needed help, Egypt failed to muster its army to avert the catastrophe, but the main reason for this was Israel's rejection of the LORD. Thus, while Israel's dependence on Egypt proves fatal for her existence, Egypt herself loses her hold on the Nile Delta and political relevance for her neighbours.

7.6.2. "A reminder of sin when they turned to them" (16a)

Egypt's new relation with the house of Israel is directly related to her new existence as a Low Kingdom. This new identity of Egypt brings her closer to Israel, even so far as to become God's people like Israel. This, in turn, gives hope of salvation to Israel.

The Hebrew verb זכר (*qal* "to remember"; *hiphil* "to remind," "mention," "praise") occurs 219 times in the OT.[98] An extensive use of this verb in the OT and its fairly numerous occurrences in Isaiah (26x), Jeremiah (17x and Lamentation 7x), and Ezekiel (23x) show the importance of this verb in the prophetic books. Its noun form מַזְכִּיר ("recorder," "chronicler") occurs 9 times.[99] In Ezek 29,16 מַזְכִּיר means reminding or remembrance.[100]

W. Schottroff remarks, "zkr connotes an active relationship to the object of memory that exceeds a simple thought process."[101] Rightly so, זכר, as a verb or as a noun, is used frequently to refer to God's past saving deed (Ps 77,6f.12; 119,52; 143,5) for Israel. This is a basis for the sacred Writers of the OT to use זכר to warn and instruct Israel (Mic 6,3-5; Isa 17,10). No wonder then, that its prophetic usage takes mostly God's perspective in reference to His past saving deeds for the people.[102] Furthermore, זכר is also used quite regularly in Israel's Praise to Yahweh ("whose sin the LORD does not count" Ps 32,2; cf. 42,7; 63,7; 77,4), in the thanksgiving of the community (Ps 136,23; cf. 115,12) or in supplication to the LORD ("Do not remember our sins for ever" cf. Isa 64,8 see also Jer 20,9). On the

---

[97] KEIL, *Jeremiah and Lamentations*, COT 8, 49.

[98] LISOWSKY, *Konkordanz*, 444-446, and SCHOTTROFF "זכר to remember," in *TLOT* I, 381f.

[99] LISOWSKY, *Konkordanz*, 774.

[100] Compare the occurrences of זכר in *hiphil*, in LISOWSKY, *Konkordanz*, 446.

[101] SCHOTTROFF, "זכר to remember," in *TLOT* I, 383.

[102] SCHOTTROFF, "זכר to remember," in *TLOT* I, 386.

other hand, זכר may also convey a "harmful intention" in the sense of remembering the harm done by someone and its usage in Ezek 29,16 seems to express this. But its basic meaning is associated with the faculty of mind, i.e., memory.[103]

From the above explanation and the texts relating to the usage of זכר and its semantic meaning, it becomes quite clear that it has to do with the faculty of mind that collects experiences, events, places, people, and other things into its memory and helps someone to recall it. Thus, unlike God, who does not remember His people's past sin but overlooks it and forgives them (cf. Isa 43,25; Jer 31,34),[104] Egypt called Israel's past guilt to mind, but something is being said about Egypt in Ezek 29,16 that indicates a change: "Egypt will not be a reminder of guilt (עָוֹן) for the house of Israel." The former becomes an object that helps the latter to call to memory her past actions. It is a positive development in so far as Egypt's future and her role towards Israel is concerned. Something positive is said of Egypt, which reflects her changed role towards Israel. Egypt will cease to be persuasion for Israel, and will no longer cause her to neglect her covenant fidelity with the LORD. Egypt's previous role will be a thing of the past, a mere reminder of her sinful indulgences and nothing more.

The relation of מַזְכִּיר to עָוֹן, making it into a noun phrase, "reminder of sin", in this verse is noteworthy.[105] The substantive עָוֹן occurs 231 times in the OT and its basic meaning is "to bend," "curve," "turn aside" or "twist."[106] In a theological sense, pertaining to formally disqualifying "certain actions, behaviours, or circumstances and their consequences," it is usually translated as "guilt" and "iniquity," and one comes to its realisation when one is confronted by God.[107] In this sense, Egypt being a reminder of Israel's iniquity implies that in God's saving deed for Egypt, even Israel is confronted by God, causing her to remember her iniquity - her past perverse actions - which were against the demands of her covenant relationship with Him. This action on behalf of Israel is to be viewed as a realisation of her guilt and her conversion to God. Just as the salvation of Sodom and Samaria prompts Jerusalem's salvation (Ezek 16,53-63), Egypt's salvation gives a new hope and impetus to Israel's salvation.

The Deuteronomic instructions, emphasizes Israel's need to remember (זכר) and observe God's commandments, which insists on the individual experiences of God's saving deeds (cf. Deut 5,15; 7,18; 8,2.18; 9,7; 15,15; 16,3.12; 24,9.22;

---

[103] SCHOTTROFF, "זכר to remember," in *TLOT* I, 383-384.

[104] Compare with Hos 14,10, and Jer 44,21, which remind people that the LORD remembers their sin to punish them. See SCHOTROFF, "זכר to remember," in *TLOT* I, 386.

[105] There are 29 occurrences in the OT: Pentateuch 5x; Deuteronomic History 4x; Writings 9x; and Prophets 11x.

[106] KNIERIM, "עָוֹן ʿāwōn perversity," in *TLOT* II, 862-866.

[107] KNIERIM, "עָוֹן ʿāwōn perversity," in *TLOT* II, 863.

25,17).[108] Taking Deut 8,2-6 as a paradigm of how God deals with Israel, N. Lohfink highlights this aspect of the verb remember (זכר), which insists upon recalling God's past saving deeds for Israel.[109] The instruction goes further to show its purpose, namely, to know (ידע) what was in their hearts (i.e., their arrogance and consequently to humble them), and finally to encourage them to keep (שמר) his commandments. Their failure to keep His commandment ultimately means that they do not heed His covenant because they do not even remember what He has done for them. Thus, it indicates a close relationship between מַזְכִּיר and עָוֹן. Israel is to remember God's saving deeds for her and this constitutes the sole motive to keep His commandments whereas, Israel's failure to keep them, qualifies her as guilty before the LORD.

God makes Egypt a sign by which Israel will come to realise her own guilt: Egypt becomes a reminder of Israel's past actions. In this sense, מַזְכִּיר עָוֹן ("reminder of guilt" or, "to remember guilt") has been used as a formulaic expression in Ezek 29,16 (see also 1Kgs 17,18; Hos 8,13; 9,9).[110] Therefore, things are not merely political here, i.e., Egypt persuading Israel to have an alliance with her and the latter succumbing and thereby being unfaithful to the LORD, while Egypt continues to play the "spoiler" or "tempter". Rather, there is a deeper theological issue involved here, namely, persuaded by Egypt's boasting, Israel has thrown her trust on the power of Egypt. By doing so, Israel has turned away from the covenant that she entered into with the LORD and has refused to keep His commandments. It amounts to Israel's utter disregard and arrogance, and her unfaithfulness to Him. Instead, she has turned to Egypt from where the LORD had brought her with a mighty hand. In doing so, Israel has sinned, but so has Egypt as the latter acted to provide Israel a political guarantee and be a saviour to her and thus collaborated in Israel's sinful act.

Israel and Egypt have both denounced the LORD. God's saving deeds as the Saviour of Israel from the slavery in Egypt and as the Creator of Egypt in countering her hubris are easily ignored by both Israel and Egypt, which have sought to build a future of their own, without relying on the LORD. This attitude of Egypt and Israel is cleansed away by God's final saving deed for Egypt. There is no more projection of Egypt as an enemy of Israel, but as the one that is like Israel herself, as the one that is set as a nation beside Israel.

---

[108] SCHOTTROFF, "זכר to remember," in *TLOT* I, 387.

[109] LOHFINK, *Das Hauptgebot*, 125-136.

[110] KNIERIM, "עָוֹן *ʿāwōn* perversity," in *TLOT* II, 863.

7.7. "And they will know that I am the Lord GOD" (16b)

The last verse of the salvation oracle (16b), "And they will know that I am the Lord GOD," expresses the ultimate purpose of the oracle of God's judgment against Egypt. It has to do with brining Egypt to a knowledge of the LORD[111] and to a recognition of His sovereignty: *firstly*, over the nation, which Pharaoh must acknowledge and submit to, and *secondly*, to live with other nations in peace and equanimity as God's people and a neighbour of Israel.

The Hebrew root ידע ("to know," "perceive") occurs frequently in the OT[112] and its usage describes special relationship between God and Israel. The verb shows a close relationship with the Hittite verb *šek-/šak- (-za)*, Akkadic *Eidû(m) (ana)*, and the Ugarit *Ydᶜ*, which mean, "to acknowledge", i.e., "mutual legal recognition" particularly in the Near Eastern Treaties.[113] But Hebrew ידע does not derive from them although they provide sufficient ground for its usage in a similar sense, for, while זכר ("to remember") relates to the faculty of mind (i.e., "memory"), ידע relates to that of heart, as such, to inner "perception" or to affective knowledge.[114] In this sense, the final affirmation, "and they will know that I am the Lord GOD" (16b) does not relate to the intellectual knowledge of God. The Egyptians know this from His saving deed for Israel when God took them out of Egypt with mighty hands (cf. Deut 4,34; see also 29,2; Ex 19,4ff.). For Egypt, to acknowledge the LORD as God relates to the inner perception of their hearts, leading them to humble submission, attaching themselves intimately to Him. It happens as a result of their experience of His saving deeds for them, just as He did for Israel (i.e., the covenant).

The construction of ידע with כִּי (ידע + כִּי) in 16b is a formulaic statement of recognition: "so that they will know..."/"they will know that..." and it reflects the result of God's previous deeds.[115] In other words, remembering all His saving deeds makes an appeal to the hearts of the people, leading them to submit themselves to Him. It elicits acknowledgment of His deeds in their hearts, leading them to acknowledge Him as their LORD and God.[116] It is a fitting response to Him

---

[111] Knowledge of God as the result of his judgment is a common theme in the prophets, cf. EICHRODT, *Hesekiel 19-48*, 227.

[112] SCHOTTROFF, records 994 occurrences (99x in Ezek); see his "ידע *ydᶜ* to perceive, know," in *TLOT* II, 508-521; also BOTTERWECK, "יָדַע *yāda*", in *ThWAT* III, 479-511, esp. 484.

[113] HUFFMON, "The Treaty Background of Hebrew *yādā*," *BASOR* (1966), 31-37, cf. 34; see also SCHOTTROFF, "ידע *ydᶜ* to perceive, know," in *TLOT* II, 515.

[114] SCHOTTROFF, "ידע *ydᶜ* to perceive, know," in *TLOT* II, 515.

[115] SCHOTTROFF, "ידע *ydᶜ* to perceive, know," in *TLOT* II, 519.

[116] ZIMMERLI deals with God's self-revelation formula: "I am the LORD," the recognition formula: "Thus they shall know that I am the Lord GOD," and the word of proof formula: "I the LORD have spoken," in his „Ich bin Jahwe", *Geschichte und Altes Testament*, BHT 16, 179-209, „Die Erkenntnis Gottes nach dem Buch Ezechiel," (Zürich, 1954), und „Das Wort des Göttlichen

from every creature on earth and reflects both their special relation with Him and also their salvation. It means that God is ultimately acknowledged and acclaimed as the LORD of the Universe and as the God of all, by all. He brings this final purpose to fulfillment when He fulfils His promise of salvation for Egypt. It removes her hubris and the stigma as Israel's enemy by making her humble and obedient through her judgment of forty years, and makes her His people like Israel by giving her the free gift of salvation.

7.8. Conclusion:

The salvation of Egypt has a positive significance for the nations around her and for the house of Israel. God makes Egypt small and humble. This is a great change in her character. From a great and powerful nation, Egypt has been reduced in size by locating her in the land of Pathros. Egypt is no more a threat to the nations because she has given up her role of domination and rule over them. Instead, she now learns to live with them as neighbours in peace and equanimity, which gives a hope of salvation to them as well.

The salvation to Egypt presents a still more wonderful message for the house of Israel. A new situation in which God creates through salvation for Egypt removes past blots from Egypt in her relation to the house of Israel. Thus, he brings Egypt and Israel together by removing all past memory of enmity and stigma of a tempter. Egypt no longer stands as a manipulator who persuades Israel to trust in her power and influence, causing her to break away from her covenant loyalty to the LORD. Instead, Egypt becomes a sign for Israel, a reminder not just of her past "unfaithfulness", but much more of God's past saving deeds, which causes her to return to Him more earnestly than ever. Restoration of Egypt becomes a sign for Israel's covenant fidelity to the LORD and a source of hope for her salvation.

God's salvation for Egypt finally reveals its ultimate purpose for her when, seeing His saving deeds, she comes to acknowledge God's sovereignty, thereby giving Him due place and honour. Thus, as against her past arrogance (32,2), pride (29,3b.9b), and unreliability (29,6b-7), all that characterised her past behaviour, constituted her guilt and a blot to her name, Egypt finally becomes a humble nation, and one of God's people through her faithful relationship with Him, even standing next to Israel as a paradigm of His salvation to her.

Selbsterweises (Erweiswort)", *Mélanges Bibliques* (Paris 1957), 154-164. (cf. *Gottes Offenbarung*, Bd. 19, 11-40; 41-119; 120-132), respectively.

CONCLUSION

In concluding the present study, on God's dealing with Egypt in the oracle of judgment against Egypt in Ezekiel 29,1-16,[1] some of its findings can be usefully summarized. An overview of the oracles of judgment against the nations (Ezek 25,1-32,32) in *chapter one* shows that the oracles of judgment against Egypt comprise a large part (Ezek 25-32) of such oracles and raise certain, interesting questions. Why is Egypt given such prominence in the oracles against the nations? Why are the judgments against Pharaoh and Egypt so severe? The answer is clearly that Egypt, by her hubris and by her political alliance with Israel to stand against Babylon, directly confronts God's sovereignty and attempts to impede His plan of salvation for Israel. Egypt fails to see that Babylon is, after all, not just an enemy of Israel, but primarily an instrument, a sword of judgment, through which God has chosen to fulfil His plan of salvation for Israel and, as they become linked, for Egypt as well. Therefore, Egypt's alliance with Israel against Babylon is contrary to God's will.

There are seven oracles of judgment against Egypt and six of them begin with a date formula. The first (29,1-16) and the last oracles of judgment (29,17-21) are placed together, but this placement interrupts the chronological sequence of the oracles. As such, 29,17-21 is considered a secondary addition.[2] Similarly, 30,1-19, which lacks a date formula, is placed after the last oracle, and is considered to be a secondary addition because it interrupts the thematic unity of 29,1-16; 30,20-26; 31,1-18; 32,1-16 (cf., Pharaoh),[3] although it could still be seen as tracing the development of judgment against Egypt in 29,17-21 (cf. 32,17-32). Ezek 29,13-16 is not an oracle of judgment but of salvation for Egypt, and it stands between the first and the last oracle of judgment, making a bridge between them. The first oracle (29,1-12) looks forward to the oracle of salvation with hope, while the last oracle (29,17-21), which is a revision of the previous oracles of judgment against Egypt in the light of Tyre's submission to Nebuchadnezzar of Babylon (29,17-21), looks back at the salvation oracle with faith, knowing that the restoration belongs integrally to God's judgment. The other four oracles follow a chronological sequence (30,20; 30,1; 32,1.17) and describe breaking of Pharaoh's might and the destruction of Egypt by sword.

Chapter two notes some of the difficulties of the text of Ezek 29,1-16, and points out particular aspects of Ezekiel's literary style, especially in the oracles against the nations. Texts that pose certain interpretative difficulties have been

---

[1] The original dissertation dealt with the first two oracles of judgment against Egypt, i.e., Ezek 29,1-16 and 29,16-30,19.

[2] ZIMMERLI, *Ezechiel 1-24*, 697.

[3] ZIMMERLI, *Ezechiel I-24*, 697.

pointed out by D. Barthélemy, especially with regard to the plural form of MT הַתַּנִּים ("jackals")/הַתַּנִּין ("crocodile"), whether to read MT עֲשִׂיתִנִי with or without pronominal suffix נִי־ in 29,3, whether MT תִּקָּבֵץ ("be gathered") should be read as תקבר ("be buried") in 19,5, and if MT וְהַעֲמַדְתָּ ("you caused to stand") should not be amended to וְהִמְעַדְתָּ ("you caused to shake") in 29,7. Except in 29,7, where the MT needs to be amended, changes in the rest of the cases do not seem necessary. On the other hand, in 29,14b, the better reading of MT וַהֲשִׁבֹתִי (שׁוּב) is as in LXX, καὶ κατοικιῶ = וְהוֹשַׁבְתִּי (יָשַׁב "and I will cause to dwell") to show the dynamic development of the salvation oracle. In addition, the use of the MT עַל instead of the commonly expected preposition אֶל in 29,2, shows the peculiar literary form that Ezekiel uses to draw a sharp contrast in the command to the prophet.

Chapter three highlights some of the structural and literary features of the first oracle of judgment (29,1-16). The oracle is a series of three, related sub-oracles and the sub-oracle of hope at the end integrally belongs to it, even if the particle כִּי does not indicate salvation as a consequence of God's judgment. The oracles use both classical forms and other forms peculiar to Ezekiel, and these forms determine the literary units. The more usual form וַיְהִי + date is absent in 29,1; instead, the verse begins with a preposition בְּ + date, which is an intentional variation, cautioning the reader of a break and the beginning of a new section. The use of דבר in v.1 (n.) and v.3 (vb) causes an inclusion of the word-event and the indicative-imperative construction, דַּבֵּר וְאָמַרְתָּ "speak and say," to emphasize the significance of the word-event in the oracle. The use of "Pharaoh, king of Egypt...and all Egypt" (v.2), crerates an overall frame for the first oracle, telescopically indicating its breadth of development through vv.3-16. The oracles of judgment (3b-6a; 6b-9a; 9b-12) use the metaphors of the "big crocodile" and the "staff of reed" to identify the roles of Pharaoh and of the land of Egypt, respectively. The third oracle repeats the proud saying of Pharaoh (v.3b), makes an "inclusion" of all three oracles and establishes their overall unity, indirectly bringing out the role of the Nile, which becomes clear from the judgment against the land of Egypt (9a.12a). The oracles of judgment use figurative language but the oracle of salvation (vv.13-16) is spoken plainly.

The use of the "message" and the "recognition" formula make the first two oracles remarkable (cf. the recognition formula also in v.16). The highlights of God's judgment appear in the figures of the "wilderness" (v.5), "sword" (v.8), "waste and desolation" (vv.9.10.12), and "dispersion" (v.12), and are described by the verbs נטשׁ, נפל (v.5), נתן (vv.4.5.10) and היה (vv.6.9.12), which highlight God's judgment. Ezekiel has used the particles הִנְנִי, לָכֵן, יַעַן in accusation, judgment, and in giving a warning in the oracles of judgment, making them highly compact, while his use of כִּי in v.13 offers an interpretative key to the oracle of salvation.

The motif "house of Israel"[4] appears once in each of the judgment and the salvation oracles (vv.6.16; cf. v.21), with a central placement that attracts strong focus, and thus structure that comes from the oracles against Egypt, serve as a model.

Special mention needs to be made of the nexus between the first and the last oracles of judgment against Egypt, which occurs before the conclusion of the third chapter. It offers an important explanation of the larger context of the salvation oracle (29,13-16), which logically extends to 29,17-21 and 30,1-19. The last oracle 29,17-21 (26th April 571 B.C.), which is placed next to the first oracle 29,1-16 (6th January 585 B.C.), displays a redactor's reinterpretation of the prophet's previous oracles against Egypt in the light of the fulfilment of his oracles against Tyre, leaving no one in doubt about the genuineness of his oracles. Thus, by placing it before both the other chronologically ordered oracles (30,20-32,32) and the undated oracle (30,1-19) that precedes them, he inserts the last oracle (29,17-21) after the first oracle (29,1-16) and thereby strongly emphasizes the fulfilment of the last oracle of judgment against Egypt and her salvation. How concretely and in what detail they are going to be fulfilled does not affect the prophet's personal faith in God's revelation.

The semantic analysis in *chapter four* reveals the central and vital role of the divine name יהוה in the word-event formula as He who brings accusation and announces judgment against Pharaoh and Egypt, so that they may come to recognize His sovereignty. The use of the title "Pharaoh" as a proper name and "king of Egypt" as his designation identifies him with "all Egypt." Pharaoh's association with the "Nile-crocodile" and his "saying" come into direct confrontation with God's sovereignty. The saying of the crocodile ultimately expresses a hubris that is the real motive for God's judgment. The use of "heaven" and "earth" in the announcement of the judgment (v.5) is a reference to God's entire creation, affirming His sovereign authority.

The description of the "staff of reed" and its behaviour in connection with the "house of Israel," point out the "unreliable" nature of Egypt. This brings into focus the culpability of Egypt with regard to God's plan for Israel, namely, resisting God's sovereign plan of salvation for Israel by tempting Israel to unfaithfulness. Bringing a sword against Egypt for her involvement with Israel is a reminder for the latter that her desolation and captivity is God's handiwork.

The repetition of the "saying" of the crocodile in the third oracle shows the main accusation and motive for God's judgment against Pharaoh and Egypt. Here, God's judgment enumerates the implications of the judgment, i.e., the significance of the "waste and desolation," which the sword of the LORD brings upon the land. It means devastation of the land through war and captivity. For the house of Israel,

---

[4] The "house of Israel" occurs 17 times in the book of Ezekiel. See ZIMMERLI, *Ezechiel 1-24*, 169.

however, it is a sign of God's purpose that Israel has been exiled and her land desolated.

The promise of restoration of Egypt is closely connected with her judgment. The interpretative key כִּי (v.13) makes this quite clear and shows that salvation is an integral part of God's judgment. Salvation rather than punishment is the ultimate purpose of God's judgment, which leads Egypt to acknowledge Him.

A study of the meaning and usage of the Hebrew verb קבץ concerning God's action of gathering in *chapter five* makes it clear that, as used in the Bible, this verb relates to God's shepherding care for His people. Although many of its occurrences signify a gathering of Israel to judgment, God nonetheless ultimately gathers them to show his salvation. The study shows that קבץ denotes a fundamental concept of God's saving action and it is his prerogative to gather and save people. It describes the beginning of God's saving action for His people, Israel, but in Ezek 29,13, it is used once to describe the restoration of Egypt. A very similar construction of the oracle of salvation for Egypt, like that for Israel, suggests that Ezekiel intentionally draws a similarity between God's dealing with Egypt and with Israel. God's action of gathering the Egyptians reveals that even their dispersion through the countries is God's own action (= judgment), which includes per se, his action to gather them together at the end of a definite period. It does not depend on any merit of the people but on God's own concern and love for them. It reveals the inner nature of God's goodness and there lies the source of salvation.

In *chapter six*, another fundamental concept of God's saving activity שְׁבוּת שׁוּב is discussed in an attempt to point how, despite much discussion of its meaning, "restore fortunes," "return the captivity" or "bring back captivity," its reference to God's fundamental, saving action has not yet been sufficiently understood. Though in the pre-exilic period, the verb's meaning related to restore fortunes, and the exilic and post-exilic situation led to interpret it in more concrete sense, as "to bring back from captivity." Just like God's action to gather together, to "bring back from captivity" is also His own prerogative. He gathers the dispersed from the peoples and it is He who also brings back their captivity. Without God's intervention, such change in the historical-political situation of people is not possible. For, in the end result, it is He who makes the situation possible that allows the captives to be brought back from captivity and settle in their own land. As such, to bring back from captivity has a specific goal.

Beyond the historical-political meaning of the expression, there lies a deeper theological meaning. This is the restoration of Egypt, i.e., a bringing back of the captives to settle them in Pathros, their native land where their roots as Egyptians lie (cf. Isa 11,1). This signifies both their territorial and political restoration, which is equally linked to their historical origin. However, it has an important theological significance, which means bringing them back to the LORD through inner conversion of their hearts. In contrast to the initial hubris of Egypt, her return to the LORD in humble submission to His sovereignty displays this theological significance. Ezekiel uses the expression מַמְלָכָה שְׁפָלָה "low kingdom" to describe the restoration of Egypt in Ezek 29,14 and to convey this sense.

Chapter seven provides an explanation of the oracle of salvation to Egypt. It shows that the judgment of Egypt has a set term of "40 years," at the end of which God's saving intervention is expected, and will arrive when He begins to gather the scattered and dispersed of Egypt. The beginning of the oracle of salvation displays a strong influence of the exodus tradition and exilic theology. This influence is seen further in God's promise to bring back the captives of Egypt to the land of Pathros, to the land of their origin and to make them a low kingdom. The "land-giving" to Israel is supposed to be a concrete realization of the goal of Israel's exodus, which God repeats when He brings back their captives from Babylon. Even before Israel could take possession of the land for the first time, however, God makes them His people by testing them (i.e., by making them humble) in the desert. Now, God's action of bringing back the captives of Egypt to Pathros, and making them a "low kingdom," are accredited God's own privilege, which He grants to Egypt when He settles them there and makes them a low kingdom. From Egypt's former position of pride, God makes her low, and this is His privileged action that Egypt receives from Him just as Israel has. It is the low and the humble who inherit the land (Mt 5,5); God has not only given the Egyptians possession of their native land by establishing them there, but made them a low kingdom, with a new status and dignity.

This last action that God performs for Egypt fulfils His larger plan of salvation for the nations and for Israel, causing them to acknowledge His sovereignty. The nations can live in equanimity and peace in a new dispensation without any fear of being dominated by Egypt. The act has a still deeper meaning for Israel: she will not be tempted by Egypt to apostasy again, but may live in total fidelity to God. Thus, the salvation of Israel is not pushed to the side in the restoration of Egypt, but on the contrary, it strengthens her hope of salvation. On the other hand, Egypt is given the dignity of being one of God's people, similar to Israel, and placed beside her even as His dealing with Egypt becomes a paradigm for Israel's restoration and salvation.

Returned to her original roots in the southern land (Pathros), Egypt receives a new identity - a "lower" kingdom in a geo-political sense, but still more, a "low" kingdom in a theological–political sense. This classification of Egypt is central to the oracle of salvation and displays a deeper motive for God's salvation of Egypt. God humbles the pride of Egypt and she acknowledges the sovereignty of the LORD[5] and recognizes her proper place in His plan for the nations.

---

[5] RENZ, *The Rhetorical Function of the Book*, 93.

ABBREVIATIONS

1. Journals and series and abbreviated titles

AB	The Anchor Bible
ABD	The Anchor Bible Dictionary
ANET	*Ancient Near Eastern Texts Relating to the Old Testament*
ATD	Das Alte Testament Deutsch
BASOR	*Bulletin for American Studies of Oriental Research*
BDB	BROWN, DRIVER, and BRIGGS (ed.), *Hebrew and English Lexicon of the Old Testament,*
BEThL	Bibliotheca Ephemeridum Theologicarum Lovaniensis
BibetOr	Biblica et Orientalia
BJRyL	Bulletin of the John Rylands Library
BKAT	Biblischer Kommentar Altes Testament
BThB	*Biblical Theology Bulletin*
BZAW	Beihefte zur Zeitschrift für die alttestamentliche Wissenschaft
BZWANT	Beiträge zur Wissenschaft vom Alten und Neuen Testament
CBQ	*The Catholic Biblical Quarterly*
CBR	*Currents in Biblical Research*
CFThL	Clark's Foreign Theological Library
COT	Commentary on the Old Testament
EH	Europäische Hochschuleschriften
FOTL	The Forms of Old Testament Literature
FzAT	Forschung zum Alten Testament
FzB	Forschung zur Bibel
HALOT	*The Hebrew and Aramaic Lexicon of the Old Testament*
HAR	*Hebrew Annual Review*
HAT	Handkommentar zum Alten Testament
HCOT	Historical Commentary on the Old Testament
HSM	Harvard Semitic Monographs
HThKAT	Herders Theologischer Kommentar zum Alten Testament
HThKNT	Herders Theologischer Kommentar zum Neuen Testament
IB	The Interpreter's Bible
ICC	The International Critical Commentary
IEJ	*Israel Exploration Journal*
JAOS	*Journal of American Oriental Studies*
JBL	*Journal of Biblical Literature*
JBQ	*Journal of Biblical Quarterly*
JNSL	*Journal of Northwest Semitic Languages*

JPS	The Jewish Publication Society
JSOT	*Journal for the Study of the Old Testament*
JSOT.Suppl.	Journal for the Study of the Old Testament Supplement Series
JTS	*Journal of Theological Studies*
KHAT	Kurzer Handkommentar zum Alten Testament
MVAG	Mitteilungen der Vorderasiatischen (-Ägyptischen) Gesellschaft
NAC	New American Commentary
NCB	New Century Bible
NCBC	The New Century Bible Commentary
NEB.AT	Die Neue Echter Bibel. Kommentar zum Alten Testament
NIB	New Interpreter's Bible
NIBC	New International Biblical Commentary
NICOT	New International Commentary of the Old Testament
OTL	Old Testament Library
OTS	Old Testament Studies
PTMS	Pittsburgh Theological Monograph Series
RBC	*Revue Biblique Cahiers*
SBL	*Society of Biblical Literature*
SBL.MS	Society of Biblical Literature Monograph Series
SBS	Stuttgarter Bibel Studien
SFEG	Schriften der Finnischen Exegetischen Gesellschaft
SP	Sacra Pagina
SSB	Stuttgarter Studien zur Bibel
StBTh	Studien zur Biblischen Theologie
TB	Theologische Bücherei
THAT	Theologisches Handwörterbuch zum Alten Testament
ThWAT	Theologisches Wörterbuch zum Alten Testament
TLOT	Theological Lexicon of the Old Testament
UCOP	Universities of Cambridge Oriental Publications
VT	*Vetus Testamentum*
VT.Suppl.	Vetus Testamentum Supplements
WBC	Word Biblical Commentary
ZAW	*Zeitschrift für die Alttestamentliche Wissenschaft*
ZDMG	*Zeitschrift der Deutschen Morgenländer Gesellschaft*
ZDPV	*Zeitschrift des Deutschen Palästina-Vereins*

2. Grammatical and other abbreviations & signs

=	it denotes/means or it is translated
<	derives from
//	parallel to
abs.	absolute

adj.	adjective
adv.	adverb
BHS	Bibia Hebraica Stuttgartensia
ch.(s)	chapter(s)
consec.	consecutive
cstr.	construct
dat.	dative
ed.	editor/edited by
EIN	Einheitsübersetzung (German)
Eng. trans.	English translation
ESV	English Standard Version of the Bible
f.	feminine
fn.	footnote
FS	Festschrift
impf.	imperfect
indef.	indefinite
intrans.	intransitive
KJV	King James Version of the Bible
LXX	Septuaginta
LXX^B	Codex Vaticanus
m.	masculine
n.	noun
NIV	New International Version of the Bible
NJB	Neue Jerusalemer Bibel
NKJ	New King James Version of the Bible
No.	number
pf.	Perfect
pl.	plural
prep.	Preposition
pron.	pronoun
RSV	Revised Standard Version of the Bible
sg.	singular
subj.	subject
suff.	Suffix
trans.	translation
v./vv.	verse/verses
vb.	verb
x	occurrences/times

BIBLIOGRAPHY

Concordances, Dictionaries and Grammars

ANDERSEN F. I., and A. D. FORBES. *The Vocabulary of the Old Testament*, Rome: Pontifical Biblical Institute, 1989.

BROWN, F., S. R. DRIVER, and C. A. BRIGGS. *Hebrew and English Lexicon of the Old Testament*, Oxford: Clarendon Press, 1951.

BUTTRICK, G. A. (ed.), *The Interpreter's Bible*, Vol. 6, Nashville: Abingdon Press (1956), 41-63.

DAVIDSON, B. *The Analytical Hebrew and Chaldee Lexicon*, 2nd ed., Grand Rapids, Michigan: Zondervan Publishing House, 1850.

FARBY, H.-J., and H. RINGGREN (eds.), *Theologisches Wörterbuch zum Alten Testament*, zehn Bände, Stuttgart. Berlin. Köln: W. Kohlhammer Verlag, 1973-2000.

FREEDMAN, D. N. (chief ed.), *The Anchor Bible Dictionary*, Vol. 2, (New York: Doubleday, 1992), 321-412.

JENNI, E., and C. WESTERMANN (eds.), *Theological Lexicon of the Old Testament*, 2. Vols., Eng. trans. by M. E. BIDDLE from *Thoelogisches Handwörterbuch zum Alten Testament*, zwei Bände (München: Chr. Kaiser Verlag; und Zürich: Theologischer Verlag, 1976); Peabody, Massachusetts: Hendrickson Publishers, 1997.

JASTROW, M. (compiler), *A Dictionary of the Targumim, the Talmud Babli and Yerushalmi, and the Midrashic Literature*, Vol. II, New York: Pardes Publishing House Inc., 1950.

JOÜON, P., and T. MURAOKA, *A Grammar of Biblical Hebrew, Part One: Orthography and Phonetics*; and *Part Two: Morphology*, Rome: Pontifical Biblical Institute, 1991.

KAUTZSCH, E. (ed.), Eng. trans. by A. E. COWLEY, *GESENIUS' Hebrew Grammar*, Oxford: Clarendon Press, 1910, reprint 1988.

KECK, L. E. (ed.), *The New Interpreter's Bible*, Vol. VI, Nashville: Abingdon Press, 2001.

KOEHLER, L., and W. BAUMGARTNER. *Hebräisches und Aramäisches Lexikon zum Alten Testament*, Vol. III, Leiden: E. J. Brill, 1983.

KOEHLER, L., and W. BAUMGARTNER. *The Hebrew and Aramaic Lexicon of the Old Testament*, Study Edition, 2 Vols., Leiden, Boston, Köln: Brill, 2001.

LAMBDIN, T. O. *Introduction to Biblical Hebrew*, London: Darton, Longman & Todd, 1971.

MANDELKERN, S. *Veteris Testamenti Concordantiae Hebraicae atque Chaldaicae*, Graz, Austria: Academische Druck und Verlagsanstalt, 1975.

WOLFGANG, H., and W. WOLFAHRT. *Lexikon der Ägyptologie*, Band IV, Wiesbaden: Otto harrassowitz, 1982.

VOGT, E. *Lexicon Lingquae Aramaeicae: Veteris Testamenti*, Rome: Pontifical Biblical Institute, 1971.

ZORELL, F. (ed.), *Lexicon Hebraicum et Aramaicum Veteris Testamenti*, Rome: Pontifical Biblical Institute, 1948-1954.

Commentaries

ALLEN, L. C. *Ezekiel 1-19*, WBC 28, Dallas, Texas: Word Books Publishers, 1994.

__________. *Ezekiel 20-48*, WBC 29, Dallas, Texas: Word Books Publishers, 1990.

__________. *Psalms 101-150*, WBC 21, Waco, Texas: Word Books, Publishers, 1983.

ANDERSEN, A. A. *The Book of Psalms*, Vol. 2, NCB, London: Oliphants, 1972.

ANDERSEN, F. I., and D. N. FREEDMAN, *Amos: A New Translation and Commentary*, AB 24A, Garden City, New York: Doubleday & Co., 1989.

__________. *Hosea*: A New Translation and Commentary, AB 24, Garden City, New York: Doubleday & Co., 1980.

__________. *Micah: A New Translation and Commentary*, AB 24E, Garden City, New York: Doubleday & Co., 2000.

BECKER, J. *Esra. Nehemia*, NEB 25, Stuttgart: Echter Verlag, 1990.

BERTHOLET, A. *Hesekiel*, HAT 13, Tübingen: J. C. B. Mohr, 1936.

__________. *Das Buch Hesekiel*, KHAT 12, Freiburg in Breisgau. Leipzig. Tübingen: J. C. B. Mohr (Paul Siebeck), 1897.

BEUKEN, W. A. M. *Jesaja 1-12*, HThAT, Freiburg. Basel. Wien: Herder Verlag, 2003.

BLENKINSOPP, J. *Ezekiel:* Interpretation: A Bible Commentary for Teaching and Preaching, Louisville: John Knox press, 1990.

BLOCK, D. I. *The Book of Ezekiel 1-24*, NICOT 33/1, Grand Rapids, Michigan: W. B. Eerdmans, 1997.

__________. *The Book of Ezekiel 25-48*, NICOT 33/2, Grand Rapids, Michigan: W. B. Eerdmans, 1998.

BRAULICK, G. *Deuteronomium II*, 16,18-34,12 NEB 28, Stuttgart: Echter Verlag, 1992.

BRIGHT, J. *Jeremiah*, AB 21, Garden City: Doubleday & Co., 1965.

BROWNLEE, W. H. *Ezekiel 1-19*, WBC 28, Waco, Texas: Word Books, Publishers, 1986.

CARROLL, R. P. *Jeremiah: A Commentary*, OTL, Philadelphia: The Westminster Press, 1986.

CHRISTENSEN, D. L. *Deuteronomy 21:10-34:12*, WBC 6B, Nashville: Thomas Nelson Publishers, 2002.

CODY, A. C. *Ezekiel: With an Excursus on Old Testament Priesthood*, OTM 11, Wilmington, DE: Michael Glazier, Inc. 1984.

COOKE, G. A. *The Book of Ezekiel*, ICC 19, Edinburgh: T. & T. Clark, 1936.

COOPER Sr., L. E. *Ezekiel*, NAC 17, Nashville: Broadman & Holman Publishers, 1994.

CORNILL, C. H. *Das Buch des Propheten Ezechiel*, Leipzig: J. C. Hinrichs'sche Buchhandlung, 1886.

CRAIGE, P. C. *Ezekiel*, DSB, Philadelphia: The Westminster Press, 1983.

_________. *Psalms 1-50*, WBC 19, Waco, Texas: Word Books, Publishers, 1983.

CRENSHAW, J. L. *Joel*, AB 24C, New York: Doubleday, 1995.

DAHOOD, M. *Psalms III, 100-150*, AB 17A, Garden City, New York: Doubleday & Co. 1970.

DAVIES, W. D., and D. C. ALLISON. *The Gospel According to Matthew*, Vol. I, ICC 1/1, Edinburgh: T. & T. Clark, 1988.

DEISSLER, A. *Zwölf Propheten: Hosea. Joël. Amos*, NEB 4, Stuttgart: Echter Verlag, 1981.

DRIVER, S. R., and G. B. GRAY. *The Book of Job*, ICC 13, Edinburgh: T. & T. Clark, 1971.

DRIVER, S. R. *Deuteronomy*, ICC 5, 3rd ed., Edinburgh: T. & T. Clark, 1896, 1902.

DUHM, D. B. *Das Buch Hiob*, KHAT 16, Tübingen: J. C. B. Mohr (Paul Siebeck), 1897.

_________. *Das Buch Jeremia*, KHAT 11, Tübingen: J. C. B. Mohr (Paul Siebeck), 1901.

EICHRODT, W. *Der Prophet Hesekiel: Kapital 1-18*, 1. Teilband, 22/1, Göttingen: Vandenhoeck & Ruprecht, 1959.

_________. *Der Prophet Hesekiel: Kapital 19-48*, 2. Teilband, 22/2, Göttingen: Vandenhoeck & Ruprecht, 1966.

ELLIGER, K. *Deutero Jesaja 40,1-45,7*, 1. Teilband, BKAT 11/1, Neukirchen-Vluyn: Neukirchener Verlag, 1978.

FISCH, S. *Ezekiel: Hebrew Text and English Translation with an Introduction and Commentary*, London, Jerusalem, New York: Socino Press, 1978.

FOHRER, G. *Ezechiel*, HAT 13, Tübingen: J. C. B. Mohr Verlag, 1955.

FUHS, H. F. *Ezechiel I, 1-24*, NEB AT 21, Würzburg: Echter Verlag, 1984.

_________. *Ezechiel II, 25-48*, NEB AT 22, Würzburg: Echter Verlag, 1988.

GNILKA, J. *Das Matthäusevangelium 1,1-13,58*, HThKAT, 1/1, Freiburg. Basel. Wien: Herder Verlag, 1986.

GRAY, G. B. *The Book of Isaiah 1-39*, Vol. I., ICC 17/1, Edinburgh: T. & T. Clark, 1912.

GREEN, Joel B. *The Gospel of Luke*, NICNT 3A, Grand Rapids: W. B. Eerdmans Publishing Co., 1997.

GREENBERG, M. *Ezekiel 1-20*, AB 22, Garden City, New York: Doubleday, 1983.

GREENBERG, M. *Ezekiel 21-37*, AB 22B, Garden City, New York: Doubleday, 1998.

__________. *Ezechiel 1-20*, HThKAT, Freiburg in Breisgau: Herder Verlag, 2001.

HALS, R. M. *Ezekiel*, FOTL 19, Grand Rapids, Michigan: W. B. Eerdmans, 1989.

HEINISCH, P. *Das Buch Ezechiel*, HAT VIII, Bonn: Peter Hanstein Verlag, 1923.

HERRMANN, J. *Ezechiel*, KAT 11, Leipzig-Erlangen: A. Deichertsche Verlag, 1924.

HOLLADAY, W. L. *Jeremiah 2:* Chapters 26-52, *A Commentary on the Book of the Prophet Jeremiah*, Minneapolis: Fortress Press, 1989.

HOSSFELD, F.–L., and E. Zenger. *Die Psalmen 51-100*, HThKAT 23/2, Freiburg. Basel. Wien: Herder Verlag, 2000.

IRSIGLER, H. *Zefanja*, HThKAT 43, Freiburg. Basel. Wien: Herder Verlag, 2002.

JEREMIAS, J. *Der Prophet Hosea*, Göttingen: Vandenhoeck & Ruprecht, 1983.

JOHNSON, L. T. *The Gospel of Luke*, SP 3, Collegeville, Minnesota: The Liturgical Press: 1991.

JONES, D. R. *Jeremiah*, NCB 30, London: HarperCollins Publishing Group, 1992.

MÜLLER, H.-P., O. KAISER, and J. A. LOADER. *Das Hohelied/Klagelieder, Das Buch Ester*, ATD 16/2, 4. Aufl., Göttingen: Vandenhoeck & Ruprecht, 1992.

KAISER, O. *Der Prophet Jesaja: Kapitel 13-39*, Göttingen: Vandenhoeck & Ruprecht, 1973.

KEIL, K. F. *Biblischer Kommentar über den Propheten Ezechiel*, Leipzig: Dörffling und Franke, 1882.

__________. *Ezra Nehemiah*, Commentary on the Old Testament, Vol. 4, Eng. trans. by J. MARTIN and M. EASTON, Peabody, Massachusetts: Hendrickson Publishers, 1996.

__________. *Jerimiah Lamentations*, Commentary on the Old Testament, Vol. 8, Eng. trans. by J. MARTIN and M. EASTON, Peabody, Massachusetts: Hendrickson Publishers, 1996.

__________. *Ezekiel. Daniel*, Commentary on the Old Testament, Vol. 9, Eng. trans. by J. MARTIN and M. EASTON, Peabody, Massachusetts: Hendrickson Publishers, 1996.

__________. *Minor Prophets*, Commentary on the Old Testament, Vol. 10, Eng. trans. by J. MARTIN and M. EASTON, Peabody, Massachusetts: Hendrickson Publishers, 1996.

KEOWN, G. L., P. J. SCALISE, and T. G. SMOTHERS. *Jeremiah 26-52*, WBC 27, Dallas, Texas: Word Books, Publishers, 1995.

KESSLER, R. *Micha*, HThKAT 40, Freiburg in Breisgau: Herder, 1999.

KILIAN, R. *Jesaja II. 13-39*, NEB, AT 32, Stuttgart: Echter Verlag, 1994.

KITTEL, R. *Die Psalmen*, KAT 13, Leipzig: A Deichertsche Buchhandlung, 1914.

KOOLE, J. L. *Isaiah III, 40-48*, Vol. 1, HCOT 3/1, Kampen, the Netherlands: Kok Pharos Publishing House, 1997.

KOOLE, J. L. *Isaiah III, 49-55*, Vol. 2, HCOT 3/2, Kampen, the Netherlands: Kok Pharos Publishing House, 1998.

__________. *Isaiah III, 56-66*, Vol. 3, HCOT 3/3, Kampen, the Netherlands: Kok Pharos Publishing House, 2001.

KRAETZSCHMAR, R. *Das Buch Ezechiel*, HAT 3/1, Göttingen: Vandenhoeck & Ruprecht, 1900.

KRAUS, H.-J. *Psalmen 1-59*, BKAT 15/1, 5. Aufl., Neukirchen-Vluyn: Neukirchener Verlag, 1978.

__________. *Psalmen 60-150*, BKAT 15/2, 5. Aufl., Neukirchen-Vluyn: Neukirchener Verlag, 1978.

MACHINTOSH, A. A. *Hosea*, ICC 21A, Edinburgh: T. & T. Clark, 1997.

MARSHALL, I. H. *The Gospel of Luke*, NIGTC 3, Granville, Australia: The Paternoster Press, 1879.

MARTI, K. *Das Buch Jesaja*, Tübingen: J. C. B. Mohr Verlag, 1900.

MAY, G. (Introduction and Exegesis), and E. L. ALLEN (Exposition). "The Book of Ezekiel," in G. A. BUTTRICK (ed.), *The Interpreter's Bible*, Vol. 6, Nashville: Abingdon Press (1956), 41-63.

MCKANE, W. *Jeremiah*, Volume II, XXVI-LII, ICC 18B, Edinburgh: T. & T. Clark, 1996.

NELSON, R. D. *Deuteronomy: A Commentary*, OTL, Louisville, London: Westminster John Knox Press, 2002.

NEWCOME, W. *An Attempt toward an Improved Version, a Metrical Arrangement, and an Explanation of the Prophet Ezekiel*, Dublin: R. Marchbank, 1788.

NIELSEN, E. *Deuteronomium*, HAT I/6, Tübingen: J. C. B. Mohr (Paul Siebeck) 1995.

OSWALD, J. N. *The Book of Isaiah: Chapters 1-39*, NICOT 29/1A, Grand Rapids; Michigan: W. B. Eerdmans, 1986.

PAUL, S. *Amos: A Commentary on the book of Amos: A Critical and Historical Commentary on the Bible*, Hermeneia, Minneapolis: Augsburg Fortress Publishers: 1991.

PEAKE, A. S. *The Book of Isaiah 40-48*, Vol. II, ICC 17/2, Edinburgh: T. & T. Clark, 1912.

POHLMANN, K.-F. *Das Buch des Propheten Hesekiel (Ezechiel): Kapitel 20-48*, ATD 22/2, Göttingen: Vandenhoeck & Ruprecht, 2001.

__________. *Das Buch des Propheten Hesekiel (Ezechiel): Kapitel 1-19*, ATD 22/1, Göttingen: Vandenhoeck & Ruprecht, 1996.

RENKEMA, J. *Lamentations*, HCOT, Leuven: Peeters, 1998.

RUDOLF, W. *Esra und Nehemia*, Samt. 3 Esra HAT 20, Tübingen: J. C. B. Mohr (Paul Siebeck), 1949.

RUDOLF, W. *Jeremia*, HAT 12, Tübingen: J. C. B. Mohr (Paul Siebeck), 1958.

SEDLMEIER, F. *Das Buch Ezechiel*, Kapitel 1-24, NSKAT 21/1, Stuttgart: Verlag Katholisches Bibelwerk, 2002.

SMITH, J. M. P., W. H. WARD, and J. A. BEWAR. *Micah, Zephaniah, Nahum, Habakkuk, Obadiah and Joel*, ICC 22, Edinburgh: T. & T. Clark, 1912.

STRAUSS, H. *Hiob*, 2. Teilband 19, 1-42, 17, BKAT 16/2, Neukirchen-Vluyn: Neukirchener Verlag, 2000.

TIGAY, J. H. *Deuteronomy*, JPSTC, Philadelphia: Jewish Publication Society, 1996.

Vawter, B., and L. J. Hoppe, *Ezekiel. A New Heart*, ITC, Grand Rapids, Michigan: W. B. Eerdmans, 1991.

VLAADINGERBROEK, J. *Zephaniah*, HCOT, Leuven: Peeters, 1999.

VOLZ, P. *Der Prophet Jeremia*, KAT 10, Leipzig: A Deichertsche Verlagshandlung, D. Werner Scholl, 1928.

WATTS, J. D. W. *Isaiah* 1-33, WBC 24, Waco, Texas: Word Books Publisher, 1985.

————. *Isaiah* 34-66, WBC 25, Waco, Texas: Word Books Publisher, 1987.

WEVERS, J. W. *Ezekiel*, NCB 33, Johannesburg: Thomas Nelson & Sons, 1969.

WHYBRAY, R. N. *Proverbs*, NCBC 24, Grand Rapids, W. B. Eerdmans, 1994.

WILDBERGER, H. *Jesaja 1-12*, 1. Teilband, BKAT 10/1, Neukirchen-Vluyn: Neukirchener Verlag, 1972.

————. *Jesaja 13-27*, 2. Teilband, BKAT 10/2, Neukirchen-Vluyn: Neukirchener Verlag, 1978.

WOLFF, H. W. *Joel und Amos*, BKAT XIV/2, 2. Aufl., Neukirchen-Vluyn: Neukirchener Verlag, 1969.

————. *Hosea*, BKAT XIV/1, 2. Aufl., Neukirchen-Vluyn: Neukirchener Verlag, 1965

WRIGHT, C. J. H. *Deuteronomy*, NIBC, Peabody, Massachusetts: Hendrickson Publishers, 1996.

ZENGER, E. *Stuttgarter Altes Testament: Einheitsübersetzung mit Kommentar und Lexikon*, Stuttgart: Katholische Bibelanstalt, 2004.

ZIMMERLI, W. *Ezechiel 1-24*, BKAT 13/1, Neukirchen-Vluyn: Neukirchener Verlag, 1969.

————. *Ezechiel 25-48*, BKAT 13/2, Neukirchen-Vluyn: Neukirchener Verlag, 1969.

Books and Monographs

ALING, C. F. *Egypt and Bible History from Earliest Times to 1000 BC*, Grand Rapids, Michigan: Baker Book House, 1981.

BARNES, W. H. *Studies in the Chronology of the Divided Monarchy of Israel*, HSM 48, Atlanta, Georgia: Scholar Press: 1991.

BARR, J. *The Semantics of Biblical Language*, Oxford: Oxford University Press, 1961.

BARTHELÉMY, D. *Critique Textuelle de L'ancien Testament*, Tome 3, Ézéchiel, Daniel et les 12 Prophètes (Göttingen : Vandenhoeck & Ruprecht, 1992), 239-244.

__________. *Preliminary and Interim Report on the Hebrew Old Testament Text Project*, Vol. 4, Prophetical Books I: Ezekiel, Daniel, Twelve Minor Prophets: Text Project-4, New York: United Bible Societies, 1980.

__________. *Preliminary and Interim Report on the Hebrew Old Testament Text Project*, Vol. 5, Prophetical Books II: Ezekiel, Daniel, Twelve Minor Prophets: Text Project – 4, New York: United Bible Societies, 1980.

BOADT, L. *Ezekiel's Oracles against Egypt: A Literary and Philological Study of Ezekiel 29-32*, BibetOr 37, Rome: Pontifical Biblical Institute, 1980.

BREASTED, J. H. *Geschichte Ägyptens*, German trans. by H. RANKE, Zürich: Phaidon Verlag, 1974.

BRIGHT, J. *A History of Israel*, 3rd ed., Philadelphia: Westminster Press, 1981.

CHILDS, B. S. *Introduction to the Old Testament as Scripture*, London: SCM Press, 1979.

CLEMENTS, R. E. *Old Testament Prophecy: From Oracles to Canon*, Westminster: John Knox Press, 1996.

CORRAL, M. A. *Ezekiel's Oracles against Tyre: Historical Reality and Motivations*, BibetOr 46, Rome: Pontifical Biblical Institute, 2002.

CROW, L. D. *The Songs of Ascent (Psalms 120-134): Their Place in Israelite History and Religion*, SBL Diss. Series 148, Atlanta, Georgeia: Scholars Press, 1996.

DAY, J. *God's Conflict with the Dragon and the Sea: Echoes of a Canaanite Myth in the Old Testament*, UCOP 35, Cambridge: Cambridge University Press, 1985.

DIETRICH, E. L. שׁוּב שְׁבוּת: *Die Endzeitliche Wiederherstellung bei den Propheten*, Giessen: Alfred Töpelmann Verlag, 1925.

DONNER, H. *Geschichte des Volkes Israel und Seiner Nachbarn in Grundzügen*, 2. Teil, 3. Aufl., Göttingen: Vandenhoeck & Ruprecht, 2001.

DUGUID, I. M. *Ezekiel and the Leaders of Israel*, VT.Suppl. LVI, Leiden, New York, Köln: E. J. Brill, 1994.

EHRLICH, A. B. *Randglossen zur Hebräischen Bibel: Ezechiel und die kleinen Propheten*, 5. Band, Leipzig: J. C. Hinrichs'sche Buchhandlung, 1912.

FECHTER, F. *Bewältigung der Katastrophe: Untersuchungen zu ausgewählten Fremdvölkersprüchen im Ezechielbuch*, BZAW 208, Berlin. New York: Walter de Gruyter, 1992.

FRANKFORT, H. *Ancient Egyptian Religion*, New York: Harper Brothers, 1961.

GALAMBUSH, J. *Jerusalem in the Book of Ezekiel: The City as Yahweh's Wife*, SBL Diss. Series 130, Atlanta, Georgia: Scholars Press, 1002.

GALIL, G. *The Chronology of the Kings of Israel and Judah: Studies in the History and Culture of the Ancient Near East*, VT.Suppl. IX, Leiden: E. J. Brill, 1996.

GARSCHA, J. *Studien zum Ezechielbuch: Eine redaktionskritische Untersuchungen von Ez 1-39*, EH, Frankfurt am Main: Peter Lang, 1975.

GASTER, T. H. *Myth, Legend, and Custom in the Old Testament: A Comparative Study with Chapters from Sir James G. Frazer's Folklore in the Old Testament*, New York, Evanston: Harper & Row Publishers, 1969.

GOTTWALD, N. K. *The Politics of Ancient Israel*, Louisville, Kentucky: Westminster John Knox Press, 2001.

GRETHER, O. *Name und Wort Gottes im Alten Testament*, Giessen: Alfred Töpelmann Verlag, 1934.

GUNKEL, H. *Schöpfung und Chaos in Urzeit und Endzeit: Eine religions-geschichtliche Untersuchung über Gen 1 und Ap Joh 12*, Göttingen: Vandenhoeck u. Ruprecht, 1895.

HARFORD, J. B. *Studies in the Book of Ezekiel*, Cambridge: Cambridge University Press, 1935.

HARRIS, J. R. (ed.), *The Legacy of Egypt*, Oxford: Clarendon Press, 1971.

HARRISON, R. K. *Introduction to the Old Testament*, London: Inter-varsity Press, 1971.

HAYES, J. H., and P. K. HOOKER, *New Chronology for the Kings of Israel and Judah*, Atlanta: John Knox Press, 1988.

HAYES, J. H. (ed.), *Old Testament Form Criticism*, San Antonio: Trinity University Press, 1974.

HERNTRICH, V. *Ezechielstudien*, Beihefte, ZAW 61, Giessen: Töpelmann, 1932.

HERRMANN, J., *Ezechielstudien*, Leipzig: Deichertsche Verlag, 1908.

HÖLSCHER, G. *Hesekiel: Der Dichter und das Buch: Eine Literarische Untersuchung*, BZAW 39, Giessen: Alfred Töpelmann Verlag, 1924.

HOSSFELD, F.–L. *Untersuchungen zu Komposition und Theologie des Ezechielbuches*, FzB 20, Würzburg: Echter Verlag, 1977.

HOWIE, C. G. *The Date and Composition of Ezekiel*, SBL MS 4, Philadelphia: Society of Biblical Literature, 1950.

IRWIN, W. A. *The Problem of Ezekiel: An inductive Study*, Chicago, Illionis: University of Chicago Press, 1943.

JAGERSMA, H. *A History of Israel, Part I: The Old Testament Period*, Eng. trans. by J. BOWDEN from the Dutch *Geschieenis van Israël het Oudtestamentlische Tijdvak*, London: SCM Press, 1982.

JAHN, G. *Das Buch Ezechiel: Auf Grund der Septuaginta hergestellt*, Leipzig: Eduard Pfeifer Verlag, 1905.

KLEIN, R. W. *Ezekiel: The Prophet and his Message*, Columbia, South California: University of South California Press, 1998.

KRÜGER, T. *Geschichtskonzepte im Ezechielbuch*, BZAW 180, Berlin, New York: Walter de Gruyter, 1989.

KUTSCH, E. *Die Chronologischen Daten des Ezechielbuches*, OBO, Göttingen: Vandenhoeck & Ruprecht, 1985.

LAMPARTER, H. *Zum Wächter Bestellt der Prophet Hesekiel*, BAT 21, Stuttgart: Calwer Verlag, 1968.

LANG, B. *Ezechiel: Der Prophet und das Buch*, EdF 153, Darmstadt: Wissenschaftliche Buchgesellschaft, 1981.

LOHFINK, N., and E. ZENGER. *The God of Israel and the Nations: Studies in Isaiah and the Psalms*, Eng. trans. by E. R. KALIN from *Der Gott Israel und die Völker: Untersuchungen zum Jesajabuch und zu den Psalmen*, Collegeville, Minnesota: Liturgical Press, 2000.

LOHFINK, N. *Das Hauptgebot: Eine Untersuchung Literarische Einleitungs-fragen zu Dtn 5-11*, AnBib 20, Rome: Pontifical Biblical Institute, 1963.

LUST, J. (ed.), *Ezekiel and his book*, BEThL 74, Leuven: Leuven University Press, 1986.

MAIER, M. P. *Ägypten – Israels Herkunft und Geschick: Studie über einen theo-politischen Zentralbegriff im hebräischen Jeremiabuch*, Österreichische Biblische Studien 21, Wien: Peter Lang, 2002.

MAY, H. G. (ed.), *Oxford Bible Atlas*, 3rd ed., New York: Oxford University Press, 1984.

MEIN, A. *Ezekiel and the Ethics of Exile*, New York: Oxford University Press, 2001.

MILLER, J. M., and J. H. HAYES. *A History of Ancient Israel and Judah*, Philadelphia: Westminster Press, 1986.

MISSEL, N. *Ezechielfragen*, Oslo: I Kommisjon Hos Jacob Dybwad, 1945.

NIBBI, A. *Canaan and Canaanite in Ancient Egypt*, (place and publication not available), 1989.

OSTERLOH, E. *Die Offenbarung Gottes in der Fremde: Die Botschaft des Buches Ezechiel*, München: Chr. Kaiser Verlag, 1939.

OTTO, E. *Das Deuteronomium im Pentateuch und Hextateuch*, FzAT 30, Tübingen: Mohr und Siebeck (2000), 153-155.

PARKER, G. (ed.), *The Times Atlas of World History*, 4th ed., London: Times Books Limited, 1993.

PARKER, R. A., and W. H. DUBBERSTEIN, *Babylonian Chronology 626 B.C–A.D. 45*, Chicago: University of Chicago Press, 1942; and Providence: Brown University Press, 1956.

PERLITT, L. *Deuteronomium-Studien*, FzAT 8, Tübingen: Mohr und Siebeck, 1994.

POHLMANN, K.–F. *Ezechielstudien: Zur Redaktionsgeschichte des Buches und zur Frage nach den ältesten Texten*, BZAW 202, Berlin. New York: Walter de Gruyter, 1991.

PREMSTALLER, V. *Fremdvölkersprüche des Eezechielbuches*, FzB 104, Würzburg: Echter Verlag, 2005.

PRICHARD, R. *Ancient Near Eastern Texts*, 2nd. Ed., Princeton, New Jersey: Princeton Univ. Press, 1955.

REDFORD, D. B. *Egypt, Canaan, and Israel in Ancient Times*, Princeton, New Jersey: Princeton University Press, 1992.

REIMER, D. J. (ed.), *Deuteronomy: Issues and Interpretation*, OTS, Edinburgh: T. & T. Clark, 2002.

RENZ, T. *Rhetorical Function of the Book of Ezekiel*, Leiden: Brill, 1999.

REVENTLOW, H. G. *Wächter über Israel: Ezechiel und seine Tradition*, BZAW 82, Berlin: Töpelmann, 1962.

RUPRECHT, E. „Das Nilpferd im Hiobbuch: Beobachtungen zu der so genannten zweiten Gottesrede", *VT* 21 (1971), 209-231.

ROOKER, M. F. *Biblical Hebrew in Transition: The Language of the Book of Ezekiel*, JSOT.Suppl. 90, Sheffield: JSOT Press, 1990.

SCHÖPLIN, K. *Theologie als Biographie im Ezechielbuch*, FzAT 36, Tübingen 2002.

SEDLMEIER, F. *Studien zu Komposition und Theologie von Ezechiel 20*, SSB 21, Stuttgart: Katholisches Bibelwerk Verlag, 1991.

STACEY, D. W. *Prophetic Drama in the Old Testament*, Westminster: Epworth Presss, 1990.

STIPP, H.-J. *Das masoretische und alexandrinische Sondergut des Jeremiabuches: Textgeschichtlicher Rang, Eigenarten Triebkräfte*, Freiburg in Breisgau: Universität Freiburg Verlag; und Frankfurt am Main: Anton Hain, 1994.

STIPP, H.-J. *Jeremia im Parteienstreit*, Frankfurt am Main: Anton Hain, 1992.

THIEL, W. Die Deuteronomistische Redaktion von Jeremia 26-45, WMANT 52, Neukirchen-Vluyn: Neukirchener Verlag, 1981.

TORREY, C. C. *Pseudo-Ezekiel and the Original Prophecy*, New Haven: Yale University Press, 1930; and New York: Ktav Publishing House, Inc., 1970.

VAN DE MIEROOP, M. *A History of the Ancient Near East ca. 3000-323BC*, Oxford: Blackwell Publishing, 2004.

VAN DIJK, H. J. *Ezekiel's Prophecy on Tyre (Ezek 26,1–28,19): A New Approach*, BibetOr 20, Rome: Pontifical Biblical Institute, 1968.

VEIJOLA, T. (ed.), *Das Deuteronomium und Seine Querbezeichnungen*, SFEG 62, Göttingen: Vandenhoeck & Ruprecht, 1996.

VOGELS, W. *God's Universal Covenant: A Biblical Study*, Ottawa, Canada: University of Ottawa, 1979.

VOGT, E. *Untersuchungen zum Buch Ezechiel*, AnBib 95, Rome: Pontifical Biblical Institute, 1981.

WALTKE, B. K., and M. O'CONNOR. *An Introduction to Biblical Hebrew Syntax*, Winona Lake, Indiana: Eisenbrauns, 1990.

WATSON, W. G. E. *Classical Hebrew Poetry: A Guide to its Techniques*, JSOT.Suppl. 26, Sheffield: JSOT press, 1984.

WESTERMANN, C. *Grundformen prophetischer Rede*, BEvTh 31, München: Chr. Kaiser Verlag, 1960.

WISEMAN, D. J. *Chronicles of the Chaldeaean Kings: 626 -556 B.C.*, London: British Museum, 1956.

ZENGER, E. *Einleitung in das Alte Testament*, Fünfte, gründlich überarbeitete und erweiterte Auflage, Stuttgart: Kohlhammer Verlag, 2004.

ZIMMERLI, W. *Die Erkenntnis Gottes nach dem Buch Ezechiel, eine theologische Studie*, ATANT 27, Zürich: Zwingli Verlag, 1954.

________. *Gottes Offenbarung: Gesammelte Aufsätze zum Alten Testament*, München: Chr. Kaiser Verlag, 1963.

ZUNZ, L. *Bibelkirtisches II: Ezechiel*, ZDMG 27 (Wiesbaden: Steiner, 1873), 676-681.

Articles

BALTZAR, D. „literarkritische und Literarhistorische Anmerkungen zur Heilsprophetie im Ezechiel-Buch", in J. LUST (ed.), *Ezekiel and his book*, BEThL 74, Leuven: Leuven University Press (1986), 166-181.

BAUMANN, E. „שׁוּב שְׁבוּת: Eine exegetische Untersuchung", in *ZAW* 73 (1929), 17-44.

BAUMGÄRTEL, F. „Zu den Gottesnamen in den Büchern Jeremia und Ezechiel", in *Verbannung und Heimkehr: Beiträge zum 70. Geburtstag von W. Rudolf*, Tübingen: J. C. B. Mohr (1961), 1-30.

BEN-YASHAR, R. G., and M. ZIPOR, „שׁוּב שְׁבוּת/שְׁבִית", in *ThWAT*, Band VII (1993), 958-965.

BLAU, J. "Zum angeblichen Gebrauch von את vor dem Nominativ", in *VT* 4 (1954), 7-19.

BLAU, J. „Reste des i-Imperfekts von zkr, qal", in *VT* 11 (1961), 81-86.

BLOCK, D. I. "God in Prophetic Tradition: A New Look at Ezekiel 38,17," in *VT* 42 (1992), 154-172.

BOADT, L. "Rhetorical Strategies in Ezekiel's Oracles of Judgment," in J. LUST (ed.), *Ezekiel and His Book*, BEThL 74, Leuven: Leuven University Press (1986), 182-200.

________. "Textual Problems in Ezekiel and Poetic Analysis of Paired Words," in *JBL* 97/4 (1978), 489-499.

________. "The Function of the Salvation Oracles in Ezekiel 33-37," in *HAR* 12 (1990), 1-21.

BORGER, R. „Zu שׁוּב שׁבו/ית", in *ZAW* 66 (1954), 513-316.

BOTTERWECK, J.G. "עָדַ yāda '", in *ThWAT*, Band III (1992), 479-512.

BRACKE, J. M. "šûb šᵉbût: A Reappraisal," in *ZAW* 97 (1985), 233-244.

BRUEGGEMANN, W. "Israel's sense of Place in Jeremiah," in J. JACKSON and M. KESSLER (eds.), *Rhetorical Criticism: Essays in Honour of J. Muilenburg*, PTMS (1974), 149-165.

BUDDE, K. „Zum Eingang des Buches Ezechiel", in *JBL 50* (1931), 20-41.

CASSUTO, U. "The Arrangement of the Book of Ezekiel," in *Biblical and Oriental Studies I* (Jerusalem, 1973 from Original Hebrew of 1946), 25-32.

CAZELLES, H. «L'expression šubh šebhut viendrait-elle del'accadien d'Asarhaddon?», in *GLECS* 9 (1960), 57-60.

CLASSEN, W. T. "Speaker-Oriented Functions of Kî in Biblical Hebrew," in *JNSL* 11 (1983), 32.

DAY, P. L. "Adulterous Jerusalem's Imagined Demise: Death of a Metaphor in Ezekiel XVI," in *VT* 50/3 (2000), 285-309.

DRIVER, G. R. "Ezekiel: Linguistic and Textual Problems," in *Biblica* 35 (1954) 145-159; 299-312.

__________. "Studies in the Vocabulary of the Old Testament: V," in *JTS* 34 (1933), 33-44.

__________. "Studies in the vocabulary of the Old Testament: VI," in *JTS* 34 (1933), 375-385.

EISING, H. „זָכַר", in *ThWAT*, Band II (1977), 571-593.

EISSFELDT, O. „אָדוֹן", in *ThWAT*, Band I (1973), 62-78.

EISSFELDT, O. „Schwerterschlagene bei Hesekiel", in *Studies in Old Testament Prophecy: FS T. H. Robinson*, Edinburgh: T. & T. Clark (1950), 73-81.

ELLIGER, K. „Ich bin der Herr- euer Gott", in *Kleinen Schriften zum Alten Testament*, TB 32, München (1966), 211-231.

ENGELKEN, K. „שָׁפֵל", in *ThWAT*, Band VIII (1995), 438-444.

FARBY, H.-J. „שׁוּב", in *ThWAT*, Band VII (1993), 1118-1176.

FINEGAN, J. "The Chronology of Ezekiel," in *JBL* 69 (1950), 61-66.

FITZMYER, J. A. "The Aramaic Suzerainty Treaty from Sefire in the Museum of Beirut," in *CBQ* 20 (1958), 463-464.

FREEDMAN, D. N., B. E. WILLOUGHBY, and H.-J. FARBY. „נָשָׂא", in *ThWAT*, Band V (1986), 626-643.

FREEDY, K. S., and D. B. REDFORD. "The Dates of Ezekiel in Relation to Biblical, Babylonian and Egyptian Sources," in *JAOS* 90 (1970), 460-484.

GERSTENBERGER, E. "בטח bth to trust," in *TLOT*, Vol. I (1997), 226-230.

GOTTWALD, N. K. "Laken: Its Functions and Meanings", in J. JACKSON and M. KESSLER (eds.), *Rhetorical Criticism: Essays in Honour of J. Muilenburg*, PTM (1974), 254-284.

GROSS, W. "Israel und die Völker: Die Krise des YHWH-Volk-Konzepts im Jesajabuch", in E. ZENGER (ed.), *Der Neue Bund im Alten: Zur*

Bundestheologie der beiden Testamente, Qestiones Disputatae 146 (Freiburg. Basel. Wien: Herder, 1993), 149-168.

HAAG, H. „בֶּן־אָדָם", in *ThWAT*, Band I (1973), 682-689.

HASEL, G. F. „כָּרַת", in *ThWAT*, Band IV (1984), 355-367.

HAYES, J. H. "The Usage of Oracles against Foreign Nations in Ancient Israel," in *JBL* 87 (1968), 81-92.

HÖFFKEN, P. „Zu den Heilszusätzen in der Völkerorakelsammlung des Jeremiabuches", in *VT* 27 (1977), 398-412.

HOUK, C. B. "בֶּן־אָדָם as Literary Criteria in Ezekiel," in *JBL* 88 (1969), 184-190.

HUFFMON, H. B. "The Treaty Background of Hebrew *Yāda*," in *BASOR* 181 (1966), 31-37.

JENNI, E. "גָּדוֹל *gādôl* great," in *TLOT*, Vol. I (1997), 303-307.

JEPSEN, A. „בָּטַח", in *ThWAT*, Band I (1973), 608-615.

JOÜON, M. «Notes Philologiques sur le Texte Hébreu D'Ezéchiel», in *Biblica* 10 (1929), 304-312.

JÜNGLING, H.W. "Eid und Bund in Ez 16-17", in E. Zenger (ed.), *Der Neue Bund im Alten: Zur Bundestheologie der beiden Testamente*, Qestiones Disputatae 146 (Freiburg. Basel. Wien: Herder, 1993), 113-148.

KAISER, O. „חֶרֶב I", in *ThWAT*, Band III (1982), 160-164.

KAISER, O. „חֶרֶב II", in *ThWAT*, Band III (1982), 164-176.

KENNEDY, J. F. "Hebrew pithôn Peh in the Book of Ezekiel," in *VT* 41 (1991), 233-235.

KITCHEN, K. A. "History of Egypt: Chronology," in *ABD*, Vol. 2, 321-331.

KNIERIM, R. "עָוֹן *c̔āwōn* perversity," in *TLOT*, Vol. II (1997), 862-866.

KOCH; K. „חָטָא", in *ThWAT*, Band II (1977), 857-870

KOCH; K. „עָוֹן", in *ThWAT*, Band V (1986), 1160-1177.

KOHN, R. L. "Ezekiel at the Turn of the century," in *CBR* 2/1 (2003), 9-31.

KUTSCH, E. "כרת *krt* to cut off," in *TLOT*, Vol. II (1997), 635-637.

LABUSCHAGNE, C. J. "The Particle hēn and hinnē," in *Syntax and Meaning*, OTS XVIII, Leiden: Brill (1973), 1-14.

LAMBDIN, T. O. "Egyptian Loan Words in the Old Testament," in *JAOS* 73 (1953), 145-155.

LOHFINK, N. "Fortschreibung? Zur Technik von Rechtsrevisionen im Deuteronomischen Bereich, erörtet an Deuteronomium 12, Ex 21,2-11 und Dtn 15,12-18", in T. VEIJOLA (ed.), *Das Deuteronomium und Seine Querbezeichnungen*, SFEG 62 (Göttingen: Vandenhoeck & Ruprecht, 1996), 127-171.

MALAMAT, A. "The Last Kings of Judah and the Fall of Jerusalem: A Historical-Chronological Study," in *IEJ* 3 (1968), 137-155.

MARK, M. "Ewiger Bund als radikalisierte Treue: Zur rhetorischen Strategie von Ezechiel 16", in F. SEDLMEIER (ed.), *Gottes Wege Suchend: Beiträge zum*

Verständnis der Bibel und ihrer Botschaft (Würzburg: Echter Verlag, 2003), 203-252.

MEYER, I. „שָׁמַם", in *ThWAT*, Band VIII (1995), 241-251.

MOMMER, P. „קבץ", in *ThWAT*, Band VI (1989),1144-1149.

MULDER, M. J. „Die Partikel Jaᶜan", in *Syntax and Meaning*, OTS XVIII (Leiden: Brill, 1973), 49-83.

MÜLLER, H.-P. „המם", in *ThWAT*, Band II (1977), 449-454.

MULLO WEIR, C. J. "Aspects of the Book Ezekiel," in *VT* 2 (1952), 97-112.

MURNANE, W. J. "History of Egypt: New Kingdom," in *ABD*, Vol. 2, 348-353.

OREN, E. "'Migdol' Fortress in North-Western Sinai," in *Qad* 10 (1977), 71-76.

OTTO, E. „Das Deuteronomium 4: Die Pentateuchsredaktion im Deuteronomiumsrahmen", in T. VEIJOLA (ed.), *Das Deuteronomium und Seine Quer-beschreibungen*, SFEG 62, Göttingen: Vandenhoeck & Ruprecht, 1996.

PREUSCHEN, E. „Die Bedeutung von שׁוּב שְׁבוּת im Alten Testament", in *ZAW* 15 (1895), 1-74.

REVENTLOW, H. G. "Die Völker als Jahwes Zeugen bei Ezechiel", in *ZAW* 71 (1951), 33-43.

RINGGREN, H., and H.-J. FARBY. „מִצְרַיִם", in *ThWAT*, Band IV (1984), 1099-1111.

RINGGREN, H. „פוּץ", in *ThWAT*, Band VI (1989), 544-547.

SÆBØ, M. „Grenzbeschreibung und Landideal: Mit besonderer Berücksichtigung der *min-ʿad-* Formel", in *ZDPV* 90 (1974), 14-37.

SCHARTZ, B. J. "Ezekiel's dim view of Israel's restoration," in M. S. ODELL and J. T. STRONG (ed.), *The Book of Ezekiel: Theological and Anthropoligical Perspectives*, SBL Symposium Series 9 (2000), 43-67.

SCHOORS, A. "The Particle kī," in *Oudtestamentische Studiën*, Deel XXI, Leiden: E. J. Brill (1981), 240-276.

SCHOTTROFF, W. "ידע *ydᶜ* to perceive, know," in *TLOT*, Vol. II (1997), 508-521.

__________. "זכר *zkr* to remember," in *TLOT*, Vol. I (1997), 381-388.

SCHUNCK, K. „כָּרָה", in *ThWAT*, Band IV (1984), 318-322.

SCHWALLY, F. „Die Reden des Buches Jeremia gegen die Heiden XXV XLVI-LI", in *ZAW* 8, Giessen (1888), 177-217.

SEDLMEIER, F. „Wider die Selbstvergottung: Der Fürst von Tyrus und sein Selbstverständnis nach Ez 29,1-10", in T. BRANDSCHEIDT and T. MENDE (ed.), *Schöpfungsplan und Heilsgeschichte: FS Ernst Haag zum 70. Geburtstag* (Trier: 2002), 271-297.

SOGGIN, A. „שׁוּב שְׁבוּת", in *THAT*, Band II (1976), 884-891.

SPALINGER, A. "History of Egypt: 3D Intermediate-Saite Period (Dyn. 21-26)," in *ABD*, Vol. 2, 353-364.

STEINER, R. C. "Does the Biblical Hebrew Conjunction -וֹ Have Many Meanings, One Meaning, or no Meaning at All?," in *JBL* 119/2 (2000), 249-267.

STENDEBACH, F. J. „שָׁנָה", in *ThWAT*, Band VIII (1995), 324-340.

STOLZ, F. "נשׂא *nś'* to lift, bear," in *TLOT*, Vol. II (1997), 769-774.

SWANEPOEL, M. G. "Ezekiel 16: Abandoned Child, Bride Adorned or Unfaithful Wife," in P. R. DAVIES and D. J. A. CLINES (eds.), *Among the Prophets: Language, Image and structure in the Prophetic Writings,* JSOT.Suppl. 144 (Sheffield: JSOT Press, 1993), 84-104.

TALMON, S. „קָץ", in *ThWAT*, Band VII (1986), 84-92.

TSEVAT, M. "The Neo-Assyrian and Neo-Babylonian Vassal Oaths and the Prophet Ezekiel", in *JBL* 73 (1959), 199-204.

VAN ROOY, H. F. "Parallelism, Metre and Rhetoric in Ezekiel 29, 1-6," in *Semitics* 8 (1982), 90-105.

VOGELS, W. «Restoration de l'Égypte et Universalisme en Ez 29,13-16», in *Biblica* 53 (1972), 473-494.

WASCHKE, E.-J. „רָבַץ", in *ThWAT*, Band VII (1993), 320-325.

WATSON, W. G. E. "The Hebrew Word-pair 'sp//qbs," in *ZAW* 96 (1984), 226-434.

ZIMMERLI, W. "The Special Form and Tradition-Historical Character of Ezekiel's Prophecy," in *VT* 15, Leiden: E. J. Brill (1965), 515-527.

__________. „Das Wort des göttlichen Selbsterweises (Erweiswort): Eine prophetische Gattung", in TB 19, 2. Aufl., München: Chr. Kaiser Verlag, 1969, 120-132.

__________. „Die Eigenart der Prophetischen Rede des Ezechiel", in *ZAW* 66 (1954), 1-26.

ZOBEL, H.-J. „מָעַט", in *ThWAT*, Band IV (1984), 1030-1036.

__________. „רָדָה", in *ThWAT*, Band VII (1993), 351-357.